1993

University of St. Francis
GEN 943.03 H871m
Hsia, R. Po-chia,
The myth of ritual murder :

3 0301 00094490 6

SO-AID-580

THE MYTH OF RITUAL MURDER

Jews worshipping the Devil. In the background, three Jews kneel in worship of a statue of the Devil on a column. In the foreground, two outraged Christians turn to a lord who is holding a sword in his right hand and a whip in his left, the symbols of justice. From *Ein seltzame kouffmanschatz*. Reproduced courtesy of Stadtarchiv Freiburg.

The Myth of Ritual Murder

Jews and Magic in Reformation Germany

R. PO-CHIA HSIA

Yale University Press   New Haven and London

LIBRARY
College of St. Francis
JOLIET, ILL.

Copyright © 1988 by Yale University.
All rights reserved.
This book may not be reproduced, in whole
or in part, including illustrations, in
any form (beyond that copying permitted by
Sections 107 and 108 of the U.S. Copyright
Law and except by reviewers for the public
press), without written permission from the
publishers.

Designed by James J. Johnson
and set in Palatino Roman types by
Keystone Typesetting Co., Orwigsburg, Pennsylvania.
Printed in the United States of America by
Edwards Brothers, Ann Arbor, Michigan

Library of Congress Cataloging-in-Publication Data

Hsia, R. Po-chia, 1953–
    The myth of ritual murder.

    Bibliography: p.
    Includes index.
    1. Blood accusation.   2. Jews—Germany—Persecutions.
3. Jews—Germany—History—1096–1800.   4. Germany—
Ethnic relations.   5. Magic—Germany—History—16th
century.   I. Title.
BM585.2.H74   1988   943'.004924   88–5727
ISBN 0–300–04120–9 (cloth)
        0–300–04746–0 (pbk.)

THE PAPER IN THIS BOOK MEETS THE GUIDELINES FOR
PERMANENCE AND DURABILITY OF THE COMMITTEE ON
PRODUCTION GUIDELINES FOR BOOK LONGEVITY OF THE
COUNCIL ON LIBRARY RESOURCES.

10 9 8 7 6 5 4 3

943.03
H871m

Contents

147,988

Illustrations

Acknowledgments

Many friends and colleagues have been encouraging during times when I doubted the wisdom of this project. Steven Ozment, David Sabean, and Gerald Strauss read the manuscript and offered valuable suggestions. I am further thankful for the opportunities to test my ideas at the Society of Fellows at Columbia University, at the Sixteenth Century Studies Conference (1984), at the Leo Baeck Institute, New York, and at the European History Seminar at Syracuse University; lecture audiences at Cornell University, at the University of Massachusetts at Amherst, and at Yale University have offered stimulating questions and criticisms. Jane Abray, Ruth Angress, Philip Bohlman, Uwe Gertz, Sander Gilman, Joseph Roisman, Ursula Seitz-Gray, and Charles Wood have helped along the way with suggestions, ideas, and various favors.

In Germany, the dedication of the archival staffs is exemplary. Dr. H. Andernacht of Frankfurt, Fritz Reuter of Worms, and Dr. H. Wunschel of Bamberg have been especially helpful. Grants from the National Endowment for the Humanities, the German Academic Exchange Service, the Cornell University Humanities Council, and the American Society for Church History made possible several research trips; the generosity of the John Simon Guggenheim Foundation enabled me to complete the manuscript during 1986–87. For the support of my colleagues at Cornell and the courtesy of the historians at Dartmouth, who offered me an office and their hospitality, I would like to extend my warmest appreciation. I. G. Marcus and Ralph Davis reminded me of the modern origins of the legend of Rabbi Loew (chap. 9); for a more detailed treatment of Ulrich Zasius's views of the Jews, there is a recent biography: Steven Rowan, *Ulrich Zasius: A Jurist in the German Renaissance, 1461–1535* (Frankfurt, 1987); G. R. Elton and C. Friedrichs have pointed out other minor errors. To them, I wish to express my appreciation. At Yale University Press, Charles Grench and Laura Jones Dooley have been most helpful with their suggestions and enthusiasm. Finally, this book is for Pamela, whose good sense and historical judgment have been indispensable.

Abbreviations

ADB	*Allgemeine Deutsche Biographie*
HHHStA	Haus-, Hof- und Hauptstaatsarchiv Vienna
-RHR	Reichshofrat
HStA St	Hauptstaatsarchiv Stuttgart
HWDA	*Handwörterbuch des Deutschen Aberglaubens*, ed. Hanns Bächtold-Stäubli and E. Hoffmann-Krayer. 10 vols. Berlin, 1927–42.
N.F.	Neue Folge
Osiander	*Andreas Osianders Schrift über die Blutbeschuldigung*, ed. Moritz Stern. Kiel, 1893; reprint, Berlin, 1903.
SCJ	*Sixteenth Century Journal*
StA Lu	Staatsarchiv Ludwigsburg
StA Mb	Staatsarchiv Marburg
-PA	Politisches Archiv des Landgrafen Philipp
StA Nb	Staatsarchiv Nürnberg
StA Wü	Staatsarchiv Würzburg
StdA Fb	Stadtarchiv Freiburg
StdA Ff	Stadtarchiv Frankfurt
StdA Wo	Stadtarchiv Worms
Urkunden	*Urkunden und Aktenstücke zur Geschichte der Juden in Regensburg, 1453–1738*, ed. Raphael Straus. Munich, 1960.
WA	*D. Martin Luthers Werke. Kritische Gesamtausgabe*
WA-Br	*Briefwechsel*
WA-Tr	*Tischreden*
ZGF	Zeitschrift der Gesellschaft für Beförderung der Geschichts-, Altertums- und Volkskunde von Freiburg
ZGO	Zeitschrift für die Geschichte Oberrheins

CHAPTER ONE

Introduction: Ritual, Magic, and Murder

URING HIS STAY IN ENGLAND BETWEEN 1773 AND 1774, Georg Christoph Lichtenberg (1742–99), the Göttingen professor of mathematics and astronomy famous for his incisive *Aphorisms*—those witty commentaries on contemporary mores and culture that won the later admiration of Goethe and Hegel—wrote a number of letters home that reflected on his observations of the London theater. Enchanted by Shakespeare, Lichtenberg never failed to record his reactions to performances of the various masterpieces. In his third "English letter," dated 30 November 1775, Lichtenberg recalled a visit to a performance of *The Merchant of Venice*, with the famous Shakespearean actor Carl Macklin (McLaughlin) in the role of Shylock. "When he [Macklin, as Shylock] came out," Lichtenberg remembered, "he was greeted with three rounds of applause, with each lasting fifteen seconds. One cannot deny that, to see this Jew is more than enough for all childhood prejudices against this people to be awakened suddenly again in the most lawabiding man."[1] This was said in the century of the Enlightenment—the time of Moses Mendelssohn and of Gotthold Ephraim Lessing's *Nathan the Wise*, a play to honor the wisdom of the Jewish patriarch—by a man who was the star of the newly founded and immensely prestigious university at Göttingen. A simple remark betrays all the historical complexities between two peoples whose fates were so tragically intertwined.

Like many leading intellectuals of the German *Aufklärung*, Lichtenberg was the son of a Lutheran pastor. Those childhood prejudices of a "most lawabiding man," perhaps, reflected the ambivalent attitude of German Protestants toward Jews. Fear and hatred of Jews was nourished by the many children's rhymes and stories that represented the Jews as

---

1. Georg Christoph Lichtenberg, *Vermischte Schriften*, vol. 3 (Göttingen, 1867), p. 266.

horrifying creatures of the Devil;[2] most terrifying of these tales, to children and their parents alike, must have been the legends of child sacrifice, the alleged ritual murders of Christian children by Jews, whereby the innocent victims were slowly tortured and bled to death.[3] The legend consisted of the belief that Jews required Christian blood for their ritual and magic. Numerous motives were imputed to the Jews: they allegedly used Christian blood in preparing matzo, for anointing rabbis, for circumcision, in curing eye ailments, in stopping menstrual and other bleedings, in preventing epileptic seizures, removing bodily odors, and to ward off the evil eye, to make amulets, love potions, and magical powder, and to paint the bodies of the dead.[4]

In Europe, the first documented case of ritual murder persecution was the alleged martyrdom of the English boy William of Norwich in 1148.[5] At least seven other accusations of ritual murder occurred in the

2. Cf., e.g., the children's rhymes about Jews in the Saarland collected by Nikolaus Fox in *Saarländische Volkskunde* (Bonn, 1927).

3. There is an immense literature on the blood libel. For scholarly and critical introductions to the subject, see Hermann L. Strack, *The Jew and Human Sacrifice*, trans. Henry Blanchamp (New York, 1909), based on the original and influential work, *Der Blutaberglaube in der Menschheit: Blutmorde und Blutritus* (Munich, 1892), which discusses the best known cases of alleged ritual murders from Antiquity to the 19th century. Strack was professor of theology at the University of Berlin; his book was intended to discredit the new wave of child murder accusations against Jews at the end of the 19th century. A similar work of scholarship discrediting the blood libel was written by Daniel Chwolson (Khvol'son), professor of Hebrew and Oriental languages at Saint Petersburg, who was appointed to an imperial commission to investigate ritual murder charges against Russian Jews. His 1880 Russian book was translated as *Die Blutanklage und sonstige mittelalterliche Beschuldigungen der Juden: Eine historische Untersuchung nach den Quellen* (Frankfurt, 1901). See also Hugo Hayn, ed., *Übersicht der (meist in Deutschland erschienenen) Literatur über die angeblich von Juden verübten Ritualmorde und Hostienfrevel* (Jena, 1906), which is a compilation (although quite incomplete) of 121 sources related to ritual murder and Host desecration cases in history. For an overview from the perspective of a leading German folklorist of the 20th century, see Will-Erich Peuckert, "Ritualmord," in *HWDA*, 7, cc. 727–39. Peuckert lists a rather comprehensive bibliography of printed literature on ritual murder accusations, but his chronology of such accusations inevitably reflects the inaccuracies and confusion of some of the older chronicles and polemic writings. Two works by Jewish scholars focus on the publication of papal documents condemning ritual murder trials. See Moritz Stern, ed., *Die päpstlichen Bullen über die Blutbeschuldigung* (Berlin, 1893), and Cecil Roth, ed., *The Ritual Murder Libel and the Jew: The Report by Cardinal Lorenzo Ganganelli (Pope Clement XIV)* (London, 1934). For examples of the political character of the debate in the late 19th and early 20th centuries, see Leopold Lipschiltz, *Christliche Zeugnisse gegen die Blutbeschuldigung der Juden* (Berlin, 1882), a collection of testimonies by Christian professors, theologians, and bishops from Germany and the Netherlands condemning the blood libel, and Albert Hellwig, *Ritualmord und Blutaberglaube* (Minden, 1914), which introduces the subtle and pernicious argument that Jews might not have murdered Christian children for ritual purposes but for magical-medical cures.

4. Cf. Peuckert, "Ritualmord," *HWDA*, 7, c. 734.

5. Strack, *Jew and Human Sacrifice*, p. 177.

TABLE 1. Frequency of Ritual Murder Accusations

	Century				
	12th	13th	14th	15th	16th*
German-speaking lands	2	15	10	14	12
England	2	7			
France	2	1	4		
Spain	1	1			4
Italy			1	6	
Bohemia	1		1		3
Poland				2	8
Hungary				1	3
Total	8	24	16	23	30

*Peuckert's figures are based entirely on secondary literature. For the 15th and 16th centuries, more cases of ritual murder trials and accusations can be found in archives. The figures presented here are meant to indicate some general patterns rather than the absolute numbers of incidents.

Source: Peuckert, "Ritualmord," HWDA 7, cc. 727–31.

twelfth century: two in France, two in Germany, and one each in England, Bohemia, and Castile.[6] The number of accusations multiplied threefold during the thirteenth century, dropped slightly in the fourteenth, and reached its apex in the fifteenth and sixteenth centuries (see table 1).

This pattern of distribution suggests that ritual murder accusations became quite widespread by the thirteenth century and reached their climax in the fifteenth and sixteenth centuries. The seemingly low figure of the fourteenth century must be seen in the context of the massive pogroms associated with the Black Death of midcentury, during which entire Jewish communities in the Holy Roman Empire were destroyed. Geographically, these accusations spread eastward like an epidemic from England and France across the German-speaking lands of Central Europe—where it spent its full fury during the sixteenth century—and began to plague Eastern Europe by the late fifteenth and early sixteenth centuries, with accusations increasing, especially in Poland, in the seventeenth and eighteenth centuries.[7] The disappearance of the blood libel from Western Europe after the fourteenth century can be explained by the expulsion of Jews from England and France. Accusations in Mediterranean countries, where Jewish communities had settled since Roman

6. Peuckert, "Ritualmord," HWDA, 7, cc. 728–29.
7. For figures of the 17th and 18th centuries, see Peuckert, "Ritualmord," HWDA, 7, cc. 731–33.

times, were rare; almost all cases were limited to the fifteenth century, when preachers of the mendicant orders played a crucial role in raising charges against Jews.[8]

As an expression of anti-Semitism, the blood libel was much more virulent than Host desecration accusations, which often accompanied ritual murder charges. Like the blood libel, Host desecration cases—when Jews were blamed for stealing or buying the consecrated Host in order to torture Christ—rose steadily in the late Middle Ages and died out after the Reformation: seven cases were known in the thirteenth century, thirteen in the fourteenth, twenty in the fifteenth, and five during the sixteenth century.[9]

Another striking fact emerges from the distribution of ritual murder cases: the blood libel was particularly prominent in the German-speaking lands of Central Europe. In the Holy Roman Empire, ritual murder charges, trials, and executions reached a climax in the fifteenth and sixteenth centuries; thereafter, judicial investigations began to dwindle, although the belief of Jewish child murder remained widespread and strong well into the nineteenth century. The period from the mid-fifteenth to the early seventeenth century, in particular, appears crucial in the history of anti-Semitism, not least because of its contemporaneous conjunction with the religious and social upheavals of the Reformation and Counter-Reformation.

Sources on these alleged ritual murders before the mid-fifteenth century are few and unreliable; the chronicles that recorded these cases are generally inaccurate, uncritical, and deeply biased as historical sources. Often only a few lines of information describe a purported ritual murder. The medieval chronicles depict a scenario far removed from the actual historical reality; beyond naming the alleged victims, perpetrators, motives for the killings, dates, places, and punishments, they provide insufficient context for the analysis and interpretation of these persecutions.

Beginning with the second half of the fifteenth century documentation becomes more abundant. A bewildering variety of sources—"confessions" of the Jews, protocols of official investigations, judicial records, legal briefs, minutes of city council meetings, correspondence between magistrates, princes, and emperors, folk songs, tales, broadsheets, woodcuts, pamphlets, chapbooks, theological writings, and personal reminiscences—shed light on the complexity of the blood libel. In some instances, as we shall explore in later chapters, a ritual murder trial can be

8. For the role played by Dominicans and Franciscans in instigating late medieval ritual murder charges, see Jeremy Cohen, *The Friar and the Jews: The Evolution of Medieval Anti-Judaism* (Ithaca, 1982), pp. 42–44, 239–340, 244.

9. Figures computed from Will-Erich Peuckert, "Jude, Jüdin," in *HWDA*, 4, cc. 819–20.

reconstructed in its entirety. While a disturbing similarity can be found in all alleged ritual murders, the sources also reveal significant patterns of variation. If the persistent similarity of accusations can be likened to the basic character of an epidemic whose symptoms are uniformly discernible in all those afflicted, then the historical variations in ritual murder cases must resemble the individual social contexts surrounding the outbreaks of this particular pestilence of anti-Semitism.

Writing about the blood libel is hazardous. There is always the temptation to begin a dialogue with the past, the impulse to refute the historical accusations against victims of a past age. But at issue is not the veracity of ritual murder—that was thoroughly discredited in the late nineteenth century by scholars who set out to refute the renewed charges of ritual murder in a time of heightened anti-Semitism[10]—rather, the task for historians is to reconstruct and interpret the elusive reality, the motives and functions behind these fantastic fabrications of ritual murder. While the charges against the Jews were unfounded, the ideas that sustained the blood libel were real enough to send hundreds of innocent victims to their deaths.

To many Christians, ritual murder was a real event; the discovery of murdered children furnished the material evidence necessary to convict the Jews. For the Jews themselves, and for a minority of Christians, ritual murder was a superstition, a lie, and an excuse for persecution. The study of the history of the blood libel, hence, must necessarily be the analysis of different interpretations of reality: the object is to elucidate the production of social knowledge in its specific historical structure and to explain how cultural symbols acquired their power and signification. Moreover, ritual murder discourse in the fifteenth and sixteenth centuries must be understood as fundamentally a discourse of Jewish magic and Christian antimagic, with the Jews appearing as involuntary partners in an unequal interlocution, struggling against the roles assigned to them as murderous magicians.

Well before the twelfth century, before the first ritual murder accusation was raised in Europe, Jews had already acquired a firm magical reputation in the Mediterranean world. Combining Canaanite, Egyptian, Babylonian, and Hebraic magical beliefs in their religious rites, Jews embodied a distinct, exotic civilization in the eyes of the Greeks and Romans.[11] As fortune-tellers, healers, physicians, and sometimes as

10. See esp. Strack, *Jew and Human Sacrifice*, and Roth, *Ritual Murder Libel*.

11. On ancient Jewish magic, see Joshua Trachtenberg, *Jewish Magic and Superstition: A Study in Folk Religion* (Philadelphia, 1939), pp. 11–12; for Greek perceptions of Jews as magicians, see Marcel Mauss, *A General Theory of Magic*, trans. Robert Brain (London, 1972), p. 31; for Roman views, see John Gager, *The Origins of Anti-Semitism* (New York, 1983), pp. 107–8.

charlatans, some Jews peddled their magical arts just as others practiced their mercantile and artisanal trades in the Roman Empire. While Jewish folk religion might have reaped the scorn of Cicero and his fellow members of the Roman senatorial class, it was only in medieval Christian Europe that Jewish magic came to be seen as essentially demonic. In its fight to establish orthodoxy, the medieval church gradually eroded away the conceptual distinctions between heretics, magicians, and Jews, attacking all as enemies of true religion.[12]

By the late fifteenth century, on the eve of the Reformation, there existed an extensive Christian folklore concerning Jewish magic. On the more prosaic side, Jews were reputed to be highly skilled fortune-tellers, medicine men, and treasure hunters.[13] More bizarre stories narrated the prowess of the Jewish magician: a Jew changes a woman into a mare because she spurns a youth; the magician Zambres kills an ox with a single word; a Jew can conjure the Devil; he commits murder by making and destroying wax figures; he can transform himself into a werwolf.[14] Some Jews, not surprisingly, tried to make a living by exploiting these Christian beliefs, selling talismans and amulets, presenting themselves as fortune-tellers and magicial healers, and enjoying, apparently, considerable success.[15] Others encountered a more hostile reception, as did the unfortunate man who tried to sell a talisman to Duke Albrecht of Saxony for protection against sword wounds and paid for it with his life when the incredulous duke tested the talisman's efficacy by running his sword through the peddler.[16]

Three cultural themes underlay this powerful idea of Jews as magicians: the cabalistic belief and practice of word magic in the religion and medicine of medieval Jews; the potency of blood, a belief found in all folk cultures; and, finally, the salvific power attributed to human sacrifice in late medieval Christianity, as reflected in the magical notions projected onto the sacrament of the Mass and eucharistic sacrifice.

The notion that Jews as sorcerers practiced ritual murder was entirely constructed by Gentiles. But, apart from the attribution of blood magic, the Jews of medieval Europe did possess a rich magical lore; it

---

12. This point is forcefully argued in Edward Peters, *The Magician, the Witch and the Law* (Philadelphia, 1978), pp. 12–13, 94; Joshua Trachtenberg, *The Devil and the Jews* (New Haven, 1943), pt. 2.

13. Cf. Trachtenberg, *Jewish Magic*; Peuckert, "Jude, Jüdin," cc. 811–12.

14. Peuckert, "Jude, Jüdin."

15. For Christian-Hebrew amulets, see T. Schrire, *Hebrew Amulets: Their Decipherment and Interpretation* (London, 1966), pp. 69–72. For the persistent reputation of Jews as magicians in modern Germany, see Günther Dammann, *Die Juden in der Zauberkunst*, 2d ed. (Berlin, 1933).

16. The story was told by Luther as an illustration of the folly of Jewish magic. See *WA Tr* 5, no. 5567.

derived in part from a tradition of occult learning, the mystical way known as the *Kabbalah*, and was in part a reflection of the practice of folk medicine.

Kabbalah, meaning "tradition," refers to the mystical philosophy and practice derived from biblical commentaries. Based on the mystical significance and symbolism of letters and words in Hebrew, cabalistic thought flourished in the thirteenth century. Divided into two branches, the speculative was concerned with motions of the universe and their spiritual significations, and the practical focused on tapping the spiritual energies of cosmic movements for magical control.[17]

Speculative Kabbalah was central to the development of Christian mystical philosophy during the Renaissance. With the revival of neo-platonism in the fifteenth century, such cabalistic texts as *Zohar* (*The Book of Splendor*) exerted a profound influence on a circle of Christian intellectuals, among whom Pico della Mirandolla and the German humanist Johannes Reuchlin were the leading figures.[18] Reuchlin first gave Christian scholars a systematic introduction to the principles of the Kabbalah in his *De arte cabalistica* (1517).[19] A fascination with occult knowledge and the will to control the forces of the cosmos sustained this intellectual interest in the Kabbalah well into the seventeenth century, but far more widespread, though less intellectually prominent, was the fame of practical Jewish magic among the Christian folk.

Demons of all sorts populated the religious folklore of medieval Jewry; theirs was a world haunted by diseases and disasters, often induced by evil spirits. Magical formulas, gems, amulets, talismans, medical cures, omens, dreams, and divinations filled this imaginative universe founded on a real life of perpetual insecurity and frequent brutality.[20] Only the sacred Word and personal piety supplied true defenses against the misfortunes of life. Of the many rabbinic prescriptions

17. The fundamental works are Gershom Scholem, *Major Trends in Jewish Mysticism* (New York, 1974), and Scholem, *On the Kabbalah and Its Symbolism* (New York, 1965); see also Marcia Reines Josephy, *Magic and Superstition in the Jewish Tradition* (Chicago, 1975).

18. For a survey of Christian Kabbalah, see Frances A. Yates, *Giordano Bruno and the Hermetic Tradition* (Chicago, 1964), esp. pp. 84–116, and Yates, *The Occult Philosophy in the Elizabethan Age* (London, 1979); see also Cecil Roth, *The Jews in the Renaissance* (Philadelphia, 1977), pp. 112ff. For an English translation of selections from the *Zohar*, see Gershom Scholem, ed., *Zohar: The Book of Splendor* (New York, 1949).

19. For Reuchlin's lifelong study of the Kabbalah, see Max Brod, *Johannes Reuchlin und sein Kampf* (Stuttgart, 1965), pp. 80–84, 90–118, 271ff. Reuchlin's *De arte cabalistica* has been translated into English by Martin and Sarah Goodman (New York, 1983). For a general survey of Christian scholarship on Judaism in the 15th and 16th centuries, see Jerome Friedman, *The Most Ancient Testimony: Sixteenth Century Christian Hebraica in the Age of Renaissance Nostalgia* (Athens, Ohio, 1983).

20. The classic study of medieval Jewish popular culture is still Trachtenberg's *Jewish Magic and Superstition*.

for making amulets, the *Sefer Raziel* (c. 1230) of R. Eleazar ben Judah of Worms (1176–1238) was the most comprehensive.[21] A typical Hebrew amulet contained the magical name of God, the tetragrammaton, snippets of biblical texts, and names of angels. Different amulets were made for the promotion of health, fertility, and the protection of mother and child, to ward off the influence of the evil eye, to prevent miscarriages, for safety on journeys, and for the inducement of general well-being.[22]

Hebrew amulets were also in demand outside Jewish communities, and by the fifteenth century, Christian-Hebrew amulets, on which the names of Christ and the saints were inscribed, had made their appearance as new prophylactic objects. With the publication of Cornelius Agrippa's writings on the occult, many of which were compilations of secret magical formulas, Christians could finally consult their own handbook to make charms and amulets.[23] Word magic was not alien to Christianity; the many benediction formulas of the medieval church for consecration and exorcism resemble the operations of a magical language. Some benediction formulas blessed water, salt, bread, wine, holy oil, candles, crops, vegetables, and animals; some reconsecrated polluted wells and banished thunder, infertility, and danger; some protected mothers and babies during childbirth and travelers on the road; some cured the sick; some exorcised demons; and some stopped the flow of blood, the essence of all life.[24]

In Judaic, Christian, and Germanic folklore immense power was ascribed to blood, especially human blood.[25] According to Mosaic laws, Jews had to refrain from tasting blood because it contained the spirit of living beings; hence, animal or human blood was a polluting element (Lev. 17). In the *Nibelungenlied* (5.2054), blood was imbibed to renew strength because it was widely believed that blood contained the power of the soul. Blood was used in love potions to spellbind lovers in the Middle Ages; this ritual persisted into the modern period in the folk customs of Baden, Hesse, Bohemia, and Oldenburg.[26] As the embodiment of life, blood was also thought to be desired by the dead, giving rise to the legend of vampires.

Blood was more than a substance of life; it became the symbol of the

21. Schrire, *Hebrew Amulets*, p. 3; Trachtenberg, *Jewish Magic*, p. 76; Josephy, *Magic and Superstition*.

22. Schrire, *Hebrew Amulets*, p. 50.

23. For the writings of Heinrich Cornelius Agrippa von Nettersheim (1486?–1535), see his *Magische Werke*, 5 vols. in 3 (Berlin, 1921); see also Charles Nauert, *Agrippa and the Crisis of Renaissance Thought* (Urbana, 1965).

24. For an exhaustive study of medieval Christian benedictions, with numerous examples, see Adolph Franz, *Die kirchlichen Benediktionen im Mittelalter*, 2 vols. (Freiburg, 1909); on Christian amulets, see ibid., 2:435–37.

25. Stemplinger, "Blut," in *HWDA*, 1, cc. 1430–42; Strack, *Jew and Human Sacrifice*.

26. Stemplinger, "Blut."

living spirit. Thus, with blood one could sign a contract with the Devil, an old Saxon belief that found its way into the Faust legend in the sixteenth century, when the unscrupulous magician signed over his soul with his own blood. Fortified by the power of the Devil, Faust the magician could even triumph over the crafty Jews; by cutting off his own leg as a collateral to a Jewish moneylender, in the end he won back not only his leg but more than his share of wealth.[27]

Furthermore, blood was painted on door posts to keep away witches and demons. It was also used for many cures in folk medicine: in medieval and early modern rabbinic *Responsa*, the blood of a he-goat, dried in the sun, was recommended as a general medicine;[28] among Oriental Jews, the blood of circumcision was used for writing the tetragrammaton on talismans for protection against pestilence;[29] in Christian Bavaria, to relieve cramps at childbirth, a father would let the mother taste the blood from his finger;[30] and blood, used with the consecrated Host, represented a potent remedy against sickness for medieval Christians.[31]

Beginning at the end of the twelfth century, when the church promoted the doctrine of transubstantiation—whereby bread and wine, consecrated by a priest during Mass, were transformed into the body and blood of Christ while retaining their outward appearance—devotion to the Mass and to the Eucharist rapidly gained popularity among the laity.[32] As a representation of Christ's sacrifice, the Mass was depicted in gruesome detail in sermons, stained glass windows, sculpture, and paintings.[33] Perceived as an reenactment of the passion of Christ, the salvific power of the Mass was often reduced to the single moment of the elevation of the Host, all else being a mere prelude.[34] Periodically, preachers and bishops condemned the disorder during the reading of Mass: the elevation of the Host often degenerated into a moment of commotion as the people scrambled into the choir to behold the Eucharist, hoping to reap benefits from beholding the sacred.[35]

27. *Historia von D. Johann Fausten dem Weitbeschreyten Zauberer und Schwarzkünstler*, ed. Richard Benz (Stuttgart, 1977), pp. 81–83.

28. H. J. Zimmels, *Magicians, Theologians, and Doctors: Studies in Folk-medicine and Folklore as reflected in the Rabbinical Responsa (Twelfth–Nineteenth Centuries)* (London, 1952), p. 125.

29. Zimmels, *Magicians*, p. 163.

30. Stemplinger, "Blut."

31. See chap. 7.

32. The fundamental works are: Adolph Franz, *Die Messe im deutschen Mittelalter: Beiträge zur Geschichte der Liturgie und des religiösen Volkslebens* (Freiburg, 1902), and Peter Browe, *Die Verehrung der Eucharistie im Mittelalter* (Munich, 1933; reprint, Freiburg, 1967).

33. Franz, *Die Messe im deutschen Mittelalter*, p. 730.

34. Franz, *Die Messe im deutschen Mittelalter*, p. 32; Browe, *Verehrung der Eucharistie*, pp. 36–38.

35. Franz, *Die Messe im deutschen Mittelalter*, p. 32; Browe, *Verehrung der Eucharistie*, p. 49.

The demand to see the sacred represented a new piety of the Middle Ages: cabinets were opened to show off reliquaries; relic holders, monstrances, and other church objects were invented to satisfy the desire for this "holy gaze." The elevation of the Host, the display of the Corpus Christi on the monstrance, and eucharistic processions were also introduced at the end of the twelfth century to help satisfy this new devotional need.[36] To see is to establish contact. For the laity, to behold the sacred was to create a direct bond between themselves and the sources of sanctity. "Holy gaze" operated essentially in a functional and mechanical way; an action, "seeing," supposedly resulted in benefits to the beholder; it thus worked in the same way that magic is said to operate: a direct causal relationship is established between action and effect.[37]

Not surprisingly, then, popular eucharistic piety nourished a vast paraphernalia of practices and ideas that existed alongside the official rituals of the medieval church; magical notions played a prominent role in this parasacramental eucharistic devotion, despite repeated condemnations by the ecclesiastical professionals. The consecrated Host was used for two purposes: to protect oneself or to hurt others.

One of the most popular uses of the Eucharist was in love magic: according to popular legends, if a woman kissed a man with a Host in her mouth, he would always be true to her; prostitutes would apply the Eucharist as a sexual device to seduce men; the Host, grounded into powder, served as an essential ingredient in love potions.[38] Other powers were attributed to the sacrament of the altar: it protected one against the dangers of life and limb, it helped one to achieve wealth and fortune, it saved one from drowning, it induced fertility, in humans as well as in beasts and insects, and, finally, its presence kept the Devil at bay.[39]

Put to evil use in black magic, the Host could cause the destruction of life and property. It seems to have been applied frequently in abortions, if one is to believe the Franciscan preacher Berthold of Regensburg (d. 1272), who in his sermons warned women not to abuse the Eucharist in abortions.[40] In stories dating from the fifteenth century, the Eucharist was also reputedly used by witches in the preparation of magical potions, whose ingredients included bone powder and the blood of children.[41]

36. Anton L. Mayer, "Die heilbringende Schau in Sitte und Kult," in *Heilige Überlieferung: Festschrift für Ildefons Herwegen* (Münster, 1938), pp. 234–62; here, p. 234.

37. Mayer, "Die heilbringende Schau," pp. 235–36, 239; for a theoretical discussion of magical operations, see Mauss, *Magic*, pp. 18–24.

38. Peter Browe, "Die Eucharistie als Zaubermittel im Mittelalter," *Archiv für Kulturgeschichte* 20 (1930), pp. 134–54, here, pp. 135–37.

39. Browe, "Die Eucharistie als Zaubermittel," pp. 137–40.

40. Browe, "Die Eucharistie als Zaubermittel," p. 141.

41. Browe, "Die Eucharistie als Zaubermittel," pp. 141–42.

To separate true religion from the contagion of vulgar magic, the medieval church mustered its forces to combat the ritualistic use of the Eucharist in popular magic: excommunications were pronounced; the Inquisition turned its attention to reported abuses; mendicant preachers admonished layfolk to adhere to the boundary between the sacred and the diabolic; delinquent clerics who sold the Host or who practiced eucharistic magic themselves were severely disciplined; and measures were adopted to safeguard against the theft of the Host.[42] According to these medieval legends, compiled by generations of monks, friars, and bishops, Christ himself often punished the culprits who had desecrated his sacrifice by turning his body, in the form of the stolen and abused Host, into bloody human flesh.[43]

Ironically, the magical abuse of the Eucharist reflected the very success of the doctrine of transubstantiation: the consecrated bread had become much more than a symbol of Christ's Passion; in popular devotion, the Host was literally Christ's body, as legends told of the miraculous transformations of the Host into the bleeding flesh of Christ and the Child Jesus, and as the crucified Christ and the sacrament of the altar acquired the same significance in Christian iconography. The theme of sacrifice—the Crucifixion—loomed even larger in the fourteenth and fifteenth centuries. Numerous crucifixes and paintings of the Passion from this period document this development. At the same time, passion masses became common; they celebrated specifically the endless sufferings of Christ: there were masses "of the Lord's Countenance," "of the wounds of Christ," "of the Five Wounds," "of the crown of thorns," "of the lance," and "of the chains of the Lord."[44] Similarly, masses were read in commemoration of the joys and sorrows of Mary, of the Child Jesus in the Temple, and in honor of Saint Anne, the reputed mother of Mary in popular devotion.[45] In identifying themselves with Christ's real pains and human sufferings, the layfolk of late medieval Germany did not worship Christ in isolation: for them, the historic Jesus lived in a social world of parents, cousins, and kinsfolk that included Mary, Joseph, Saint Anne, and his siblings; and it was the image of the "Holy Clan" (die heilige Sippe), that offered the common people a ready point of identification with their own social nexus.[46]

42. Browe, "Die Eucharistie als Zaubermittel," pp. 145–52.

43. Cf. Peter Browe, "Die Hostienschändungen der Juden im Mittelalter," *Römische Quartalschrift für christliche Altertumskunde und Kirchengeschichte* 34 (1926): 167–97; Browe, *Die eucharistischen Wunder des Mittelalters* (Breslau, 1938).

44. Franz, *Die Messe im deutschen Mittelalter*, p. 157.

45. Franz, *Die Messe im deutschen Mittelalter*, pp. 161–69.

46. On the "Holy Clan" and the cult of Saint Anne, see John H. Bossy, *Christianity in the West, 1400–1700* (Oxford, 1985), pp. 10–11.

As a sacrament of peace, the partaking of the eucharist represented a ritual of communal harmony and Christian solidarity, and the children of a Christian community symbolized its innocence before God. What greater sacrilege could be committed against divinity and community when Christian children, martyrs like Christ, were kidnapped and slaughtered?

From the middle of the fifteenth century, the accusation of child murders against Jews in the Holy Roman Empire sounded louder and louder, and trials of ritual murder reached a crescendo in the generations before the Reformation. Between 1520 and 1570, efforts were made to suppress ritual murder trials by a conjunction of imperial interdictions and Jewish self-defense. After 1570, trials of ritual murder began to decline in the central German lands of the Holy Roman Empire, but the discourse of ritual murder and child kidnappings would persist in a divided Christendom.

Chronologically, this study begins with the 1470 case in Endingen, the earliest ritual murder trial with extensive extant documentation. In chapters 2 through 6 I describe the intensification of ritual murder and host desecration trials leading up to the Reformation—incidents that often revealed major political conflicts within the empire—and the consolidation of a discourse of ritual murder in the learned and popular cultures of the time. The impact of the Reformation, the elevation of religion over magic, and imperial interdiction of ritual murder trials are discussed in chapters 6 through 8. In a final chapter I analyze the disintegration of the late medieval ritual murder discourse and its transformation and survival into the eighteenth century in both Lutheran and Catholic Germany.

Four themes inform this history of the blood libel in late medieval and early modern Germany; they form the analytical structure that frames the flesh of chronological narrative.

First, there is the question of ritual murder as historical and social knowledge. For the simple folk and learned professors of late medieval Germany, ritual murder was a fact; Jewish magic existed. How was this "knowledge" created? Who transmitted this knowledge of the Jews and by what means? Who received this knowledge? How was knowledge practiced and modified in social and political actions?

Second, it is essential to remember that knowledge does not exist separate from institutions of power. In tracing the rise and decline of ritual murder discourse, and in analyzing the reasons for the suppression of ritual murder trials, we must focus on the political conflicts between the emperors and territorial princes, between the central imperial government and local authorities. Above all, special attention must be paid to judicial practice in the matter of ritual murder trials and to the ideology behind legal discourse and practice.

The third theme may be described as the relationship between the historical phenomenon of child murders and its representation as ritual murder. Facts never speak for themselves; interpretations create knowledge. What is the significance, then, of a particular mode of representation, and how is it related to other representations of the same phenomenon? In late medieval and early modern Germany, stories told of the Devil, of witches, and of werewolves killing children; Jews were not the only alleged child kidnappers. Why was ritual murder discourse the most prominent genre of representing child murders in the fifteenth and sixteenth centuries? What led to its decline in the second half of the sixteenth century?

Fourth, I address the role of the Reformation as it affected the relationship between learned and popular discourses of ritual murder. The elegant conceptual distinction between elite culture and popular culture belies the immensely complicated and confusing interactions between varieties of ritual murder discourse. For the learned world, one can distinguish between theological, legal, and medical discourses on ritual murder; in folk culture, a vast array of songs, tales, woodcuts, and practices transmitted this knowledge of Jewish magic. Who influenced whom? Where did the culture of the elite and the culture of the people meet? Did ideas circulate across social strata? Did they filter down from above or did they swell up from the common folk? In analyzing ritual murder discourse as cultural history, I hope to suggest some answers to these questions.

Finally, I hope to tell a good story. This book is based on numerous stories of ritual murder, told by Christians and Jews, Lutherans and Catholics, lawyers and theologians, thieves and magistrates. In sifting through their tales, as recorded in judicial records, political correspondence, folk songs and stories, woodcuts and paintings, theological expositions and legal treatises, I have paid as much attention to the "storytellers" themselves as to their stories. Their social background, their historical setting, their narrating techniques, and their social audience, in addition to the functions and contents of their tales, provided the sources and inspiration for this study. Theirs as well as mine are tales of morality; the discourses of ritual murder were about "sacrifice" and "justice"; this book concerns the practice of a knowledge that had tragic consequences for a people.

CHAPTER TWO **Endingen**

AUSTRIAN BREISGAU

 ITUATED BETWEEN THE BLACK FOREST AND THE RHINE, the Breisgau is a lush, fertile region irrigated by the Rhine and its tributaries with narrow, long, agricultural valleys extending from the elongated river plain gently upward onto the slopes of the Black Forest. The Breisgau occupies the heartland of the Upper Rhine valley and is today that part of Germany which borders on France and Switzerland. Settled in early Germanic times by the Alemanni, the Upper Rhine had a pattern of civilization resembling a parallel string of towns on both sides of the Rhine, with Strasbourg, Colmar, and Mulhouse on the left bank, and Karlsruhe and Freiburg on the right, running from north to south, and with Basel located at the lower tip of the long pocket, astride the Rhine.[1] Father Rhine, as the nineteenth-century German poet Friedrich Hölderlin praises, nourishes its children, and the economy of the region depended on the ready communication afforded by the grand river. With the elevation of the terrain the rich agricultural valleys give way to vineyards; in the later Middle Ages, viticulture was of great importance both to Alsace and to the Breisgau.[2] The rich pastures also supported a flourishing animal husbandry: horse and cattle markets could be found in the second half of the fifteenth century in Strasbourg, Freiburg, and Basel.[3] A wide variety of handicraft and mercantile trades grew up on the basis of a fertile agrarian economy; cities like Strasbourg, Colmar, Freiburg, and Basel became centers for the wine trade, for food and leather processing, and for the many other occupations that characterized the guild economy of

---

1. On the Breisgau, see the articles in the special issue of the *Oberrheinische Heimat* 28 (1941).

2. See L. J. Mone, "Zur Geschichte des Weinbaues vom 14. bis 16. Jahrhundert in der Schweiz, Wirtenberg, Baden, Hessen und Rheinpreussen," *ZGO* 3 (1852), pp. 257–99.

3. See L. J. Mone, "Zur Geschichte der Viehzucht vom 14. bis 16. Jahrhundert in Baden, Wirtenberg, Elsass, Baiern," *ZGO* 3 (1852), pp. 398–414.

the later Middle Ages. In the late fifteenth century, a Freiburg merchant with moderate capital would roam as far south as Basel and as far north as Frankfurt to trade his merchandise.[4]

The geographical, cultural, and economic unity of the Upper Rhine, however, belied its political division in the late fifteenth century: the territorial presence of the imperial Hapsburg dynasty, both in the Franche-Comté and in the Breisgau, posed a constant threat to the autonomous, republican aspirations of the Alsatian free cities and the Swiss Confederation. Politically, the Rhine formed a dividing line between the quasi-city republics of Alsace—Strasbourg, Rosheim, Obernai, Sélestat, Kaysersberg, Colmar, Münster, and Mulhouse—and the Hapsburg Further Austria (Vorderösterreich), formed around the core of Breisgau, the Black Forest, and parts of Alsace and Switzerland, with Ensisheim in Alsace as the provincial capital and Freiburg in Breisgau as its intellectual and economic center. An added dimension of tension was represented by the emergence of the Swiss Confederation after the original revolt of the peasant communities of Uri, Unterwalden, and Schwyz against the Austrian Hapsburg authorities and the subsequent incorporation of other urban and rural communities into the antinoble confederation of "the common men."[5] The fifteenth century witnessed the growing political influence of the mountainous cantons and the emergence of a "free" communal Swiss political model, whose influence extended well into South Germany, as exemplified by the urban alliance linking Zurich with Strasbourg by means of the Rhine.[6] Proud of their civic traditions and weary of the territorial ambitions of the Hapsburgs, the citizens of the imperial and free cities and the Swiss cantons harbored suspicions of the territorial ambitions of the imperial dynasty.[7] But free citizens could determine their body politic without having to bend to the will of noble lords; civic freedom emboldened the magistrates and townsfolk of the Alsatian and Swiss cities to expel their Jews in the wake of the Black Death of 1348–50, despite the imperial protection accorded to this religious minority. Communal revolts, by which patrician regimes were overthrown or forced to share power with the guilds, often accompanied

4. The account book of the Freiburg merchant Marx Hoff shows his wide-ranging travels; see Steven Rowan, ed., "Die Jahresrechnungen eines Freiburger Kaufmanns 1487/88," in Stadt und Umland, ed. Erich Maschke and Jürgen Sydow (Stuttgart, 1974), pp. 227–77.

5. For a succinct summary of the communal movement in Switzerland and South Germany, see Peter Blickle, Gemeindereformation: Die Menschen des 16. Jahrhunderts auf dem Weg zum Heil (Munich, 1985), esp. pp. 167–96.

6. The alliance between Strasbourg and Zurich was celebrated in a long panegyric by Johann Fischart: Das Glücksfahrt Schiff von Zürich (1577).

7. For a succinct analysis of the political divisions in the Upper Rhine, see Thomas A. Brady, Turning Swiss: Cities and Empire, 1450–1550 (Cambridge, 1985).

the pogroms. Where the principle of communalism triumphed, even if Jews were permitted to return, their legal and social status became severely restricted; but for a few cases, Jews were forbidden to acquire citizenship.[8] In contrast, where the authority of the nobility remained strong, Jews were granted the right of residence, often against the wishes of the common men. In their dynastic territories, the Hapsburgs encouraged Jewish settlement in order to benefit financially from the protection fees and taxes levied from the Jews. In 1446, the Hapsburg territorial government issued a decree in Further Austria threatening prompt prosecution of anyone who injured or killed Jews.[9] The free citizens were, so to speak, *"Judenfrei,"* whereas the subjects of the Austrian regime in Breisgau, with the exception of the powerful city of Freiburg, had to tolerate the Jews of their lord.

Located on the road between Breisach and Riegel, the little town of Endingen in Breisgau perches on the north slope of the Kaiserstuhl, a high point of 557 meters overlooking the surrounding flat river valley. With a population of about two hundred households, or roughly one thousand souls, in 1470,[10] Endingen was a small market town for the surrounding countryside. Corn and wine represented the chief commodities; most Endingers cultivated a patch of land, either as their major source of income or as an important secondary occupation. Grain, wine making, and barrel making were the three leading trades. The first handicraft guild, the shoemakers, did not appear until 1415, and the first guild ordinance dates back to 1447.[11]

The Endingers enjoyed limited political rights. Around 1470 Endingen became a member of the third estate in the Provincial Estates (*die Landstände*), which collectively represented the towns and the peasant communities of Further Austria. In 1467, the community of Endingen consisted of a *Bürgermeister*, a town council, and citizens; a civic court of ten members served as the lower court for civic and minor criminal cases. But as a territorial town the political autonomy of Endingen had clear limits. The administration of criminal justice had been pawned by the Austrian archdukes in order to raise cash for the perennial financial

8. On the pogroms associated with the Black Death, see the thorough and thoughtful article by Alfred Haverkamp, "Die Judenverfolgungen zur Zeit des Schwarzen Todes im Gesellschaftsgefüge deutscher Städte," in Alfred Haverkamp, ed., *Zur Geschichte der Juden im Deutschland des späten Mittelalters und der frühen Neuzeit* (Stuttgart, 1981), pp. 27–93.

9. See Selma Stern, *Josel of Rosheim: Commander of Jewry in the Holy Roman Empire of the German Nation,* trans. Gertrude Hirschler (Philadelphia, 1965), p. 4.

10. In 1475 Endingen's population was estimated at 200 herds, see Erich Keyser, ed., *Badisches Städtebuch* (Stuttgart, 1959), p. 215.

11. For Endingen's economy and political structure, see Keyser, ed., *Badisches Städtebuch,* pp. 215–16.

needs of the Hapsburgs. For most of the fourteenth and fifteenth centuries, the lords of Üsenberg, local noblemen, administered justice for the Hapsburg authorities; in 1467, the town's justice was administered by the nobleman Martin von Staufen. One of the hallmarks of subjection to feudal lordship was the need to tolerate Jews: in 1331, some Jews lived in Endingen under the protection of the lord of Üsenberg; and in 1427, Duke Friedrich of Austria promised the townsfolk that he would not force them to accept Jews, a promise the Hapsburg did not keep.

THE TRIAL

At Easter 1470, the charnel of Saint Peter's Parish Church in Endingen caved in and had to be demolished. Removing bones from the charnel for reburial, workers came across the remains of a man, a woman, and what looked like two small, headless corpses. Someone remembered that eight years ago, in 1462, many Jews had gathered in the house of Elias to celebrate Passover and a poor beggar family had been given refuge by Elias. Suspicion of murder soon fell on the Jews of Endingen. It is not clear exactly who brought up the charges in 1470: oral legend and the subsequently composed *Judenspiel* have the Bürgermeister and the town council of Endingen writing to Archduke Sigismund in Innsbruck, who had inherited the Hapsburg lands on the Upper Rhine; another account has Ludwig, the lord of Lichtenberg, as the initiator of the inquiry. In any event, the matter came to the attention of Archduke Sigismund, who then instructed Karl, margrave of Baden, his governor, or *Statthalter*, to take charge of the investigation. Karl of Baden ordered the arrest of the Endingen Jews.[12]

On 24 March the magistrates arrested Elias of Endingen and his brothers, Eberlin and Mercklin. Thus began the notorious Endingen ritual murder trial, which resulted in the execution of the three brothers and the expulsion of the rest of the Jewish families. Five major sources of very different degrees of reliability document the Endingen ritual murder trial: the first is a record of the interrogation of the three Endingen Jews, Elias, Eberlin, and Mercklin, deposited in the city archive of Freiburg; the second, a copy of the confessions of Elias, Eberlin, and Mercklin and those of three Jews subsequently arrested in Pforzheim, deposited in the city archive of Strasbourg; the third, again a copy of the confessions of Elias and Mercklin of Endingen and of four Pfrozheim Jews, in addition to two imperial mandates, deposited in the city archive of Frankfurt; the fourth, a ballad, "The Song of the Parents and Innocent Children"; and

---

12. See StdA Ff Ugb 44t, 8 folios, unnumbered.

the last, a play commemorating the occasion, the *Judenspiel* of Endingen.[13]

The Freiburg copy of the confessions is probably the earliest account we have of the alleged murder—the arrest and confessions of the Pforzheim Jews came later—and any reconstruction of the real event has to begin here. We must, however, approach this document with extreme caution because the guilt of the Jews had already been assumed, as the opening sentence of the record clearly indicates. It is worth quoting the confessions at length:[14]

> On the Saturday before Easter Sunday [24 March] in the year of Our Lord [14]70, Elias, Jew at Endingen, was held and questioned as to what he knew of the murder committed some years ago in Endingen by the Jews, because one knows well, that nobody else but the Jews had committed the murder [*dann man wisse wol, das den morde nieman annders gethon hab, dann die juden*]. First, he should answer whether he knew that some years ago several poor people had used his shearing shed as lodging. To this, Elias the Jew answered without any torture or pain that some time back, perhaps eight years ago, some poor people were resting on his lane and would have liked to have some lodging—they were a man, a woman, with two children and a small horse. Whereupon his wife Serlin invited these poor people into the shed, where they could find plenty of straw for their beds. The poor people then went into the shed with their two children. After that Elias was asked . . . as to who had murdered them and who else were present. To this Elias the Jew

13. The original record of the confessions has been lost, but a copy of it was transcribed by the Freiburg city council; Heinrich Schreiber published it in his *Urkundenbuch der Stadt Freiburg im Breisgau*, vol. 2 (Freiburg, 1829), pp. 520–25. In editing the Endingen *Judenspiel*, Karl von Amira has reedited the confessions, correcting some of Schreiber's mistakes; the confessions, the Play of the Jews, and "The Song of the Parents and Innocent Children" are collected in his *Das Endinger Judenspiel* (Halle, 1883). In the Frankfurt city archive under signature Ugb 44t, a manuscript by Dr. Jorge Ehinga, imperial chamber procurator, contains somewhat shorter and slightly different versions of the confessions of Elias and Mercklin and the confessions of four other implicated Jews, which are missing in the Freiburg copy as transcribed by Schreiber and Amira (StdA Ff, Ugb 44t, folios 1–6). Two letters by Emperor Friedrich III that shed new light on the trial are also to be found under the same archival signature. These documents have been published by Isidor Kracauer; see "L'affaire des Juifs d'Endingen de 1470: Prétendu meurte de chrétiens par des Juifs," *Revue des études Juifs* 17 (1888), pp. 236–45. The Strasbourg manuscript has been published, without much critical commentary, by Georg Wolfram: "Prozessakten eines angeblich durch Juden verübten Christenmords zu Endingen," *ZGO* N.F. 2 [41] (1887); pp. 313–21.

14. I am translating here from the published version by Karl von Amira, which is essentially the same as Schreiber's transcription, except for minor spelling differences. The confessions of Elias and Mercklin in the Frankfurt city archive are incomplete but contain some minor variations. The variant readings are pointed out in subsequent notes. The confessions of Elias, Eberlin, and Mercklin in the Strasbourg manuscript are identical to the Freiburg version published by Schreiber and Amira.

answered: the murder was committed in the same night in his shed by
Mennlin the Jew, Mercklin the Jew, Leoman the Jew,[15] Hesman the
Younger, a Jew, Matthew the Jew, and an alien vagabond Jew.[16] They
helped one another to commit the murder and in the same night they
carried the four murdered persons out the back door of the shed into the
lane, passing by the house of Cunlin Binder on the way to the charnel.
Elias was then asked whether he was in the shed at the same time and
what he had done. To this he answered: he was not inside the shed but
kept watch by the house. . . . He was told by the other Jews to wait
there; he did their bidding, but went to the shed anyway to find out
what the other Jews were doing with the poor folks, and through a crack
in the door, he saw how each of them took one person and murdered
them with sickles and then carried the very same murdered persons out
the back door to the charnel. He also said that his brother Eberlin was
waiting in the street near the bridge. Elias the Jew said that the Jews then
carried the blood of the young children in a glass and their heads into his
room.

In confessing to being a witness of the gruesome murders, instead of
being a killer himself, Elias was trying to gain some respite and a lighter
sentence. Except for the first question, which he answered voluntarily,
torture was undoubtedly applied during the rest of the interrogation.
Eventually, enough pain produced the desired answers. Elias confessed
further to the magistrates that Mennlin and Hesman wanted to buy his
silence but that he did not take any money from them. They then threatened his life and warned him not to go before the Jewish elders; if he
should denounce them, they would implicate him in the murder as well.
Later Mercklin gave his wife, Serlin, money to buy her silence. Elias
found out that the bodies were buried in the charnel house in the Christian cemetery. In the subsequent counsel to cover up the "crime," during
which Elias was present, the Jews agreed to the pretense of praying so
that people would not become suspicious of any cries of the poor folks
they might have heard. It was the time, after all, when the Jews of
Endingen were celebrating the Feast of the Tabernacle. Later, Mennlin
told Elias that he sold the blood to Leo, a rich Jew in Pforzheim, and that
the foreign vagabond Jew rode away with the horse.[17] When asked by
the magistrates about the heads of the parents, Elias said he only saw the

15. In the Frankfurt manuscript of Elias's confession, he says that Leoman was from
Sélestat (Schlestett) in Alsace.
16. The confession of Smolle, the son of Mennlin, names Helyan (=Elias), Eberlin,
Mercklin, Berman, the old traveling Jew, and Leo, the young Jew. See StdA Ff Ugb 44t.
17. In the Frankfurt manuscripts, Berman confessed that he brought the blood of the
children to Leo of Pforzheim and that Smolle was the foreign Jew who rode away with the
horse.

heads of the children. Finally, at the end of a lengthy interrogation, Elias described the children as a boy and a girl.

Eberlin's ordeal came next. According to the interrogation record, he confessed without torture.[18] Probably the sight of the instruments of pain was enough to secure his cooperation. A new element emerged in Eberlin's testimony. He told of a counsel in Elias's house in which the decision was taken to murder the Christian family; his own task in the plot was to keep watch by the bridge. He repeated the information given by Elias that six men—Mennlin, Hesman, Mercklin, Leoman, Matthew, and a foreign Jew—had committed the murder. More gory details came out. The Jews who carried the blood of the children and their heads into Elias's room, where several old and young Jews were waiting, were bloody and had to wash the blood off their arms. According to Elias, the bodies of the victims were buried in the charnel so that if they were discovered, people would suspect Christians and not Jews of the crime. But when the magistrates questioned him about the blood, Eberlin seemed to have trouble satisfying his inquisitors:

> After that Eberlin the Jew was asked what the Jews did with the Christian blood and to say why the Jews needed it. In reply he answered badly [Darvff hat er schlechtlich geantwurt], that the Jews need Christian blood for their circumcision.[19]

Furthermore, Eberlin also said he saw the heads of the two children; that Leoman gave him ten guldens to buy his silence; that Mennlin and the foreign Jew went away with the blood and the two heads; that they murdered first the adults and then the children; and that the Jews back in the house conspired to make a loud cry while the others were slaughtering the Christians in the shed in order to drown out their death cries. Moreover, Eberlin stated that Serlin, his sister-in-law, had given the poor Christians some milk earlier in the evening to make them sleep more soundly. At the end of his interrogation, the clerk recorded:

> Thus all that is written down has been confessed to by Eberlin without torture, and he begged to be allowed to become a Christian, that he wanted to be and remain a good Christian until his end, and that he wanted to do all that a pious Christian would do.[20]

While fear might have overwhelmed Eberlin and broken his spirit even without torture, the third brother, Mercklin, tried to be courageous. Two days later, on Monday, 26 March, the magistrates interrogated a more defiant Mercklin:

18. Amira, *Judenspiel*, p. 94.
19. Amira, *Judenspiel*, p. 95.
20. Amira, *Judenspiel*, p. 95.

He was asked what he knew of the murder in Endingen, which his two brothers, Elias and Eberlin, had each on their own confessed as to who had committed the murder and how it was done. To this Mercklin the Jew replied: if his brothers had said so, you should know well enough. Why do I need to say anything?[21]

The magistrates rebuked him and told him that it did not matter what his brothers had said, they also wanted to hear about it from him. He was tortured and admitted "with many enforced words" to the crime, including his own role in killing the woman by slitting her throat, that the foreign Jew killed the husband, and that the parents were awake but the children were asleep when they were killed. After they had murdered the parents, they then slaughtered the children and collected their blood. Since he was the strongest, he carried the body of the man to the cemetery, while the other Jews carried the woman and the headless children. At the cemetery, Mennlin climbed up the bone hill, dug a hole, and threw the bodies into it, covering them up with bones.[22]

The magistrates then asked Mercklin whether the Jews had used the blood of the adults:

To that he answered no; they did not collect the blood of the adults, only the children's. Mercklin was then asked why they had killed off the adults if they did not use their blood. To that he answered: they did it because they wanted to have the children. Afterwards, Mercklin was asked as to why Jews need Christian blood. To that he answered in many words, saying at first that Jews need Christian blood because it has great healing power [*dann es sye gar heilsam*]. We would not be satisfied with this answer and told him he was lying, that we knew why they need it because his brother Eberlin had told us already. To this Mercklin said that Jews need Christian blood for curing epilepsy. But we replied: Why then is your son an epileptic? And we would not be satisfied with the answer. Mercklin then said further that Jews need Christian blood for its taste because they themselves stink. But we would not be satisfied with the answer and told him he was lying, and must tell us the truth, because his brother Eberlin told us a different story; now he must also tell us the truth. To this he answered badly that he wanted to tell us the truth, that he saw it cannot be otherwise . . . but that Jews need Christian blood for circumcision. Mercklin was then asked once more about the aforementioned things and [we] reproached him: if you Jews all know so well that Christian blood is good and salutary [*heilsam*], why don't you make your own blood salutary and accept baptism? To that he answered, it is the devil's work.[23]

21. Amira, *Judenspiel*, pp. 95–97.

22. In the Frankfurt manuscripts, Smolle, the son of Mennlin, confessed to this act, and not Mennlin, as implicated by Mercklin. Mercklin's own confession in the Frankfurt manuscript also names Smolle and not Mennlin in climbing the bone hill.

23. Amira, *Judenspiel*, p. 97.

Even a proud, defiant man like Mercklin could not stand up to repeated torture. It is clear from the testimony on the alleged Jewish use of Christian blood that the poor man was utterly confused. He obviously had some ideas of Christian blood superstitions and seemed to have been desperately seeking the correct answer that would satisfy the magistrates and end his torture. Eventually, he came upon the expected "truth." "Justice" came swiftly. The end of the interrogation protocol recorded the Jews' execution by burning on 4 April.

What can we make of this judicial record of confessions to a heinous crime? It would be tempting to dismiss it as propaganda, a document of hatred reflective of anti-Jewish prejudices and Christian superstitions and practically worthless as a historical record. Certainly it is useless as a documentation of an event, the alleged crime, because, in all probability, even if these were violent deaths, the Jews did not commit them. In other words, the crucial question concerns not a murder; at issue is the fabrication of the "event" of a ritual murder out of diverse fragments of social reality: the discovery of the bodies, the long-standing suspicion of Jews, their incarceration and judicial torture, and their execution. The interrogation record represents an attempt to create coherence out of troubling disparate facts; it is itself less a documentation of a historical event than a testimony to the process of cultural representation that blamed Jews for child murders and sent them to their deaths.

The unreliability of the interrogation record as a judicial document is borne out by a comparison with the confessions from the city archives of Frankfurt and Strasbourg, which contain some telling variations. Aside from the three main characters—the brothers Elias, Eberlin, and Mercklin—there is a coterie of accomplices whose identities remain shadowy in spite of zealous official investigation. The Freiburg copy of the interrogation record, on which the traditional tale of the Endingen trial is based, names Elias, Eberlin, Mercklin, Mennlin, Leoman, Hesman, Matthew, an unnamed foreign Jew, Serlin (Elias's wife), and Leo of Pforzheim. The Frankfurt manuscript contains, in addition to the condensed versions of the confessions of Elias and Mercklin, long confession by Smolle, the son of Mennlin, and shorter ones by Berman, Leo of Pforzheim, and Leo the Young Jew. These men were arrested in Pforzheim and interrogated by Karl of Baden after the three brothers had been executed. While Berman might have been the Hesman named by Elias, the two sets of confessions vary significantly, especially regarding the confusion of roles. In one set of confessions, Mennlin sold the children's blood to Leo of Pforzheim; in the other, it was his son, Smolle. In one, Mennlin climbed the bone hill to dig a hole in order to dispose of the bodies; in the other, it was again Smolle. In one confession, Mercklin suffered repeated tortures and gave many answers before he admitted, to the satisfaction of his interrogators, that Jews needed Christian blood for circumcision; in the other, he confessed right away to the alleged secret purpose behind the Jewish use of Christian blood. The Frankfurt version omits Eberlin's confession altogether, while the Strasbourg manuscript records the confessions of the three brothers but only three of the four Pforzheim Jews' testimonies; Leo the Younger's confession is missing. Evidently, the three copies amount to three variants of the same ritual murder confessions. According to any principle of jurisprudence, serious questions must be raised as to the accuracy of the confessions, especially if they contain contradictory information on roles in a murder case.

If these confessions are opaque as text of a judicial inquest, they are, however, richly revealing of the context in which they were generated, and by "decoding" this text in its political and religious context we can begin to reconstruct the historical process behind the so-called Endingen ritual murder.

Compared to the Frankfurt and Strasbourg manuscripts, which seem unstructured in legal format, lacking the exact dates of interrogation and the precise questions asked, the Freiburg copy is a model of procedural clarity. The Freiburg copy recorded the confessions according to the guidelines for judicial clerks specified in the 1507 Bamberg Criminal Code, which served as a model to the 1532 criminal code of Emperor Charles V, the *Carolina*: the clerks were to record carefully the times and places of each interrogation, the questions asked, and the answers given by the suspects.[24] By contrast, the six confessions in the Frankfurt manuscript lack details and structure. And why should Eberlin's confession be missing? A bad transcription of the original interrogation records might have produced the discrepancy, but it suggests that the lucid narrative structure of the Freiburg copy is the result of a synopsis, a redaction of the contradictory notes taken during the interrogations; it represents a "clean" copy, its clear chronology and sequence of events superimposed on the confused and spontaneous utterings of the men under torture.[25] Moreover, internal evidence also suggests that the confessions were highly dubious as judicial records; contradictions and tensions in the confessions are clearly evident from a close reading of the text. First, the

24. *Carolina*, arts. 181–91. I have used the 1900 edition by Kohler and Scheel. See Josef Kohler and Willy Scheel, eds., *Die peinliche Gerichtsordnung Kaiser Karls V: Constitutio Criminalis Carolina [Die Carolina und ihre Vorgängerinnen: Text, Erläuterung, Geschichte, 1]*, (Halle, 1900; reprint Aalen, 1968), pp. 96–99. Similar guidelines for jurisprudence were already in practice in the early 16th century; Heinrich Zoepfl has shown the textual similarities between the *Carolina* and the 1507 Bamberg Criminal Code. See Zoepfl, ed., *Die peinliche Gerichtsordnung Kaiser Karls V. nebst der Bamberger und der Brandenburger Halsgerichtsordnung . . . mit den Projecten der peinlichen Gerichtsordnung Kaiser Karls V. von den Jahren 1521 und 1529* (Heidelberg, 1842).

25. In the 1504 Freiburg ritual murder trial, information came out that the Endingen Jews were forced to confess to their guilt. See chap. 5.

guilt of the Jews was already assumed in the opening sentence: "One knows well that nobody else but the Jews had committed these crimes." In addition, the interrogation record minimized the application of torture: Elias confessed "without any torture and pain (*one alle marter vnd wethun*)," according to the Freiburg manuscript; in the Frankfurt manuscript, he confessed "out of free will and uncoerced (*fryes willens vnd ungezwungen*)"; Eberlin also confessed "without torture (*one alle marter*)." But there is evidence to contradict this. After Karl of Baden executed the three brothers, Emperor Friedrich III wrote a stern letter, rebuking the margrave because he had, without imperial approval, "on account of the alleged murder of some Christians at Endingen in Breisgau imprisoned several Jews, condemned some of them to death, and held others in prison under severe torture and pain."[26]

The terror and confusion faced by the three brothers and the other Jews arrested by Karl of Baden is easily imagined. Thrown into cold, damp, dark cells, often without ventilation, dragged before the rack and the pulley, iron fetters around their legs, necks, and arms, and forced to confess to a spurious murder eight years past, the Jews would have to muster superhuman strength to maintain their innocence. The ubiquitous instrument of torture in Europe before the French Revolution was the *strappada*, by which the suspect's hands were tied together behind his back with a rope, which was then thrown over a beam. Hoisted in midair, the poor fellow was left to hang for some time; often weights were added to his feet to increase the strain on the arms and back muscles (see fig. 1). A few jolts usually sufficed to loosen joints as well as tongues, and only the hardiest did not break down and confess.[27] Apparently Eberlin broke down without actually undergoing torture, and the stronger Mercklin was also eventually reduced to confess. Both Elias and Eberlin tried to save their lives by confessing to acting as accomplices, hoping, perhaps, if not for pardon, then for imprisonment, mutilation, or a relatively quick death by the sword. Other ways of execution, as prescribed by the *Carolina* and the Bamberg Criminal Code, were much more painful: death

26. Letter of Emperor Friedrich III to Karl, margrave of Baden, 5 May 1470: "vns ist angelangt wie du in crafft unser keyszerlich bevelh so du von vns haben solt oder auss deins selbs furnemen geschicht vnd handlunghalb so sich an ettlichen Cristen menschen zu Enndingen in Breyszgaw sollen ergangen haben ettlich Juden zu Vengknuss genomen der ettlich vom leben zum tode bracht, ettlich nach in vengknuss mit sweren martt vnd pein haltest" (StdA Ff Ugb 44t).

27. On the introduction of torture and the inquisitorial process into medieval jurisprudence, see Henry C. Lea, *Superstition and Force: Essays on the Wager of Law—the Wager of Battle—the Ordeal—Torture* (Philadelphia, 1866); pp. 353*ff.* deal with Germany. For descriptions of the instruments and methods of judicial torture in Europe before the French Revolution, see Edward Peters, *Torture* (New York, 1985), pp. 67*ff.*; for illustrations of the torture instruments of the ancien régime, see John H. Langbein, *Torture and the Law of Proof: Europe and England in the Ancien Régime* (Chicago, 1977), pp. 18–26.

Wie der Graue den juden wyter
peinlich ließ fragē vñ der jud sich eins kampffs erbodt.

Figure 1. The strappada. A Jew is undergoing judicial torture. Note the weight tied to the man's feet. From Thomas Murner, *Die Entehrung Mariae durch die Juden*, reproduced in *Jahrbuch für Geschichte, Sprache und Literatur Elsass-Lothringen* 21 (1905).

by fire, by quartering, by the gallows, or by drowning, by having one's limbs broken on the wheel or by being buried alive, or by being tortured with red hot pincers before execution.[28]

28. *Carolina*, art. 192. Richard van Dülmen argues that these gruesome rituals of death were intended as demonstrations of magisterial authority over the ruled (*Theater des Schreckens: Gerichtspraxis und Strafrituale in der frühen Neuzeit* [Munich, 1985]).

147,988

College of St. Francis Library
Joliet, Illinois

The brothers' confessions did not save them. Karl of Baden condemned all three to death. As the Endingen *Judenspiel* commemorated,
the three brothers were stripped, wrapped in dry cowhide, tied to horse-
tails, dragged to their execution ground, and burnt (see fig. 2).[29] The
dragging of condemned criminals to execution sites was a customary
practice at the time; it signified the denigration of the murderers to the
level of beasts, men who had lost their human reason.[30] For Jews, this
kind of humiliation was not unusual. When Michael the Jew was executed for theft in Dortmund in 1486, he was hung at the gallows between two dogs, a particularly degrading mode of execution for Jewish
criminals that gradually disappeared during the sixteenth century (see
fig. 3).[31] Death by burning for a murder was exceptional: men who
committed premeditated murders were normally broken on the wheel
and left to die; murders mitigated by anger or other circumstances
deserved death by the sword; and women who killed infants were
drowned.[32] Only heretics and black magicians were burnt.[33] To Christians of the late fifteenth century, the Jews of Endingen embodied a
despicable cross of both.

Let us return for a moment to the interrogation record. Having
examined its reliability as a judicial document, we conclude that it contains inaccuracies of testimony and prior assumption of guilt. If it appears
highly ambivalent as a historical and legal document, upon which the
Jews were sent to their deaths, how is it to be interpreted? One strategy
would be to examine it as a social text, a discourse,[34] in which various
social voices made use of the ensemble of religious, political, legal, and
magical vocabularies to contest and define the nature of social reality;

29. "Derwegen soll mans schleiffen auss,/meniglich zue einem grauss;/darnach ge-
worffen in dass feur/und da verbrent gantz ungeheur" (Amira, *Judenspiel*, lines 1672–75).
30. See *Carolina*, art. 193 "Vom Schlayffen": "Item wo durch die vorgemellten enndt-
lichen vrtheill einer zum todt erkannt, beschlossen wirt, das der vbellthätter ann die
Richstat geschleyft werden soll, so sollenn die nachvollgenden wortlin ann der andern
Vrtheill, wie obsteet, auch hangen, Allso Lautende: Vnnd solle darzu vff die Richstat durch
die vnvernunfftigen thier geschlayfft werden."
31. See the Dortmund chronicle of Dietrich Westhoff in *Die Chroniken der westfälischen
und niederrheinischen Städte*, Bd. 1: *Dortmund, Neuss (Die Chroniken der deutschen Städte vom 14.
bis ins 16. Jahrhundert Bd. 20]*, ed. Historische Kommission bei der Bayerischen Königlichen
Akademie der Wissenschaften (Leipzig, 1887), p. 349.
32. See *Carolina*, arts. 131 (infanticide), 133 (abortion), 137 (murder).
33. See *Carolina*, art. 109, and Zoepfl, ed., *Bamberger . . . Halsgerichtsordnung*, art. 131,
"Straff der Zauberey," p. 44.
34. For the concept of discourse as social knowledge and as a guide to practical action,
see David W. Sabean, *Power in the Blood: Village Discourse and Popular Culture in Early Modern
Germany* (Cambridge, 1984), pp. 195–96.

Wie der Graue den juden ließ
schentlichen uß schleyffen zu dem galgen.

Figure 2. A Jew dragged to execution. From Thomas Murner, *Die Entehrung Mariae durch die Juden,* reproduced in *Jahrbuch für Geschichte, Sprache und Literatur Elsass-Lothringen* 21 (1905).

perhaps then can we begin to understand the multiplicity of meaning the language of accusation had for the participants.

Three structural levels to this ritual murder discourse can be distinguished. The first, or fundamental, level was also chronologically the earliest phase: the initial rumor and gossip when the bodies of the mur-

Wie der Graue den Juden ließ er-
henckte mit zweyen riiden/vnd verbrenne vnd dem galgen.

Figure 3. A Jew hung between dogs. This gruesome manner of execution mimicked a reversed Crucifixion: Christ was crucified between two thieves. From Thomas Murner, *Die Entehrung Mariae durch die Juden,* reproduced in *Jahrbuch für Geschichte, Sprache und Literatur Elsass-Lothringen* 21 (1905).

dered Christians were discovered in the bone hill of the charnel. People immediately suspected the Jews. This initial process can be described as the appropriation of an immemorial legend—one transmitted by village gossip, chronicles, folk songs, tales, pictorial depictions, sculptures, pilgrimages, and shrines—namely, that Jews had murdered Christian children in the past and that blood played a central role in Jewish magic. The first phase of the ritual murder discourse thus activated a tradition about Jews and applied this "knowledge" toward explaining and resolving an immediate problem in daily life. In Endingen, a murder needed to be solved. The dialogue during this initial phase took place between an impersonal discourse and a particular actor: the impersonal discourse of ritual murder was articulated in part by historical events (ritual murder trials in the past), transmitted by the various media of popular culture, sanctioned by some ecclesiastical authorities, confirmed by the judicial actions of lords and magistrates, and authenticated and recorded in chronicles; the particular actor could be a peasant, a burgher, a nobleman, a prince, a town council, or a community. In the case of Endingen, the trial record refers to an impersonal, unspecified source—rumors, gossip, or popular discourse—which has come to take the place of truth "because one knows well that nobody else committed the murder but the Jews." As we shall see later, however, this was not exactly how suspicion first befell the Jews.

The second level or phase of a ritual murder discourse moved from accusation to official investigation. Now the murmurs and whispers of popular gossip became submerged in the official voice of the judicial apparatus and the protestations of the suspects. The interlocution took place between officers of the law in the Holy Roman Empire—princes, magistrates, and bailiffs, who acted both on the discourse of ritual murder and the common laws of the empire—and the accused Jews, who were interrogated under judicial torture to confess to the crimes. Naturally, the dialogue was uneven, since the magistrates called in witnesses, weighed the evidence, and applied torture, while the Jews tried steadfastly to maintain their innocence or broke down and confessed under fear and pain in this unequal power play. Legends of Jewish magic, which helped to trigger the initial accusation, were thus further reinforced by the confessions of the imprisoned. In the Endingen trial, Leo of Pforzheim, who was supposed to have purchased the children's blood from the Endingen Jews, confessed that some eighteen or twenty years back, he and his father had attended a circumcision. He saw red liquid in a cup and asked his father what it was. His father answered that it was Christian blood necessary for circumcision.[35] The moment of "truth" extracted under torture in 1470 in fact retroactively validated ritual murder trials in the past; in ritual murder discourse, past and present engaged in a self-affirming historical dialectic, through which social knowledge produced eternal truths, and experience and interpretation formed a seamless whole.

At this stage the discourse turned political: city councils exchanged

35. StdA Ff Ugb 44t, "bekanthenisse Leo des Judden."

queries and warnings about other possible ritual murders, and jurisdic-
tions were often contested, as when Emperor Friedrich III reproached
Karl of Baden for summarily executing imperial Jews. Read as a social
text, the Endingen confessions resemble the write-up of an originally
unspoken and unarticulated dialogue, one that already existed in the
minds of the magistrates and was finally written as text when the Jews
were forced to utter their lines. The scenario of the "murder" was a
confused montage of legends about Jews and biblical and parabiblical
narratives woven into a meaningful whole by the central "fact" of a
murder-sacrifice. No one would have missed the identification between
the poor murdered Christian family and the Holy Family: the description
of the husband and wife, their two young children, and their small horse
in the shed, spending their night on straw, must have represented to the
Endingers the image of Joseph and a pregnant Mary sojourning with
their donkey in a stable in Bethlehem. The Christians were slaughtered in
Elias's shearing shed like innocent lambs, like Jesus victims of the blood-
thirsty Jews with their butcher knives.

The religious subtext and the social context of the Endingen trial
record are manifest in the third and final level of this ritual murder
discourse. After three gruesome days of torture, the climax of the investigation was not the admission of murder by Mercklin but the confession
of motive: that Jews killed the children for the healing and salutary power
of Christian blood. Without Christian blood, there would be no circumcision; without the even greater power of Christian sacrifice, Jewish magic
was impotent. Christianity triumphed. Eberlin wanted to convert and
live out the rest of his life as a good Christian; Mercklin admitted to the
greater efficacy of Christian blood and confessed that the Devil was
preventing the Jews from conversion. Only the sentencing and the public
executions of the Jews remained. Banished were the discordant voices of
unequal contestation during the interrogation: the "crime" had been
confessed, the cries of the evildoers muted. Replacing the sound and fury
of angry accusation, stern interrogation, and tormented protestations
was the calm voice of unison between Jews and Christians; both parties
now swore to the "truth" of the ritual murder and its inevitable detection
and punishment. During this final phase, the discourse resounded in the
voice of a vindicated and triumphant Christian community. The public
execution itself served as a dramatic representation of the evil of Jews and
the triumph of Christianity: the convicted were burnt as minions of the
Devil, as black sorcerers, and, only incidentally, as murderers. The narrative structure of the interrogation record reflected the tripartite structure
of the ritual murder discourse; crucial was not the actual deaths of the
Christians but the meaningful representation of otherwise unknowable
reality. As such, the record of the judicial proceedings resembled the

dramatic structure of the Endingen Jewish play, which "was [a] bloody faction . . . a tragedy [with] a beginning, a middle, and a sad outcome."[36]

A BALLAD

If a critical reading of the interrogation record and the *Judenspiel* opens a window into the mental universe of the Christians of late medieval Germany, a historical question still remains unanswered. What happened? Why was it that the alleged murders, supposedly committed in 1462, waited eight years to be uncovered? And who denounced the Jews? Ironically, possible answers to these questions are provided not by the judicial documents of interrogation but by a folk song, "The Ballad of the Parents and the Innocent Children."[37] This song contains some startling information that may provide the clue for reconstructing the historical context behind the trial. Given the biased nature of the official records, it is all the more important to read the cultural products of ritual murder discourse in a critical way for their possible historical content. The text of the ballad follows:

1.
What do I want to sing and tell you
of a woman and a man
and two small children, yes children?

2.
They passed through Endingen town,
they came in front of the Jew's door,
lodging they could not find, not find.

3.
Jew, will you not let us stay for the night?
The Jew, he said: with all my heart,
go rest in the shed on straw, on straw.

4.
And they came into the shed on straw,
there they praised God and Our Lady,
that they lodging had found, had found.

5.
And it was around midnight
when the Jews held counsel,
what to do with them, with them.

36. Amira, *Judenspiel*, lines 1875–77.
37. See "Lied von den eltern und unschuldigen kindern," in Amira, *Judenspiel*, pp. 100–102.

6.
The Jewess, she gave false counsel:
we will strike them all dead,
no one can say a thing, a thing.

7.
And it was around midnight,
Jacob the butcher said to his wife:
listen, the Jew hits his wife, his wife.

8.
Oh no, I think it's not his wife,
but the poor folks on straw,
they strike their children, their children.

9.
And when it was light in the morn'
Jacob the butcher into the Jew's house stepped:
Jew, where are your guests, your guests?

10.
I sent them first thing morn'
out the city gate away,
must have been half past six, past six.

11.
Oh Jew, you lie to my face,
the horse is still in your stall,
eating hay from your stack, your stack.

12.
Jacob the butcher will not let things stand,
he goes to the Bürgermeister,
wants to tell him things, yes things.

13.
Jacob Butcher, you are a clever man,
you can just let things be,
they will bring you money, yes money.

14.
Before I will let things lie still,
I will rather lose my possessions,
and my young, fresh life, yes life.

15.
Eight and a half years went by,
Jacob experienced much with the Jews,
his possessions are all gone, all gone.

16.
When Jacob was a poor man,
God showed a miracle one day,
the charnel caved in, caved in.

17.
They bloom like a rose tree,
their fragrance like a pilgrim staff,
before God they are four angels, yes angels.

The crucial character, as revealed by the ballad, was the butcher Jacob, a neighbor of Elias. He was the one who heard something in the night, suspected the Jews, confronted Elias, and denounced the Jews to the Bürgermeister. Other matters might have been involved. Perhaps Jacob borrowed money from Elias and they had a dispute over interest and repayment, an all too common quarrel between Jews and Christians in this period. Maybe the two competed: Elias had a shearing shed where he kept animals, and butchering was one of the trades Jews practiced in fifteenth-century Germany. Material self-interest could easily breed resentment. In any case, both the ballad and the Endingen *Judenspiel* single Jacob out as the courageous man who suspected Elias and went before the Bürgermeister.[38] In both accounts, the Bürgermeister dismissed the accusation, instead asking Jacob to leave the matter alone. It was not unlikely that Jacob's quarrel with his Jewish neighbor was well known in a small town of one thousand, and without material evidence, an accusation of murder was insufficient to warrant an investigation. But eight years later, in 1470, when the charnel was being demolished, bodies were found. Eight years would have been long enough for bodies to decompose; whatever was found underneath the pile of bones in 1470 certainly did not belong to the alleged murder victims of 1462. But eight years later, Jacob was financially ruined; he was "a poor man" and bitter, too. It is more than likely that he started the rumor circulating again of the Passover of 1462 and the alleged ritual murder. Jacob never appeared in any of the extant judicial records. Once the judicial apparatus bestirred itself, his presence no longer mattered; he receded into the background as the folk hero of the ballad and the Jewish play. Moreover, by this time, the political climate had changed. The town was about to buy back its judicial autonomy from the lord of Üsenberg, the protector of the local Jews.

In 1467, on the death of his brother and cousin, Martin von Staufen inherited the lordship of Üsenberg. Following custom, the citizens of Endingen swore allegiance to Martin, but with the new proviso that if they could have recourse to better justice, Martin would not stand in their way of redeeming the judicial autonomy of the town, which had been pawned by the Hapsburg archdukes to the lords of Üsenberg.[39] Two

---

38. For the argument of the play, which summarizes the plot, see Amira, *Judenspiel*, lines 59–134, esp. 108–16 (pp. 20–23).

39. Oath of allegiance sworn on 22 Oct. 1467; for text, see Heinrich Maurer, "Urkunden zur Geschichte der Herrschaft Üsenberg," in ZGF 5 (1879–82), pp. 193–326, here p. 312.

years later, the townsfolk sold a municipal bond to a Strasbourg citizen and raised five hundred guldens to buy back the town's independence.[40] Martin, however, refused to return justice to the town council because this right was pledged to his relatives by the Hapsburgs in exchange for a loan of more than one thousand guldens.[41] The dispute was eventually settled by arbitration; in November 1470, the city council of Freiburg suggested a compromise: eight hundred guldens, plus restitution by Endingen to the nobleman for damages to his interests—namely, the execution of the Jews and the confiscation of their properties.[42] In other words, the Endingen ritual murder trial took place in the middle of a confrontation between the townsfolk and their noble lord, who was also the protector of the Jews. The crux of the conflict was, as we have just seen, the power of jurisdiction: Who should pronounce justice, the lord and his bailiff or the town council elected by the citizens? In the battle to assert communal solidarity and autonomy, the Jews were tempting scapegoats. A sensational murder trial would bring the matter before higher authorities; a conviction of the Jews would vindicate the townsfolk and humiliate the lord.

Once the three brothers were arrested, interrogated, and executed, the trial took on a life of its own. Names of other Jews mentioned in the confessions led to other arrests and interrogations. Elias, Eberlin, and Mercklin were arrested on 24 March; they died on 4 April. In less than two weeks, Karl of Baden and the territorial government in the Breisgau had gathered enough information from forced confessions to suspect a widespread Jewish conspiracy. Named in Elias's confession, Leo of Pforzheim was arrested with three other Jews in his house. Leo was a prominent Jew in Baden who had been granted protection in 1463 by Friedrich, elector of the Palatine. Perhaps his arrest also reflected underlying political tensions about which the documents are silent.[43] From the confessions of these four Jews, extracted under torture, Endingen seemed to be the tip of an iceberg. Smolle, Mennlin's son, confessed to knowledge of another child murder. In 1465, according to Smolle, a five-year-old Christian shepherd boy from Wörde was kidnapped and sold for twenty-two guldens to a rich Nuremberg Jew by the name of Moses of

40. On 20 Oct. 1469, Duke Sigismund of Austria allowed the city of Endingen to sell a bond of 500 guldens to Claus Duntzenheim of Strasbourg at 4% interest; see Maurer, "Urkunden," p. 230.

41. See letter of Duke Sigismund to Endingen, 15 July 1470 (Maurer, "Urkunden," pp. 230–31).

42. For the text of the arbitration recommendations by Freiburg, dated 29 Nov. 1470, see Maurer, "Urkunden," pp. 312–15.

43. See J. A. Zehnter, "Zur Geschichte der Juden in der Markgrafschaft Baden-Baden," ZGO N.F. 11 [50] (1896), pp. 337–441, here p. 346.

Freyberg. He, Smolle, and another man, Abraham, hired themselves out
to kill the boy.[44] Further, Smolle admitted that some ten or eleven years
back (1459/60), he had talked a poor woman in Speyer into selling her
own child for thirty guldens; he then resold the child to the rich Jew Lazar
of Worms. The Worms Jews then killed the child for its blood and buried
its body near the Jewish cemetery.[45] The confessions of Leo and Berman
implicated the Jews of Worms, Frankfurt, Nuremberg, Sélestat, and
Pforzheim.[46] In other words, the Endingen trial could have served as the
basis for the persecution of almost all the major Jewish communities of
the Holy Roman Empire. The Frankfurt Jews tried to save themselves the
only way they could; they offered a generous monetary contribution to
the coffers of the emperor to buy his good graces.[47]

Reminded of the usefulness and the compliant loyalty of the Jews,
Emperor Friedrich III intervened forcefully to stop the escalation of persecutions. On 5 May Friedrich wrote a stern letter to Karl of Baden
declaring that Karl had imprisoned, tortured, and executed Jews solely
on his own will and without imperial sanction. Moreover, Karl was about
to confiscate the properties of all the Jews in his territory. Friedrich
commanded Karl to desist immediately:

> By Our Roman Imperial Might We recommend earnestly and firmly
> ask that you leave the Jews unharmed in regard to the aforementioned
> matter, and also to free all the Jews which you have imprisoned, without
> compensation and upon the receipt of this letter, and further by the
> authority of Our Imperial Mandate and order . . . not to undertake
> anymore violence against a single Jew or Jewess so as to avoid Imperial
> and Our great displeasure.[48]

Finally, Emperor Friedrich admonished Karl of Baden that if he had any
complains against the Jews, he should raise them with the emperor

44. StdA Ff Ugb 44t, "Smollen Juden Bekanthenisse."
45. "Smollen Juden Bekanthenisse."
46. Copies of the confessions of the three Endingen brothers have not turned up in the
city archives of Worms and Nuremberg and the Staatsarchiv of Nuremberg.
47. See Kracauer, "L'affaire d'Endingen," p. 237, and his Geschichte der Juden in Frankfurt a. M. (1150–1824), 2 vols. (Frankfurt, 1925), vol. 1.
48. Letter of Friedrich III to Karl von Baden:

"So empfehlen wir dem lieb von Römisch Keyszerlicher Macht ernstlich vnd vesterlich
gepietende daz du die gemelten Judischeyt der vermalten sachenhalb vnangelangt vnd
vnbekumert bliben auch die gefennge so du nach Ingefencknuss hast, derselben
fengknuss seind etlich vnd alles verzihen nach antwurtung diss brieffs on entgeltnuss
ledig vnd mussig lassest vnd ferner in crafft vnser keyszerlichen briefe vnd bevelh ob
die an dich vnd ander mit den von vns aufgegeinge beschehen weren nach dein selbe
eygen furnemen, oder auss dennoch ander [gewaltsenn]? wider einich Juden oder
Judin nichtz handelst furnemst noch tust, in einich wise als lieb die sey unser und des
Reichts swere ungnad zumeyden" (StdA Ff Ugb 44t).

according to law; what he was doing with the Jews was both arbitrary and without imperial permission. On the same day, an imperial mandate went out to "princes, both spiritual and secular, counts, free lords, city councils, servants, headmen, officeholders, curators and overseers, Bürgermeisters, judges, councillors, citizens, and communes, and all imperial subjects" condemning the arbitrary imprisonment, judicial torture, and execution of the Endingen Jews by Karl of Baden. The emperor informed his subjects that he had commanded Karl to free the Jews without bail and to refrain from confiscating their property or harming their persons, and he further enjoined the imperial estates to insure that the Jews come to no harm.[49]

The four Jews of Pforzheim had already died at the stake; but apparently Karl of Baden complied with Friedrich's wishes, and no more Jews were arrested.[50] For the burghers of Endingen, the trial represented a triumph for their communal Christian politic: by destroying the Jews in the town, the Endingers not only did away with an alien cultural and religious minority but also freed themselves from the intrusion of noble power, under which the Jews had previously been protected; moreover, they gained a privilege from Emperor Friedrich III, renewed by Emperor Maximilian in 1517, not to tolerate Jews in the future.[51] The ritual murder trial was the cause célèbre of the community; it occurred simultaneously as the town redeemed its juridical autonomy from Martin von Staufen. The process represented nothing less than the victory of a Christian civic community over the Jews and, by implication, over their noble protector as well.

THE JUDENSPIEL

Victory called for celebration. Sometime after the burning of the three brothers, a play was written to commemorate the supposed ritual murder and its vindication. Thomas Mallinger recorded its performance in 1616 in his diary:

> In Endingen a solemn comedy was performed: it was about several innocent children secretly killed by the Jews who used to live there, an act for which they were arrested, convicted, and thrown into the flames and burnt. The corpses of the children are still at hand and on display. Visitors from neighboring towns and villages are asked and invited to this comedy, in which stately instruments and voices are used for music.

49. Imperial mandate of Friedrich III to the estates of the empire, StdA Ff Ugb 44t.
50. Kracauer, "L'affaire d'Endingen," p. 237.
51. See imperial privilege, 29 Dec. 1517 (Maurer, "Urkunden," p. 135); see also Adolf Lewin, *Die Juden in Freiburg i. Breisgau* (Trier, 1890), p. 93.

Thousands come from neighboring places to attend upon and see this comedy.[52]

The text of the Endingen Jewish play drew from the interrogation records, from oral legends, and from the abundant imagination of its anonymous author. The *Judenspiel* resembled the passion plays of many other German-speaking communities in that it was performed at Easter and celebrated, in essence, the triumph of Christianity over Judaism. Performances attracted spectators from neighboring communities well into the nineteenth century.

Divided into a prologue, an argument, eight acts and an epilogue, the drama calls for forty-eight players, including nine roles for the Jews. It was performed, as mystery and passion plays were, in open air, either in the market square or in front of a church. A platform with a backdrop and perhaps a canopy would have sufficed to excite the natural imaginations of the spectators. The prologue gives the leitmotiv for the following action: the prophecy and example of Christ already foreshadowed the hatred Jews would harbor against Christians; Jews have killed not only their own prophets and Christ but have also poisoned wells to murder Christians en masse.[53] Another player then steps onto stage to recite the argument, or summary, of the play: he tells of the gathering of Jews in Old Endingen to celebrate the Feast of the Tabernacle, and how a Christian beggar family could not find a hospice to take them in. He then describes the false hospitality of Elias and Serlin, the gruesome murder and the disposal of the bodies, Jacob the butcher's courageous confrontation with the Jews, the inaction of the Bürgermeister, and, finally, God's miracle in exposing the bodies when the charnel was demolished eight years later. The Jews confess without torture, and the player tells the spectators that "it shall not be missing that they are judged and burnt to death, as you shall see in this play, which is true and based on past fact."

The first three acts take place in 1462. They represent the arrival and murder of the Christian family. Elias is the major character and dominates the first act. Described as a learned rabbi, Elias is portrayed with power and passion and is given many lines and dramatic scenes. He is the one who calls the other Jews to a counsel to plot the murder of the Christians. Revenge is the motive. Elias praises God for the Feast of the Tabernacle, about which the Jews are going to celebrate:

> That I have oft' celebrated Passover with jubilation,
> give me great peace that I may praise thee also

---

52. From the diary entry of 24 Apr. 1616, cited by Amira, *Judenspiel*, p. 1.

53. The legend of well poisoning emerged in the wake of the Black Death; see Schreiber, *UB Freiburg I*, pp. 378–83.

in yonder high heaven there above.
The might of Christians may fall soon at hand,
which has truely shamed in all lands,
in the whole world, our people, with the vilest abuse.

Abraham, Mennlin, Mercklin, Leoman, Hess, Matthew, and a foreign
Jew all voice their hatred of Christians and add that "moreover, Christian
blood is good and useful for many things" (lines 211–12). Mercklin wants
Christian blood to flow like a well; Leoman will slaughter Christians like
dogs. Pleased by the consensus, Elias vows to destroy Christians just as
his ancestors have done, "according to the commandments of our religion."

The second act opens with the arrival of the poor Christians. The
faceless bodies discovered in 1470 are given names: it is Irus, with his
wife and children. They are forced to seek shelter with the Jews because
the Christians turn them away. The play reminds the spectators of their
duty of Christian charity; the tragedy of 1462 happened because "no one
does his best for the poor people of the world, whom God himself had
chosen." Sara gives shelter and milk to Irus and his family and immediately informs Elias of the arrival of the potential victims. A counsel is
called, all Jews appear on stage, and they volunteer for the gruesome
murder. Elias promises that he will divide up the blood. The children are
to be "butchered like sheep." The murder scene takes place right on stage
with Irus and the woman shouting out murder before their throats are
slit. Jacob the butcher hears the death screams, but his wife tells him to go
back to sleep and let the Jews mind their own business.

In act 3, we see Jacob and another neighbor, Cunlin, discussing the
noises they have heard last night. Right away, they both suspect the Jews
of some evil deed. Jacob confronts Elias in his house and demands to
know the whereabouts of the Christian family. Elias replies that they
have left. Jacob calls him a liar, saying that Irus's horse is still in the
stable. Elias says he bought it from the family. Now fully convinced of
foul play, Jacob goes to the Bürgermeister and denounces Elias, but he is
turned away.

In act 4, eight years have gone by and Jacob has dropped out of sight.
The charnel is about to collapse, and the bones have to be removed and
reburied. The workmaster and two burghers are working in the charnel
when the men turn pale as ghosts: they come across undecomposed
bodies underneath a pile of bones. The parish priest is called in, but he
does not want to have anything to do with the undecomposed and
headless bodies. He treads on the bodies and immediately becomes lame
in every limb. While being carried off stage, he begs God for mercy and
forgiveness for his sin of disbelief. The Bürgermeister and councillors are

convinced of a miracle because the bodies smell like roses. They put them on display in the church.

Jacob's accusation suddenly comes to mind, and in act 5, the Bürgermeister sends for Elias. When asked, Elias confesses promptly and accuses "foreign Jews" of having committed the murder. He names them. Nonetheless, the Bürgermeister puts "the old Jew" in chains and sends for his brother Eberlin. In act 6, also a short scene, Eberlin confesses to having kept watch. He is likewise put in chains. Four burghers are sent to fetch the third brother from the Hochburg, the castle of the local lord.

Many scenes follow one another in quick succession in act 7. The burghers of Endingen present their noble lords with the murder case. The lord of Hochburg hands over Mercklin, who also promptly confesses. The Bürgermeister then writes to Archduke Sigismund in Innsbruck. In an interlude, two men are cured miraculously after visiting the displayed bodies in the church: a blind man can see and a lame man can now walk, thanks to the "two innocent children." Meanwhile, the postmaster brings news from Innsbruck: Karl of Baden will preside over the case.

The final and longest scene is also the dramatic climax, with a large cast to represent the various jurors and judges. Justice is served; the verdict is pronounced. It takes place before the town hall, with the knight of Hochberg, the bailiff, as the plaintiff, the lord of Stauffen as the mace-bearer, and ten players representing the jurors sent by the cities of Freiburg, Basel, Villingen, Sélestat, Neuenburg, Colmar, Ketzingen, Endingen, Waldkirch, and Emendingen. While the previous acts contain an element of historical reality, this final triumphant scene of judgment is entirely the product of the playwright's imagination. The confessions of the three Jews are read aloud; when asked about their veracity, Elias, Eberlin, and Mercklin are permitted only to utter "yes." The jurors advise the death sentence, in accordance with Mosaic and imperial law. Moreover, in the words of the "lord" of Sélestat:

> since they spilled innocent blood,
> one cannot let the matter stand,
> but that they must be sentenced,
> and Imperial law suffices,
> that they be sentenced to death,
> and God may give us grace.
> For I think if this murder
> remains unpunished, God will
> punish us eternally and always
> cast us out of his kingdom.

In pronouncing the death sentence, the lords proclaim that justice is served and that no violence has befallen the Jews. In the final scene, the

Jews are dragged to be burnt; comic relief is provided by three boys who eagerly stone the Jews. When the stage is cleared, a sole actor comes on to deliver the epilogue, describing how the Jews have been bound hand and foot and "burnt down to powder, dust, and ash." He reminds the spectators that God will leave no sin undiscovered or unpunished: "O, dear, pious Christian . . . do good, fear God, hold his commandments . . . that you may go forth from misery into life . . . without end in all eternity."

The Endingen *Judenspiel* is, of course, a morality play, and morals are derived from the perceptions of reality. The identities of the four bodies remain forever hidden. Whatever their fate in life, the burghers of Endingen succeeded in constructing a meaningful and moving story out of what would otherwise have been just another reminder of the violence and meaninglessness of life. Fragmented events now acquired a unifying structure in the ritual murder discourse; violence was transformed into sacrifice, victims into martyrs, bodies into relics, tragedy into triumph, and death into life. The Christian family would live on, not only in folk memory, in the ballad, and in the performance of the Jewish play, but also in the ongoing salvific economy of a Christian community. Miracles were reported, and Saint Peter's in Endingen, which housed the relics, became a pilgrimage site for the region.[54]

But had there been a murder in the first place? Perhaps Elias was right, and the vagabond family had simply moved on. No crime existed after all. The only murders that took place were in the townsfolk's fantasies, conjured by vivid imaginations of horror, inspired by a belief in Jewish magic, and excited by a haunting rumor spread by a Jew hater.

Ritual murder discourse transformed an unsolved murder or fantasy into material for its own reproduction: it expressed itself in the confessions, in the interrogation record, in a ballad, in oral legends, and in a morality play. Two central themes ran through this discourse: murder-sacrifice and judgment. The representations of the Endingen "murders" provided a discursive outlet for the unspeakable crimes committed against the family, especially the children, who were cruelly beheaded. The discourse created a more meaningful, coherent, alternative explanative model, that argued for the dialectical opposition between the two binary opposites of Jew/murderer/magician and Christian/victim/believer, between black, demonic magic and life-giving, godly religion. At a deeper level, ritual murder discourse produced the powerful experience of sacrifice so central to the self-expression of late medieval piety in a century of the imitation of Christ and the many moving and gruesome

54. See "Miracula quaedam und Wunderzeichen, so sich durch Intercession und Fürbitte der lieben Kinder und Märtyrer alhie zu Endingen zugetragen," cited in Amira, *Judenspiel*, p. 4.

depictions of the Crucifixion. A ritual murder discourse involved two sacrifices: by murdering the Christian family, Jews reenacted the Crucifixion, giving a historical event a salvific immediacy and power that the commemorative mass could not rival; by exposing the "crimes" of the Jews and avenging the "murders," sacrificing the evildoers to the offended deity, the townsfolk celebrated the triumph of Christianity and avenged and vindicated the historical Crucifixion of Jesus. A ritual murder discourse functioned as a form of *imitatio Christi*. Just as the Christian community dispensed justice, so, too, could pious Christians expect divine justice at the end of the world. The solemnity of the final act of judgment in the Endingen *Judenspiel* must have excited the eschatological imaginations of the "dear, pious Christian" spectators. To German Christians of the late fifteenth century, who understood their religion from various ecclesiastical sacraments and rituals, iconographical motifs, and biblical narratives, the twin themes of murder-sacrifice and judgment must have represented the essence of the salvific message.

Poignantly, sacrifice and judgment also reinforced the salvific message for the Jews. Their fate was to suffer, survive, and remember. Elias, Eberlin, and Mercklin were great-uncles of Josel of Rosheim, who became an energetic spokesman and leader for the Jewish communities in the Holy Roman Empire during the reign of Charles V. His own father, who was just a boy at the time of the trial, fled Endingen and escaped death. Josel remembered the bitter fate of his relatives and of the other Jews in his memoirs.[55]

Endingen was also remembered in Freiburg. The confessions of the Jews were transcribed in the *Kopialbuch* of the city of Freiburg. The Kopialbuch was a compilation of the most important legal documents of the city: it served as a record of the civic privileges, laws and customs, and more important business transactions, and was, in sum, a duplicate of the original diplomatics (*Urkunden*), which may be damaged or lost through time. It served as both a legal compendium and a historical reference for the practice of government. When the confessions of the Endingen Jews passed into the Kopialbuch, the trial of 1470 became uncontestable history, the ritual murder a fact. In the words of the play's prologue, "the many rogish tricks [of the Jews] against pious Christians are proven by history and evidenced by chronicles."[56] A story became history.

55. See memoirs of Josel of Rosheim: Isidor Kracauer, "Rabbi Joselmann de Rosheim," memoirs, section 1, in *Revue des études Juifs* 17 (1888): 84–105, and Selma Stern, *Josel of Rosheim: Commander of Jewry in the Holy Roman Empire of the German Nation*, trans. Getrude Hirschler (Philadelphia, 1965), pp. 4–6.

56. "Desgleichen gar vil schelmen stuckh /begangen, und gar manchen duckh /den frommen christen sy bewisen, /d'history, cronickh dis erwisen" (Amira, *Judenspiel*, lines 41–45).

CHAPTER THREE **Consolidation of a Discourse**

HE ENDINGEN TRIAL OF 1470 REMAINED A REGIONAL AF-
fair. Four years later, however, another ritual murder
trial on the periphery of the empire, in Trent, quickly
won widespread attention. In fact, during the two generations before the Reformation, the various legends,
histories, memories, and "cases" of ritual murder co-
alesced into a single tradition of discourse. Alleged
magical murders of Christian children by Jews not only furnished the
stuff of stories and histories but also reinforced the social knowledge
about Jews as expressed in ritual murder discourse; and, for Christians in
the Holy Roman Empire, these stories of murder served as a harbinger of
worse crimes in the future if nothing were done about the "Jewish
problem." In short, the consolidation of an unified discourse on ritual
murder and Host desecrations created a moment of synthesis between
past memory and present experience; tradition acquired the aura of
historical truth. Crucial to this cultural consolidation was the appearance
of moveable type printing, which provided the means for rendering
insignificant the often indistinguishable boundary between elite and
popular culture, between written and oral traditions.[1] Behind the many
chapbooks, song sheets, broadsheets, and printed woodcuts describing
these purported ritual murders and host desecrations, one detects more
than an amorphous popular anti-Semitism: the conscious creators of a
clearly articulated political message were hard at work to shape public
opinion. Through focusing on two well-known trials of the 1470s, the
ritual murder trial in Trent and the Host desecration trial in Passau, we
will examine the cultural representations of these events, the agents of

1. For the impact of printing on the cultural and intellectual changes in early modern
Europe, see the stimulating but not always persuasive argument of Elizabeth Eisenstein,
*The Printing Press as an Agent of Change: Communications and Cultural Transformations in Early
Modern Europe*, 2 vols. (Cambridge, 1979).

cultural transmission, and the various media by which the discourse on Jewish magic was articulated.

SIMON OF TRENT

No case illustrates this process of a ritual murder discourse in the making better than the publicity generated by the death of Simon of Trent. During Easter of 1475 in the north Italian city of Trent, which lay between the Venetian Republic and the Austrian Tirol, a two-and-a-half-year-old boy named Simon was found missing by his parents. His father, Andreas, a tanner, went before the local judge, the *podestà*, and accused the Jews of kidnapping and murdering his child.[2] In conjunction with Bishop Hinderbach of Trent, the secular authorities acted quickly; they rounded up the Jews and put them under severe torture. The chief suspect, Samuel, the leader of the local Jewish community, was badly tortured for two months before he was burnt on 21 June. Many other Jews, including some German Jews who were visiting Trent, were likewise tortured, forced to confess, and executed throughout 1474 and 1475. In this first trial, presided over by Bishop Hinderbach and the city officials, the Jews pointed to a Swiss, a man named Zanesus, as the real murderer. Zanesus had lost a lawsuit against Samuel and was apparently trying to frame him. On account of the excessive torture and judicial irregularities found in the report of the proceedings received by Pope Sixtus IV, another trial was decreed for 1476, with the Bishop of Ventimiglia presiding instead of Bishop Hinderbach. The second trial at Trent and Roveredo established that the confessions of guilt had been extorted under severe torture; moreover, a Christian citizen of Trent also accused Zanesus of the child's murder. During a third trial in Rome during 1477 and 1478, the probity of Bishop Hinderbach's conduct and the legality of the first trial formed the main issues. Although Pope Sixtus IV did not declare the trial invalid, he warned the bishop not to cause further harm to the Jews. In any event, popular piety rapidly overtook the legal scruples of the ecclesiastical authorities: miracles began to be attributed to the little martyr boy, Trent became a pilgrimage site, and Simon was beatified by the Curia. The impact of Trent on the history of Italian Jews does not belong to our story; in the empire, however, it became sensational news.

A heavy traffic in people, goods, and ideas linked northern Italy with the south German cities in the second half of the fifteenth century and the first decades of the sixteenth century. From Venice, Asian spices,

2. For a partial transcription and translation of the trial record, see Strack, *The Jew and Human Sacrifice*, pp. 193–200.

Mediterranean foods, and Italian silk and woolen fabrics went north to the great financial and industrial cities of Augsburg, Nuremberg, and Ulm; from the Germanic north came students who enrolled in the law faculties of the Italian universities, merchants who did business in the *Fondaco Tedesco*, the German "factory," in Venice, bookmen who were prominent in the incipient Venetian printing industry, and, naturally, clerics, pilgrims, and soldiers who traveled further south.[3] For the Jewish communities of the two countries, there were also many family and business ties. In Mantua, the Jewish community consisted of immigrants from Germany and adhered to Ashkenazic rites.[4] In Venice, business and family bonds of the Jewish community transcended the Alps: in 1470, the doge wrote to the city council of Nuremberg on behalf of a certain Lazarus; in 1471, the doge Nicolaus Tronus again interceded on behalf of Cressonus Michael's daughter, who was residing in the Jewish community in Nuremberg, that she be allowed to emigrate with all her possessions to Roveredo in Venetian territory.[5] Not surprisingly, news of the Trent murder quickly spread to the nearby city of Venice, which had a large German population. The first printed account of the ritual murder trial to appear in German came from the printing press of Hans von Rheine, who had settled first in Vicenza and later in Venice to ply his trade.[6] The account appeared as a long poem composed by a Matthäus Kunig and was printed in octavo.[7] It was much more than a description of "the horrible death" of Simon; the poetic voice intruded repeatedly to demonstrate the "truth" and to agitate for a particular course of political action against the Jews.

For Kunig, the essence of the ritual murder was its imitation of the crucifixion. The poem did not give a precise reason as to why Jews might need to shed young Christian blood beyond the vague verse: "they must have Christian blood/in this Easter time."[8] But the torments were described vividly: stretched out "crosswise," tortured in many ways, the

3. On the economic connections between Italy and Germany in the 15th century, see Hermann Kellenbenz, *The Rise of the European Economy: An Economic History of Continental Europe from the Fifteenth to the Eighteenth Century* (London, 1976), pp. 150–51.

4. Cf. Moritz Stern, ed., *Urkundliche Beiträge über die Stellung der Päpste zu den Juden* (Kiel, 1893), no. 70, p. 74; no. 80, pp. 81–82.

5. StA Nb, Reichsstadt Nürnberg, Repertorium 2b, Urkunden nos. 3414, 3415, 3419, 3460.

6. For the importance of German printers in the first decades of the Venetian book trade, see Martin Lowry, *The World of Aldus Manutius* (Ithaca, 1979), chap. 1.

7. See the poem "Vom heiligen Simon" in Rocus von Liliencron, ed., *Die historischen Volkslieder der Deutschen vom 13. bis 16. Jahrhundert*, 5 vols. in 4 (Leipzig, 1867), vol. 2, no. 128, pp. 13–21. The poet names himself on line 419 and the printer on lines 437–38.

8. "Sie müsten haben Christen plut/zu düser osterlichen zeit" ("Vom heiligen Simon," lines 22–23).

boy Simon finally "tilted his head to his right/and gave up his noble spirit."[9] Through the invented dialogue spoken by the Jews, Kunig made an explicit comparison between Simon and Jesus, as if the language of Christ's Passion was not clear enough.[10] In narrating the judicial proceedings that followed the discovery of the body, Kunig exonerated Zanesus and praised the podestà and the captain of Trent. The poet admonished Archduke Sigismund of Austria not to accept money from the Jews and to deal harshly and justly with the culprits.[11] The hero who earned full poetic praise was the "most reverend Bishop of Trent," who would enjoy heavenly bliss next to the boy saint Simon.[12]

Through Kunig's printed poem and through "eyewitness accounts" repeated by German students, merchants, and clerics returning from Italy, the legend of Simon of Trent became well known in the Holy Roman Empire. A celebrated ritual murder had become a symbol of political propaganda. In his chronicle of the reign of Count Friedrich I of Palatine, Matthias von Kemnat retold the story in great detail.[13] For the chronist, the "evil of the Jews" served as a critique of "the princes, lords, and the cities who give the evil ones so much freedom" in their plan to destroy the Holy Roman Empire.[14] Ultimately, however, responsibility lay with the head of the realm, as Kemnat appealed to Friedrich III: "Oh Emperor, Emperor! You are their lord and say they are yours. Now look at how you woo and protect the enemies of Jesus Christ who are also your own enemies. How can Jesus love you, when you love and give shelter to his oppressor and murderer?"[15]

9. For the description of the torture, see "Vom heiligen Simon," lines 100–120. For his death, see lines 154–55: "es naigte sein haubt auf sein rechte seiten/und gab auf seinen edelen gaist."

10. "Vom heiligen Simon," lines 118–25.

11. "Und herzog Sigmunt von Österrich/hochgeporn und so lobelich,/nim von den ketzern weder gold noch gelt,/so hastu lob in aller welt" ("Vom heiligen Simon, lines 289–92).

12. See "Vom heiligen Simon," lines 375–98.

13. Kemnat's chronicle is printed in *Quellen zur Geschichte Friedrichs des Siegreichen*, ed. Conrad Hoffmann, vol. 1 (Munich, 1862), pp. 1–141; for the ritual murder at Trent, see pp. 119–26.

14. "Vnd ist ein gros wonder, so die hunde vns so gefere vnd feindt sint, das die fursten vnd herren, desgleich die stede den boswichten so gros freiheit geben vnd so uil vbersehen vnd ire groste feinde bei ine erneren, dan die verfluchten juden teglich rach vber die christen schrien vnd betten, vnd besunderlich alle tag bitten sie vmb die zerstorung des romischen reichs" (*Quellen zur Geschichte Friedrichs des Siegreichen*, ed. Hoffmann, pp. 124–25).

15. "O keiser, keiser! du bist ir herre vnd sagst, sie sein dein. Nw merck, wie du die fiende Jesu Christi vnd auch dein eigen feinde friest vnd hegest. Wie mag dich Jesus lieb haben, so du sein durchechter vnd morder lieb hast, behusest vnd behoffest?" (*Quellen zur Geschichte Friedrichs des Siegreichen*, ed. Hoffmann, p. 126).

For many Germans, the Jews symbolized the troubles of the empire, and among the "crimes" of the Jews, ritual murder stood out as the most heinous. Whereas the impact of the ritual murder trial in Endingen was restricted by and large to the Upper Rhine, the martyrdom of Simon of Trent in foreign Italy lent credence to the suspicions of murder long harbored against German Jews. Many city chronicles had an entry on Trent: the tragic death of this little boy seemed to have touched a universal chord of human fear and sympathy.[16] The "history" of the murder was told repeatedly in a variety of formats; the narrative became the essential mode for remembering child murders and Jewish magic.

A multiplicity of forms characterized the transmission of ritual murder discourse; they can be divided into the categories of print, orality, and iconography, and many cultural objects and processes combined more than one media type. Of the two German sources on Trent mentioned thus far—Kunig's poem and Kemnat's chronicle—one was printed, sold, and read, while the other remained in manuscript. They belonged, essentially, to the realm of cultural products accessible primarily through literacy. Where dissemination by printing was involved in the fifteenth century, one must necessarily be talking of urban cultural products: printers, poets, writers of vernacular literature, booksellers, and readers—in short, the creators, producers, and consumers of a commercialized culture—were overwhelmingly urban dwellers. It was primarily the townsfolk of late medieval Germany who incorporated these stories of ritual murder and Host desecration into their own understanding of history, a consciousness that placed civic history as the fulcrum of human experience and equated the political fortunes of the urban republic with the general salvific progress of Christendom.[17] With its teleologically unending and ever-unfolding narration of divine and human events, the chronicle represented the means by which stories of ritual murder received the authority of historical verification.

As one of the most popular chronicles of the late fifteenth century, and certainly a landmark in German book printing, Hartmann Schedel's *Book of Chronicles from the Beginning of the World* (1493) provided a compendium of all important divine and human events, while its physical beauty celebrated the glory of Nuremberg craftsmanship.[18] The son of a rich

16. For example, Simon of Trent is mentioned in Koelhoff's Chronicle of Cologne; see Anna-Dorothee von den Brincken, "Die Juden in der Kölnischen Chronistik des 15. Jahrhunderts," in *Köln und das rheinische Judentum: Festschrift Germania Judaica 1959–1984*, ed. Jutta Bohnke-Kollwitz et al. (Cologne, 1984), pp. 63–74.

17. For a persuasive argument on the historical consciousness as reflected by medieval German city chronicles, see Heinrich Schmidt, *Die deutschen Städtechroniken als Spiegel des bürgerlichen Selbstverständnisses im Spätmittelalter* (Göttingen, 1958).

18. Hartmann Schedel, *Liber Chronicarum cum figuris et imaginibus ab initio mundi*

Nuremberg merchant, Hartmann Schedel studied at Leipzig before pursuing his medical training at the University of Padua around the time of Trent ritual murder trial. His chronicle was an almost unaltered rewriting of the chronicle of Jacob Philip Foresti of Bergamo.[19] In terms of scholarship, Schedel's erudition was unremarkable, but the chronicle represented a cultural enterprise that involved the economic and intellectual elites of Nuremberg—in political power and territorial possessions, certainly the most important imperial city around the turn of the century. *The Nuremberg Chronicle,* as it came to be called, was published by Anton Koberger, the largest printer in Germany. Born into a patrician family that had achieved prominence through banking and goldsmithery, Anton counted among his friends the leading merchants, artists, and humanists of Nuremberg. Sebald Schreyer and Sebastian Kammermaister, the two most important patrons of the chronicle, were leading patricians; the 2,165 woodcuts that grace the book were carved by Michael Wohlgemut, Wilhelm Pleydenwurff, and their workshop, where the young Albrecht Dürer trained as an apprentice; and the German translation, which appeared in the same year, was the work of Georg Alt, scrivener of the city treasury.

In scope, the *Schedel Chronicle,* or *Nuremberg Chronicle,* begins with the creation of the universe and ends 6,692 years later in A.D. 1493, the year of its publication. The myriad events since the creation cluster around four major themes: sacred history includes biblical events and church history; secular history tells of the rise and fall of kings, centering on the Holy Roman Empire and its cities; the history of natural disorders includes such items as miraculous weather, blood rains, unnatural births, and monsters; finally, there is the history of human monstrocities. Under this last theme the reader can find the various "crimes" against Christianity perpetrated by Jews, witches, and heresiarchs. The Jews are depicted, both in words and in woodcuts, engaging in acts of violence against Christianity: piercing the images of Christ, crucifying the boy William of Norwich, murdering Richard of Paris, and torturing the Host in Deckendorf.[20] Persecutions of Jews are also vividly depicted: the bloody "Rindfleisch" pogroms at the end of the thirteenth century, and the massive executions in the wake of the Black Death.[21] Naturally,

---

(Nuremberg: Anton Koberger, 1493). On the cultural milieu of Nuremberg and the economics and mechanics behind the production of the Schedel chronicle, see Adrian Wilson and Joyce Lancaster, *The Making of the Nuremberg Chronicle* (Amsterdam, 1976).

19. Wilson and Lancaster, *Nuremberg Chronicle,* p. 26.

20. See Schedel, *Liber Chronicarum,* Nuremberg edition, folios 168, 201^v, 210, 230^v; Augsburg Schönsberger pirate edition, folios 168^v, 189, 225, 231^v, 258^v.

21. Schedel, *Liber Chronicarum,* Nuremberg edition, folios 220^v, 230^v; Augsburg edition, 247^v, 258^v.

Simon of Trent is not forgotten. The original Nuremberg edition devotes half of a folio page to depicting the boy's "martyrdom"; the accompanying woodcut, beautifully carved, shows nine Jews, all named, holding the boy on a table while they bleed him to death, collecting his blood in a bowl (see fig. 4).[22]

Altogether, some fifteen hundred Latin and one thousand German copies of The Nuremberg Chronicle were printed, a rather large press run for the time, especially in view of the price of the book.[23] In 1496 the Augsburg printer Johann Schönsberger pirated the whole work and published a German edition in small folio format, with the original illustrations recut in smaller, and much inferior, reproductions. This cheaper edition captured the market in a short time. Schönsberger also pirated the Latin edition in 1497 and reprinted the German edition in 1500.[24] Together, the Koberger and Schönsberger editions reached a wide distribution; copies of the chronicle were sold in Prague, Vienna, Budapest, Danzig, Lübeck, Augsburg, Munich, and Paris.[25] The "history" of ritual murders thus became part of the general culture of Europe, thanks to the dissemination made possible by this technical innovation of the Germans, the printing press.

Whereas The Nuremberg Chronicle represented one extreme of the book market spectrum, in terms of workmanship and price, at the other end cheap pamphlets, broadsheets, and chapbooks could be had for a few pennies. Around 1498, Johann Zainer of Ulm printed a broadsheet to commemorate Simon of Trent. On the single sheet was a short poem beginning with the verse, "I am called Simon the child," typeset around a woodcut depicting the ritual murder.[26] Unlike the voluminous Nuremberg Chronicle, this broadsheet was meant to be read aloud and heard more than it was meant to be read in the privacy of the study. Most likely intended for storytellers or for those who told stories on the side for entertainment and money, the poem's meter and brevity served as

22. Schedel, Liber Chronicarum, Nuremberg edition, folio 254^v–255; Augsburg edition, folios 285^v–286^v.

23. On the estimated press runs, see Peter Zahn, Neue Funde zur Entstehung der Schedelschen Weltchronik (Nuremberg, 1974). On estimations of the size of usual press runs, see Miriam U. Chrisman, Lay Culture, Learned Culture: Books and Social Change in Strasbourg, 1480–1599 (New Haven and London, 1982), p. 5. On the price of The Nuremberg Chronicle, we know that the rival, pirated, and cheaper Augsburg edition sold for two guldens; this figure comes from the provenance of a Schönsberger Augsburg edition in the Yale Beinecke Library.

24. Wilson and Lancaster, Nuremberg Chronicle, p. 191.

25. Wilson and Lancaster, Nuremberg Chronicle, pp. 229ff.

26. Simon ain kind bin ich genant/zu triendt wol in dem wälschen lant [Ulm: Johann Zainer, ca. 1498]. See Einblattdrucke des XV. Jahrhunderts: Ein bibliographisches Verzeichnis, ed. Kommission für den Gesamtkatalog der Wiegendrucke (Halle, 1914), p. 352, no. 1324.

Das sechst alter

Symon das sellig kindlein zu Trient ist anii.xri.tag des Mertzen nach der gepurt Cristi.M.cccc.lxxv.iar.in 8 heyligen marterwochen in der statt Trient von den iuden getödt vnd ein martrer Cristi worden. dann als die iuden in derselben statt wonende it offten nach irem sytten begeren wolten vnd doch kein cristenliche plüt zu gepiauch irs vngesewiten piots hetten do biachten sie diss kindlein verstolen in Samuelis eins iuden haws. in solcher gestalt. an dem diitt tag voi offten vmb verspeizeit sasse diss kindlein voi seins vaters thür in abwe'sen seiner eltern do nehme sich Thobias ein iüdischer veireter zu disem kindlein das noch nit dieymal zehen mo'nat alt was. dem redet er mit schmaychlenden woite zu vnd trüg es pald in das haws Samuelis. Als nw die nacht herfiele do fiewrten sich Samuel Thobias Vitalis Moyses Israhel vnd Mayer voi der synagog vber vergiessung cristenlichs pläts. Vnw entplössieten sie das kindlein vnd legten ime ein faciletlein vmb sein helsslein das man es nit schieyen hören möcht vnd spanneten ime sein ermlein auss. schnytten ime eistlich sein mälich glid lem ab vnd auss seinem rechten wenglein ein stücklein vnd stachen es allenthalben mit scharpffen spitzigen sta'cheln hefftein oder nadeln. einer die hend der ander die füsslein haltende. vnd als sie nw das plüt grawsamlich gesammelt hetten so hüben sie an lobsang zesingen vnd zu dem kindlein mit hönischen bedroewoiten zesprechen Nym hin du gehangner Jhesu also haben die etwen vnsser eltern gethan. also sollen alle cristen in hymel. auff eiden vnd meer geschend werden. diewil verschied das vnschuldig marterlein. die iuden eyleit zum nachtmal vnd assen von dem plüt das vngesewerte zu schmahe Cristo vnsserm hayland vnd wouffen dë totë leichnä in ein fliessends wasser nahent bey irem haws vnnd hielten it offten mit fiewden. Die bekümerten eltern süchten it verloins kindlein. das funden sie vber diey tag in dem fluss. Als solchs an Johansen von Salis den edeln burger von Bixen kaiserlicher rechten doctoi vnd dessmals öbersten pfleger gelanget do hiess er nach den iudë greiffen vnd sie mit marter anziehen. also das sie nach oidnung ansagten wie sie dise missthat beganngen hetten. vnd darauff waiden sie mit gepürlicher straff auffgeiilgt. Als der leichnam auff befelhe Johasen hinderbachs bischoffs daselbst bestattet waidt do fieng er allspald an in wunderzaichen zescheinen vnd auss allen cristenlich en gegenten zu dise heilliges kindes grab ein zulawff zewerden. davon dan dise statt nicht kleine auffing vnnd zunemung empfunden hat. vnd die burger daselbst haben disem leichnam ein schöne kirchen auffgeichtet.

Dergleichen vbeltat haben auch die iuden vber fünff iar darnach in dem stettlein Mota in foriaul gelegë mit eitödtung eins andern kinds begangen. darumb waiden der teter diey gefangi gein Venedig gefüert vnd nach grawsauser peyn veistenfft.

Je Türcken zohen abeieins in nydern Misiam vnd waiden mit grosser schlacht einydeigelegt. Darnach eiobeiten die Genueser die grossen statt Capham die die Türcken noch inhetten. aber dieselb statt kome in disem iar durch veirettereey vnd dargebung eins Genuesischen burgers widcrumb in der Türcken gewalt.

Figure 4. Simon of Trent. From the *Nuremberg Chronicle* of Hartmann Schedel (1493).

mnemonic devices, while the woodcut told its own story to the illiterate; innkeepers, pilgrims, students, soldiers, balladeers, journeymen, and all sorts of people on the roads comprised the vast throng of storytellers and listeners in this age.[27] Besides being related in taverns, at home, in

27. On storytellers and the social context of storytelling, see Elfriede Moser-Rath, "Some Thoughts on Historical Narrative Research," in *German Volkskunde: A Decade of Theoretical Confrontation, Debate, and Reorientation (1967–1977)*, ed. and trans. James R. Dow and Hannjost Lixfeld (Bloomington, 1986), pp. 221*ff.*; Linda Dégh, *Folktales and Society: Story-Telling in a Hungarian Peasant Community*, trans. Emily M. Schossberger (Bloomington, 1969), while focusing on the 20th century, provides helpful insights into the social context of storytelling in early modern Europe, see esp. pp. 51–52, 67–81.

workplaces, and on the road, stories were also told in churches by clerics; the numerous exempla of the lives of saints and sinners, in fact, furnished preachers with lively and poignant anecdotes to hold the attention of their audiences.[28] In the half-century after Gutenberg, printing accelerated and multiplied the channels of interaction between forms of communication; thus reading, writing, narrating, hearing, and seeing, taken together, helped to constitute a sense of the meaningful experience of the divine.

Textual and oral communications often exhorted readers to act. Printed woodcuts not only told stories to the illiterate; their centrality in texts was a response to the deep emotional need in late medieval piety for achieving a sensual bond between the mundane and the divine. The image of little martyr Simon in the woodcut of the broadsheet represented a readily accessible icon for those who could not undertake the pilgrimage to Trent to behold and touch the blessed boy; paper and picture served as substitutes in the pious yearning for redemptive flesh.[29]

PASSAU: MIRACLE OF THE HOST

While Trent was too far away for most German pilgrims, the episcopal city of Passau on the Danube became one of the most important pilgrimage sites in South Germany during the last decades of the fifteenth century. In 1478 a Christian servant in Passau, Christoph Eisengreishamer, was arrested for theft. He confessed to the authorities that in 1477 he had been sent as a messenger to Prague by two Passauer Jews, Unger and Mandel. On his return trip he told the two Jews that he could procure the Eucharist for them, since he had often heard that Jews would secretly purchase the sacrament, whereupon, according to his confession, they agreed. Thereafter, he broke into St. Mary's in Freyung, took eight Hosts, and sold them to the two Jews for one gulden. He further confessed that in 1477 he stole seven Hosts and sold them to the Jew Süttel of Regensburg. The Passau magistrates arrested and tortured many Jews; and, although their testimonies conflicted, the magistrates concluded that the chanter Mandel had secretly smuggled the Hosts into the synagogue, where two men, Veidl and Vetterl, stabbed Christ's Body

28. On the clergy as storywriters and storytellers, see the important collection on popular narrative and the Reformation. Confessional polemics between Catholics and Protestants gave new life to the medieval tradition of legends and exempla. See Wolfgang Brückner, ed., *Volkserzählung und Reformation: Ein Handbuch zur Tradierung und Funktion von Erzählstoffen und Erzählliteratur im Protestantismus* (Berlin, 1974). The article by Rudolf Schenda in the collection is especially helpful; see his "Hieronymus Rauscher und die Protestantisch-Katholische Legendenpolemik."

29. On the centrality of woodcut illustrations in propagating the messages of the early evangelical movement, see Robert W. Scribner, *For the Sake of Simple Folk: Popular Propaganda for the German Reformation* (Cambridge, 1981).

with a knife until blood flowed and the Eucharist turned itself into a young boy. The Jews then allegedly threw the Hosts into an oven from which two angels and doves flew out of the flames.[30] Suspecting again a widespread conspiracy, the Passau magistrates extracted further confessions under torture to the effect that the Jews had sent some hosts to Prague and to Regensburg.[31] On 10 March 1478 all purported participants in the Host desecration were condemned to death: four Jews accepted baptism to die a quicker death of decapitation; Veidl and Vetterl, the accused torturers of the Hosts, were themselves tormented with glowing pincers and then burnt, an excruciating form of execution shared by their accusor, Eisengreishamer. Altogether, forty Jews and their families accepted baptism; the rest were expelled. The synagogue was razed in 1479; on its site, the Church of Our Savior was completed in 1484.[32]

Reports of miracles and cures multiplied immediately after the executions, and Passau became a famous pilgrimage site. To cater to these pilgrims, a broadsheet was printed in 1480 to be sold as a memento. The twelve woodcuts of the broadsheet form a tripartite narrative panel; captions printed over each block of woodcuts elaborate on the story (fig. 5). The first block of four woodcuts show Eisengreishamer stealing and selling the Hosts to the Jews, who then carry them to the synagogue to be stabbed. The second block portrays the arrest and decapitation of the four baptized Jews; the second woodcut on this block depicts the miracle of the incombustible Host: two angels and doves fly from the oven, and the Host appears in the shape of a little boy. The final block of woodcuts depicts the gruesome executions and the erection of the pilgrimage church on the site of the razed synagogue. As a pictorial narrative and a pious memento, this broadsheet increased the popularity of the pilgrimage to Passau; it was reprinted some twenty years after the event in Nuremberg and Augsburg.[33]

The 1478 Passau Host desecration trial reveals the dynamics of the cultural transmission of anti-Semitic prejudices. The event was transmit-

---

30. For the Passau Host desecration trial, see the poem by Fritz Fellhainer, composed in 1490, published in Liliencron, *Historische Volkslieder*, vol. 2, pp. 142–46, no. 153. See also V. M. Schmid, "Zur Geschichte der Juden in Passau," in *Zeitschrift für die Geschichte der Juden in Deutschland* 1:2 (1929), pp. 119–35.

31. For the correspondence between Passau and Regensburg, see *Urkunden*, no. 438 (p. 151); Sebastian von der Albin, marshal at Passau, wrote to Regensburg about Eisengreishamer's confession. See also chap. 4.

32. See Anton L. Mayer, "Die Gründung von St. Salvator in Passau—Geschichte und Legende," *Zeitschrift für bayerische Landesgeschichte* 18 (1955), pp. 256–78.

33. The Nuremberg reproduction was by Kaspar Hochfeder, dated to ca. 1497; the Augsburg edition, ca. 1500, was by Johann Froschauer; see *Einblattdrucke des XV. Jahrhunderts*, p. 290, nos. 1079, 1080.

Figure 5. Host desecration at Passau. The twelve scenes and verses narrate, from left to right and top to bottom, the alleged theft and torture of the Host. From the broadsheet *Ein grawsamlich geschicht geschehen zu Passaw von den Juden als hernach volget.*

ted by a variety of forms with different functions in the communications process; one can speak of a multiplicity of the media. Each form of communication repeated a basic structure of the perception of reality; in other words, a unity of discourse was manifest. Finally, with the stories of Trent and Passau in the 1470s, legends of ritual murders and Host desecrations began to converge, resulting in a standardized type of ritual murder discourse in which prepubescent boys and eucharistic devotion played the central roles.

Regarding the multiplicity of media, three distinct types of communication can be discerned according to function. The "primary source" of the supposed Passau desecration was the interrogation record—that is, an official document. A copy of this judicial document was sent by the Passauer magistrates to Regensburg because the testimony in Passau pointed to a possible connection with the ongoing Regensburg ritual murder trial. As such, the dynamics of judicial exchange between city councils was reminiscent of the process of the Endingen case in 1470. And, as we shall see in chapter 4, this exchange of judicial records provided for the accumulation of documentary "evidence" of magic and murder against the Regensburg Jews. A second category of communicative media commemorated the piety of the event. Hence, a monk in the cloister of Ebersberg copied excerpts of the interrogation record for the edification of his monastic brothers, and a pilgrimage church was built in Passau as a monument to the power of the Eucharist.[34] A final type of communication operated through the marketplace rather than the institutional channels of city governments and the church. The 1480 broadsheet depicting the Host desecration in woodcuts and verse was a commodity: it was produced to be sold in massive quantities and for a profit. As such, it relied on the commercial and geographical networks of communication for its distribution, networks that often coincided with the routes of pilgrimage. With the return of the pilgrims to their homes, the story of Passau and the fame of its sanctity gained a wider circulation.

A fundamental structural unity amounting to a unified discourse underlay the multiplicity of communicative functions and cultural forms. The form of the discourse was the narrative: a ritual murder or a host desecration was essentially a story; it was a tale with a dialectical morality, of the wickedness of Jews and their magic, and of the power and efficacy of Christianity. The titles of many broadsheets and chapbooks reflected the narrative essence: "A Cruel Story . . . ," "A Miraculous Story . . . ," "A True Tale . . . ," or simply "The Story of . . ." or "The History of. . . ." In the discourse on Jewish magic, the distinction between history and story disappeared; both were defined by the word *Geschichte*. History, a story, has a narrative beginning, a turning point, and a satisfying end. What was being created in the two generations between 1470 and the Reformation, and what is revealed here, was a process of cultural creation that literally made historical and salvific reality out of fragments of inexplicable facts, an ideology of anti-Semitism, and the imaginative powers of a deeply pious society. What was

34. The manuscript is in the Staatsbibliothek Munich, cod. Germ. 753, printed in *Niederbayerische Monatsschrift* (1916), pp. 52f. Cited by W. M. Schmid, "Geschichte der Juden."

being created, in short, was historical meaning. The basic narrative structure revealed itself not only in the varied forms of writing on ritual murders; musical and visual arts of Jewish magic also partook in the storytelling. The twelve woodcuts in the 1480 Passau broadsheet represented a reproduction of the altar panels and wooden carvings often found in pilgrimage churches. These painted or carved pictures provided the iconographic counterparts to the textual narratives; they could be found in the pilgrimage churches in Endingen and in Rinn, Tirol, also the site of a purported ritual murder.[35] They were narrative pictures, stories without words. Woodcut illustrations in broadsheets and chapbooks disseminated the "aura" of these narrating icons of pilgrimage churches; they made commercially available a portion of that sanctity and grace that flowed from the blood of the young Christian martyrs, their spirits eternally captured in the sites of their violent deaths by these artistic representations. Sequentiality was also an important element in rendering this cultural material into musical forms. Balladeers of the fifteenth and sixteenth centuries often went on pilgrimages, where they earned money by singing to fellow travelers. Printed song sheets began to appear around this time, turning what many nineteenth-century folklorists and musicologists termed folk songs into commodities for sale.[36] Balladeers used these printed song sheets for their trade; for their performances, they often displayed a banner on which a sequence of pictures, similar to the woodcut stories of the broadsheets, served as visual aids for the audience in following the tale and as mnemonic devices for themselves.[37]

The main function of a narrative is to provide the means for an ordering of reality, whereby individual events and facts can be arranged sequentially, causatively, and meaningfully. The publicity generated by Trent and Passau in the 1470s helped to coalesce the two traditions of ritual murder and Host desecration discourses. In the legends of ritual murders before Trent, both in Germany and in other lands, the victims were mostly boys ranging in age from infancy to adolescence. In a few

35. For Endingen, see Amira, *Judenspiel;* for the panel of legends at Rinn (Judenstein), see Gustav Gugitz, *Österreichs Gnadenstätten in Kult und Brauch,* vol. 3: *Tirol und Vorarlberg* (Vienna, 1956), pp. 64*ff.*

36. See Rolf Wilhelm Brednich, "The Song as a Commodity," in Dow and Lixfeld, eds., *German Volkskunde,* pp. 203–11. Leopold Schmidt argues persuasively that the printed songs (*Flugblattlieder*) gathered in the 19th century and naively described as *Volkslieder* were really the *Gesellschaftslieder* of the 15th and 16th centuries. See his "Flugblattlied und Volksgesang," in a collection of his essays: *Volksgesang und Volkslied: Proben und Probleme* (Berlin, 1970), pp. 108–13, here p. 108.

37. See Leopold Schmidt, "Geistlicher Bänkelgesang: Probleme der Berührung von erzählendem Lied und lesbarer Bildkunst in Volksdevotion und Wallfahrtsbrauch," in Schmidt, *Volksgesang und Volkslied,* pp. 223–37; see also Elsbeth Janda and Fritz Nötzoldt, *Die Moritat vom Bänkelsang, oder das Lied der Strasse* (Munich, 1959).

cases, however, the victims were not boys: legend had it that in 1266 an old woman in Forcheim sold a seven-year-old orphan girl to the Jews, who tortured and bled her to death;[38] and in 1470 in Endingen, as we have seen, the victims were two parents and their two children. After the 1470s, reports of ritual murders generally identified the alleged victims or missing children as boys between infancy and age seven, the age of childhood. At work was the gradual standardization of ritual murder discourse, in which variant models from the past were displaced by the motif of the violent deaths of young male children. The driving force behind this standardization was the increasingly central function of ritual murder discourse as a form of the imitation of Christ, in which the representations of the boy victims and the Child Jesus became fused and ritual murders came to be identified with Host desecrations.

Passau was meant to celebrate, of course, the triumph of the Eucharist; the episode also served to demonstrate the real presence of Christ in the Host. The very indestructibility of the sacrament testified to the triumph of Christ's Crucifixion and Resurrection. According to the 1480 broadsheet, the Host turned into the figure of the Christ Child in the oven: the transformation from Host into a child illustrated the doctrine of transubstantiation, whereby the consecrated bread embodied the human and celestial flesh of Christ; the incombustible Host, moreover, signified the eternity of Christian truth, a motif continued after the Reformation when Luther's image took on the aura of incombustibility.[39] This graphic depiction of the doctrine of real presence was not new; medieval legends and sermons abound in such examples: Hugh of Saint Victor saw the Child Jesus in the host and chatted with him; a monk, while celebrating Mass, felt he was eating the Child Jesus; on another occasion, the Child Jesus refused to be eaten by a doubting priest.[40] But the Christ Child manifested himself especially when attacked by Jews. A sermon told this story:

> In Cologne, a Jew always wanted to dispute with Christians about the real presence and to mock the Eucharist. One Easter, he went to church in disguise and received the Host. He then ran to a hidden corner of the church, took the Host out of his mouth, held it in his hands, and saw a little child smiling at him. Petrified that the Christians would kill him, he put it back into his mouth, where it turned hard as stone. He heard a voice in the air saying: "Do not give what is holy to dogs." He spat the child out, hid it under his cloak, and tried to leave the church. At the

38. The story of the Forcheim ritual murder of 1266 comes from a 13th-century manuscript; it is published in Friedrich Pressel, *Geschichte der Juden in Ulm* (Ulm, 1873), pp. 41–42.

39. See Robert W. Scribner, "Incombustible Luther: The Image of the Reformer in Early Modern Germany," *Past and Present* 110 (1986), pp. 38–68.

40. These examples are cited by Schenda, "Hieronymus Rauscher," pp. 230ff.

door he saw a devil waiting who threatened to kill him the moment he
set foot outside. The Jew then buried the child in the churchyard, but the
devil was still waiting for him. As the churchgoers were leaving, he
grabbed hold of one of them and asked him to get the priest. After
listening to his story, the priest summoned the Christians and dug the
child-Host out of the earth. A voice then cried out: "Crucified, died,
buried, and resurrected from the dead." They all saw the Christ Child in
the form of a Host. The bishop then forced all the Jews to go to church,
where the sacred object was put on display on the altar. The angels then
announced: "He is ascended unto Heaven and is seated at the right
hand of God." And through this miracle, all the Jews were converted.[41]

To the churchgoers nothing depicted more vividly the doctrine of transubstantiation, whereby human flesh and salvific bread partook of the
same form. These medieval exempla also described other torturers of the
Host; some legends accused unbelieving women of Host desecration,
thus providing a crucial link between witch hunts, infanticide, and accusations of child murders in a later age.[42]

Beginning with the 1470s, the descriptions of ritual murders as mock
crucifixions featured much more prominently; the discourse on the death
of Simon of Trent would set a new pattern for subsequent ritual murder
narratives. The martyred boys, like the Eucharist, would also bleed to
show God's mercy and sorrow; and both the corpses and the Host were
put on display as salutary objects. A parallel development was the assimilation of child murder accusations in Host desecration trials. Whereas
the original accounts of Passau told of Host desecrations, a poem to
commemorate the event composed in 1490 accused Veigl of Passau, one
of the principal "suspects," of purchasing a child from a man in Schärding who was himself executed for the crime.[43] In the most nefarious Host
desecration trial, the 1510 Brandenburg case, the confession of ritual
murder was also extracted from the tortured Jews and added to their
litany of "crimes."[44]

41. From Pelbart von Temesvar, *Pomerium Sermonum Fratris Pelbarti de Themeswar*
(Hagenau, 1515/16), folio Ee 5v; the text is quoted by Schenda, p. 231. My citation summarizes rather than translates the tale.

42. For legends of women commiting Host desecrations, see Schenda, "Hieronymous
Rauscher," pp. 231–33. For the connections between the child murders, witchhunts, and
accusations of Jewish ritual murders and Host desecrations, see chap. 7.

43. See the poem by Fritz Fellhainer in Liliencron, *Historische Volkslieder*, vol. 1, p. 145,
stanza 20: "Nun merkt fürpass in meinem gedicht:/zu Schärding hat man ainen gericht,/der
hat verkauft sein kindlein ain knaben gut/den Juden gein Passaw in ir stat,/Veigl Jud im das
bezalet hat,/zwelf schilling umb unschuldigs plut."

44. See *Ein wunderbarlich geschichte: Wye dye Merckischen Juden das hochwirdig Sacrament
gekaufft vnd zu martern sich vnderstanden. Anno domini 1510* (Nuremberg: Hieronymus
Höltzel), sig. A3ʳ; see also A. Ackermann, *Geschichte der Juden in Brandenburg* (Berlin, 1906),
pp. 34–54.

A FOLKLORE IN THE MAKING

The intensification of magical charges against Jews in the last decades of the fifteenth century must be understood in the larger context of increasing popular piety in Germany. This religious renewal expressed itself in the imitation of Christ, in the veneration of saints, in Marian and eucharistic devotion, in the popularity of pilgrimages, and in agitated millenarian expectations.[45] To complement this positive outburst of religious energies, the enemies of Christianity and the Holy Roman Empire consequently also received a sharper attention. Alongside the literature on ritual murders and Host desecrations were other anti-Judaic writings: some attacked the Talmud, some defended Christian doctrines, and still others represented the initial polemical efforts to convert German Jews.[46] And, on a more general level, the early printing presses also turned out many pamphlets, chapbooks, broadsheets, and learned treatises to warn Christians about the Ottoman Turks and witches.

It has been pointed out that the total output of anti-Semitic literature by the printing presses was small, especially in view of the spectacular explosion of pamphlets in the early years of the evangelical movement.[47] But this is not the crucial point. What mattered was not the number of pamphlets published but the relationship of this specific corpus of printed culture to other cultural forms of anti-Semitism. In the decades before the Reformation, the limited nature of anti-Judaic print testified rather to a broad Christian consensus on the Jews: their religion was condemned, their wealth envied, their magic much feared. Polyphony of voices often represents dissent; but where consensus exists, the cultural expressions of underlying ideas assumes an almost ritualistic character. In the case of anti-Semitism in the late medieval empire, printed culture served essentially to propagate and to render into reproducible textual documentations the prior experiences of Jewish "crimes," which had already been amply depicted in nontextual forms in legends, folktales, songs, altar panels, paintings, pilgrimage churches, and carnival and Easter plays. The advent of printing and the role it served in transmitting anti-Semitic ideas involved a complex process: printing gave rise to at-

45. On late medieval piety in Germany, see Will-Erich Peuckert, *Die grosse Wende: Das Apokalyptische Saeculum und Luther* (Hamburg, 1948), and Willy Andreas, *Deutschland vor der Reformation* (Stuttgart, 1959).

46. For a catalog of early Judaica (writings about Jews) in the University Library of Frankfurt (previously in the Stadtbibliothek), see Aron Freimann, ed., *Stadtbibliothek Frankfurt a. M. Katalog der Judaica und Hebraica*, vol. 1 (Frankfurt, 1932).

47. This is the argument of Heiko A. Oberman; see his "Zwischen Agitation und Reformation: Die Flugschriften als 'Judenspiegel,'" in Hans-Joachim Köhler, ed., *Flugschriften als Massenmedium der Reformationszeit* (Stuttgart, 1981), pp. 269–88; here, pp. 287–88.

tempts at the systematic collection of religious folklore; it also made possible the commercialization of specific religious events. The printed book was only one of the many cultural forms that transmitted ideas about Jews.

In the history of the collection of folktales and folk songs, the sixteenth century is the first period when one can discern a folklore in the making, a fact often overlooked when folklorists have traced the history of their discipline back to the Enlightenment. Oral and manuscript traditions of medieval piety—legends of miracles, saints' lives, pious histories, tales of demonic horror—underwent systematic collection and publication in the sixteenth century.[48] A good example was the making of the Deckendorf legend. According to tradition, the Jews of this small town in Lower Bavaria went to a Christian woman to ask her to steal the Host at Easter. Having obtained the Eucharist, they tried the usual tortures; as expected, the Host bled, turned into a child, and remained simply indestructible. This gruesome sacrilege was discovered because a sentinel heard Mary lamenting the murder of her child near the house of the Jews (fig. 6). In a fury the townsfolk burnt the Jews, who were also accused of well poisoning, and a great number of miracles were reported. The Host desecration of Deckendorf took place in 1337. For more than a century and a half, the story of Deckendorf was transmitted primarily through oral and pilgrimage traditions. The 1492 *Nuremberg Chronicle* included an entry on it. In 1520, nearly two hundred years after the event, a poem, published in Augsburg, commemorated the wonders of the Host.[49] The poet, whose identity remains unknown, told his readers that he actually went to Deckendorf to ask the townsfolk about the Host desecration; through the efforts of this protofolklorist, the oral tradition of Deckendorf was preserved in print and survived to our time.[50]

A second point that cannot be emphasized enough was the commercial aspect of popular printing. Folklore was meant to be marketed. Written by clerics and literate laymen, produced by printers in the larger cities, and peddled by hawkers and booksellers along the pilgrimage routes, broadsheets, chapbooks, and poems of Host desecrations and ritual murders depended on pilgrimage sites as primary points of marketing. The physical appearance of this genre of popular print reflects their character as mass commodities: usually printed in small, octavo "pocket" size, the products often featured woodcuts to enhance their aesthetic appeal, and they had such catchy titles as "A Miraculous Tale"

48. See Wolfgang Brückner, "Historien und Historie: Erzählliteratur des 16. und 17. Jahrhunderts als Forschungsaufgabe," in Brückner, ed., *Volkserzählung und Reformation*, pp. 13–123.

49. *Von Tegkendorff das geschicht wie die Iuden das hailig sacrament haben zugericht* [Augsburg: S. Otmar, 1520].

50. *Von Tegkendoff*, sig. A¹ᵛ–A².

Figure 6. Mater Dolorosa. The Virgin Mary is pierced by the sword of sorrow for the death of her son, a motif extended to the iconography of alleged ritual murders and Host desecrations. From *Ein seltzame kouffmanschatz*. Reproduced courtesy of Stadtarchiv Freiburg i. B.

or "A Pretty New Song" to arouse the curiosity of potential customers. When an alleged ritual murder was discovered in 1540 in the village of Sappenfeld in the Upper Palatinate, a printer came out with a new product: "A Pretty New Song of What recently happened between Two Jews and A Child in Sappenfeld."[51] Like many chapbooks, this song sheet was short, containing only four pages, and it was cut in even

51. *Ein hübsch new lied von Zweyen Juden/vnd einem Kind/zu Sappenfelt newlich geschehen* [s.l., 1540?].

I. 777

1540?
Jews
7

Ein hübsch new lied / von
Zweyen Juden / vnd einem Kind /
zů Sappenfelt newlich geschehen / Im thon / Es geht sich
gegen der sumer zeit / zc.
Oder im thon / Jch weyß nit
was der gylgen brist / zc.

*

6

Figure 7. Ritual Murder of Sappenfeld. Title page of *Ein hübsch new Lied / von zwei Iuden / vnd einem Kind / zu Sappenfelt newlich geschehen*. Reproduced courtesy of the British Library (actual size).

Figure 8. Simon of Trent at the Brückenturm in Frankfurt. Reproduced courtesy of the Historisches Museum Frankfurt. Photograph kindly supplied by Frau Ursula Seitz-Gray.

smaller format on sheets only one-sixteenth of a folio page. A crude woodcut on the title page depicts a child tied to a pillar with cut wounds all over his body; a long-bearded Jew wearing a *Judenhut* and holding a knife and a dish, approaches the dead or dying boy (fig. 7). The song had been composed especially for the occasion, and the lyrics of this gruesome murder could be sung to the tune of two traditional cheerful folk melodies—"Time passes well in summer time . . ." or "I know not the Lily breeze . . ."—as the printer helpfully suggested. As a product of the connections between popular piety and the marketplace, this little song sheet represented an ingenious conjunction of music, text, and picture.

The importance of cities as centers of cultural dissemination is obvious: anti-Semitic pamphlets, like all forms of popular literature, were first printed and sold in the cities. Just how firmly anchored anti-Semitism was in the urban culture of late medieval Germany can be seen in two other examples of propaganda that did not rely on the printed word: a painting on the city wall of Frankfurt, and the carnival plays of Hans Folz of Nuremberg.

News of the Trent child murder soon reached the imperial city of Frankfurt am Main, which had a small Jewish community in the late fifteenth century.[52] Outraged by the alleged ritual murder, the burghers painted the "martyrdom" of Simon of Trent on the wall under the arch of the Brückenturm, or Bridge Tower, the busiest gate of the city, as a sort of warning to visitors (fig. 8).[53] This gruesome depiction exceeded even the

52. See Kracauer, *Geschichte der Juden in Frankfurt a. M.*, vol. 1, p. 205. In the late 15th century, when the ghetto was enclosed, there were fewer than twenty households and a total of about one hundred Jews. The period of rapid expansion was the late 16th century.

53. See chap. 9.

woodcut in the *Schedel Chronicle* in gore. Whereas the Nuremberg artists relied on the confessions of the Jews to reconstruct the scene of the "murder," the Frankfurt wall painting exuded a spirit of bloodthirsty realism. At eye level, a visitor entering the city gate would see a painting depicting the boy Simon nailed down on a board, with blood wounds inflicted by awls all over his body. The iconography of the Brückenturm painting aimed at exciting a revulsion against the Jews, just as paintings and sculptures of Christ, Mary, and the saints filled Christians with grace and hope for eternal salvation. Thus for late medieval Christians, both types of artistic representations—Christian sacrifice and Christian triumph—fortified a feeling of piety, deepened an awareness of Christian boundary, and heightened a sense of danger, for the display of salvation and the display of damnation were but two episodes in the same story.

The demonization of Jews was a prominent theme in the carnival plays of the Nuremberg *Meistersänger* Hans Folz. A new dramatic form which first appeared in Lübeck and Nuremberg in the 1430s and 1440s, the carnival play was preeminently a form of entertainment in the cities.[54] At Shrovetide, especially on Shrove Tuesday, or Mardi Gras, troupes of players under their leaders would burst into taverns, surprising and delighting the guests by performing short sketches of fifteen to thirty minutes. The players created space simply by moving furniture around, and they wore a minimum of costumes. A great deal of burlesque and obscenity characterized the dialogues and gestures of the players, in keeping with the general atmosphere of license and merrymaking on the eve of Lent. After the quick performances, a herald would apologize for any offensive remarks, claiming the license of carnival; amid applause and laughter, he would go around the guests for a collection. Then just as swiftly, the players made their exit and went on to another tavern.

Socially, carnival plays grew out of the life of the guilds. In Lübeck, they were put on by young merchant apprentices from patrician families; in Nuremberg, journeymen from the handicraft guilds acted as players in farces written by guild masters. The most prolific writer of Nuremberg carnival plays was the barber-surgeon Hans Folz. Born in the Rheinish city of Worms, Folz moved to Nuremberg in 1459, where he wrote more than a hundred carnival plays before his death in 1513. Most of these were very short; a great number mocked the stupidity of rustics, others provided obscene humor at the expense of women, while a few of the longer pieces targeted the Jews.[55]

---

54. See Dieter Wuttke, "Versuch einer Physiognomie der Gattung Fastnachtspiel," in D. Wuttke, ed., *Fastnachtspiele des 15. und 16. Jahrhunderts* (Stuttgart, 1973), pp. 401–19.
55. The older edition of carnival plays by A. von Keller is still indispensible; see

In one of his longer carnival farces, "The Play of the Duke of Burgundy," Folz had Philip (1478–1506), son of Emperor Maximilian I, visiting Nuremberg to attend a carnival play.[56] In this farce a player, presumably dressed as a duke, strode into the room where the tavern guests were sitting. A prophetess, Sibella, accompanied by her virgin maids, then presented herself to the duke. The purpose of her visit was to expose the lies of the Jews because "some Jewish rabbis/have proclaimed in all lands/that their messiah is coming." Five players introduced themselves as the false messiah and four Jews; they were now to rule over all kingdoms and lord over Christians. Mocked by the court jester, the Jews begged their messiah to scare the Christians, whereupon the actor playing the messiah produced a fire-breathing dragon. Sibella admonished the dragon "by the power of Jesus" that it should do no harm here until "[she] has clearly revealed/what this magic means"; she then exposed that the Jews were in league with the Antichrist. Sibella interrogated the Antichrist-messiah as to his ancestry; the rabbis stubbornly proclaimed their faith in him and agreed to suffer whatever punishments the duke might mete out if their messiah was proven false. Sibella offered the false messiah a drink, stating that if he could protect himself from its power, she would believe him. Swearing many nonsensical (and comical) Hebrew names, the false messiah drank the potion, fainted, and died. Sibella conjured him back to life and asked him to confess to the purpose of his trickery and magic. The resurrected Antichrist-messiah confessed that, constringed by Christian might, he could no longer hide his secret: for more than 1,400 years the Jews had hated, killed, and robbed Christians. He lamented:

> Oh how many are the young children
> who are stolen and killed
> and made red with their pure blood;
> kidnapped from you Christians
> to mock the annual birth of
> Jesus, which you celebrate eternally;
> so that we, filled with hate and envy,
> find all our joys driven away.
> And the Messiah still doesn't come
> and no comfort is given us.

All that remained was to determine the punishments for the Jews. Folz seized on this dramatic moment to appeal to the sadistic and scatological humor of his audience. The duke asked heathens, his knights, the fool,

---

Fastnachtspiele aus dem fünfzehnten Jahrhundert, 3 vols. [Bibliothek des literarischen Vereins in Stuttgart, vols. 28–30] (Stuttgart, 1853).

56. Keller, Fastnachtspiele, pt. 1, no. 20, pp. 169–90.

and his wife as to the appropriate punishments for the Jews. In turn, sadistic replies alternated with scatological jokes: their tongues were to be torn out; they were to be stuffed with powder and ignited; they should be forced to eat feces; once a year they were to sit in the public latrine; some recommended burning them, others suggested stripping and freezing them. In the end, a sow was led into the room, and the actors playing the Antichrist and the Jews, egged on by the fool and his wife, pretended to suck milk and eat feces to the merriment of the audience. After the scene with the *Judensau*, the court master ordered the fool to bind the Jews, to take them from the city, and to carry out the sentence, presumably, death by burning. Having rewarded the virgin maids of Sibella, the duke and his court exited to the sound of pipes.

Folz skillfully presented all the stereotypes of Jews in this carnival play. Dramatic representations of the Jewish messiah, the demonic nature of Jews, the Judensau, ritual murders, and Jewish magic occurred in the context of slapstick comedy and scatological humor. In two other anti-Semitic plays, "The Carnival of the Antichrist" and "Emperor Constantine," Folz again ridiculed the Jews as children of the Antichrist and enemies of Christians.[57] While carnival lent a certain license to Folz's hateful creativity, through his poems he expressed a deep hostility toward Jews, accusing them of Host desecrations at Deckendorf and Passau; it was a hatred nurtured both by his religious feelings and by economic resentment.[58]

In Frankfurt, Jewish magic and ritual murder were painted on the very stones of the city's wall as an integral part of urban identity. The painting remained there, in spite of protestations, until the reforms of Emperor Joseph in the 1770s.[59] In Nuremberg, the tradition of carnival plays endured throughout the sixteenth century, although after the Reformation the magistrates succeeded in suppressing other forms of carnival celebrations, such as the mummery parade of the *Schelmbartlauf*.[60] One can not, however, find in the later plays the vulgar anti-Semitism expressed in the carnival farces of Hans Folz. In 1499, with imperial

57. Keller, *Fastnachtspiele*, pt. 2, pp. 597*ff.*, no. 68, "Der Entkrist Vasnacht," and pp. 796*ff.*, no. 106, "Kaiser Constantinus."

58. The *Knittelvers* of Hans Folz has a variable metric pattern within each verse, the *Meisterlieder* have different rhyming patterns, and the *Reimpaarsprüche* are poems composed of many pairs of rhyming verses. For references to Deckendorf and Passau, see *Die Meisterlieder des Hans Folz*, ed. August L. Mayer (Berlin, 1908), no. 76:6, p. 301, line 170. For his other anti-Semitic poems, see "Der falsche Messias," "Judas der Ketzerapostel," "Christ und Jude," and "Jüdischer Wucher," in Hans Folz, *Die Reimpaarsprüche*, ed. Hanns Fischer (Munich, 1961).

59. See chap. 9.

60. Gerald Strauss, *Nuremberg in the Sixteenth Century* (Bloomington, 1976), p. 215.

permission, the city council expelled Jews from Nuremberg. The literary works of Hans Folz had helped to prepare public opinion for the cleansing of the body politic.

Standardized, commercialized, and widely disseminated, ritual murder discourse also served overt political purposes. In the fifteenth century, most German Jews settled in towns, especially in the imperial cities, where they enjoyed the protection of the emperor, their nominal overlord. Letters of safe conduct, residence permits, and the permission to pursue a livelihood were paid for with heavy taxes to the emperors or holders of regalian rights over Jews. Many imperial city governments found themselves in the unenviable position of having to protect the emperor's Jews in the face of growing conflicts between citizens and Jews, and open hostility toward the religious minorities and the regimes that protected them on the other. In the first half of the fifteenth century, especially in the 1420s and 1430s, Jews were expelled from most of the imperial cities in the Rhineland. Beginning with the 1470s, a new wave of expulsion affected the imperial cities in Bavaria, Swabia, and Franconia.[61] While the charge of usury was raised again and again, the accusations of ritual murder and Host desecration proved far more powerful in providing the emotional and judicial impetus for the expulsion of Jewish communities. The discourse on Jewish magic provided a rhetorical framework for political persecutions. What Hans Folz tried to accomplish, using the license of carnival, the magistrates of Regensburg attempted, resorting to political trials. The targets were the same: the Jews and their magic. For the Jewish community of Regensburg, the 1470s were indeed a dark time.

61. See Markus J. Wenninger, *Man bedarf keiner Juden mehr: Ursachen und Hintergründe ihrer Vertreibung aus den deutschen Reichsstädten im 15. Jahrhundert* (Cologne, 1981), pp. 244ff. Wenninger argues that urban anti-Semitism was primarily fiscal and economic and that the authorities often took the lead. He neglects the political tensions within the cities and ignores the religious factor.

CHAPTER FOUR **Regensburg**

I N THE FOURTEENTH AND FIFTEENTH CENTURIES, THE JEW-
ish community in the imperial city of Regensburg was
the largest in the Holy Roman Empire, but it was a
community that had outlived its golden age.[1] The elders remembered a time when their ancestors advanced credit to the city patriciate to support long-
distance trade and raised large loans for the secular
lords and prelates of the church. But the pogroms of 1349–50 and increasing imperial taxation led the Jewish community, like the larger city in
which it existed, into a prolonged period of economic decline. Crippled
by repeated financial exactions, the Regensburg Jews were unable to
sustain large-scale credit operations and were forced to lend money to
lesser customers—petty nobility, small merchants, artisans, shopkeepers, and local clergy.[2] To the extent that Jews became more impoverished—their financial strength gradually sapped by a greedy monarchy and their legal disputes with citizens increasing in acrimony and
volume—their civic value, in the eyes of the magistrates, also eroded. By
the mid-fifteenth century, the erstwhile policy that favored Jews became
a policy of restrictions.[3] Duke Ludwig of Bavaria-Landshut, whose territory surrounded the imperial city, expelled Jews from his territory in
1450. In 1454 the popular Italian Franciscan preacher Capistrano aroused
great religious fervor on his tour of Germany, while the papal legate
Nicolaus of Cusa also called for stricter control of Jews; many diocesan

---

1. Raphael Straus has written the definitive studies on the Regensburg Jewish
community; see: *Die Judengemeinde Regensburg im ausgehenden Mittelalter* (Heidelberg, 1932),
and *Regensburg and Augsburg*, trans. Felix N. Gerson [Jewish Communities Series] (Philadelphia, 1939). Extant documents related to the history of this community have been
published by Straus as *Urkunden und Aktenstücke zur Geschichte der Juden in Regensburg, 1453–
1738* (Munich, 1960).

2. Straus, *Regensburg and Augsburg*, pp. 40–43.

3. Straus, *Regensburg and Augsburg*, pp. 127–29.

synods, such as Würzburg and Bamberg, stipulated a distinctive dress for Jews.[4]

The religious revival in the second half of the fifteenth century coincided with a new economic upturn. Many South German cities prospered as manufacturing centers of wool, fustian, iron, precious metals, and armaments and as major centers of international finance. However, the rise of Nuremberg, Augsburg, and Ulm—the most spectacular success stories—was also built on the decline of older centers of trade. For Regensburg, the competition from nearby Nuremberg proved fatal, and as the Danubian city struggled to recover its prosperity, the alleged wealth of its Jews appeared a tempting target.[5]

A COMMUNITY UNDER SIEGE

In six years, from 1470 to 1476, the Jews of Regensburg were accused of ritual murder and Host desecration on four occasions. More than any previous or subsequent events, the Regensburg trials showed how those in power could consciously exploit magical notions and religious fervor to serve a particular political end. This sordid affair involved three parties: the bishop of Regensburg, Duke Ludwig of Bavaria-Landshut, to whom the regalian rights over Jews had been pawned, and the city fathers, who sought to protect their own jurisdictional authority over the Jews. The fate of the Regensburg Jews would hang in precarious balance between the cooperations, contestations, and machinations of these three powers. But before the hurricane of persecutions eventually struck in 1476, the Jewish community had been battered by the storms of Host desecrations and ritual murder on three previous occasions.

On 4 May 1470 a young Jew by the name of Kalman was arrested and interrogated by Hans Ebran, ducal judge in Landshut. The interrogation record called him "a renegade" because he once expressed the desire to convert but eventually decided to return to his family.[6] According to his testimony, about a year earlier, on Good Friday, he witnessed a Christian procession and was much impressed by its pomp and ceremony. Afterwards, dressed as a Christian, he listened to a sermon by the suffragan bishop. Thinking that he might want to convert, Kalman began to visit and talk with the suffragan bishop. He also dined once with the Augustinians, who impressed him with the "order and honor" they showed

---

4. Straus, *Judengemeinde*, p. 23.
5. Straus, *Judengemeinde*, pp. 68ff.
6. *Urkunden*, no. 111, pp. 29–30; Carl Theodor Gemeiner, *Regensburgische Chronik*, vol. 3 (Regensburg, 1821), pp. 456–59.

him; "in all his days among the Jews he had not seen such decorum
[*Zucht*]," as the young catechumen himself put it. By this time, Kalman
was lodging with the bishop and receiving catechism lessons. But the
young man had not severed his ties with his family, and he secretly
visited the Jewish quarter. His brother and friends tried hard to dissuade
him. Kalman's fervor was cooled by the indignations heaped on him by
the bishop's cook, who cursed him, called him a scoundrel, and threatened many times to drag him over the dinner table by his hair. Only the
other servants saved Kalman from these beatings. After repeated humili-
ations, the young man decided that he had had enough, and he went
back to his family. The Jews received him with great joy: Rabbi Aron
kissed his foot, and on the night of his return, thirty of his brethren
celebrated with him the return of the prodigal son.

Rejoice on one side was matched by anger on the other. Baptized
Jews who returned to their old faith were often burnt as renegades, and
although Kalman had not yet received baptism, the ecclesiastical authorities were determined to make an example of him: surely it was really the
Jew's own fault that he turned from Christianity. During the first interrogation, obviously under duress, Kalman had already admitted that
Jews still wrote books against the Christian faith and that they kept these
books from their young men until their faith in Judaism had been tested.

It is unclear whether Kalman was tortured, but the poor man must
have been petrified. If the episcopal officials treated him as a renegade,
his fate would be sealed. On 6 May, Judge Hans Ebran faced Kalman and
urged him to speak the truth about a list of articles to which he was to
answer.[7] Anxious to cooperate and to save himself, Kalman confessed
that the rabbis of the community were writing blasphemous books about
the birth of Christ; that the Jews uttered other blasphemies against Christianity; and that a fellow Jew, Maier, wanted to convert with his young
son so that the boy could grow up and earn a better living but that Maier's
wife went to the other Jews, who then bound Maier on all fours, telling
Kalman that they were sending Maier away but instead drowning him or
burying him alive. Finally, Kalman confessed that Rabbis Israel, Byman,
and Jossel, and his own brother had tried to persuade him to help them
steal and torture the Host.

On this occasion, the magistrates seemed to have supported the
Jews and interceded on their behalf with the duke.[8] On 18 June, Duke
Ludwig instructed his judge Hans Ebran to pass judgment on Kalman on

7. For the notarial record of the second interrogation, see *Urkunden*, no. 112, pp. 30–
31.

8. *Urkunden*, no. 113, p. 31.

the charge of blasphemy against Christ and Mary.[9] Kalman was sentenced to death by drowning.[10]

Four years later, in March 1474, Hans Veyol, a baptized Jew, was arrested for theft. During his interrogation he told magistrates that he had sold a seven-year-old boy to the chief rabbi, Israel of Brünn, who was promptly arrested. For twenty years, Rabbi Israel had acted as the leader for not only the Regensburg Jews but also other smaller Jewish communities, mediating family disputes, settling business disagreements, and pronouncing bans on those who disobeyed rabbinic authority.[11] A condemnation of Israel would be tantamount to an attack on the entire community. Before the magistrates had a chance to interrogate the rabbi, Emperor Friedrich III wrote and ordered his immediate release.[12] At the same time, the city council heard from King Wladislaus of Bohemia, who informed the magistrates that he had placed Israel under his personal protection on petition by Rabbi Manasse of Prague, the son of the venerable Rabbi Israel.[13]

With such highly placed patrons protecting Rabbi Israel, the magistrates returned to questioning his accusor on 30 March. At first, Veyol admitted to lying; he had falsely implicated Israel in order to prolong or save his own life. But then he changed his statement and once more accused Israel of buying the child from him. After repeated vacillations, the magistrates lost patience. At nightfall, they took Veyol and Israel to a stone on the bank of the Danube, pretending that both men would be thrown into the river. Once again, they admonished Veyol to speak the truth and unburden his soul. Thinking that he was facing his final moments, Veyol confessed to the magistrates that everything he had said was true, except for the false accusation against Israel; he had done this out of hatred and in the hope of saving his own life. The two men were then led back to prison. Seeing that they had no real grounds to pursue the investigation, the magistrates wanted to end the matter quickly; they feared that the old, sick Israel might die in prison.[14]

On 16 April, after reporting to Emperor Friedrich on the new twist of

9. *Urkunden*, no. 114, p. 31.

10. Gemeiner, *Chronik*, p. 459.

11. A 1455 civic document described the leadership role of Rabbi Israel; see *Urkunden*, no. 13, p. 4.

12. Emperor Friedrich wrote twice to the city council, on 12 and 16 March, threatening the city fathers with his imperial displeasure; see *Urkunden*, nos. 141, 143, p. 38.

13. There were two letters from King Wladislaus, dated 18 March and 28 May (*Urkunden*, nos. 144, 150, pp. 38, 40–41).

14. For a transcript describing this extraordinary interrogation, see *Urkunden*, no. 145, p. 39.

events, the magistrates released Israel.[15] On 4 May, Veyol was drowned on the charge of false testimony, theft, and receiving multiple baptisms for money, once in Regensburg and once in Hungary.[16]

Scarcely a year had passed before yet another charge of Host desecration was raised against the leaders of many Jewish communities, and again by a baptized Jew. In 1475 Reichart of Mospach was caught stealing in Regensburg. During his interrogation, he told a fascinating tale of his life. Baptized in 1464 in Würzburg, he had changed his name from Isaac to Reichart. He wandered everywhere, to Bohemia, Moravia, Holland, the Rhineland, Brandenburg, Alsace, and Württemberg, to Rome, Trent, Bern, Bamberg, and Nuremberg. When the occasion suited him, he presented himself as a Jew, even to the point of accepting two other baptisms and two other Christian names, Johann and Francis. At other times, he showed off his Christian piety, wearing a paternoster around his neck. According to his own testimony, he had married three women and had stolen from all, Christian and Jew, peasant and merchant. Fact and fantasy became fused when this charlatan of many identities told the magistrates of several thefts of the Host, implicating the Jews of Krautheim, Bamberg, and Regensburg in torturing the Eucharist.[17]

There is no further news of Reichart. But his fantastic testimony came at a time when the Jews were becoming a political problem for the city council. For more than twenty years, the Regensburg Jews had been engaged in pawnbroking and retailing to earn their livelihood. Crippling taxes had dried up their capital; moreover, ceilings on interest rates and the angry denunciation of usury had turned moneylending into an unattractive and dangerous business. Hence, pawnbroking and retail trade increasingly displaced the credit business as occupations for most urban Jews.[18] Pawnbroking drew in all sorts of goods, including stolen silver and gold from churches, and the restitution of stolen goods found in pawnshops to their original owners gave rise to numerous lawsuits between Jews and Christians.[19] The Regensburg magistrates discussed

15. *Urkunden*, no. 148, p. 40.

16. *Urkunden*, no. 149, p. 40.

17. *Urkunden*, no. 211, pp. 64–66.

18. For the growing importance of retail trade and pawnbroking as Jewish occupations, see Renate Overdick, *Die rechtliche und wirtschaftliche Stellung der Juden in Südwestdeutschland im 15. und 16. Jahrhundert dargestellt an den Reichsstädten Konstanz und Esslingen und an der Markgrafschaft Baden* (Konstanz, 1965), pp. 60–62, 90, 122–28; see also Straus, *Judengemeinde*, pp. 94–96.

19. A list of complaints that extended back as far as 1443 was drawn up by the magistrates of Regensburg in 1475. The Jews had accepted all manner of stolen goods—primarily gold, silver, clothing, and forged bonds (*Urkunden*, no. 168, pp. 44–47).

this situation with Duke Ludwig and the bishop because pawnbrokerage represented, in real economic terms, a disguised credit and retail trade market that linked the city and the hinterland outside the city council's jurisdiction. There was talk of following Duke Ludwig's example a generation back in expelling the Jews.[20]

In the first months of 1475, it seemed that Emperor Friedrich might withdraw his protection of the Regensburg Jews because they could not come up with their quota of the Burgundian war taxes; the emperor even warned the Jews that their synagogue could be closed.[21] This was the signal many had been waiting for. Things got uglier for the Jews during the summer months. Hans Notscherff, the city treasurer (*Kämmerer*) and a member of the city's Inner Council, was an outspoken enemy of the Jews.[22] He and his confederates on the city council encouraged what amounted to an economic boycott: the city court refused to enforce the collection of debts for Jews, their traditional liberties were curtailed, and, following the magistrates' lead, many citizens refused to pay debts or sell goods to the Jews; threats of violence were uttered.[23]

Economic tensions became dangerously explosive in the face of religious passions. About a year before the boycott, in April 1474, during the ritual murder trial of Rabbi Israel, the Dominican Peter Schwarz had engaged the Regensburg rabbis in a disputation on the nature of the true messiah.[24] The friar's fervor was more a testimony to his missionary zeal than to his knowledge of Judaism, but the Regensburg colloquy nevertheless represented one of the most serious attempts to introduce an element of dialogue into the familiar pattern of forced conversions. Schwarz's treatise, which emerged from this rather one-sided dialogue, became a standard theological handbook for the refutation of Judaic doctrines and was translated, adapted, and reprinted into the early Reformation years.[25] When the campaign against Jewish moneylending got

20. *Urkunden*, nos. 212–13, p. 66; Straus, *Judengemeinde*, pp. 40–41.

21. See Friedrich's letter to the Regensburg Jews, dated 19 Jan. 1475 (*Urkunden*, no. 173, pp. 49–50; see also nos. 157, 159, 162, 182, 183).

22. Straus, *Judengemeinde*, p. 66.

23. See Emperor Friedrich's letter of 9 Aug. 1475 to the city council protesting the failure of the magistrates to protect the Jews (*Urkunden*, no. 189, pp. 54–55).

24. Peter Schwarz (1434–84) was born in Kaaden, Bohemia. After joining the Order of Preachers, he studied in Salamanca, where he learned Hebrew and acquired some knowledge of the Talmud and rabbinical writings. For the Regensburg colloquy, Schwarz enjoyed the backing of Duke Ludwig, Bishop Heinrich, and the city council (*Urkunden*, no. 147, p. 40).

25. The account of the disputation was first published in 1475 by Conrad Fyner of Esslingen under the title *Tractatus contra perfidos Judaeos de conditionibus veri Messie*. It contained the first Hebrew characters printed in Germany and was, moreover, the first non-Hebrew book in which printed Hebrew characters appeared. The Hain repertorium

under way a year later, the clergy readily supplied the moral backing, openly preaching against Jewish usury and blasphemies from the pulpits, apparently with the approval of Bishop Heinrich of Regensburg.[26]

In September, the Inner Council deliberated the matter with the Council of Forty-five, the larger council—which consisted of guildsmen and merchants not included in the patrician inner ruling circle—and decided pro tempore to renew protection for the Jews.[27] But events soon made a mockery of this document of protection.

THE SHOW TRIAL

In early 1476, Bishop Heinrich of Regensburg traveled to Rome. On his return journey, he paused in Trent and obtained a copy of the confession of Wolfgang, a German Jew accused of participation in the murder of Simon of Trent.[28] This confession, extorted under torture, named more than twenty Regensburg Jews in a supposed ritual murder in 1467.[29] On his return to Regensburg in March, the bishop urged Duke Ludwig and the magistrates to seek "justice."

The decision to arrest the implicated Jews was made by a handful of men in secret: perhaps a half-dozen magistrates (including Treasurer Hans Notscherff, the self-professed Jew-hater we have met), consulted Duke Ludwig on how to proceed with the trial against the Jews. In a meeting between delegates of the city council and the ducal councillors, the two parties agreed to support one another, to arrest the named Jews, and to draw up inventories of their properties.[30] At other meetings, the

---

number is 11885 N227. A German translation came out in 1477, also by Fyner of Esslingen, with the title *Der Stern des Meschiah*. A later work, published anonymously, was very similar to Schwarz's account. It appeared under the title *Phareta catholice fidei: Siue ydonea disputatio inter Christianos et Judeos;* there were two 1495 editions, from Ulm and Cologne (by Heinrich Quentell), and a 1518 reprint by Johann Weissenburg of Landshut. The Nuremberg surgeon and Meistersänger Hans Folz translated this work into German; for the printed text of the translation, see *Die Meisterlieder des Hans Folz*, ed. August L. Mayer (Berlin, 1908), pp. 372–401.

26. See the mandate of Friedrich to Bishop Heinrich, dated 12 Aug. 1475 (*Urkunden*, no. 190, p. 55) and letter of petition by the Jewish community to the bishop, dated 8 Nov. 1475 (*Urkunden*, no. 207, p. 63).

27. *Urkunden*, nos. 203–4, pp. 61–62.

28. See Straus, *Judengemeinde*, p. 35; Aron Freimann, "Aus der Geschichte der Juden in Regensburg von der Mitte des 15. Jahrhunderts bis zur Vertreibung im Jahre 1519," in *Beiträge zur Geschichte der deutschen Juden: Festschrift zum 70. Geburtstage Martin Philippsons* (Leipzig, 1916), pp. 79–95, here p. 83; Stern, "Regensburger Judenprozess," p. 4.

29. The text of Wolfgang's confession, dated 11 Nov. 1475, is printed in *Urkunden*, no. 208, p. 63, and in Stern, "Regensburger Judenprozess," pp. 10–11. Wolfgang was asked whether he knew of ritual murders in other cities besides Trent; when he said no, he was tortured and named the Regensburg Jews.

30. *Urkunden*, no. 218, p. 68.

inner circle deliberated on how to present the arrest to the emperor as a fait accompli and how much the Council of Forty-five should be told; they also decided to inventory the properties of all Jews in the city.[31]

On 29 March the magistrates arrested six Jews; on 9 April they imprisoned eleven more men;[32] a list of the Jews' properties was immediately drawn up.[33] Most of those arrested were leaders of the community: they helped to collect the Jewish tax, arbitrated disputes between Jews, and stood out as the most prestigious and richest members of the Regensburg community. In arresting them, the city council and the duke wanted more than to render "justice" in an alleged ritual murder; it was nothing less than a political plot to commit judicial murder. In early April, city delegates and the duke discussed measures to interrogate the Jews and ways to freeze their assets.[34] Duke Ludwig gave his councillors secret instructions to ensure that the city would not cheat him of his fair share of the confiscated properties.[35] The Jewish quarter was sealed by guards, the assets of all Jews were frozen,[36] and Jews were forbidden to leave Regensburg.

Shortly after their arrest, the first six men—Rabbi Jossel, Samuel Fleischacker, Simon of Worms, Sayer Straubinger, Mair Heller, and Hayim Hirsch—were interrogated under torture.[37] A list of twenty-five questions was drawn up:

> Interrogation: these are the questions one should ask every Jew: a Christian child is missing here in Regensburg and he was brought to the Jews, to whom he was sold, tortured, killed, and buried. Our lords want to have knowledge of this . . . if a Jew begins to speak, one should ask him article by article which are listed below, and write down truefully what he really said: 1) Which Jews brought and purchased the child? 2) If such a child was brought among the Jews, interrogate the person or persons in question; 3) How much money did he pay? 4) What time and day of the year did he buy the child? 5) What is the name of the child? 6) Whence was the child carried? To whose house? 7) Were there any Jews present when the child was tortured? 8) What was done to the child at

---

31. See notes of several meetings (*Urkunden*, no. 222, p. 69).

32. *Urkunden*, nos. 226–27, pp. 70–71. The 17 men were: Schmoel (=Samuel) Fleischman, Mair Schmalman, Sayda Straubinger, his son Isaac, Simon of Worms, David of Gmund, Mayr Heller, Rabbi Jössel of Kelheim, Moses of Gmund, Moses of Bamberg, Eberlin son of Jacob, Abraham Heller, Joshua the chanter, Abraham of Kitzing, Hirsch, Süssel son of Jacob, and Ansel of Happburg.

33. *Urkunden*, no. 228, p. 71; Stern, "Regensburger Judenprozess," pp. 10–11.

34. *Urkunden*, no. 223, p. 70.

35. *Urkunden*, nos. 224–25, p. 70.

36. A list of the members of the 72 Jewish households was drawn up: altogether 146 adults (excluding children, servants, and students) are named. For a published list of the names, see Moritz Stern, "Der Regensburger Judenprozess," pp. 12–17.

37. *Urkunden*, no. 234, pp. 73–74.

first? 9) What did each [of the assembled] Jew do? Who held the child? Who tortured him? 10) How much money did each Jew give to participate? 11) How was the child's blood collected? 12) Which Jew took the blood of the child? 13) Which Jew was the first and the last to kill the child? 14) What was done with the child afterwards? 15) Where was the child buried? 16) Did they bury the child together? 17) To which Jews was the blood given? 18) What was the blood used for? 19) Do they need blood from a Christian child every year and why? 20) How were the needles used? 21) How were the pincers used? 22) Why was a handkerchief tied around the child's throat? 23) How was the foreskin on the penis cut off and which Jews cut off the penis and what was done with it? 24) Was more flesh cut from his body? And for what purpose? 25) Which Jewesses knew about this and what did they have to say?[38]

It seems probable that this guideline for the interrogation followed the model of the trial in Trent. In fact, before the magistrates interrogated the prisoners, the confession of the Jew Wolfgang was read to them.[39] The Regensburg magistrates sought not justice but a duplication of the ritual murder trial in Trent. Since Rabbi Jossel and Samuel were named as chief suspects by Wolfgang, the rabbi was interrogated first. Under repeated torture on 30 March and 1 April, immediately after his arrest, he confessed and named other Jews.[40] Of the five others, Samuel and Simon broke down immediately and confessed.

The courage of the others did not outlast their physical endurance. All seventeen were tortured more than once, with ducal and episcopal officials attending many of the sessions; Jossel was questioned four times between 30 March and 15 April. This terse note of the proceedings suffices for us to imagine the torments of the prisoners:

> Abraham was tied [with a stone] and hoisted up 12 times; confesses nothing. The Chanter (Joshua) is broken, was tied; confesses nothing. Black Eberlin . . . was tied and hoisted up 13 times . . . Big Abraham was tied [and hoisted]; confesses nothing. Süssel . . . was tied [and hoisted]; confesses nothing. Moses of Gmund was tied [and hoisted], was broken; confesses nothing. Ansel was tied [and hoisted]; confesses nothing.[41]

Eventually, six men—Jossel, Samuel, Eberlin, Abraham of Kitzing, Simon, and Süssel—confessed, while the others held out. As judicial evidence, the magistrates had little to go on; the conflicting testimony and fragmentary nature of the event reflected only the spontaneous and confused words of the tortured.

38. *Urkunden*, no. 230, pp. 72–73.
39. *Urkunden*, no. 234, p. 73.
40. *Urkunden*, no. 244, p. 78.
41. *Urkunden*, no. 247, p. 80.

Jossel admitted to buying a child from a Christian beggar woman eight years ago at Christmas. According to Samuel, the murder took place at Passover; he also named another murder twelve or fourteen years in the past. For Eberlin, the ritual murder happened at Christmas; the scene of the crime was the cellar in Jossel's house. Abraham of Kitzing "confirmed" the scene of the crime but placed the murder seven years in the past. Simon's confession corroborated Abraham's statement of time but placed the murder in the synagogue. As for motives, only one defendant gave an answer. Samuel admitted that Jews smeared Christian blood on matzo and that he himself painted Christian blood under his eyes, apparently to ward off the evil eye.[42] These confused statements reflected the fantastic tales spun by terrified men in order to please their tormentors; the victims were attempting to anticipate the murder scenario envisioned by their persecutors. Hence, Samuel's assertion of blood-smeared matzo was really his understanding of Christian eucharistic devotion, whose association of consecrated bread with Christ's blood must have been known to the Jews. That blood could serve as a magical substance to repel the power of the evil eye was Samuel's ingenious idea to anticipate Christian beliefs in blood magic, for any Jew would have found it utterly disgusting to use blood for ritualistic purposes.[43] While these fragments give us an insight into the function of the confessions—as raw material for a ritual murder discourse to be written subsequently by Christians, as mirror reflections of Christian magical beliefs and eucharistic piety, unwillingly and imperfectly recreated by Jews—they did not add up to hard legal evidence. Furthermore, Jossel and Simon retracted their confessions, citing duress under torture.[44] To clinch the case, material proof was needed.

Meanwhile, news of the arrest had reached the imperial court. Six years earlier, the emperor had acted too late to save the Jews of Endingen. This time, he reacted swiftly. On 15 April, Friedrich III ordered the city council to release the Jews without bail and to turn them over to him;[45] Duke Ludwig received another edict ordering him to enforce the mandate.[46] Fearful of incurring imperial wrath, the bishop asked the duke and the city not to mention his name but promised to support their

42. *Urkunden*, no. 244, pp. 78–79.

43. To ward off the harm of the evil eye, Jewish folk beliefs prescribed the use of charms and amulets, not blood; see Trachtenberg, *Jewish Magic*, pp. 56, 97, 139–140, and Zimmels, *Magicians*, p. 140.

44. *Urkunden*, no. 245, pp. 79–80.

45. *Urkunden*, nos. 231–33, p. 73. For a full description of the letter, see Stern, "Regensburger Judenprozess," pp. 25–26.

46. Friedrich's letter to Duke Ludwig is printed in Joseph Chmel, ed., *Actenstücke und Briefe zur Geschichte des Hauses Habsburg im Zeitalter Maximilian's I*, vol. 3 (Vienna, 1858), p. 566.

endeavor through quiet diplomacy.[47] The magistrates also stopped the inquisition; they left the Jews alone, except for Jossel and Simon, whom they again tortured into confessing.[48] To secure wider support, the Inner Council briefed the Council of Forty-five on the proceedings and swore its members to secrecy.[49] With the bishop distancing himself from the whole affair, the magistrates asked Duke Ludwig to intercede on their behalf to secure imperial permission for the expulsion of Jews.[50]

Surprised by the energetic negative response from the emperor, Notscherff and his associates worked hard to uncover the material evidence. On 22 April workers and peasants were sent to Jossel's house to tear up the cellar. After three days of digging, they found human bones. In the presence of representatives from the city, the duke, and the bishop, two physicians and two surgeons, all employed by the city, examined the exhumed bones. They testified that the bones were human and that they came from four skeletons of children ranging in age from three to six.[51] The use of medical testimony in the Regensburg case was unique among ritual murder trials. Leaving aside the question of the sophistication of fifteenth-century forensic medicine, contemporaries voiced grave doubts about the authenticity of the material evidence.[52] According to a legal brief in defense of the seventeen Jews and presented at the imperial court, the excavation was not supervised by disinterested parties: soldiers and authorities were not called in until the third day, and one soldier actually expressed his distrust of the workers entrusted with the digging. Some thought that the bones had been planted to frame the Jews; men were seen removing bones from the Christian cemetery.[53] Moreover, the city treasurer was heard to have boasted that if the synagogue was not destroyed, his name would not be Hans Notscherff.[54]

47. On 19 April the ambassadors of Regensburg at the imperial court reported to Duke Ludwig that they found the emperor "almost angry (etbas fast zornig)" with the arrest (Urkunden, no. 236, p. 74). Around this time, the duke, the bishop, and the city met to discuss a common strategy to deal with the emperor (Urkunden, no. 240, pp. 75–76).

48. Urkunden, no. 242, p. 77.

49. Urkunden, no. 247; Stern, "Regensburger Judenprozess," p. 28.

50. Urkunden, no. 250, pp. 81–82.

51. For the medical testimony, see Urkunden, no. 255, pp. 82–83.

52. Medical training in German universities at this time lagged behind the standards of Italian universities. Learned physicians would have only read theoretical texts at the universities; practical experience was disdained. In the 1470s, the University of Freiburg had this curriculum for medical students: the entire first year is given over to lectures on Avicenna; the second year is devoted to Galen; the third and fourth years consist of lectures on Hippocrates, Almansor, and again Avicenna. See Ernst T. Nauck, Zur Geschichte des medizinischen Lehrplans und Unterrichts der Universität Freiburg i. Br. (Freiburg, 1952), p. 82.

53. From a 1477 petition by a lawyer representing the imprisoned Jews at the imperial court (Urkunden, no. 425, pp. 144–48).

54. Urkunden, no. 425, n. 1, pp. 144f.

Again, on 10 May, Friedrich ordered the city to hand over the seventeen Jews.[55] He also sent Marshal Heinrich von Pappenheim as imperial plenipotentiary to Regensburg.[56] The emperor's intervention not only stopped the ritual murder trial in its tracks but also threatened the city's traditional jurisdictional autonomy. The magistrates protested that they could not hand over the Jews without the consent of Duke Ludwig, since Friedrich had pawned the regalian rights on Jews to the Bavarian;[57] they claimed, moreover, to be defending the lives and property of the Jews against the commoners.[58] While the magistrates stalled the imperial plenipotentiary, both the bishop and the duke wrote to Friedrich III on behalf of the city. Bishop Heinrich implored the emperor not to jeopardize an undertaking that would strengthen Christian faith and claimed that the Jews had already confessed.[59] Duke Ludwig sent an ambassador to Friedrich reminding the latter that no king had ever interfered with the jurisdiction of an imperial city and that the regalia over Jews had been pawned to Bavaria.[60]

By mid-July, Friedrich's patience wore out. He instructed the Imperial Fiscal Chamber to summon the city council to face charges of disobedience and appointed Marshal Heinrich Vogt as his new plenipotentiary.[61] Vogt persuaded both the duke and the bishop to distance themselves from the city. Feeling their political isolation, on 17 August the Regensburg magistrates freed the wives and children of the seventeen imprisoned Jews from house arrest.[62] By late August, the city faced the threat of an imperial ban, which would ruin its trade and expose its merchants to predatory princes and robber barons.[63] Nevertheless, Notscherff and his colleagues stood firm, despite moments of doubt, for the city council was now caught between the emperor and the many citizens who were clamoring for "justice," encouraged by the clergy, who denounced Jews in their sermons, unaware of the political machinations behind the trial and fully convinced of the murderous intent of the Jews.[64] The city bailiff, Hans von Fuchsteiner, a nobleman who enjoyed

55. *Urkunden*, no. 268, p. 86. For the complete text, see Stern, "Regensburger Judenprozess," p. 29.

56. Pappenheim was appointed on 29 April and arrived in Regensburg on 16 May (*Urkunden*, nos. 259 273, pp. 84, 87, and Chmel, *Actenstücke*, p. 567).

57. See city's reply to Pappenheim, (*Urkunden*, no. 274, pp. 87–88).

58. See city's reply to Pappenheim, ca. 17 May 1476, (*Urkunden*, no. 280, p. 89).

59. See episcopal letters to Friedrich, dated 27 April and May (*Urkunden*, nos. 257 and 283, pp. 83, 90).

60. *Urkunden*, no. 284, pp. 90–92.

61. *Urkunden*, nos. 297–98, p. 95, and Chmel, *Actenstücke*, p. 570.

62. *Urkunden*, nos. 313–14, pp. 100–101.

63. Cf. the threat of Marshall Vogt (*Urkunden*, no. 317, p. 102).

64. There was a meeting of the city council in August to decide on whether to release the Jews (*Urkunden*, no. 326, p. 110).

the counsel of Duke Ludwig, a close political ally of Notscherff, and under whose authority the trial was being conducted, drew up two legal briefs to answer the charge of disobedience. The city's position was that a crime had been committed, that the Jews had confessed, that justice must run its course, and that nobody, not even the emperor, could obstruct justice. Moreover, Fuchsteiner refuted imperial regalian rights over the Jews by claiming that the constitutional concept of Jewish imperial cameral servitude, a theory advanced by Friedrich II in 1236 to bind all Jews in the Empire directly to his person, was invalid in view of the prior claim of the church, advanced by Pope Innocent IV, that Jews as serfs belonged to all Christians. The Regensburgers were playing a dangerous game in adopting Guelf political ideology and advancing communal rights over and against imperial sovereignty.[65]

A delegation went to Vienna. Its members were instructed to argue that a murder must not remain unpunished, that the common man would never stand for it, that an uprising would result, and that even the city fathers must fear for their own safety. The delegates were told to counter the rumor that some Jews had died under torture, to which end the city supplied a notarial certificate testifying that all seventeen were still alive,[66] but they were also to claim that the Jews themselves had produced the corpse and the bloodstained clothes, which was untrue.[67] In any case, the emperor refused to grant them an audience. On 2 September Friedrich revoked the right of the city to impose capital

65. The influence of canon law and Guelf political ideology points to an interesting connection between South Germany and Italy that can only be touched on here. But Fuchsteiner's arguments refuting imperial regalian rights over Jews are worth quoting; in answering the statement of the Imperial Fiscal Chamber that Jews are under the sole sovereignty of the emperor and the empire ("Das dy selb Judischait mit der öberchait allain dem Kaiser und dem . . . Reich zusten"), Fuchsteiner writes: "Item quod Judeis propter demerita sua post passionem Domini venditi sunt non Cesari sed ominibus indistincte, ut generales servi omnes haberentur, non quod propterea aliquod privilegium sortiretur." And further: "Judeis non sunt veri servi camere Imperialis proprie loquendo, quia propria possident etc. sed improprie dicuntur servi, videlicet respectu pene et servicii, in quibus sunt obnoxii camere etc. Sic in casu proprietatis Judeis licet proprie loquendo non sint servi Imperii sive camere Imperialis, tamen respectu territorii iuris, quo obnoxii sunt, appellari servi camere possunt. Licet enim Judeis servi appellentur, verum est, quod sunt servi peccati respectu perpetue damnacionis et hoc propter delictum ipsorum per mortem Christi, quo ipsi perpetue servituti sive captivitati subiecti sunt." And in response to the charge of disobedience of the emperor, Fuchsteiner invokes papal authority: "Item cum hoc crimen contingit ecclesiam, poterant in defectu Principis secularis per Papam compelli ad faciendam iusticiam, ergo debebant." See *Urkunden*, nos. 323–24, pp. 104–9.

66. On 2 September the magistrates instructed two public notaries to visit the cells, talked to all 17 prisoners, and drew up a certificate (*Urkunden*, no. 332, pp. 112–13).

67. *Urkunden*, no. 328, pp. 100–11.

punishment.[68] At this time, the city stood alone; Duke Ludwig had advised the Regensburgers that he would not jeopardize his friendship with Friedrich over some Jews.[69] By late September, the city seemed ready to compromise: the city council sent one of its own, Jeronimus Reich, to the imperial court, arming him with a bunch of documents to "prove" the guilt of the Jews. Included were Wolfgang of Trent's confession, the confessions of the Regensburg Jews, and the medical report on the exhumed human bones. But Reich was also instructed to come to an agreement with the emperor, to get him to lift the ban on capital punishment, and to ensure that the city could recover its legal expenditures.[70] In private, some magistrates vented their frustration by wishing that the Jews would all suffocate in jail.[71] In any event, Friedrich was now preoccupied with the Burgundian War. At the imperial court, the Jews did not lack supporters; they accused the Regensburgers of burying the bones themselves.[72]

Those involved in initiating the prosecution had miscalculated badly. Not only could they not lay their hands on the imagined vast wealth of the Jews but the city had paid out large sums for its diplomatic missions and for the Jews' imprisonment. Worse, it had incurred imperial disgrace and was threatened with a ban. Even the legal foundation of the trial had been called into question. The Regensburgers were desperate to extricate themselves from their quagmire.

On 6 January 1477 Hans von Fuchsteiner and his fellow Regensburg diplomats at the imperial court wrote to the city council and suggested that their colleagues should acquire a copy of the judicial confessions of the Endingen Jews executed by Margrave Karl of Baden seven years earlier.[73] The city fathers hurriedly sent messengers to Margrave Christoph, Karl's son, and to the city councils of Pforzheim and Baden; by 20 January, they had received copies of the confessions, which they forwarded to their ambassadors in Vienna by the end of the month.[74] These preparations, however, were in vain, because Friedrich had no time to grant the Regensburgers an audience. Finally, on 25 May after thirty weeks of waiting, Hans von Fuchsteiner received an audience with the emperor. His arguments made no impressions on Friedrich, who in-

68. *Urkunden*, no. 330, p. 112. For the complete text, see Stern, "Regensburger Judenprozess," p. 33.

69. Stern, "Regensburger Judenprozess," p. 34.

70. *Urkunden*, no. 341, p. 115.

71. Stern, "Regensburger Prozess," pp. 34–35.

72. See city council's instructions to its delegates at the imperial court, 8 Dec. 1476 (*Urkunden*, no. 358, p. 121).

73. *Urkunden*, no. 374, p. 128.

74. *Urkunden*, nos. 375, 376, 377, 380, pp. 128–30.

formed the Regensburger that a decision would be made by the Imperial Fiscal Chamber at its next court session. And although Hans Notscherff himself went to Vienna, the emperor was determined to wait out the Regensburgers.[75] Both parties—the city council and the Jews—appealed to the papal legate Alexander to plead their case before the emperor.[76] By now, the case had dragged into its second year: the magistrates were discouraged but had not completely given up; the Jews were still languishing in jail, although they were no longer subject to interrogation and torture.

The new year brought the Regensburgers fresh hopes. Not far down the Danube, the Jews of Passau had been arrested. In February 1478, Hans Friesshaimer, a member on the city council and a cousin of Treasurer Hans Notscherff, was sent to inquire of the case. He asked the marshal of Passau whether the arrested Jews had confessed to any knowledge of the Regensburg ritual murder; he also advised the Passauers to convict their Jews quickly, before the emperor could intervene.[77] On 22 February a letter from Passau informed the Regensburg magistrates that the servant (Christian Eisengreisshaimer) who had denounced the Passau Jews also confessed that he had sold some Hosts stolen from a church in Wenng to the Jew Sündel of Regensburg.[78] To the Regensburgers, this promised a break in the deadlock. A conviction in Passau would bolster their own case; moreover, a network of Jewish conspiracies stretching from Trent to Regensburg to Passau could be exposed. The magistrates informed their Passau colleagues that although they did not know the whereabouts of Wenng, two villages by the names of Weinttingen and Wintzer were close to Regensburg. The accused Sündel had been away for two years at the imperial court trying to defend his brethren, but his son Süttel was at home.[79] In their eagerness to tie the two trials together, the Regensburg magistrates arrested Süttel on 6 March, ironically ignoring the "evidence" of a false confession. Under torture, Süttel named a man, Joseph, and a woman, Pelein, Jacob's widow, as accomplices in this travesty of justice; Pelein was arrested but

75. *Urkunden*, nos. 396, 400, 403, 412, pp. 135–37, 139.
76. *Urkunden*, nos. 424–25, pp. 144–48.
77. Hans Friesshaimer apparently belonged to the anti-Semitic faction in cty government. In 1473 his wife was involved in a lawsuit against a Jewish woman, Josepin of Kelhaim (*Urkunden*, no. 133, p. 36); for his report on the consultation with the Passauers, see *Urkunden*, no. 436, pp. 150–51. The marshal informed him that the Passau Jews had not confessed to knowledge of the Regensburg ritual murder trial but they had not been asked; he also rejected Friesshaimer's suggestion of a quick execution because the stolen sacrament had not been found.
78. *Urkunden*, no. 438, p. 151.
79. *Urkunden*, no. 443, p. 153.

was too sick to be interrogated.[80] Naturally, Notscherff forwarded these confessions, together with copies of the Passau confessions, to the city's diplomats at the imperial court.[81] A copy of Süttel's confession was also sent to Nuremberg because the identity of this Joseph could not be established among Regensburg Jews. It seems probable that the Regensburgers might have altered reported facts to fit circumstance: Eisengreisshaimer's original Passau confessions made no mention of Nuremberg, but when the whole Passau-Regensburg case was presented to the Nuremberg city council, Eisengreisshaimer's confession included a theft of Hosts from two churches in Nuremberg.[82] The motive was obviously to extend the anti-Jewish trials to yet another imperial city and to forge, if possible, a common urban front against the emperor, a plan that failed when no Nuremberg Jew fit the description.[83]

Time was running out for Regensburg. While the magistrates were trying to exploit the Host desecration trial in Passau, Friedrich III warned of the revocation of all civic freedoms and the status of imperial city for Regensburg.[84] He also undertook to forestall further persecutions. At the request of the Salzburg Jews, who feared that charges of Host desecration and child murder from neighboring Passau would spill over and destroy their own community, Friedrich wrote to the archbishop of Salzburg on 12 March, bidding him not to instigate judicial proceedings against Jews on rumors and unfounded charges and to investigate any possible accusations with seriousness and an unprejudiced disposition.[85] Back in Regensburg, the magistrates briefly considered an appeal to the Papacy but dropped the idea because it would have cost the city fifty or sixty thousand florins, ten times what the city had already spent on the trial.[86] Moreover, the city council was split, with one party ready to compromise and the other determined to pursue the affair to the bitter end.[87] In mid-

---

80. *Urkunden*, no. 444, p. 153.

81. *Urkunden*, nos. 445, 453, pp. 153, 155–56.

82. Eisengreisshaimer's confession was copied in the 1478 Ratschlagbuch of Nuremberg; see Arnd Müller, *Die Geschichte der Juden in Nürnberg, 1146–1945* (Nuremberg, 1968), p. 46 and n. Müller, however, inaccurately reports this case as a local accusation, and not as originating from Regensburg.

83. See letter from Nuremberg to Regensburg, 9 Mar. 1477 (*Urkunden*, no. 450, p. 155).

84. *Urkunden*, nos. 437 and 442, pp. 151, 153.

85. Joseph Chmel, ed., *Sammlung von Actenstücken und Briefen zur Geschichte des Hauses Habsburg in dem Zeitraum von 1473 bis 1576*, 1. Abteilung: *Das Zeitalter Maximilians's I*, vol. 2 (Vienna, 1855), p. 342.

86. For a draft of the appeal to the Papacy, dated 24 March, see Straus, *Urkunden*, no. 459, pp. 157–58; for Friesshaimer's memorandum to drop the appeal and to concede to the emperor, dated 16 April, see no. 466, pp. 159–60.

87. Gemeiner, *Chronik*, p. 605.

April, the Regensburg ambassadors indicated their willingness to concede and to guarantee the safety of the Jews; on 8 May, Friedrich revoked the interdict on capital punishment, dropped the citation at the Imperial Fiscal Chamber, declared Regensburg to be again in the grace of the Holy Roman Empire, and ordered the release of the seventeen Jews charged with ritual murder as well as Süttel and Pelein.[88] In Regensburg, Notscherff, the leader of the die-hards, was replaced in the councillor election by a moderate, thus opening the road to a political settlement.[89]

In essence, the Regensburg ritual murder trial was over in May 1478, but negotiations over fines and payment procedures dragged on for another twenty-eight months. The newly arrested Süttel and Pelein were released on 26 November 1478 after they had agreed to pay for the cost of their imprisonment.[90] But the seventeen imprisoned Jews could not raise the enormous sums stipulated in the agreement between emperor and city: ten thousand florins to Friedrich for securing their freedom, five thousand florins to repay the city for the cost of the trial and their upkeep in jail, and another eight thousand florins, a fine imposed on Regensburg by the emperor that the city was determined to pass on to the Jews.[91] Eventually, the Jewish community was able to raise enough money, and payment plans were worked out; on 4 September 1480, fifty-four months after their arrest, the seventeen were released. One of the most protracted ritual murder trials at last came to a close.[92]

SURVIVAL AND EXPULSION

Even in this well-documented trial, relatively little is known about the individual victims. It seems that almost all the arrested were visible leaders of the community: Jössel was rabbi, Joshua was chanter, while others, men like Ansel, Mair Schmalman, Mair Heller, and Simon of Worms, were tax collectors in the community. Their high visibility probably accounted for their being named and arrested in the first place. Aside from confessions extracted under torture, the victims remained silent about their ordeal. The only voice of the Jews in jail was indirect. A note, in Yiddish, was found in the cell of Pelein, the woman arrested in

88. Straus, *Urkunden*, nos. 466–67, pp. 159–60, nos. 470–71, p. 161. For Friedrich's order to Regensburg of 18 May not to torture Süttel and Pelein, see also Chmel, *Actenstücke*, pp. 101–2.

89. Gemeiner, *Chronik*, p. 616.

90. *Urkunden*, nos. 496–97, p. 168.

91. *Urkunden*, nos. 475, 479, 482, 485, 490, 494, pp. 162–68.

92. *Urkunden*, nos. 514–15, p. 174. For the promissory note of the Jews to the emperor, see Chmel, *Actenstücke*, pp. 121–22; Stern, "Regensburger Judenprozess," pp. 34–47.

connection with the alleged Passau-Regensburg Host desecration. Apparently sent by a friend, it reads: "Dear friend, my dear crown, I have written often to you, but you do not answer, is it because you cannot on account of the torture? Tomorrow, I will go and speak to the magistrates to see if I can bring the matter to a good end, to try to get you out."[93] The men released in September 1480 resumed their normal lives with a stoic matter-of-factness. Many reoccupied positions of leadership within the community, collecting Jewish taxes for the city council that had imprisoned and tortured them. Some got into legal disputes with other Jews over the question of tax assessments to repay the city over the cost of their long internment, a financial burden shared by the entire community.[94] All seventeen and their descendants were cited by the magistrates in a complaint to the imperial government in 1518 over tax arrears.[95] Most would live to witness another wave of anti-Semitic violence in the 1490s; Isaac Straubinger, probably the youngest of the seventeen, survived to experience the complete expulsion of the Jewish community in 1519.[96]

Although the magistrates failed to expel the Jews through the ritual murder trial, their successors in 1519 succeeded. Tensions between citizens and Jews did not subside after 1480. In 1493 a wave of anti-Semitic violence broke out; throughout the 1510s, frequent complaints, especially by the guilds, were made about Jewish economic competition in retail trade. In 1513 another popular unrest claimed the lives of several patrician councillors. In 1519 encouraged by the sermons of Balthasar Hubmaier, the new cathedral preacher who attacked Jewish usury and blasphemy from the pulpit, and exploiting the weakness of imperial government immediately after the death of Emperor Maximilian I, Friedrich's successor, the Regensburgers expelled the entire Jewish community—some eight hundred men, women, and children.[97]

In spite of persistent anti-Semitism, the trial of 1476 represented a watershed. Imperial opposition discredited the ritual murder and host desecration trials in Regensburg. Personal prejudices of some of the magistrates and the overall political considerations had clearly stretched the framework of legality and jurisprudence to the breaking point. After 1480, another ritual murder trial would have lost credibility from the

93. *Urkunden*, no. 502, p. 170.
94. *Urkunden*, no. 697, pp. 239–41.
95. *Urkunden*, no. 965, p. 343.
96. *Urkunden*, nos. 563, 670 (Ansel of Happburg), no. 651 (Süssel), nos. 586–88, 605–6 (Mair Schmalman), no. 651 (Sayda Straubinger), no. 577 (Simon of Worms), no. 680 (Jössel of Kelheim), no. 697 (Moses of Gmund), no. 676 (Abraham Heller), and no. 676 (Abraham of Kitzing); for Isaac Straubinger, see nos. 1144–45.
97. Straus, *Regensburg and Augsburg*, pp. 155ff.

start; and even in times of heightened anti-Semitism, the magistrates refrained from accusations of Jewish magic and murder.

The only other occasion on which a charge was brought before the magistrates was in June 1513. Two burghers, Georg Gebhart and Georg Reitmair, reported on a couple who were seen taking children into the Jewish quarter.[98] Gebhart claimed he saw a man and a woman taking a boy and an infant into the ghetto. Reitmair swore he saw the couple and three children sitting at an inn near the Jewish quarter; when they came out, the woman had only one child. He also claimed to have heard from the innkeeper's wife that the man drank a glass of wine and asked how much the Jews would pay for a child. The magistrates questioned nine more witnesses, who could provide nothing conclusive: some saw only one child; others saw them go inside the Jewish quarter; still others heard the man offering to sell the child, but not to the Jews. In any case, the magistrates arrested the couple who were staying at the inn, tortured them, failed to get confessions, and found out they had the wrong man. To prevent an uproar, they arrested Gebhart and Reitmair instead. The whole case had come to naught. It seems that the two zealous burghers were Jew-haters; apparently they tried a second time to undermine the Jews and were punished in January 1518 by imperial mandate.[99]

Three crucial themes emerge from our analysis of the events in Regensburg and illuminate the context and dynamics of ritual murder discourse. First, the language of magic in the 1476 trial had a relatively weak voice; the case of Regensburg shows that ritual murder trials must be understood in their concrete political settings as well. Reflected in the language of accusation was not only the vocabulary of Christian piety and fervor but also a field of political reference. The specific discourse of Jewish magic was embedded in the larger discourse of anti-Semitism: the depiction of ritual murder represented but one of the many voices of anti-Semitism. After 1480 this specific language proved inadequate and politically ineffective as a means of expressing anti-Semitism; instead, the language of the moral economy was voiced in the many petitions, lawsuits, and sermons that denounced Jewish moneylending, pawnbroking, and retailing. According to the language of this moral economy, the Jews were ruining much more than the prosperity of an imperial city; they imperiled the way of life and the moral and social fiber of a Christian community in crisis. In the end, this language of moral economy proved more effective (though less dramatic) in ridding the civic community of its religious minority because it both reinforced the message of and was incorporated by the early Reformation movement.

98. For their and others' testimonies, see *Urkunden*, no. 799, pp. 279–80.
99. *Urkunden*, no. 951, p. 337.

Second, the Regensburg ritual murder trial revealed two sources of tension. The first was between the emperor and the city council, and the events of 1476–80 can be interpreted as a defense of civic liberties and urban autonomy against imperial intervention. The second was between the magistrates and the citizens over the treatment of Jews, which led to the two popular uprisings in 1493 and 1513. In the 1476–80 ritual murder trial, the magistrates were playing a double game: they initiated the trial, negotiated for allies, and jealously guarded knowledge of the political machinations from the citizens—sometimes even from the larger Council of Forty-five—while allowing popular feelings to mount against the Jews; to Friedrich III, however, the city fathers presented themselves as men of order and justice who were protecting the Jews from mob violence while seeking to punish a real crime. In the end, the patrician regime found itself caught between a civic commune it tried to manipulate and the Jewish community it was forced to protect by the emperor. One of the causes of the civic unrest of 1493 was the charge of corruption directed at the patrician councillors; ironically, the citizens' committee cited as an example of patrician venality the reward of ten guldens to former councillor Hans Friesshaimer for his service as ambassador to the imperial court during the ritual murder trial.[100] The conflict between authorities and citizens was a recurring theme in policies toward Jews in late medieval and early modern Germany.[101]

The final theme is the intersection of ritual murder and learned discourses. When the magistrates summoned physicians to examine the exhumed bones, they were also opening legal thinking to the influence of learned medical discourse. In the case of Regensburg, the testimony of the medical experts played a minor supporting role for the case of the prosecution, but it signaled an increasing academic concern with alleged ritual murders. From a discourse in which the languages of common law and popular piety provided the mode of perception and description, the new academic interest in ritual murder supplied a new vocabulary drawn from a new jurisprudence, Roman Law, and from the arguments of theology.

A generation later, and under a different emperor, all three themes would again emerge in yet another ritual murder trial. This trial took place in 1504 in Freiburg, in Austrian Breisgau, not far from Endingen.

100. *Urkunden*, no. 626, p. 212. For the unrest leading up to the election of a new city council and the purge and arrests of members of the old council, see Gemeiner, *Chronik*, pp. 789–840.

101. For a more detailed argument and other political examples, see R. Po-chia Hsia, "Die Juden im Alten Reich: Einige Bemerkungen zu einer Forschungsaufgabe," in *Stände und Gesellschaft im Alten Reich*, ed. Georg Schmidt (Wiesbaden, forthcoming).

CHAPTER FIVE **Freiburg**

HE LARGEST CITY IN THE BREISGAU, FREIBURG STRADDLES the crossroad between Alsace and the Black Forest, between north Baden and Switzerland. Traveling from west to east in 1503, it took Duke Philip of Burgundy and his party one day to reach Freiburg from Ensisheim, the capital of the Austrian Upper Rhine, and another two days from Freiburg to reach Villingen in the Black Forest.[1] In the thirteenth century, Freiburg developed rapidly as the gateway to the silver mines of the mountains, and after the silver ores were exhausted, the city continued to flourish as the major regional market town.[2] Entering Freiburg in the summer of 1503, Philip of Burgundy and his retinue were greeted by two hundred militiamen dressed in white; Philip found Freiburg to be "a good and very beautiful city, full of wells, and situated in a fertile and beautiful country."[3]

In 1500 the city had a population of between 6,000 and 6,500.[4] The burghers had used their prosperity to build magnificent churches: construction of the Münster began in the early thirteenth century and was completed in the sixteenth century. In addition, there were five male religious houses, three crusading orders, and seven female cloisters; Freiburg's university was founded in 1457.[5]

In the thirteenth and fourteenth centuries, when Freiburg enjoyed

1. For Freiburg's central geographical location and the travel routes and times around 1500, see the 1503 travel journal of Philip the Handsome, duke of Burgundy: Ulrich Crämer, ed., "Eine Reise durch Schwaben, Tirol und die Rheinlande im Jahre 1503," in *Alemannisches Jahrbuch* (1956), pp. 371–403.

2. On the economy of medieval Freiburg, especially on the role of the city as a market town and center for silver mining in the Breisgau, see Hektor Amman, "Freiburg und der Breisgau in der mittelalterlichen Wirtschaft," *Oberrheinische Heimat* 28 (1941), pp. 248–59.

3. Crämer, "Eine Reise," entry under 24 August.

4. Keyser, ed., *Badisches Städtebuch*, p. 222.

5. See Leo A. Ricker, *Freiburg: Aus der Geschichte einer Stadt* (Karlsruhe, 1964), pp. 37–48.

its economic heyday, an uneasy coalition of noblemen and merchants governed the city and sat on the council. This patrician-mercantile regime gradually yielded to a guild regime during the fifteenth century, when the urban patriciate and the mercantile elite withdrew from civic politics and when Freiburg no longer formed one of the vibrant centers of international trade. The artisans' long path to political power reached a turning point in 1464 when Archduke Sigismund of Austria formally recognized the legal status of the twelve guilds and gave the guildmasters half of the twenty-four seats on the city council.[6] Guild political participation increased even more toward the end of the fifteenth century, when many patrician families withdrew from civic politics altogether. By the end of the century, in addition to the twelve guaranteed seats, the guildmasters practically dominated the city council, which by then had only a handful of patrician members.[7]

When Maximilian I succeeded Friedrich III in 1493, the Austrian lands in the Upper Rhine took on a new political significance in Maximilian's attempt to consolidate dynastic power and to strengthen imperial institutions.[8] In 1498 the Imperial Diet met in Freiburg.[9] In 1499, the city served as one of the centers of military operations in Maximilian's attempt to subjugate the Swiss Confederation. The Swabian War of 1499 resulted in the victory of Swiss peasants and townsmen and the definitive break of the confederation with the empire; it also dashed the emperor's hopes of a Hapsburg dynastic territorial bloc on the southern border of the German-speaking lands of central Europe, unbroken and stretching from the Danube to the Inn and to the Rhine.[10] Freiburg benefited from this unfulfilled imperial dream; it became the bastion of Hapsburg rule against the infectious antinoble aspirations of the Swiss and the common people of the Upper Rhine. Maximilian favored the University of Freiburg, helped the city pay its debts by forcing its cloisters to make financial contributions, and even conceded to the city the regalian right to mint gold coins.[11]

The economic importance of Freiburg to the Hapsburgs was under-

6. Ricker, *Freiburg*, p. 36.

7. *Badisches Städtebuch*, pp. 226–27.

8. On the relationship between the Hapsburgs and Freiburg, see Friedrich Hefele, "Freiburg als vorderösterreichische Stadt," in *Vorderösterreich: Eine geschichtliche Landeskunde*, vol. 2 (Freiburg, 1959), pp. 326–47.

9. See Steven W. Rowan, "A Reichstag in the Reform Era: Freiburg im Breisgau, 1497–98," in James A. Vann and Steven W. Rowan, eds., *The Old Reich: Essays on German Political Institutions, 1495–1806* (Brussels, 1974).

10. On the Hapsburg imperial vision, see R. J. W. Evans, *The Making of the Habsburg Monarchy, 1550–1700* (Oxford, 1979); on the Swabian War, see Brady, *Turning Swiss*, pp. 57–72.

11. See Ricker, *Freiburg*, p. 58.

lain by the active credit market in the late thirteenth and fourteenth centuries. Jews and Lombards were financiers and moneylenders, but with the decline of silver mining and the rise of the guilds, their importance began to diminish.[12] Disaster befell Freiburg's Jewish community in 1349. As the plague spread across the empire, people accused Jews of poisoning wells. In January 1349 the city council of Freiburg obtained confessions from Jews under torture and burnt all Jews except pregnant women and children in the city.[13] Rumor became judicial knowledge: the Freiburg Jews confessed to a major conspiracy to poison all the wells in the Breisgau, from Breisach and Endingen to Freiburg; the Christians of Basel and Strasbourg were not to be spared as well.

Remarkably, the Jewish communities survived this catastrophe; they settled in Freiburg again in the second half of the fourteenth century under the protection of the Hapsburg rulers. But in 1401 another wave of persecution struck. In May of that year, the bailiff and councillors of Diessenhofen, a small town on the South German-Swiss border, arrested the Jew Michael and charged him with paying a Christian servant to obtain Christian blood from a boy, who died from the bleeding. Under torture, Michael confessed to a widespread ritual murder coverup, implicating the Jews of Schaffhausen, Winterthur, and Zurich in child murders; he also revealed a Jewish plot to poison the air in order to slowly kill off all Christians.[14] Michael was burnt in Schaffhausen, as were many other Jews whose confessions were likewise obtained under torture. The magistrates in Freiburg received warning from their colleagues in Schaffhausen, Winterthur, and Diessenhofen and interrogated their own Jews.[15] Unable to find them guilty, the Freiburgers nevertheless decided to expel their Jews because by now the populace was agitating for action. The Freiburgers wrote to Duke Leopold of Austria, requesting permission to expel the Jews. Leopold appointed a commission, which, together with the Freiburg magistrates, proclaimed that Jews were forever banned from the city.[16] In 1411, however, Duke Friedrich gave permission to three Jewish families to live in Freiburg, an infringement of civic autonomy in the eyes of the proud burghers. As a prerequisite to renewing their allegiance to the House of Hapsburg in 1427, the citizens secured an expulsion of the Jews and a privilege to not tolerate Jews in the future.[17]

Thus, in the major towns of Further Austria, no Jews were to be

12. See Clemens Bauer, "Wirtschaftsgeschichte der Stadt Freiburg im Mittelalter," in Wolfgang Müller, ed., Freiburg im Mittelalter (Bühl, 1970), pp. 50–76.
13. See Schreiber, UB Freiburg I, pp. 378–83.
14. Schreiber, UB Freiburg I, p. 167.
15. Schreiber, UB Freiburg I, pp. 167–72.
16. Schreiber, UB Freiburg I, pp. 174–75.
17. Hefele, "Freiburg als vorderösterreichische Stadt," pp. 327–28.

found. To the burghers of the Upper Rhineland, being free of Jews symbolized the achievement of communal political autonomy, for the Jews had been forced on the communities by their Hapsburg rulers, had been protected by local noble lords, and represented an alien economic and religious minority in their midst. Freedom from Jews amounted to a fundamental civic right.

WALDKIRCH: A SMALL TOWN CRIME

In the valley of the Elz, eight miles from the proud university city of Freiburg, on the left bank of the river, and not far from the confluence of the Elz and the Rhine, is the little town of Waldkirch. In 1475, it had a population of 650, most of whom were artisans—weavers, bakers, gem polishers, butchers, millers, and vintners.[18] There were three parish churches and a Benedictine cloister. A council with twelve members, including three Bürgermeisters, represented the town. But the administration of the town, nominally under the Austrian territorial government in Ensisheim, had been enfeoffed in the early fifteenth century to the House of Staufen, whose lords became the de facto rulers of Waldkirch during that century.[19] Under the protection of Leo, Freiherr von Staufen, several Jewish families were allowed to settle before 1500. The townsfolk, however, harbored bitter memories. In 1349, the Waldkirch Jews had been accused of well poisoning and were burnt; others later settled there but were expelled in 1424.[20]

In accordance with their prohibition decree of 1401, the city fathers of Freiburg forbade the Jews of nearby Waldkirch to do business in Freiburg's market; they also denied Jews the right of passage.[21] Failing to gain concessions from Freiburg for his Jews, Leo von Staufen complained to King Maximilian, who decided in 1502 that it was unreasonable for the Freiburgers to deny Jews the right of passage, since the road south from Waldkirch ran through Freiburg.[22] The magistrates and burghers felt their civic rights infringed and their pride dented by a overlord who was partial to the Jews and their noble protector.[23]

It was against this historical background that yet another ritual murder trial took place, between March and October of 1504. Many of the

18. Keyser, ed., *Badisches Städtebuch*, p. 406.

19. Keyser, ed., *Badisches Städtebuch*, p. 407.

20. Keyser, ed., *Badisches Städtebuch*, p. 408.

21. See letter of Leo von Staufen on behalf of the Waldkirch Jews to the city of Freiburg, 21 Aug. 1500, StdA Fb, A1 XIIc, no. 25.

22. See letter of Maximilian to the city of Freiburg, 12 July 1502, StdA Fb, A1 XIIC, no. 26.

23. It seemed that the Freiburgers continued to make things difficult for the Waldkirch Jews; even after Maximilian's mandate, Leo von Staufen still had to request safe conduct for his Jews. See his letter to the city of Freiburg, 28 Dec. 1502, StdA Fb, A1 XIIc, no. 27.

sources that documented this alleged murder in Waldkirch and its subsequent trial in Freiburg have survived, allowing us to reconstruct with much greater precision the judicial process and the motivations of the different actors. Three parties were involved in what was actually two separate trials: three men—Philip Bader, Hans Gysennbrecht, and Michael Hun—played the role of accusors; the authorities in question included a noble lord, Konrad Stürtzel, the city council of Freiburg, and Maximilian I and his government; the suspects or victims were, of course, the Jews of the Hapsburg Breisgau.[24]

It all began at Easter in the village of Benzhausen in the Lordship of Buchheim, located to the northwest of Freiburg.[25] On Good Friday, the

24. The first trial that involved the death of Philip Bader's son has been recorded in only two contemporary accounts. The first is a long (809 lines) epic poem with the title *Ein seltzame kouffmanschatz wie ein man sein leiplich kind Nüwlich den Juden verkoufft hatt, und das kind zu tod gemartert worden ist*, with no date or place of publication. Fridrich Pfaff, who published the poem, has identified the printer's markings to be those of Johannes Grüninger of Strasbourg; he also argues that the anonymously published poem came from the pen of the Franciscan Thomas Murner and not from Johann Eck, as one may expect. In any event, the authorship cannot be established with documentary proof. For Pfaff's introduction to the poem, see "Die Kindermorde zu Benzhausen und Waldkirch im Breisgau: Ein Gedicht aus dem Anfang des 16. Jahrhunderts," *Alemannia* 27 (1899), pp. 247–51. Probably following Eck's memory of the trial, Pfaff puts the year of the Benzhausen trial at 1503, which is inaccurate; the year should be 1504, as other trial documents clearly show. In addition to this poem, we have a short personal recollection by Johann Eck in his *Ein Judenbüchleins Verlegung* (1541) directed against the Protestant reformer Andreas Osiander, who tried to discredit ritual murder trials. For a detailed discussion of this, see chaps. 6 and 7. Judging from internal evidence, the poem was probably composed by someone close to the Freiburg city council: it made extensive use of the confessions of Hans Gysennbrecht and Michael Hun, who were interrogated by the magistrates in the city's jail, and it strongly disapproved of the imperial intervention that led to the release of the Jews. An almost identical chapbook describing the murder at Benzhausen is at the British Library, entitled, *Ein grausame Geschicht von einem verrucktem Christen man. der sein natürliches kind den seellosen Juden verkauft hat. 1504* (4033.c.50). This chapbook differs from *Ein seltzame kouffmanschatz* only in its lack of illustrations. The confessions of Gysennbrecht and Hun, the correspondence between Freiburg and neighboring cities and the imperial government, the report of the imperial commission, and the sworn oaths of the Jews on their release are deposited in the Stadtarchiv Freiburg under signatures A1 XIIc and C1 Judensachen. Some of these documents, including the confessions of Gysennbrecht and Hun, are appended in Pfaff, although most only appear as precis and extracts. Pfaff is also incorrect in the dating of two letters: on p. 277, the letter from Freiburg to Mulhouse announcing the arrest of the Waldkirch Jews should be 19 Apr. 1504, not 1503; on the same page, the letter from Freiburg to Margrave Christoph von Baden should be 20 Apr. 1505, not 1504. I cannot locate in the Stadtarchiv Freiburg some of the letters published by Pfaff, whereas Pfaff has not included some important letters and reports concerning the trial. His transcriptions are not always accurate and need to be checked against the originals.

25. For contemporary accounts of the event, see Pfaff, "Ein seltzame kouffmanschatz" and "Ein grausame Geschicht."

Figure 9. Ritual Murder of Benzhausen. The dead boy Matthew Bader is discovered by the cowherd Andreas. From *Ein seltzame kouffmanschatz*. Reprinted courtesy of Stadtarchiv Freiburg i. B.

cowherd boy Andreas was tending his herd in the fields when his cattle's moos alerted him to the corpse of a little boy, who turned out to be one of his playmates, Matthew Bader (see fig. 9). The cries of the cowherd boy drew the villagers to the spot; judging from the pale corpse, they surmised that it had been lying there for at least three days. The body was removed and buried in the churchyard. Six days later, the father of the dead boy, Philip Bader, was arrested for theft. After he had confessed to stealing, the bailiff confronted Bader about the death of his child (one account described the boy as his illegitimate son). At first, Bader denied knowledge of the circumstances of the murder, but when he was brought to the churchyard and presented with the corpse of his child, which the authorities had dug up, he was ready to "confess." As a contemporary poem commemorating the event tells it, and in the words of Philip Bader, the mad Jews went to him and offered him money for a Christian child to celebrate Passover. Out of a throng of boys playing nearby, the Jews supposedly picked Bader's own son. They assured him,

Bader told the bailiff, that the child would not be killed; all they needed was a little Christian blood, and they intended to draw this from the Bader boy, who was barely seven years old. A bargain was concluded. Bader took his boy to the Jews in Waldkirch in exchange for a handsome sum. After this initial confession, the bailiff applied torture and Bader changed his story. Now he admitted that he was acting entirely on his own accord: he had heard that Jews pay good money for Christian blood and had drawn blood from his own son's neck to sell to the Jews. But when he approached the Jews, they turned from him and scolded him for trying to sell them animal blood. Rebuffed, Bader threw away the blood. Since his two testimonies contradicted each other, Bader was tortured further, and the village bailiff referred the case to his master, the lord of Buchheim, whose feudal jurisdiction extended over Benzhausen.[26]

The lord of Buchheim, Konrad Stürtzel (c. 1435–1509), was the former chancellor of Maximilian I. His distinguished career began in the world of learning; he served as professor of civil law at the university in Freiburg. Summoned from academics, he became a councillor in the Hapsburg provincial government in Ensisheim and later served as a ducal councillor in Innsbruck. Maximilian appointed Stürtzel to be his court chancellor, employing him in many diplomatic missions. Ennobled in 1491, Stürtzel retired in 1500 due to ill health and concentrated his energies in the management of his extensive estate around Buchheim.[27] While Stürtzel held his serf Philip Bader for further questioning, the magistrates of Freiburg took the initative to turn this investigation into a major ritual murder trial. On 20 April messengers and letters were sent by the Freiburg city council to Waldkirch, Ensisheim, Villingen, Mulhouse, and Colmar (in other words, to all the towns in the Breisgau and Alsace with a sizable Jewish community) to inform the other magistrates of the murder and to advise the immediate arrest of their Jews.[28]

On 26 April the magistrates in Villingen, a town in the Black Forest two days' journey away, wrote to the city fathers of Freiburg, informing the latter that they had heard about the alleged ritual murder in Waldkirch and had acted promptly. All Jews found in Villingen, including one

26. For the first two confessions of Philip Bader, see Pfaff, "Ein seltzame kouffman-schatz," lines 38–248. Although the poem represents a contemporary report of the trial, the facts seem highly reliable. The poet narrates both sets of confessions even though he strongly rejects Bader's second confession, attributing it to "the devil's work" to make the poor man confess in order to exculpate the Jews (lines 211–14).

27. See Jürgen Bücking, "Das Geschlecht Stürtzel von Buchheim (1491–1790): Ein Versuch zur Sozial- und Wirtschaftsgeschichte des Breisgauer Adels in der frühen Neuzeit," *ZGO* 18 (1970), pp. 239–78.

28. For the correspondence between Freiburg and neighboring towns and rulers, see Pfaff, "Ein seltzame kouffmanschatz," pp. 277–79.

who had traveled there from Waldkirch, were now securely in prison. The Villingers asked the Freiburgers for further information.[29] The next day Leo von Staufen, who had received the lordship over Waldkirch from the Austrian government, wrote to the city of Freiburg. He too had been in correspondence with Villingen. The Waldkirch Jew arrested in Villingen was the son of Lameth, the chief suspect in the murder case. Leo suggested to the Freiburgers that they should adopt a common course of action.[30] The net of arrests soon spread to other communities in the Breisgau and Alsace. The magistrates of Mulhouse and Boldwiler threw their Jews in jail, and in Colmar, Ensisheim, Stockbach, and Aha the authorities also drew up inventories of the possessions of their Jews. The outcome of the Waldkirch ritual murder case could determine the fate of all the Jewish communities in the Upper Rhine.

Under interrogation, the arrested Jews protested their innocence and said that the father Bader must in fact have killed his own child for blood money. At this point, the Freiburg magistrates consulted Stürtzel on the interrogation of Philip Bader. Once more, Bader changed his story, insisting now that the Jew Lameth of Waldkirch had purchased and killed his son. In any event, Stürtzel went ahead with the trial on his feudal estate and condemned Bader to death; as for the Jews, they were not under his jurisdiction. On 30 May, Bader was executed in Buchen. Just before his execution, he again protested his innocence: the Jews and not he had killed the boy. The gruesome death, which many witnessed, consisted of a slow, excruciating ritual of torture and dismemberment whereby Bader was tied to a board, dragged to the execution ground, mutilated by glowing pincers, broken on the wheel, and, finally, quartered for the heinous crime of killing his own child. Without evidence, the Jews had to be released.[31]

So far, the case seemed straightforward. Family violence was endemic in rural society; and killing one's child was but one step removed from child abandonment. It was possible that Bader had not intended to kill his boy and that he had merely wanted to sell blood to the Jews. In any event, once the boy had died from the wound inflicted by his father, and once the corpse was discovered, the initial fantasy of Jewish blood magic that had motivated this gruesome act in the first place also supplied the father with the ideal scenario for self-defense. The crucial point is that, to certain segments of village society, at least to its marginal elements, the discourse of Jewish magic and ritual murder was in itself neutral: what concerned these rural folks was not the intrinsic evil of

---

29. See letter from Villingen to Freiburg, 26 Apr. 1504, StdA Fb, A1 XIIc, no. 28.
30. See letter from Leo von Staufen to Freiburg, 27 Apr. 1504, StdA Fb, A1 XIIc, no. 28.
31. Pfaff, "Ein seltzame kouffmanschatz," lines 283–380.

Jewish magic, as formulated by the intellectuals, but the practical implication of magic, Jewish or otherwise. For Philip Bader, who was obviously in dire need of money, blood, even that of his own child, was just another commodity for sale; Jewish magic only turned evil when the practical consequences of the unsuccessful transaction became a threat to himself. At this point, the initial willingness to traffic with Jews changed into a self-righteous and remorseful rejection; the underlying structure of the ritual murder discourse, which motivated Bader's action and subsequent self-defense, remained intact. Mindful that Bader was a violent criminal, in some ways he reveals the culture of rural society; his example suggests that a cynical and realistic outlook on life, a strong materialism in popular culture one may say, was perfectly compatible with and actually underlied magical beliefs. In the sense that magic represented a force for wish fulfillment, it functioned in the economic universe of the villages; hence, magic in itself was not evil, but it represented a force that had to be controlled for one's benefit.[32] Bader's confessions also suggest an attempt to manipulate the authorities in order to save his own life. By fabricating an elaborate tale of ritual murder, Bader tried to focus the attention of his judges on the discourse of ritual murder and to minimize his own role in the murder.

A similar but unrelated case in Frankfurt provides comparative information to illustrate this model of behavior. In the same year, 1504, the shoemaker Bryhenn came under suspicion of the magistrates due to the sudden death of his stepson and his own hasty departure from Frankfurt. Arrested in nearby Hanau, he confessed to having struck and killed his stepson in anger. But, when threatened with judicial torture, Bryhenn said he stabbed his stepson with awls, collected the blood, and sold it to the Jew Gumprecht. The latter was arrested and interrogated under torture but maintained his innocence. When Bryhenn was condemned to death, he retracted his accusation and Gumprecht was released.[33] What these two cases imply was an ambiguity in popular culture toward Jews and alleged Jewish magic. It was precisely because blood superstitions and magical beliefs played such a powerful role in the religion and culture of the common people before the Reformation that ritual murder discourse acquired credibility and authority.[34]

32. This point has been exhaustively documented for early modern England by Keith Thomas, *Religion and the Decline of Magic* (London, 1971).

33. For a brief description of this case, see letter of Frankfurt to the archiepiscopal government in Arnsberg, 7 Oct. 1611, StdA Ff Ugb E47p. See also chap. 9.

34. On the importance of ritual and materialism in popular religion in late medieval Germany, see R. W. Scribner, "Ritual and Popular Religion in Catholic Germany at the Time of the Reformation," *Journal of Ecclesiastical History* 35:1 (1984), pp. 47–77.

THE FREIBURG CONNECTION

In any event, the release of the Jews provoked strong resentment. Soon, rumors began circulating that the Jews had a golden calf that they stroked and implored in times of need; the theme of this political satire was, of course, suspicion of official venality and resentment of Jewish wealth.[35] The case, however, was not yet closed. On 16 May a man by the name of Hans Gysennbrecht was arrested in Freiburg. At the time of his arrest, he was pretending to be a servant of the bailiff of Hochberg and was about to swindle a clothier out of some English cloth. Unfortunately for him, the bailiff was also in Freiburg at the time. When he heard of the swindle, he asked the Freiburg magistrates to arrest Gysennbrecht. It was while Gysennbrecht was in the custody of the Freiburgers, and after Philip Bader had been executed by Stürtzel with no conclusive proof against the Jews, that the swindler turned out to be, according to the city council, a messenger for the Waldkirch Jews, an accomplice in the ritual murder who was secretly carrying Christian blood for the Jews. Based on this new confession, the accusation of ritual murder was brought forth again, and the Jews were rearrested.[36]

How exactly was a swindler transformed into a ritual murder accomplice? There are simply no sources to document this remarkable and (for many) rather timely twist of events. It seems unlikely that the Freiburgers would have coerced Gysennbrecht into accusing the Jews, although that would not have been impossible, since many were convinced of the guilt of the Jews and saw their release as a gross injustice. Perhaps the magistrates had probed into possible dealings between Gysennbrecht and the Waldkirch Jews and had suggested to him, while administering judicial torture, the elements for a "good confession." Or Gysennbrecht might have spun the tale himself, hoping in some confused way to ingratiate himself with the magistrates by confessing to something they would want to hear and thereby saving his own skin. Another possibility is that he himself had actually tried to sell blood to the Jews, just like Philip Bader, if in some ways his testimony was based on fact. In any case, Hans Gysennbrecht gave a lengthy confession on 10 June:[37]

> On the Monday after Corpus Christi Day [10 June], in the year fifteen hundred and four, Hans Gysennbrecht of Sultz confessed to the statements written below:

---

35. "Man prediget von eim gulden kalb/vnd sunst noch von einer hülsen salb,/das sie in noten streichen an:/es ir gar wol gehelffen kan" (Pfaff, "Ein seltzame kauffmanschatz," lines 279–82).

36. See the report by the imperial commission to Maximilian I, 16 July 1504, StdA Fb C1, Judensachen, folio 1ʳ.

37. Gysennbrecht's confession, 7 folios, dated 10 June 1504, StdA Fb, A1 XIIc, no. 28. The parts of his confession that implicate the Waldkirch Jews are on folios 1ᵛ–3ʳ.

He confessed and said: Matthew, a Jew in Mulhouse gave him a letter and asked him to demand payment of 10 guldens from Lameth, Jew in Waldkirch . . . he was also to bring blood back to Matthew, which had been recently obtained from a murdered child. In order that the Jews of Waldkirch would give him the blood, he was to say as password that some Jews in Boldwiler,[38] Ensisheim, and Mulhouse have been arrested. And for him to carry the blood, Matthew the Jew gave him a glass. He [Gysennbrecht] also said that he threw away the letter given to him by Matthew on the road from Krotzingen to Heitersheim, on the left hand side [of the road] near a big meadow where a shrine of the Virgin stands. . . .

Also, in Tottenbach behind Waldkirch, he helped Surwasser grab and kill a boy named Toni; and helped him carry the child into the woods. Solomon the old Jew was there, and Smolle from Villingen, and a young Jew, Jacob, who now lives in Boldwiler. This took place roughly nine or ten years ago, and the child was six years old. He also gave the child the first blow. When they arrived in Waldkirch, the Jews sent him into Howenschilt's house for some refreshments. The Jews took the blood and collected it in a book, which was black on the outside and gold-plated inside. For his troubles, the Jews then gave him ten guldens: he got five from Solomon and five from Matthew.

And after the Jews had killed the child in Buch [Bucheim—Gysennbrecht was referring to the alleged murder in Benzhausen], he went with Matthew the Jew to Mulhouse and spent the night in the forest near Brissen. On Tuesday or Wednesday, they arrived in Buch and met the other Jews. There, Matthew took the blood away; he didn't know whereto. A short Jew with curly hair was there and three or four other Jews as well.

Also, he said that the father [Bader] sold the child to the Jews. He went to the Jews and said, he had a child which he wanted to give to the Jews, if they could help him with money since he was in need. He then brought the six year old child into the woods, according to the instructions given by the Jews. It happened after Easter and he and Matthew only went home on Friday.

Also, he said he knows where Surwasser buried the child: it lies about as far from Surwasser's house as it is from Freiburg to Zeringen, and is down in the valley in a meadow under a fir tree.

Also, he said the Jews kidnapped a child who belonged to a cooper in Waldkirch; he gave the first blow but didn't kill the child himself.

Also, he said that the Jews commanded him by word of mouth to kidnap a child in Bucholtz and bring it to them for which he would get ten guldens. One Jew was called Job, the other Zacharias, both were from Boldwiler.

Also he said: his companion also helped to kill and bury Sur-

38. This is either Bollschweil or Badweiler in the Breisgau.

wasser's child; he also helped to carry its blood to Joachim the Jew in Ensisheim and was to get further instructions from him. They went to Zeringen together to look for the child, and when they found it they were to bring it to Matthew and Job of Ensisheim at the corner of the hospital where the big stone lies. . . .

Also, recently, he carried blood to Ensisheim and the Jews gave him two guldens. After that, his companion carried [blood] to Boldwiler.

Gysennbrecht confessed to further thefts and murders and was sentenced to death on 20 June. The executioner tore out his flesh with glowing pincers; he was then quartered. One part of the bloody remains and the head hung from the gallows; the other three parts were sent to the three city gates.[39]

In July, after the execution of Gysennbrecht, Maximilian I appointed a special commission to tackle this explosive situation.[40] Four men headed the commission: the nobleman Christoff von Hatstat, bailiff at Lanntser, the nobleman Hanns Ymber von Gilgenberg, and two doctors of law, Johann Schad and Andreas Helmuet. They were accompanied by Nicolaus Ziegler, the chief secretary of the royal chancery, and were to be assisted by Maximilian's officers and councillors in the government of Further Austria and by the learned professors at the university in Freiburg. It was on the testimony of the two criminals, Philip Bader and Hans Gysennbrecht, that the Jews were accused of child murders, as Maximilian instructed his commissioners. Their duty was to find out what the Jews had confessed under torture and come to a recommendation on further measures concerning the imprisoned Jews in each town. Empowered to remove the Jews from the city jails, if need be, Maxmilian further admonished them that everything must be done legally, with diligence and strictness, without fear; their actions were to be influenced neither by the bribery of the Jews nor by envy, hatred, or self-interest.

Before the commissioners had arrived in the Breisgau, Ziegler had ordered the transfer of the suspects from Waldkirch to Freiburg in the name of Maximilian.[41] This small town "crime" had taken on immense political significance. With its city court, its civic penal code, and the presence of many learned doctors of law at the university, Freiburg was the natural site of judgment.

Gysennbrecht's supposed companion in the murders was a man

39. See confession of Hans Gysennbrecht, 10 June 1504, StdA Fb, A1 XIIc, no. 28, folio 4ʳ.

40. The mandate of appointment and instructions for the commissioners is undated. See StdA Fb, A1 XIIc, no. 28, 3 folios.

41. Undated note of the secretary Nicolaus Ziegler, StdA Fb, A1 XIIc, no. 28. Leo von Staufen has instructed his bailiff in Waldkirch to conduct the Jews to Freiburg.

from Reichenbächle named Michael Hun. He was arrested shortly after Gysennbrecht's execution and interrogated on 26 June.[42] Hun admitted to acting as an accomplice in the murder of Surwasser's boy Toni in Tottenbach near Waldkirch, but beyond this basic fact he provided contradictory evidence. In his memory, the murder had happened eight years ago, not nine or ten as Gysennbrecht had confessed. Moreover, two, not three, Jews were present, according to Hun: Solomon the old Jew and a young Jew with red curly hair. Hun named Gysennbrecht as an accomplice and said that the blood of the boy was brought to Villingen. For their part, they each received five guldens. Three years back, he and Gysennbrecht helped the Jews kill Koler's child in Siglaw [Siegelau], near Waldkirch; the Jews again took the blood of the child. But Hun had even more to say:

> In order that he would not feel doubtful, the Jews told him that they had asked other people to kidnap children, whether in woods, fields, or wherever, that if they kill them [the children] the Jews would make them rich and would give them good money for this. The old Jewess and the aforementioned young Jew with the red hair were especially encouraging. One time when they were getting some eggs and hay from him, they entreated him to kidnap the children who may come his way and hand them over to them for which they promised a good reward. The said Jews also bought a hen from him this time.[43]

According to Hun's testimony, the Jews of Waldkirch would not leave him alone. Once as he was going home in Waldkirch and came to the Arch Bridge, several Jews were waiting for him. They caught up with him and walked with him to the little mountain hut near the Castelberg. While walking, the Jews said to him:

> "Dear Michael, you are a poor fellow. When you need something and if you know of a child, be it young or old, take it and tell us. If you do this we will make you a lord!" He [Michael] then answered: "You dogs! That's why people call you so. I'll give you no child!" They retorted and said: "When people call us dogs, it is as if they called us gracious lords."

42. For Michael Hun's confessions, see StdA Fb, A1 XIIc, no. 28, 2 folios.

43. "Sagt, die juden haben im ouch als im nit zwyfle, ander lewten mer zu gemutet, kinder, wo sy das an komen im holcz, feld vnd wo sy das zu wegen bringen möchten, zu verslachen vnd inen dann solichs kinnd zetuoten so wolten sy die reichen vnd inen darumb guten sold geben, vnd in sonderheit hetten im die alt judin und der oben angezeigt jung rot jud vff ein zit, als sy by im eyer holen wolten, vnd auch gern hew gehept hettent, zu gemutet vnd im gebetten, das er so wol thet, vnd kinder wie er die ankomen vnd zu wegen bringen möcht, versluge vnd als dann inen die uberantwortet, darumb wolten sy im guten sold geben. Die juden obgemelt haben im dentzumal ein hennen abkoufft" (StdA Fb, A1 XIIc, no. 28). Pfaff's transcription of this confession omits a crucial sentence.

He [Michael] doesn't doubt that such a proposition had been made to many other deceitful men.[44]

At the end of his confession, Hun made no attempt to hide his hatred for the Jews and uttered a statement that undermined his credibility as a witness. He said "one should lie and do whatever, so that the Jews are destroyed because they try daily and unceasingly to bring about the ruin of Christian blood."[45] The magistrates did not sentence him right away but held him for further questioning "so that one may deal with the Jews."[46]

The witnesses, Gysennbrecht and Hun, were no novices to crime. In his long confession, Hans Gysennbrecht admitted to a long list of crimes. When first questioned under torture, he confessed to being a thief: he stole cloth in Freiburg and sold it in Waldkirch; three years earlier he stole a horse from his cousin Heinrich Gysennbrecht, to whom he owed money, and sold it for four guldens; he stole another horse and sold it for two guldens; during the fair at Basel, he stole cloth, which he sold for six guldens; at Boldwiler market, he stole cloth and sold it for six guldens; in Breisach, he stole a horse and sold it for eight guldens in Bellickenn; and at Ketzingen in the Sündgau, he sold a stolen horse for three pounds of silver. His first theft was apparently fifteen years ago. Nor did he act alone. On occasion he had help from a companion, Hans, nicknamed Big Claus, who came from Eberbach in the Hochberg valley; a second accomplice was of course Michael Hun, with whom he had also stolen two horses. This horse thief did not spare the Holy Church: he stole a silver plate from a parish priest in Mulhouse and sold it in Basel for four guldens; in 1499, when a priest in the Sündgau refused to hear his confession, he burnt down the cleric's house. More gruesome were his

44. "Lieber Michel, du bist ein armer gesell, wo du etwas bedorftest ob du dem kind wistest. Sy syen jung oder alt so verslach die und thut dann unns solichs kind, darumb wollen wir dich zu einem herren machen. Do sagte er zu jnen wider, lr Hund, dann man nempt euch also. Ich thu euch nit kindt, do sagten sy hinwider, unns ist eben wen man unns nempt hund als spreche man unns gnad Her, solich anstrengen als im nit zwyfle macht mer lurn auch geschechen sein" StdA Fb, A1 XIIc, no. 28.

45. "Item sagt man sol lugen vnd darzu thun, das die Juden vertilgt werden, dann sy sollen teglichs on underlass zu verderbnus des Cristennlichen Blutz" StdA Fb, A1 XIIc, no. 28.

Confession of Michael Hun, 26 June 1504, StdA Fb, A1 XIIc, no. 28, folio 1^v. The Ratsprotokolle also notes his confession: "Michel des armen menschen halb der mit den Juden gehandelt hat ist erkennt, man soll inne ligen lassen vnd nit richten byss man mit den Juden hanndlen" (StdA Fb, B5 [P] XIIIa, no. 9, Ratsprotokolle, 1504, folio 4^v).

46. In the poem "Ein seltzame kouffmanschatz," the magistrates made Hun confront the Jews. There is no record that this ever took place. Also, while Gysennbrecht's confession was incorporated into the poem, Hun's was not.

many highway robberies and murders. In 1496 he and Big Claus robbed and killed a man near Eltzach for 16 schillings. They soon moved on to bigger things: in 1500 he, Big Claus, Diebolt Pyss, and Zueg Herd, from Rottweil near Kaiserstuhl, killed a Strasbourg merchant on the road, took twenty guldens from him, and sold his horse in Basel for six guldens; in the same year, this gang of four murdered a man near Ensisheim and took eighteen guldens; not long after, they robbed and killed another traveler near Colmar, stealing two guldens and a horse; two others fell victim to the gang and lost their thirty-eight pounds of silver; and in 1502 yet another man was killed for only two guldens. By his own admission, Gysennbrecht had killed seven men and a boy; theft, robbery, and murder were his way of life.

Compared to Gysennbrecht, Michael Hun's crimes appeared tame. He had stolen eight schillings some six or eight years earlier in Riegel, and in the Hochberg he stole a sack of grain from the bailiff Greyer but had to return it. He once received five schillings for his silence in a murder near Hagssen. His acquaintance with Gysennbrecht apparently went back some time: in a theft at Breisach, Hun received a share of eight schillings from Gysennbrecht. The only killings he admitted were the two child murders allegedly committed at the behest of the Jews.

By no stretch of the imagination can Gysennbrecht and Hun be described as credible witnesses. But they apparently had some dealings with the Jews of Waldkirch. In his confession, Gysennbrecht told the magistrates that he first went to the Jew Lameth to demand payment of a loan on behalf of Matthew; this might have been his task. In any case, both Gysennbrecht and Hun might have had business contacts with the Waldkirch Jews, perhaps borrowing small sums of money from them, probably pawning merchandise—most likely stolen—as part of the deal, or, as in the case of Hun, selling them chicken, eggs, and hay. More perplexing questions concern the child murders: Were any killings actually committed by Gysennbrecht and Hun? It seems that they had robbed and murdered others before. And if they had murdered children, too, why? Did they perhaps try to kidnap and sell children, to Jews or to Christians? Were they child molesters who tortured and killed their young victims to gratify their perverse impulses? Or were these tales products of fantasies or the result of suggestions by the magistrates who were interrogating them? Unfortunately, the truth behind these allegations cannot be ascertained. What mattered was that their confessions of alleged ritual murders provided the "proof" required by the Freiburgers to proceed with the trial of the Jews.

In late June the Freiburg magistrates were ready to interrogate the four Jews in their custody: Lameth (Lamblin) of Waldkirch and his two sons, David and Joselin, and Jecklin from Brünlingen.[47] One of them was only a boy. A little later, a young Jew from Günzburg who was simply traveling to Freiburg was also arrested and imprisoned. The first interrogation took place at the time when Michael Hun confessed. The magistrates showed the Jews the strappada (*Vffzieher*) but did not immediately apply torture. They wanted to find out "what kinds of torture would make them confess, then one should use those against them, to make them confess to the crime, and to proceed with force when appropriate."[48]

Soon torture was used. Although the Jews steadfastly refused to confess under judicial torture, by mid-July, the magistrates had broken the will of one man. The poor Jew was willing to convert and confess if the magistrates promised to spare his life. When asked what he had heard from his parents about Christian blood, the man admitted that Jews simply need Christian blood. But, sensing a breakthrough in the case, the Freiburg magistrates now refused to guarantee his life.[49] Moreover, they decided "to break the remaining two Jews too, and to think of new tortures to make them confess. The appointed councillors are then empowered to proceed with them."[50] Still the others refused to confess. Chief royal secretary Nicolaus Ziegler feared that they might die under torture without confessing "because they know if found guilty, their faith would be completely destroyed."[51]

On 16 July the commission wrote a detailed report to Emperor Maximilian, and although the copy is unsigned, the handwriting clearly belongs to Nicolaus Ziegler, who was assisting the commissioners. Ziegler had no doubt of the guilt of the Jews even before the commission's final findings. He first reported on the interrogation of Bader, who sold his son to the Jews and was condemned to death by Chancellor

47. The four Jews are named in StdA Fb, A1 XIIc, no. 31.

48. "Der Juden halb die gefangen ligen vnnd nit an der vffziehenden marter verzehen wollen, ist erkennt man soll by dem nachricht vnnd allennthalb erfunden haben mit was marter sy gihrig zumachen gegen die soll man gegen Inen furnemen, vnnd der vbeltat gihrig machen, vnnd drueh . . . hanndlen was sich gepürt" (StdA Fb, Ratsprotokolle 1504, B5 [P] XIIIa, no. 9, folio 4ᵛ).

49. Report [by Nicolaus Ziegler] to Maximilian I, StdA Fb, C1 (Judensachen), 5 folios, here folio 2ʳ.

50. "Der Juden halb ist abermals erkennt die vbrigen zwei Juden auch zu prechen, vnd neue marter zu erdenncken damit man sy gihrig machte, vnd ist damit den geordneren räten gewalt geben mit Inen zu hanndlen" (StdA Fb, Ratsprotokolle, 12 July 1504, B5 [P] XIIIa, no. 9, folio 4ᵛ).

51. "Nu ist zubesorgen, daz sy [the Jews] nichts bekennen, sonnder er sterben dann sy wissen, wie sy schuldig erfunden werden, daz Ir glaub ganntz vertilgt wurdt" (StdA Fb, C1, folio 2ʳ).

Konrad Stürtzel on Stürtzel's family estate in Bucheim. Ziegler then wrote: "Although it is said that this evildoer exculpated the Jews at his final end, this did not actually happen; it was spread only by some bad Christians who had received money from the Jews for their benefit."[52] Based on this belief, the Jews were set free without bail, Ziegler continued, until the testimony of another Christian in Freiburg (Hans Gysennbrecht) again implicated the Jews. This time, the Jews of Waldkirch were transferred to Freiburg for interrogation. Meanwhile, the confession of another Christian (Michael Hun) supported the first testimony. Ziegler's letter then described the judicial torture of the Jews and the lack of results. He asked Maximilian to read the accompanying confessions and to recognize the open guilt of the Jews:

> Most Gracious Lord, Your Royal Majesty may judge for yourself, that the sworn testimony and confessions of the three evildoers are a firm and patent denouncement of the guilt and evil deeds of the Jews. Moreover one finds therein the time and motivation for the [murder] of the Christian children, as the contents of the sworn testimonies says. How then can the Jews be innocent?[53]

More startling information is revealed in the report, albeit not intended by Ziegler himself. After denouncing the Jews for having committed ritual child murders in the land, Ziegler cited the historical case of 1470: "The Jews of Endingen were imprisoned for the same thing and although they did not want to confess to anything, they were nonetheless all burnt because there was enough evidence [*Antzaigung*] of their evil deed, as it is now."[54]

Ziegler further accused Süss of Günzburg, a young Jew who had come to Freiburg to plead for his imprisoned brethren, of trying to bribe him, but he "turned down his beseeching." In any case, the royal secretary was of the opinion that Jews could no longer live in the Breisgau

52. "Wie wol gesagt wirdet, daz derselb ubeltetter [Philip Bader] an seinem letzten enndt, die Juden entschuldigt hab, das ist warlich nit beschehen, und wirdet allein durch ettlich bos cristen so der Juden gemiess haben, demselbs zugut also ausgeprayt" (StdA Fb, C1, folio 1ʳ).

53. "Allergenedigister Her, Euer Ku. Mt. mag selbs ermessen, daz der dreyer ubelteter urgicht und bekanntnuss, ein grundtlichs lautters antzaigen, der Juden schuld und ubeltat, gibt dartzu findet man daz die Cristen Kynnder zu der Zeit und an den Ennden, wie es die Urgichten Innhalten verlesen, wie moch dann die Juden unschuldig sein" (StdA Fb, C1, folio 2ʳ).

54. "So findet auch Euer Ku. Mt. hiebey, in geschrifft, wie die Juden in disen Lannden vor ettwevil Jaren, dergleichen ubeltaten gegen den Cristenkynndern geübt haben [fol. 2v] und als in kurtzverschid zeit, die Juden zu Enndingen, dergleichs sache halbs gefangen worden, wie wol sy nichts bekennen haben wellen, so sein sy doch alle geprendt, die weil lr ubltat genugen antzaigung verhannden was, als yetz auch ist" (StdA Fb, C1, folios 2ʳ⁻ᵛ).

because even the women would kill them. He advised Maximilian to order the transfer of the Jews out of Freiburg to Ensisheim, under the direct charge of the territorial government, because the popular mood was turning ugly; pogroms and unrest were likely.[55]

For Ziegler, history proved the "truth" of ritual murder. But his admission that the Endingen Jews did not want to confess confirms our suspicion that the so-called confessions were highly dubious as judicial documents. Beyond the judicial irregularities, Maximilian I had another reason to stop the Freiburg trial: the Jews were under the protection of the king and contributed handsomely toward the impoverished royal coffers.

Maximilian decided to intervene to save the Jews. On 16 July he wrote a strong letter of admonition to the Freiburg city council, in which he reminded the magistrates to handle the whole case "justly and according to law." Torture must be applied no more. Moreover, the young Jew from Günzburg, who had nothing to do with the case, must be released from prison at once.[56] The letter arrived just in time to spare the Jews further torture, because on 17 July the councillors were again deliberating whether they should again apply torture to extract confessions.[57] For fear of incurring royal anger, the Freiburgers decided to await further instructions.

Meanwhile, however, the Freiburgers tried to bolster their case. On 20 July the city fathers wrote to the town council of Rheinau: some years ago, so they had heard, two children were missing from Rheinau. Lameth the Jew was living in Rheinau at that time. After he had moved away, bones were discovered buried near his house, and he came under the suspicion of ritual murder. Now Lameth and others had been arrested on suspicion of murder in Waldkirch; the Freiburg magistrates asked their colleagues to furnish detailed information on the incident.[58]

Back in Freiburg, the young Jew from Günzburg, who called himself Sysslen (Süss), was thrown into jail together with Lameth, his sons, and the other Jew; the magistrates found a large sum of money on him. In the early sixteenth century, Günzburg had a prosperous Jewish community, and the young man was sent to Freiburg with bribe money to help win a

55. Ensisheim was the administrative capital of Further Austria; for a discussion of the provincial government, see Wilhelm Beemelmans, "Die Organisation der vorderösterreichischen Behörden in Ensisheim im 16. Jahrhundert," *ZGO* N.F. 22 [61] (1907), pp. 52–92, 627–56; 23 [62] (1908), pp. 195–220.

56. Letter of Maximilian to the city council of Freiburg, 16 July 1504, from Weissenhorn, StdA Fb, A1 XIIc, no. 28.

57. StdA Fb, Ratsprotokolle 17 July 1504, B5 (P) XIIIa, no. 9, folio 5ʳ.

58. The letter from Freiburg to Rheinau has been summarized by Pfaff, "Ein seltzame kouffmanschatz," p. 286.

more favorable hearing for his coreligionists.[59] According to a report written by Ziegler to Maximilian dated 20 July, Süss was accompanied by a Christian named Johannes R., who offered the royal secretary a gift of an annuity of fifty guldens (or one thousand guldens principal) plus a handsome sum of cash if he could help to secure the release of the Jews. To his master, Ziegler again declared his incorruptibility. After apprising Maximilian of current developments, Ziegler emphasized in his report that although the Freiburgers were holding Süss they were not torturing him. To conclude his report, the royal servant volunteered his assessment of the situation: "Truly, almighty lord, if the Jews should still be allowed to go about among Christians in this land, they would all be slain since resentment is growing daily against them."[60] On 5 August Maximilian wrote again, ordering the city council to release the man and send him back to Günzburg.[61] Ziegler spoke to the king on behalf of the Freiburgers, who were still convinced of the Jews' guilt, and persuaded Maximilian to permit the magistrates to hold Süss of Günzburg until the royal commission had settled the case.[62] Süss was finally released on 4 September after the Freiburgers had received another order from Maximilian.[63]

Unlike the trial in Endingen thirty-four years earlier, the magistrates in Freiburg did not have time on their side. In 1470 it took only twelve days for Karl von Baden to arrest, interrogate, and execute the Jews. In Freiburg, none of the three witnesses were completely reliable: Philip Bader admitted his guilt before death, while Gysennbrecht and Hun were hardened criminals. Moreover, a more energetic ruler now stepped in to protect the Jews. Nevertheless, the Freiburgers remained convinced of the guilt of the Jews, a prejudice shared by the royal secretary, as Ziegler's reports clearly betray.

By early September, the Freiburgers were eager to wash their hands of the whole affair. Anxious that the tortured and sick Jews might die in their custody, the city councillors entreated Ziegler to ask the king for a

59. This was at least the opinion of Nicolaus Ziegler; see the draft of a letter dated 20 August addressed to Maximilian I. The letter is unsigned but written in Ziegler's hand. Ziegler reported to the king that he had not taken any bribes from the Günzburg Jew. See StdA Fb, A1 XIIc, no. 28.

60. See letter of Ziegler to Maximilian, 20 July 1504, StdA Fb A1 XIIc, no. 28.

61. See StdA Fb, A1 XIIc, no. 29.

62. See letter of Nicolaus Ziegler to the city council of Freiburg, 9 Aug. 1504, from Offenburg, StdA Fb, A1 XIIc, no. 28.

63. See his oath of release (Urfehde), 4 Sept. 1504, StdA Fb, A1 XIIc, no. 30. See also letter of Maximilian to Freiburg, 29 Aug. 1504, in Pfaff, "Ein seltzame kouffmanschatz," p. 289.

transfer of the case to the commission and a reimbursement for the cost for holding the Jews in the city prison.[64] Maximilian also decided to take the matter out of the hands of the Freiburgers, perhaps not trusting their intentions. He first appointed Kaspar, Freiherr von Mersburg and bailiff (*Landvogt*) in Hagenau, to take custody of and provide protection for the Jews while their bail was being arranged. But Kaspar wrote to the government in Ensisheim reporting that his subjects were in an uproar about this "and would obey no orders, interdicts, letter of protection, safe-conducts, or anything, be they from royal command or from the bailiff, councillors, officers, or others."[65] In order to prevent popular unrest, Maximilian entrusted his government in Ensisheim with the difficult and thankless task of helping the Landvogt. The councillors in Ensisheim then instructed the Freiburgers to hand over the Jews to them instead. Bail was to be set at 120 guldens for the two Jews, a substantial but not crushing sum, and at another sum for the other Jew with the boy. The Freiburgers could hold the boy as surety until the amount was raised. A court day was to be set in Ensisheim after bail was arranged.[66] On 23 September Maximilian wrote directly to the Freiburg city fathers, informing them of the return of the extraordinary royal commission; his councillors in Ensisheim were now to act as royal commissioners in their

64. See letter of Freiburg to Ziegler, 5 Sept. 1504, in Pfaff, "Ein seltzame kouffman-schatz," pp. 289*f.*

65. This was reported in a letter written by the Statthalter in Ensisheim to the magistrates of Freiburg. See letter dated 2 Sept. 1504: "unns hat der wolgeborerm Herr Caspar Fryherr zu Mersperg unnd Beffert des Heiligen Richs Landtvogt zu Hagnaw geschriben. Wie sich vil underthannen diser Lanndtschafften verwandt in disem ytzigen Zug und furnemen ze mer ubel gehalten und weder gebot, verbot, Schutz, Schirm, geleit noch gar nichts. Es sig vonn Konigelicher Maiestat empheleh oder durch Landtvogt Rat Hauptlut oder andere geben. Und nemlich das etlich der euren zwen Juden und der einen Juden mit einem knaben angenomen" (StdA Fb, A1 XIIc, no. 28).

66. "Dann nachdem wir bemeltem vonn Marsperg Landtvogt zu erkennen. So dermassen nit gehandelt werden. So wer er zu solicher Schwarer Schrifft nit licht bewegt. Deshalbenn so ist vonn wegenn Kon. Mt. unnser ernstlich eruorderung an [e]uch verschaffen und beuelhende, das lr euch zu stundt der sach erkunden und by den selben so dermessen mit den Juden uber und wider Irenn Schirm im gelait gehanndelt sy gescherzt, ob sy die Schatzung empfangen haben, by iren eids pflichten und den höchstenn gebettenn verschaffen, gebietten und darob sein, das sie die selb schatzung vnverruckt zu ewren handen vberantwurten. Und lr alsdann dieselb hiehar gen Ensishaim, dem genanten herrn Landtvogt zu Recht erlegen. So wollen wir anch verschinung des nechsten hoffgerichts uff ferner hield anruffen Rechtstag ansetzen. Und bescheh umb das wass recht sein werdt. Wo aber die Schatzung noch nit geben und der Jüdisch Knab noch by Irenn handen were, alsdann die Juden deren zuvertragen unnd Innen den knaben wider zuhanden antwurten. So wollenn wir allen vliss furkeren den Lanndtvogt zu begütigen und sein fürnemen abzestellen, darmit die ewren verwitter vnruwen und Schmach verhutt werden" (StdA Fb, 1A XIIc, no. 28).

stead; the Freiburgers owed them obedience and cooperation in arranging bail and transferring the imprisoned Jews.[67]

The Freiburgers, however, held the Jews until late October, when
they again received an admonition from Ensisheim. On 28 October
Konrad Schutz, secretary of the provincial government in Ensisheim,
wrote to the magistrates of Freiburg that they must deliver the Jews to
Ensisheim within fourteen days of the receipt of his letter. Since the
weather was good, the Jews were to be sent in a wagon and handed over
to the commissioners, who alone were empowered to deal with them.
There was to be "no excuse, alternative measures, and wishes of obedience (*on alle furwort, stat thün und gehorsamen wellen*)"; and the greatest
precaution must be taken. All the documents of the trial, including the
confessions and the sworn oaths of bail, were to be sealed and handed
over to the provincial government. The entire matter must be handled
exactly in accordance with the orders of Maximilian. Finally, Schutz
expressed his desire that the Jews be removed from the land under the
semblance of law and in peace.[68]

Two days later, on 30 October, the Freiburg city council arranged for
bail. The original four—Lameth, his sons David and Jöslin, and Jecklin—
in addition to Nelius, the Jew who was arrested at a later time, posted
bond and swore an oath (*Urfehde*).[69] They had to admit to the saying,
"which had been going around the German nation for some years, that
Jews had murdered Christian boys for their blood." This was known also
in their land, just as it had happened in Trent, Endingen, and elsewhere.
On account of these misdeeds, the Jews were burnt. And some time ago,
they further swore, three Christians were caught and condemned to
death: one for killing his own son, the others for murdering other boys in

67. Letter of Maximilian I to Freiburg, 23 Sept. 1504, Munich, StdA Fb, A1 XIIc, no. 28.
68. Letter of Hofkanzler Konrad Schutz, Landschreiber in Alsace, to the city council of
Freiburg, dated 28 Oct. 1504, from Ensisheim: "Auch mit disem botten vnd furman alhie
gen Ensisheim antwurten sich nit vssern abwichen noch enderen sondern deselbs was Kon
Mt. Commissarien mit Inen handlen oder schaffen on alle furwort, stat thün vnd gehorsamen wellen. In aller gestalten als ob sy von vwer ventknus fur dieselben gefurt, vnd mit
Inen gehandelt were, in der hochsten versehung, mit genügsamen verzicken vnd das
disem botten solicher versecht abschrift auch Ir bekantnus oder vergicht vnd das kosten
vrkund gegeben, das alles verschlossen vnd versigelt werden, were mit Inen zehandlen
wissen, ob sich durch schickung des allmächtigen fügen wolte die schamtlichen Juden in
disen Landen mit gerechtem schin abzekerren als Ich hoffen wil beschehen werden. Vnd
die Juden in disem handel friederlich abnottigen so wil Ich vf min glouben vnd phlicht vth
den kesten in den xiiii tage on alles valen Vssrichten vnd vergnügen daran im kheim
mangel haben werden, Kon Mt. auch ander in der Vrfecht versehen als Ich mich des
vngezwifelt zu vth vertrosen, das wil Ich mit guttem willen getruws vngespartz Vliss vmb,
vnd wissheyt haben zuverordenen" (StdA Fb, A1 XIIc, no. 28).
69. Earlier documents mentioned four Jews; it is not clear when Nelius was arrested.

order to sell their blood. On their testimonies, which they maintained to their last end, it was the Jews who ordered the murders. It was also on royal command that the Jews were interrogated under torture in Freiburg. Now they were to be transferred under the jurisdiction of the royal commissioners in Ensisheim. They now swore that the city of Freiburg was following the royal mandate in imprisoning and torturing them and that on their eventual release they would not seek redress against the city.[70]

The sworn oath of their bail reflected the judicial principles and the extralegal assumptions under which this mistrial took place. It was on their odious reputation, their mala fama, that Jews came to be imprisoned and judicially tortured and executed in the recent past. The Germanic common law codes and the *Carolina* all admitted the accusatory principle of mala fama; the material evidence of a purported ritual murder was simply not crucial in initiating a judicial investigation.[71] What mattered was the ill-repute of the Jews, the discourse (*die Rede*) of ritual murder in the land. As we have seen, once the instruments of torture were applied, in accordance with the procedure of interrogating criminals, most men broke down. Until this point, the Freiburg magistrates were working within the confines of a vicious judicial system that produced forced confessions of guilt. But when the Waldkirch Jews refused to confess under repeated torture, and when the magistrates applied excessive physical torment contrary to royal order, the whole procedure took on a spurious character. To the end, the Freiburgers and some of the commissioners, such as Nicolaus Ziegler, remained convinced of the guilt of the Jews. And although proper judicial confessions were not forthcoming, Ziegler's report to Maximilian suggested the possibility that the Freiburg magistrates might have executed the Jews, following the historical example of the Endingen trial in 1470, if Maximilian had not intervened most forcefully to transfer the case to his territorial government.

Sometime after their extradition to Ensisheim, the Jews were set free. For the Freiburgers and their allies, it was a humiliating affair. Regardless of the probity of the investigation, most people believed in the guilt of the Jews. Whatever might have been the private convictions of the magistrates, the manifest public aim of the city council was to bring about a complete expulsion of Jews from the Breisgau. About a year after

70. See StdA Fb, A1 XIIc, no. 31.

71. On the mala fama, see *Carolina*, art. 25: "Vonn gemeinen Argkwonen vnd annzeygungen," which instructs magistrates to question the previous reputation of the suspect; art. 6, "Annemen der angegebenn vbellthalter vonn der oberkeit vnnd Ampts wegen," however, cautions the magistrates against applying torture too hastily on those arrested on account of bad reputation without prior suspicion of misdeeds.

the whole affair, on 5 April 1505, the Freiburgers wrote to Maximilian expressing their disappointment: as a result of the ritual murders of last year, the city fathers wrote, they were hoping that the Jews would at least be expelled. But to the anger of the people, nothing was done. The magistrates reminded the king that his ancestors, the Austrian arch-dukes, had granted Freiburg the privilege never to tolerate Jews and urged Maximilian to expel all Jews from the Breisgau so that Christians might not suffer from the Jews' usury and murderous intent.[72] A similar letter was sent to Margrave Christoph of Baden, the son of Margrave Karl, who had presided over the Endingen ritual murder trial in 1470, in order to enlist his support.[73] The supplication, however, went unanswered.

Looking at the trial with hindsight, it is easy to overlook the sense of injustice felt by a part of the Christian populace. Ironically, they felt that Christians, not Jews, were the victims. A contemporary poem of this event reflects the attitude of someone close to the city council, probably a cleric in Freiburg, possibly someone at the university.[74] It laments that Christian blood is despised whereas money and bribery buy freedom for the Jews:

> O pious Judge, take heed
> that the Jewish folk not despise
> Christian blood so, by which
> God on the cross redeems the earth.
> Do not turn to the golden calf.[75]

So much idolatry is in the land, the poet goes on, that St. Peter's Ship is breaking apart; evil is overwhelming Germany, and injustice marches on in Christendom. Prudently, the poet refuses to affix blame, but it is the golden calf (that is, Jewish bribery) that bought the suspects' freedom. The poet expressly excuses "the pious King Maximilian and all . . . in particular the honorable city Freiburg in Breisgau," which had handled the matter with "trust, diligence, and earnesty." The poet then reminds the reader of the ritual murder at Trent a generation ago and begs God's mercy for justice and peace.[76]

72. See letter of Freiburg to Maximilian, 5 Apr. 1505, in Pfaff, "Ein seltzame kouffman-schatz," pp. 291f.

73. See letter of Freiburg to Christoph von Baden, 20 Apr. 1505 (Pfaff dates it wrongly to 1504), in Pfaff, "Ein seltzame kouffmanschatz," p. 277.

74. See Pfaff, "Ein seltzame kouffmanschatz," pp. 248–50.

75. "O frummen richter, nemen war,/das cristen blut nit also gar/von iüdischem volck verachtet werd,/das Got am crütz erlosst vff erd,/vnd kert üch nit ans gulden kalb" (Pfaff, "Ein seltzame kouffmanschatz," lines 728–34).

76. Pfaff, "Ein seltzame kouffmanschatz," lines 742–809.

This poetic panegyric of Freiburg reflected the political culture of anti-Semitism in a city dominated by the guilds. As socioeconomic corporations, the mercantile and handicraft guilds had important religious and cultural functions: medieval guild statutes often stipulated purity of blood and religion as criteria for membership. In Freiburg the voice of the artisans was heard in city politics after the guild revolt of 1388, and in the fifteenth century, guildsmen gradually displaced the traditional patrician elite on the city council as Freiburg's long-distance trade gradually lost out to Basel and Strasbourg and as the restructuring of the city's economy enhanced the guilds' political power.[77] In the ideology of guild corporatism, the concern for civic and religious purity justified the repression of socially dangerous elements like the Jews, who by their very presence threatened the boundary and cohesion of the body politic and religious. Political defamation employed anti-Semitic rhetoric in the crisis that pitted the commons against the city council in 1492. Conrad Watzenmüller, master of the butchers' guild and leader of the opposition, was killed in a street demonstration. A supporter of the city council declared with scorn that "the King of the Jews is dead."[78]

Piety reinforced social and political solidarity, and the celebration of the body social and politic coincided with the homage to the body of Christ. The tradition of Corpus Christi processions had a long history in Freiburg.[79] By the fifteenth century, the guilds played the central role in its celebration: the order of the procession, which began at the Münster, expressed the hierarchical ranking of the twelve guilds, placing the three most powerful guilds—the tailors, shopkeepers, and butchers—in the leading positions.[80] Beginning at least in 1503, an elaborate passion play performed on the Münsterplatz crowned the procession. The different guilds and the journeymen fraternities divided up the scenes, which depicted biblical events from the creation of Adam and Eve to the resurrection of Christ.[81] As might be expected, Jews received a prominent role as enemies of Christ, whose death and resurrection embodied the mixture of sacred and secular history through which the Freiburgers and many others understood their own existence. Likewise, in the rhetoric and symbols of the poem on the Benzhausen ritual murder, the little

77. See Steven W. Rowan, "The Guilds of Freiburg im Breisgau as Social and Political Entities" (Ph.D. diss., Harvard University, 1970), pp. 116–25, 282–83.

78. Rowan "Guilds of Freiburg," p. 308.

79. See Hermann Mayer, "Zur Geschichte der Freiburger Fronleichnamsprozession," *Freiburger Diözesan-Archiv* N.F. 12 (1911), pp. 338–61.

80. For an analysis of the wealth hierarchy of the Freiburg guilds and their participation in the Corpus Christi procession, see Rowan, "Guilds of Freiburg," pp. 240, 343f.

81. Two manuscripts of the passion play have survived and were published by Ernst Martin; see his *Freiburger Passionsspiele des XVI. Jahrhunderts* (Freiburg, 1872).

child Matthew, sold by his father to the Jews, paralleled Judas's betrayal of Jesus to the Jews.[82] His "martyrdom" thus established a direct link between the Freiburgers and Christ that transcended some fifteen hundred years of history.

Although the Freiburg trial began as a belief in the discourse of ritual murder, in the end it became a political case. Myth and magic fed religious passions and provided the grammar for the articulation of a distinct legal discourse on Jews. As we shall see in the next chapter, the trial in Freiburg would have a great impact on the political, religious, and legal discourses that shaped the lives of the German Jews in the next two generations.

---

82. "Vermerken hie ein ellend that:/der crist verkaufft sein kindelein/wie Judas thet dem herren sein" (Pfaff, "Ein seltzame kouffmanschatz," lines 70–73).

CHAPTER SIX **The Professors and the Jews**

NE SHOULD LIE AND DO WHATEVER, SO THAT THE JEWS are destroyed because they try daily and unceasingly to bring about the ruin of Christian blood." Thus confessed Michael Hun to the magistrates of Freiburg. One is tempted to dismiss this statement as the ravings of a thief and murderer who confessed to his hatred for the Jews under interrogation. But anti-Jewish feeling was by no means limited to the common people, the rural folk and rougher sorts who had daily contacts with the Jews in the small towns and villages of the Upper Rhine. Writings on Jews and on their religion constituted an important part of the theological and legal discourses of the early sixteenth century, and in the two generations after the 1504 Freiburg murder trial, the "Jewish question" came to be debated by many Germans, by jurists, theologians, Catholics, and Protestants, and by Jewish converts to Christianity. For many Germans and Jewish converts in the early sixteenth century, if the accusation was that Jews conspired to "bring about the ruin of Christian blood," the answer to this alleged magical murder was religious redemption for both Jews and Christians.

It is important to understand that ritual murder discourse represented a device in which disparate experiences of religion, magic, and law were synthesized into a coherent and meaningful whole. Talking and writing about ritual murders expressed some of the deepest fears of pre-Reformation German society, an anxiety focused on the fate of its children. But discourse on ritual murder also created a possibility of salvation, and the agents of collective redemption were the innocent children. A fundamental continuity existed between the many popular beliefs in the salutary nature of human blood and body and the formal articulations of those sacramental doctrines in learned theological discourse.

In the first half of sixteenth-century Germany, the discourse on ritual murder informed much of the learned discussions on law and religion; it transcended the boundary between what many historians call "popular" and "elite" cultures. Often, the many voices of piety spoke the language of magic and antimagic: in the Holy Roman Empire these years witnessed a campaign against magic, specifically Jewish magic, and the means of combat employed by learned churchmen, both Protestant and Catholic, was the language of antimagic. In this chapter I trace the thematic centrality of ritual murder for the learned discourse of Reformation Germany by analyzing the anti-Jewish writings of three professors. One taught civil law, the other two, theology; two were Catholic, and one was Protestant. The so-called Reuchlin affair, which directly preceded Luther's appearance, must also be understood in the context of debates over the blood libel.

ULRICH ZASIUS: THE QUESTION OF FORCED BAPTISM

If Christian boys were victims of Jewish magic, perhaps Jewish boys could be saved for Christianity. At least they were still "innocent children," unlike their fathers. Concurrent with the trial in Freiburg, Maximilian, now crowned emperor, went to war with the Palatine elector over the succession of the ducal line in Bavaria. A Palatine Jew was captured by the Freiburgers, who freed him on a bond but held his young son as a hostage. The guardian of the boy, Heinrich Kolher, pastor of the Münster in Freiburg, announced that the boy desired baptism; neither the bond nor the boy, argued Kolher, should be returned to the father.[1] A lively debate followed. Kolher was supported by Ulrich Zasius, professor of civil law at the University of Freiburg, who composed a treatise in defense of baptizing Jewish children, even without their parents' consent.[2]

Zasius was most likely one of the learned professors consulted by the royal commissioners in 1504 during their investigation of the alleged Waldkirch ritual murder. A native of the imperial city of Constance, Zasius studied at the university in Tübingen, where he received his baccalaureate in 1485. Having served as a protonotary, an imperial notary, a notary of the Ecclesiastical Court of Constance, and as the city

---

1. See Guido Kisch, *Zasius und Reuchlin: Eine rechtsgeschichtlich-vergleichende Studie zum Toleranzproblem im 16. Jahrhundert* (Stuttgart and Constance, 1961), p. 1. For a summary of Zasius's views, see also Steven Rowan, "Ulrich Zasius and the Baptism of Jewish Children," *SCJ* 6 (1975), pp. 3–25.

2. The treatise "Quaestiones de paruuli Iudeorum Baptisandi" was first published in 1508 by Johann Grünniger in Strasbourg. It was reprinted in his collected works as "Quaestiones tres an Iudaei infantes sint inuitis parentibus ad baptisma auferendi." See Udalricus Zasius, *Opera Omnia*, ed. Johann Ulrich Zasius and Joachim Münsinger Vonfrundeck (Lyon: Sebastian Gryphius, 1550; reprint, Aalen, 1966), vol. 5, pp. 168–89. The pagination is that of the reprint edition.

secretary (*Stadtschreiber*) of Baden in Aargau, in 1494 Zasius accepted the position of secretary for the city of Freiburg.[3] As city secretary, Zasius kept a record of the city council meetings and took charge of its diplomatic proceedings. In addition to secretarial and administrative duties, the city secretary also took on legal tasks, including supervision of the civil court.[4] Although Zasius resigned his position as city secretary in 1496 to pursue his university studies and to teach as a schoolmaster, he maintained his contacts with the magistrates, serving for a short time as the court secretary (*Gerichtsschreiber*) and occasionally as a legal adviser to the city. In 1501 he was promoted to doctor of law (civil) and two years later joined the faculty of the university.[5] When charges were made against the Waldkirch Jews, Zasius was a doctor of both canon and civil law, someone who enjoyed the patronage of Maximilian, a young legal scholar who was rapidly acquiring a reputation, and a friend and counselor of the city magistrates. From his previous experience as city and court secretary, and with his knowledge of civic and imperial laws, Zasius must have kept himself informed of the case. His former employers and colleagues on the city council would probably have discussed the interrogations and the legal points with him as well. The ritual murder trial in Freiburg, which took place between April and October of 1504, made a deep impression on Zasius that revealed itself four years later when he defended the forced baptism of Jewish children.

The question of forced baptism of Jews was first formulated by Pope Gregory the Great (590–604) in the form of an injunction: Jews were to be persuaded and taught the doctrines of Christianity; salvation could not be forced on reluctant believers. The papal injunction, however, often went unheeded in the pogroms that followed in the wake of the crusades. With the rise of the mendicant orders in the thirteenth century, the canon law tradition prohibiting the forced baptism of Jews was gradually modified. One of the chief missions of the friars was the conversion of Jews, and through their writings on theology and their commentaries on the Bible and on the *Corpus iuris canonici*, the friars undermined the original papal prohibition against the forced baptism of Jews.[6] Around

3. See Hans Thieme, "Zasius und Freiburg," in *Aus der Geschichte der Rechts- und Staatswissenschaften zu Freiburg i. Br.*, ed. Hans Julius Wolff (Freiburg, 1957), p. 11; see also Folkmar Thiele, *Die Freiburger Stadtschreiber im Mittelalter* (Freiburg, 1973), pp. 125–27. The standard biography of Zasius is Roderich Stintzing, *Ulrich Zasius: Ein Beitrag zur Geschichte der Rechtswissenschaft im Zeitalter der Reformation* (Basel, 1857).

4. Thiele, *Freiburger Stadtschreiber*, p. 39.

5. Thieme, "Zasius und Freiburg," p. 14.

6. See Cohen, *The Friars and the Jews*, pp. 240–43; for forced conversions of Jews in the Middle Ages and for the role played by the mendicant orders, see Peter Browe, *Die Judenmission im Mittelalter und die Päpste* (Rome, 1942), pp. 28–34, 215–66. In spite of Browe's confessional bias, this is still a very useful factual study.

1235, William of Rennes wrote a commentary on Raymund of Pennaforte in which he argued for the right of princes to determine the fate of the children of slaves, since the latter, by reason of their servile status, did not enjoy parental rights. By arguing from the ecclesiastical tradition of the extension of servile status to all Jews, who collectively inherited servile status to Christians (the doctrine of *servitus Judaeorum*),[7] William of Rennes justified the baptism of Jewish children by princes without parental consent.[8] This position found its most forceful critic in the *Summa theologiae* of Thomas Aquinas. The Dominican professor refuted any arguments to deprive Jews of parental rights as contrary to nature and justice: divine law, which comes from grace, does not supersede human law, which comes from natural reason.[9] But the Franciscan Duns Scotus (1270–1308) followed the argument of William of Rennes and granted Christian princes the right to baptize the children of Jews and other unbelievers: God's higher law supersedes natural human law in the matter of salvation.[10] Hence, two contrary traditions of learned discourse came down to the early sixteenth century: one based on canon law and natural law theory, articulated by Aquinas and opposed to forced baptism; the other based on biblical commentaries, articulated by Duns Scotus and other Franciscan theologians, for the right of forced baptism by virtue of the doctrine of Jewish servitude and the power of the prince.

In his treatise, Zasius first deals with whether the children of Jews could be baptized without consent of their parents. He cites Aquinas, outlines all the arguments against forced baptism and for parental rights, but finally agrees with Duns Scotus in granting the prince the right to baptize Jewish children. In his learned and ponderous academic treatise, Zasius shows his knowledge of Scripture, canon law, the church fathers, and the scholastics. He bases his argument not only on the doctrine of

7. The basic justification is the decretal "Etsi iudeos" [c. 13, X, de iudaeis 5, 6] by Pope Innocent IV: "Etsi ludeos, quos propria culpa submisit perpetuae servituti, quum Dominum crucifixerint, quem sui prophetae praedixerunt ad redemptionem Israel in carne venturum, pietas Christiana receptet et substineat cohabitationem eorum; ingrati tamen nobis esse non debent" (cited by Zasius, "De iudaeis: Quaestio I," *Opera Omnia V*, p. 172).

8. My discussion of the canon law tradition on the baptism of Jewish children is based largely on the fundamental work by Guido Kisch; see his *Zasius und Reuchlin*, pp. 4–6, and his *The Jews in Medieval Germany: A Study of Their Legal and Social Status* (Chicago, 1949).

9. See *Summa Theologiae*, IIa IIae, qu. 10, a. 10, ad. 1: "Ius divinum, quod est ex gratia, non tollit ius humanum, quod est ex naturali ratione" (cited by Kisch, *Zasius und Reuchlin*, p. 6).

10. From Scotus's Oxford commentary on the fourth book of the Sentences, Dist. IV, Qu. IX: "Utrum parvuli ludaeorum et infidelium sint invitis parentibus baptizandi?" The commentary was composed between 1305 and 1308. Scotus writes: "Nam in parvulo Deus habet maius ius dominii quam parentes" (cited in Kisch, *Zasius und Reuchlin*, p. 6; see also p. 62, n. 20).

"Jewish servitude" but also on roman law, which gives the victors in battle proprietary rights over their captives.

At around the turn of the sixteenth century the academic study and the juristic absorption of the *Corpus iuris civilis* made rapid progress in the Holy Roman Empire.[11] In 1506, Zasius became the first German to hold the professorship of civil law at the University of Freiburg, succeeding Paulus de Cittadinis, an Italian jurist.[12] Interest in roman law was founded upon the very real historical self-identification of the Germans with the Romans: their empire represented the *translatio* of the imperial idea and institutions from the Mediterranean to central Europe. Zasius's theory of the rights of war and slavery harps back to the example of the abortive revolt of the Jews in the first century; he justifies the servile status of the Jews by historical precedent. "[Their] servitude," he writes, "was imposed upon them by captivity in a just war by the most famous Roman Emperor Titus . . . and confirmed by the mandate of Constantine the Great." Hence, history and roman law justified the present servile status of the German Jewry and the power of the prince over them. "It follows then," Zasius continues, "when the prince can sell them [the Jews] into earthly servitude by his right of dominion, he can of course transfer their children to spiritual servitude, or better said, to spiritual liberty."[13] Zasius resolves the tension between canon law and theology concerning enforced baptism with an appeal to civil law and Roman history.

Zasius's answer to the first *quaestio* is affirmative: princes have the right to baptize Jewish children without the consent of their parents so as to give them a new life, but one must be careful, Zasius pauses, so that murder does not result from this.[14] Although he concedes that tragedy

11. Gerald Strauss, *Law, Resistance, and the State: The Opposition to Roman Law in Reformation Germany* (Princeton, 1986), pp. 67–68.

12. Thieme, "Zasius und Freiburg," pp. 13–14. Zasius was promoted to the professorship of civil law on 16 June 1506; he had to lecture half an hour per day for an annual stipend of 100 guldens.

13. "Vnde non habent iudei nec bona nec res aliquas nisi in quibus ex pietate permittuntur. At talis pietas ad necessitatem trahi non debet, vt Papiniani sententia conuincitur. Non ergo quia a nobis humanitate afficiuntur, a seruitutis iugo eximi possunt, quod eis a iure non solum positiuo sed et gentium, hoc est, ex captiuitate iusti belli per clarissimum imperatorem Romanum Titum contra eos euicti impositum et, vt dicitur notari per Hostiensem, mandato Constantini magni firmatum est. . . . Cum ergo per supradicta seruitus iudeorum probata sit, quin et facultas eorum bona per principes auferendi. Sequitur, quod, cum princeps iure dominii eos in terrenam seruitutem vendere possit, etiam paruulos eorum ad spiritualiem, potius dixerim, libertatem quam seruitutem auferre posse" (Zasius, "Quaestio I," pp. 172–73).

14. "Paruuli iudeorum per terrarum principes invitis etiam parentibus auferendi et baptismi sacramento in viam salutis regenerandi sunt cautione pro viribus adhibita, ne ex hoc homicidia sequantur" (Zasius, "Quaestio I," p. 170).

might result from the forced baptism of Jewish children, the prince can be cautious in preventing parental murder. But even if some had been murdered, "it cannot be doubted," Zasius continues, "that these children killed for the faith in Christ, and thus initiated by the baptism of blood (following the holy innocents), will share eternal life."[15] Sympathy for these young Jewish children was balanced out by his hatred for the adults. German Jewry was tolerated out of Christian piety and grace, but instead, Zasius rages on, the Jews were most ungrateful. Daily they cursed Christians, exploited them with usury, refused to serve them, ridiculed Christian belief, and blasphemed against Christ.[16] Zasius continues: "But the cruelest of all, the Jews thirst after Christian blood, which these bloodthirsty bloodsuckers seek day and night. In these days and in our own land, they have spilled this [blood] more than once, as their accomplices in crime had testified to and had died for it, which I cannot speak of without feeling my heart beating with pain."[17] Zasius of course refers to the ritual murder trial four years earlier, when "the accomplices in crime," the three criminals executed by Konrad Stürtzel and the Freiburg magistrates, accused the Jews as instigators in killing Christian boys. In the moment of murder, equality existed for all children, Jewish and Christian; to Zasius, they were followers of the holy innocents, slaughtered by the order of King Herod for the sake of Baby Jesus. As sacrificial victims in the battle between the evil magic of the Jews and Christian religion, innocent children, whose young blood was spilled, offered the promise of redemption to all.

For the Jews as a people, however, Zasius has nothing but contempt. The only practical solution to "the Jewish question" was expulsion. He writes: "Why then should the princes not be allowed to eliminate such truly professed enemies, such truculent beasts, and expel them from the territories of Christians? Let that most loathsome scum sink beneath the darkness of the horizon."[18] He assures the reader that one should not

15. "Dubitari enim non potest, tales paruulos pro Christi fide occisos, atcque ita baptismo sanguinis (instar divorum innocentum) initiatos, vitae aeternae participes futuros" (Zasius, "Quaestio I," p. 179).

16. "Iudei enim christianis sunt ingratissimi, eis quotidie publicis imprecationibus, publicis execrationibus deuouent, vsuris expoliant, seruitia negant, fidem nostram emaculatissimam derident et defaedare pergunt. In nostrum saluatorem funestissimis blasphemiis, et id quidem publice, feruntur" (Zasius, "Quaestio I," p. 173).

17. "Et quod omnium est crudelissimum: christianum sanguinem sitiunt, quem dies et noctes cruentissimi isti sanguinarii querunt. Quem et in nostro territorio his diebus, quod sine cordis perculsura loqui non possumus, plus semel effudisse a sociis criminum propterea supplicio affecti delati sunt" (Zasius, "Quaestio I," p. 173).

18. "Tales itaque tam professos vere dixerim hostes, tam truculentas bestias cur non eliminare? Cur non a limitibus christianorum eminus expellere maxime principibus permittatur? Est enim isthaec spurcissima sentina cymeriis abstrudenda tenebris" (Zasius, "Quaestio I," p. 173).

fear for the disappearance of the "seed of Israel," for even if there were no Jews among Christians, there would still be "an infinite mob of the circumcised" among the infidels.[19] Zasius ends the first quaestio with three conclusions: (1) it is not only within the power but the actual duty of the princes (and other superiors of the Jews) to baptize Jewish children; (2) not only the prince, but any good Christian could, on occasion, baptize Jewish children; and (3) although it is not simple to compel adult Jews to accept baptism without some terror and coercion, force can be applied.[20]

The second and the third quaestiones are much shorter because they deal with less controversial subjects. In the second quaestio, Zasius debates the pros and cons of whether a Jewish child who seeks conversion voluntarily could be baptized. Zasius first outlines the passages from Scripture and arguments from the canonist Bartolus and the theologian Gerson concerning the right age of reason; he then concludes that a child of seven has attained sufficient rational faculty to decide on his own salvation.[21] Seven is the age of consent: a child can inherit property, decide on marriage, sin, lie, and tell the truth. Christ called small children to himself, "for theirs is the kingdom of God." Moreover, those who seek salvation are called by the grace of God, and the children of Jews who ask for baptism without the consent of their parents must be helped to win salvation.[22]

In the third quaestio, Zasius answers objections based on contractual law against the forced baptism of the child in question; the legal point being that the father had left behind a bond and his son and that he and the Freiburgers made a compact to return his child. Zasius cites Cicero and roman law to argue for the suspension of normal contractual obligations because the Palatine elector was at war with the emperor, Freiburg's overlord. Moreover, a change in status would have occurred with baptism: the boy would be freed from his "servile" status and made holy. A baptism is furthermore a public case, which would then invalidate a private contract between the Jew and the city. Finally, Zasius quotes Cicero's De officiis at length to argue for changes in circumstance, time, place, person, and thing that would amount to an invalidation of the original contract.[23]

19. "Nec timeri debet, ne pereat semen Israhel, siquidem infinita recutitorum Apellarumque faex Caspiis est montibus per Magnum Alexandrum conclusa; sunt quoque multi apud infideles, vt etiam grassabunda ista pestis, si inter christianos non ageret, satis superque talium sordium in terra relinqueretur" (Zasius, "Quaestio I," p. 173).

20. Zasius, "Quaestio I," p. 180.

21. "Filii Iudaeorum impuberes, expleto septennio, uolentes, petentesque, ad sacrum baptisma, parentibus uel inuitis, perducendi, et fonte salutis initiandi sunt" (Zasius, "Quaestio II," p. 182).

22. Zasius, "Quaestio II," pp. 18–83, rationes 1–8.

23. Zasius, "Quaestio III," pp. 185–86.

Written in the form of an academic discourse, with statements of questions, opinions, objections, counterarguments, and conclusions, the *Quaestiones de Judaeis* is a skillful and erudite treatise. Zasius cites the entire range of learned texts: the Scriptures, Cicero and Seneca, the church fathers, especially Saint Augustine, church councils, the corpus of canon and civil law, legal commentaries, and scholastic texts. Ostensibly, it served as a legal brief, similar to the many he wrote for the city of Freiburg in which the principles of jurisprudence were argued in particular cases. The treatise has in fact been read in the context of the theological and legal discourses on Jews.[24] Another dimension of the text has not received sufficient attention: the vehement anti-Semitic statements are not merely vituperations embedded in a larger academic text; rather, they reflect the emotional center from which Zasius's learned reasonings proceeded. That emotional center, "the heart beating with pain (*cordis perculsura*)," remembered the child murder of 1504, in which, as we recall, the Jews were set free by Maximilian's command. To Zasius and the magistrates who presided over the trial, there lingered, no doubt, a strong feeling of injustice, of innocent deaths unavenged, of unpacified blood. To separate a son from his father, to remove a child from his folk and kin, to immerse him in a different religion and culture thus did not represent an act of inhumanity and injustice. If it was too late to save Christian boys who had been murdered, one could still save the souls of innocent Jewish boys from their murderous, magical parents and from their false religion of death.

Zasius went on to win greater fame. At the time he wrote the *Quaestiones*, he was named a councillor to the Hapsburg government in Ensisheim. In 1514 he became a "regent" of the university at Freiburg, and his scholarly reputation attracted many students, including Johann Eck, later to become famous as Luther's opponent, and the Amerbach brothers, printers and humanists.[25] Considered one of the leading legal humanists of Germany, Zasius was an important figure in the intellectual circles of the Upper Rhine; he corresponded with Erasmus, Boniface Amerbach, Alciatus, and Beatus Rhenaus, among others.[26] When the evangelical movement swept across Germany, Zasius remained loyal to the Roman church, as did the city of Freiburg.

In 1520 the city entrusted Zasius with the task of drawing up a new civic code. The resulting legal documents, ordinances dealing with Jews, were strongly shaped by the anti-Jewish passions of 1504. On testatory

24. For example, Kisch, *Zasius und Reuchlin*.

25. See Thieme, "Zasius und Freiburg," pp. 17–18; Thiele, *Freiburger Stadtschreiber*, p. 127.

26. For Zasius's correspondence, see *Opera Omnia VII*.

rights and procedures, not only did the new civic code prohibit brothel keepers from giving legal testimony, it expressly condemned the testimonies of Jews and "open heretics," even though written law might indicate otherwise elsewhere.[27] Christians were forbidden to have any dealings with Jews; those who did would, like them, be punished. No one in Freiburg could do business with Jews, borrow money from them, buy or sell in secret, or give them lodging; those who sheltered Jews overnight were to be fined two marks silver, and repeated offenders were to be exiled.[28]

THE REUCHLIN AFFAIR

It would be an oversimplification to describe Zasius as an anti-Semite. In spite of racist overtones in his writings, any modern parallels are anachronistic. Salvation was possible for Jews, if they converted. This belief was firmly shared by a colleague of Zasius who was likewise a jurist, humanist, renowned scholar, and councillor to Emperor Maximilian I: Johannes Reuchlin, a native of Pforzheim, where four Jews died for their alleged involvement in the Endingen murder, was roughly Zasius's contemporary.[29]

In 1505 Reuchlin published an open letter to an unnamed nobleman who had asked his advice on how to convert Jews. *The German Missal* (*Tütsch Missive*) argued that the diaspora of the Jews was a manifest sign of their sins for having killed Christ and having denied his messianic identity; theirs was a collective punishment inflicted by God.[30] Moreover, Reuchlin accused the Jews of daily cursing the Virgin Mary and the apostles, "which blasphemies all Jews in this time participate in as long as they are Jews."[31] Their only hope lay in conversion, and Reuchlin generously offered to instruct the nobleman's Jews himself.[32]

The German Missal offered what seemed to Reuchlin the most hu-

27. See Ulrich Zasius, *Nüwe Stattrechten und Statuten der loblichen Statt Fryburg im Bryszgow gelegen*, folio 18ᵛ, which appears as a supplementary volume to the *Zasius Opera Omnia: Supplementum* (Freiburg, 1520; reprint, Aalen, 1968).

28. Zasius, *Nüwe Stattrechten*, folio 92ᵛ.

29. The standard biography is Ludwig Geiger, *Johann Reuchlin, sein Leben und seine Werke* (Leipzig, 1871).

30. Johannes Reuchlin, *Tütsch Missive. Warumb die Juden so lang im ellend sind* [Pforzheim: Thomas Anselm, 1505], sig. A⁴⁻⁴ᵛ. For an analysis of the missal, see Kisch, *Zasius und Reuchlin*, pp. 15–22; for a critical evaluation of Reuchlin's attitudes toward Jews, see Heiko A. Oberman, *Die Wurzeln des Antisemitismus: Christenangst und Judenplage im Zeitalter von Humanismus und Reformation* (Berlin, 1981), pp. 35–36.

31. "Das all Juden zu diser zyt so lang sy Juden sind an sölcher gotzlesterung teilhafftig syen" (Reuchlin, *Tütsch Missive*, sig. A⁵).

32. Reuchlin, *Tütsch Missive*, sig. A⁵ᵛ.

mane solution to the "Jewish question." For the Jews, conversion meant, of course, the surrender of a distinct religious identity in exchange for the promise of social and cultural integration and the end of persecutions. This was a price individual German Jews were willing to pay, not only to free themselves from the restrictive economic roles prescribed for Jews but more especially to escape from the doubly murderous role of magicians, as ritual killers, assigned to them in a Christian drama of salvation. Conversion as social redemption was also the message of Johannes Pfefferkorn, a Jewish convert from Prague who turned out to be Reuchlin's most bitter foe.

In 1507 the unknown thirty-six-year-old Pfefferkorn burst on the scene with a most remarkable work. He wrote a book entitled *Mirror of Exhortation* in which he urged all Jews to accept Christ as the Messiah.[33] He described himself as a former Jew named Joseph who was now dedicating his work to Jesus and Mary. The book is divided into three parts: the first is addressed to all Jews, whom Pfefferkorn calls "my brethren and people *(fratres et populares mei)"*; the second gives advice to religious and secular lords on methods to convert Jews en masse; and the third is a prophecy of an impending reformation and restitution.

Writing for the Jews, Pfefferkorn argues that they wait in vain because the true Messiah has already come.[34] He also asserts that some Jews recognize Christ's messianic identity but, due to their families and friends, hesitate to convert.[35] Discord plagued Jewish communities regarding the advent of the Messiah; Pfefferkorn cites the strife among the Jews of Halle in 1502 on account of the messianic preachings of a man called Lemmel.[36] It pains him, Pfefferkorn confesses, to see his brethren persist in their obstinancy, and he prays that they may open their eyes, throw away the Talmud, read the Gospels, the Mosaic Books, Psalms, and the Prophets to discover that Christ is the true Messiah.[37]

When he turns to address Christian rulers, Pfefferkorn gives advice on how to convert Jews. Usury was the main obstacle. Princes must forbid Jews from lending money, and yet they should ensure that Jews can lead honest working lives. Pfefferkorn writes: "If, therefore, you most renowned Christian ecclesiastical and lay lords want to entice and convert Jews to the Christian faith, do not allow them to practice usury; but do not suffer them to go into exile because they are already in exile

33. *Speculum adhortationis iudaice ad Christum* [Speyer: C. Hist, 1507]. A second edition was published in 1508 by M. van Werden of Cologne.
34. Pfefferkorn, *Speculum*, sig. A4-4v.
35. Pfefferkorn, *Speculum*, sig. B2-2v.
36. Pfefferkorn, *Speculum*, sig. B3.
37. Pfefferkorn, *Speculum*, sig. B3v.

from their ancient homeland."[38] Moreover, princes should send preachers to spread the word of God among Jews while confiscating their
blasphemous books, especially the Talmud.[39] Taking the Talmud away
from the Jews, Pfefferkorn argues, is not doing them violence. What is
more insidious is the popular rumor against Jews, the blood libel: "It is
said among vulgar Christians that Jews need Christian blood for circumcision, for which they kill little Christian children . . . most renowned
Christians, do not give credence to this . . . perhaps Jews can be found
and some have hitherto been found who secretly plot to kill Christian
infants, but this would not be on account of the need to have blood, but
because of their hatred and revenge against Christians."[40]

While Pfefferkorn might not have wanted to attack the ritual murder
discourse head on, he attempted to deny the magical notions associated
with blood, an underlying theme in ritual murder accusations. Pfefferkorn further criticizes his fellow Christians for uttering all sorts of contemptuous sayings about Jews, including one that has become "almost
like an adage": "It is rare that an old Jew will be a good Christian just as
old dogs are not used to chains." He writes:

> I pray that you Christians would not use this proverb, nor give it place or
> credence. For the salvation of all of us is from the Jews, and the funda-
> mentals of our faith and the edifice of our Church were first built upon
> the Jews. "Jew" is the name of peoples and nations and not religion,
> created out of proselytes from many peoples. Therefore, let us not
> scandalize them, if perhaps the Jew does not live according to the
> Christian institution and doctrine, lest we judge even our Lord Jesus,
> who had among his twelve apostles a thief and traitor.[41]

38. "Vos igitur charissimi Christiani eccliastici et seculares: si animo vobis seder
Judeos ad christianam fidem allicere et convertere, non sinite eos usuras agere, nec tamen
patiamini eos aligi in exilium, qui iam vetere sua patria exularunt" (Pfefferkorn, *Speculum,*
sig. C²ᵛ).
    39. Pfefferkorn, *Speculum,* sig. C³ᵛ⁻⁴ᵛ.
    40. "Inseram subijciamque his sup re quadam: quo vulgato fertur adversum Judeos
inani rumore sermonem refellendo cum ne nos christiani ob id ridiculi simus. Dicitur vulgo
inter christianos Judeis necessario opus esse uti sanguine christiano ad medelam propterea
eos occidere infantulos christianos: ad hoc eos feda quadam egritudine laborare. Charissimi
christiani nolite his adhibere fidem . . . redibile est inventos esse et fortasse adhuc inveniri
posse iudeos, qui christianorum infantes ad necem clam sectentur, non propter sanguinis
habendi inde necessitatem, sed odii et ultionis causa in christianos" (Pfefferkorn, *Speculum,*
sig. D¹⁻¹ᵛ).
    41. "Alius adhuc sermos inter nos christianos de iudeis vulgatus est. Jactatur quasi
adagio quodam: 'Raro iudeus senex bonus erit christianus ut seni cani non facile ad usum
adhibent vincula.' Oro vos christiani: nolite hoc uti proverbio, nec ei locum dare et fidem.
Nam et omnis nostra salus ex Judeis est, et fidei nostre fundamentum iactum, edificium
ecclesie nostre primum a Judeis superedificatum est. Judeis gentis et nationis nomen est
non religionis: et ex gentibus multi facti sunt prozeliti. Non ergo scandalizemini, si fortasse

Pfefferkorn assures his Christian readers that converted Jews would remain constant and steadfast, for the Jews had suffered so much contempt in exile for their religion. Once their obstinacy and error have been transformed by the grace of God into true faith, they would become fervent Christians.[42]

The third and final part of the work is suffused with millenarian passion and a sense of urgency. Throughout the first two parts, Pfefferkorn alternates between two identities; he feels akin to both Jews and Christians but is permanently suspended between an uncertain sense of Self and Other. His language reflects this ambivalence: he calls the Jews "my brethren and people" but distances himself when he criticizes their refusal to convert, calling them "Jews." Although no longer of one faith with them, Pfefferkorn feels their suffering and understands their courage. Christians he addresses sometimes as "us" and other times as "you"; convinced of the veracity of Christianity, he was, however, appalled by the cruelty of Christians toward Jews. The tensions and contradictions are eventually resolved in the passionate millenarian vision of the third section. Pfefferkorn the enthusiast predicts that many signs point to the great changes that would soon come. The world is full of depravity and sin, God will soon avenge the wronged and show his justice (*Justitia Dei*), there will be a reformation and a restitution, a return to a golden age; Jews and Christians, his blood and spiritual brothers, will soon be of one faith under one shepherd.[43] The princes must follow God's word, keep the peace, and exhort Jews to convert. And when the world is filled with the Holy Spirit, "where now there is war everywhere, there will be obedience"; where there is rebellion, order; where there is evil, religion; sacrilege, justice; injury, happiness; impudence, caution; wantonness, frugality; luxury, modesty; avarice, concordia; sedition, humility; ambition, love; hatred, wisdom; stupidity, faith.[44]

Born in 1470, the year of the Endingen ritual murder trial, Pfefferkorn grew up during three decades of increasingly strident anti-Jewish polemics and violence. He converted at the age of thirty-six, bringing his family with him into the new life.[45] The influence of Franciscan mille-

---

Judeus quispiam quam christianam institutionem et doctrinam non vixerit, nosipsi nos iudicemus Dominus etiam Jesus inter duodecim apostolos furem habuit et perditorem" (Pfefferkorn, *Speculum*, sig. D^{1v-2}).

42. Pfefferkorn, *Speculum*, sig. D^{2v-3}.
43. Pfefferkorn, *Speculum*, sig. D^{4}E^1.
44. Pfefferkorn, *Speculum*, sig. E^{2v}.
45. The only information on his early life comes from the prefaces of his many works. He admits to having remained in "Jewish error" for 36 years before his conversion, which would put his year of birth at around 1470. See Johannes Pfefferkorn, *Zu lob vnd Ere des aller durchleichtigsten und grossmechtigisten Fursten und herren, Herr Maximilian . . . Römischen Kaiser . . .* (Augsburg: Erhard Öglein, 1510), sig. A^{3v}.

narianism on the *Mirror of Exhortations* is unmistakable.[46] When Pfefferkorn embarked on his self-appointed mission to confiscate the Talmud
and the prayer books of the Jewish communities in Germany, he had the
ear of Kunnigund, the sister of Emperor Maximilian. Introduced by
"several pious and learned Christians" to the archduchess of Austria,
who was living under the Third Rule of Saint Francis after the death of
her husband, Duke Albrecht of Bavaria, Pfefferkorn made a very favorable impression on Kunnigund and through her intercession obtained an
imperial mandate to suppress Hebrew books.[47] Pfefferkorn then consulted the learned jurist and renowned Christian Hebraist in Pforzheim
concerning the implementation of the imperial mandate. Reuchlin, however, came to an immediate disagreement with Pfefferkorn after their
first and only meeting.[48] In 1509 Pfefferkorn and Reuchlin were appointed as two of the four imperial commissioners whose assignment
was to examine whether the books of the Jews contained blasphemies
against Christianity; the other two were a priest, Victor von Carben, also
a Jewish convert, and a Dominican named Jacob Hochstraten, inquisitor
general in Cologne.

The subsequent disagreement between Pfefferkorn and Reuchlin
turned a personal dispute into a national debate. The so-called Reuchlin
Affair has been told many times and only the barest outline needs repeat-
ing here.[49] On one side stood Pfefferkorn, supported both by the friars—
Franciscans and Dominicans—and especially by the theological faculty
of the University of Cologne; on the other side fought Reuchlin, backed
by the humanists. The exchange of *ad hominem* attacks in a series of
polemical publications began with Pfefferkorn's respectful but firm criticism of Reuchlin in the *Handt Spiegel* (1511), in which the convert reminded the learned doctor of the latter's 1505 missal to the Jews.[50] It
brought down Reuchlin's full wrath. In his reply, the *Augenspiegel* (1511),
Reuchlin scornfully dismissed Pfefferkorn as that "baptized Jew (*der
taufft iud Pfefferkorn*)" who was ignorant of Hebrew, contemptuous of

46. This has been pointed out by Oberman, *Wurzeln des Antisemitismus*, pp. 42–44.
47. Pfefferkorn, *Zu lob und Ere*, sig. A⁵ᵛ.
48. Pfefferkorn describes their short meeting in 1509 as amicable and states that they
parted on good terms (*Brantspiegell. Abzotraiben und auszuleschen eines ungegrunten laster
buechleyn mit namen Augenspiegell* [Cologne: Hermann Gutschaiff, 1512], sig. A³ᵛ. A different
story is told by Reuchlin, who reports that he strongly disagreed with Pfefferkorn on the
wording of the imperial mandate (*Augenspiegel, Warhafftige Entschuldigung gegen und wider
ains getaufften iuden genant Pfefferkorn vormals getruckt ussgangen unwarhaftigs Schmachbüchlin*
[Tübingen: Thomas Anselm, 1511], sig. A¹ᵛ⁻²).
49. For a fuller account of the Reuchlin Affair, see James H. Overfeld, *Humanism and
Scholasticism in Late Medieval Germany* (Princeton, 1984), pp. 247–97.
50. Pfefferkorn, *Handt Spiegel wider und gegen die Jüden* [Mainz: J. Schoeffer, 1511]. For
passages critical of Reuchlin, see sigs. A³⁻³ᵛ, A⁴, B¹⁻²ᵛ, C¹⁻³ᵛ, E²ᵛ⁻³ᵛ.

true learning and erudition, a liar, rabble-rouser, and money grabber.[51] Thereafter, the dispute escalated into an ugly polemical battle that haunted Reuchlin to his deathbed. The original context of the dispute, the disagreements over the treatment of German Jews, became submerged in the new battle between the camps, with the humanists in the arts faculty poking fun at the earnest friars and the scholastics, and the theologians at Cologne condemning Reuchlin for heresy. For Reuchlin, the "battle of words" meant nothing less than the defense of his beloved scholarship, the study of the Kabbalah and Hebrew books and, by extension, the protection of the civic rights of Jews as citizens (*concives*) of the empire. To the erudite linguist and jurist, Pfefferkorn was merely an ignorant rabble-rouser, a dangerous zealot who won the backing of the scholastics and the friars and, unfortunately, the attention of the emperor as well. For Pfefferkorn, Reuchlin's objections amounted to obstructionism; he felt hurt and angry at Reuchlin's learned snobbery, at the way this son of a patrician family, doctor of civil law, and imperial councillor ridiculed his own Christian fervor by dismissing him as just another avaricious Jew-convert. Ultimately, Reuchlin was faced with the charge of heresy and had to defend his own scholarly interest in the Kabbalah. Among those who rallied to his defense, whose name appeared in the antischolastic *Letters of Obscure Men*, was the Freiburg professor, Ulrich Zasius.[52] In the anti-Jewish campaigns that preceded the early Reformation years, the front lines were not always clearly drawn.

JOHANN ECK: MAGIC AND COUNTERMAGIC

The battle of books and pamphlets helped to shape a "national public opinion" among the educated elite immediately before the appearance of Luther. The works of Reuchlin and Pfefferkorn, and their respective supporters, sold well in the Frankfurt Book Fair and attracted the attention of scholars, officials, and magistrates all over Germany. Religious renewal, Christian learning, and "the Jewish problem" seemed inextricably mixed. When the evangelical movement gathered momentum after 1517 and destroyed Christian unity, the debates between the critics and defenders of the Roman church echoed in many instances the themes of ritual murder discourse. Simultaneously a war against false

51. Reuchlin, *Augenspiegel*, pt. 4: "Responsio ad Pfefferkorn," sig. H[4v]-K[6]. The following quotation is representative of Reuchlin's scornfully dismissive tone: "dass mich der taufft iud Pfefferkorn mit der unwarhait hin geben und wider got eer und recht uss geschriben und unzimlich also gegen mengklichem verunglimpfft hat/allain im selbs zu ainer unnottürfftigen müttwilligen rach/und von seiner geittigen art ab seinen elttern den iuden biss uff in kommen/das er mit mir als ain buchgrempler vil gelts möcht gewinnen" (sig. H[4v]).

52. Kisch, *Zasius und Reuchlin*, pp. 47–49.

beliefs and a struggle against Jewish magic, the battle over true religion was a campaign waged by theologians on both sides of the confessional divide; Luther and Eck, the reformer and his critic, who represented very different doctrinal positions on grace and salvation, nevertheless both argued from a similar intellectual structure against Jews. Their anti-Jewish writings reflected the underlying magical universe of the Wittenberg professor and his Ingolstadt critic.

Of the many students who studied under Zasius at the University of Freiburg, one was to win greater fame than his teacher. Johann Maier, better known as Johann Eck, was born in 1486 in the town of Eck in Swabia, from which he took his name. In 1498 the thirteen-year-old Eck registered as a student at the university in Heidelberg; a year later, he moved to the university in Tübingen, where he took his master of arts degree in July 1502. The year after, Eck continued his studies at the university in Freiburg, where in 1505 he became, as a mere youth of nineteen, lecturer on the Old and New Testaments. After receiving his licentiate in theology in 1509, he was promoted to professor of theology. In 1510 he became a doctor of theology, and in the same year he received a chair at the university in Ingolstadt. Rising steadily through the ranks of the faculty, he eventually became vice-chancellor of the university. His opposition to Martin Luther in the 1519 Leipzig debate further established his reputation as the leading defender of the Roman church and the most forceful spokesman for Catholic theology in the Holy Roman Empire. Eck was a prodigious writer. At Ingolstadt he turned out volume after volume of learned commentaries on Aristotle and on the Scriptures; he entered into fierce, sometimes acrimonious, academic debates with his colleagues, and even with his former teacher Zasius.[53] He wrote, lectured, and preached.

In 1540, a child murder in Sappenfeld rekindled the deeply buried emotions Eck had felt when he was a student in Freiburg some thirty-six years earlier. In the small village of Sappenfeld, in the diocese of Eichstätt and the County of Neuburg, a boy named Michael Pisenharter disappeared. His parents saw two Jews in the village market around the time the boy was missing; the bishop posted a reward of ten guldens for anyone who could find the boy's clothing or body. When nothing turned up, the father, Georg, went before the count of Neuburg, imploring "that he wanted to find his child amongst the wicked Jews."[54] Someone had

---

53. For Zasius's response to Eck, see his *Opera Omnia VII.*

54. The details of the Sappenfeld ritual murder case are extant in two accounts: a ballad published shortly after the event and a brief description by Eck. See *Ein hübsch new lied von Zweyen Juden/vnd einem Kind/zu Sappenfelt newlich geschehen;* see also Johannes Eck, *Ains Judenbüchlins Verlegung: darin ain Christ/gantzer Christenhait zu schmach/will es geschehe den Juden unrecht in bezichtigung der Christen kinder mordt* (Ingolstadt: Alexander Weissenhorn, 1541), sig. A2-2v.

supposedly overheard a Jewish boy telling his playmates that "the dog" was dead after it had howled for three days. Since the villagers believed that Jews called Christians dogs, they concluded that the Jews had tortured the boy for three days before he died. A shepherd then came forward with the testimony that he saw the Jews dumping the corpse in a forest. The authorities found the mutilated body: fingers and toes had been cut off; one ear had a hole; the shoulders bore three wounds, cut in the shape of crosses; the foreskin of the penis was cut off; and stab wounds, including two deep slashes, were found all over the body. The bishop, Moritz von Hutten, saw the corpse himself and ordered the arrest of Jews in his domain. The mutilated body was put on display in a church; five weeks later it bled, "showing God's mercy" and giving Sappenfeld temporary fame as a pilgrimage site.

As news of the ritual murder charge spread in the Upper Palatinate and Franconia, an anonymous booklet appeared; its title read, "Whether It is True and believable that Jews secretly kill Christian children and use their blood. A splendid text presented for everyone's Judgment."[55] The tract was composed by the evangelical preacher of Nuremberg Andreas Osiander, who defended the Jews against the blood libel and listed the possible real causes of the deaths.[56] Just the year before, Osiander had defended Nuremberg's new Protestant catechism against Eck's criticism.[57] Knowing well the true authorship of the anonymous antiritual murder discourse, Eck responded in full fury.

Refutation of a Jewish Booklet is the most massive and systematic formulation of the blood libel; Eck's volume represented the summa of learned discourse on ritual murder, a formidable defense against the first real attempt by a Christian to expose the reality behind this myth.[58] Dedicated to Bishop Christoph of Trent, in memory of the blessed boy Simon who died in 1475, Eck composed his treatise to refute the "evan-

55. Ob es war vnd glaublich sey/dass die juden der Christen Kinder heymlich erwürgen/vnd ir blut gebrauchen/ein treffenliche schrifft/auff eines yeden vrteyl gestellt.

56. The identity of the anonymous author was convincingly established in 1893 by Moritz Stern, who edited and published the tract as *Andreas Osianders Schrift über die Blutbeschuldigung* (Kiel, 1893). For a detailed analysis of Osiander's text, see chap. 7.

57. See Andreas Osiander, *Verantwortung des Nürnbergischen Catechismi, wider Johannes Eck* (Nuremberg: L. Milchtaler, 1539). Osiander's catechism emphasizes the Augustinian concept of original sin and its determination on the behavior of children; in reply, Eck defends the innocence of babies. See Johannes Eck, *Schutz Red Kindtlicher Unschuld wider den Catechisten Andre Hosander/unnd sein schmach buchlin/durch Doctor Johann Ecken zu Ingolstadt. An ain Erbern weisen Burgermeister unnd Rath der loblichen weitberümpten statt Nurmberg* (1540).

58. A brief synopsis of *Ains Judenbüchlins Verlegung* and Osiander's booklet can be found in Heinrich Graetz, *Geschichte der Juden von der ältesten Zeiten bis auf die Gegenwart*, vol. 9 (Leipzig, 1891), pp. 309–11.

gelical scoundrel (*evangelisch lumpen*)" who dared to defend the "blood-thirsty Jews" of Sappenfeld.[59]

To support his argument, Eck cites examples of fratricide from the Old Testament to illustrate the "murderous nature" of the Jews.[60] They hate Christians and would gladly have killed all.[61] They have murdered Christians in medieval France and have helped the Arabs in Spain and in the Holy Land.[62] They poisoned wells in 1348.[63] They practiced medicine only to kill Christians.[64] They blaspheme and curse Christians in their daily prayers.[65] Jews are black magicians. Eck tells the story of a Jew in Jägersdorf, Silesia, who bribed a bathmaid to give him some milk from a suckling mother; instead he got pig's milk. The Jew then poured milk into the corpse of an executed man; after his head was cut off, many piglets ran out of his neck. A few days later, all the pigs within a two-mile radius died.[66]

Blood is central to Jewish magic, according to Eck. Its nature is demonic: Jews need Christian blood to anoint their rabbis; Jewish babies are born with two tiny fingers attached to the skin of their forehead (the very image of the Devil himself), and without Christian blood it is very difficult to remove these fingers without harm to the child; above all, Jews need Christian blood to wash away the blood stain inflicted on them by God because they had crucified Christ.[67] "It is no wonder," Eck concludes, "that the Jews now buy the blood of innocent children, just as their fathers had bought the innocent blood of Jesus Christ from Judas with thirty pennies."[68] Jews plot to use the milk of Christian mothers to poison the blood of Christians; they believe that Christian blood could wash away the stains of blood from Christ. Eck's assertions reflected the fundamentally magical mental structure of a learned theologian of early sixteenth-century Germany. Medieval medical lore posited that human milk and blood were composed of the same substance.[69] In Eck's think-

59. Eck, *Ains Judenbüchlins Verlegung*, sig. A⁴.

60. Eck, *Ains Judenbüchlins Verlegung*, sig. C²ᵛ⁻³.

61. Eck, *Ains Judenbüchlins Verlegung*, sig. E².

62. Eck, *Ains Judenbüchlins Verlegung*, sig. E⁴ᵛ-F¹ᵛ.

63. Eck, *Ains Judenbüchlins Verlegung*, sig. F²⁻²ᵛ.

64. Eck, *Ains Judenbüchlins Verlegung*, sig. F³ᵛ⁻⁴ᵛ.

65. Eck, *Ains Judenbüchlins Verlegung*, sig. H¹ᵛ⁻⁴.

66. Eck, *Ains Judenbüchlins Verlegung*, sig. F³⁻³ᵛ. The charge of witchcraft against Rabbi Abraham Hirsch and other Jews came from a convicted witch. It caused widespread riots against Jews in the duchy of Jägersdorf and calls for their expulsion by the Silesian estates; see Stern, *Josel of Rosheim*, pp. 145–48.

67. Eck, *Ains Judenbüchlins Verlegung*, sig. J³ᵛ–K¹.

68. "Nit ist zu verwundern: dz die juden jetzt kaufen das blut der unschuldigen kinder, so ir väter kauft haben das unschuldig blut ɪHESU Christ vm 30. pfennig von Judas" (Eck, *Ains Judenbüchlins Verlegung*, sig. K²).

69. *HWDA* 1, "Blut," c. 1440.

ing, sympathetic magic was at work: opposites attract one another, and a sympathetic substance forces the other out. Thus Jews could use milk to poison a sympathetic substance, blood, and they need Christian blood to cleanse their own bloodstains from Christ.[70]

To be sure, there was a note of Catholic charity; Eck concedes that only a small minority of Jews, in the greatest secrecy, practiced ritual murder. But the past bore witness to the truth: in a long section on the "history" of ritual murders, Eck cites the examples of William of Norwich in twelfth-century England, Robert Gaguin of thirteenth-century France; in the empire, there were the 1261 ritual murder of a seven-year-old girl in Forchheim, the ritual murders and Host desecrations in Vienna for which three hundred Jews were burnt by Archduke Albrecht in 1420, the 1470 Endingen murders, the notorious "martyrdom" of Simon of Trent in 1475, the 1510 case in Brandenburg, and the 1529 murder in Poesing, in German-speaking Hungary.[71] In another section he recounts the parallel accusations of Host desecration: 1337 in Deckendorf, 1477 in Passau, 1492 in Sternbach, Mecklenburg, 1508 in Cracow, 1510 in Brandenburg, 1514 in Halle, and other cases in France and Spain.[72]

How was Eck convinced of these long lists of murder charges? He had read them: in chronicles, anti-Jewish polemics, and history books, in pamphlets, chapbooks, printed ballads, and broadsheets—in short, from the printed discourse on ritual murder, both verbal and visual, which had consolidated into a textual tradition between 1470 and 1540. The printed word and picture reinforced oral legends of Jewish magic, but the most important emotional moment for Eck was the memory of a personal experience that had occurred thirty-six years earlier, in 1504, when he was a student in Freiburg. Commenting on the "veracity" of ritual murders, Eck writes that he would cite all the historical examples:

> But for now one example should suffice, one I saw with my own eyes and not from hearsay. In the year 1503 [sic], as I was continuing my studies from Cologne in Freiburg, a child was missing on one of the farms near Dentzlingen. A neighbor found him in the woods, having been alerted by the bellowing of an ox. Shortly thereafter, the child's father was apprehended in Buchen on suspicion of theft. At first he feigned ignorance regarding his child, but when he was shown the body he began to sweat. Without torture he confessed that he had sold his four-year-old child to two Jews in Waldkirch for five guldens; they told him the child would not die, that they only wanted to draw some blood from him; But alas things turned out differently and the child died

70. On the theory of sympathetic magic, see Mauss, *Magic*, p. 72.

71. Eck, *Ains Judenbüchlins Verlegung*, sig. K³ᵛ–M⁴ᵛ. Eck erroneously gives the Poesing date as 1509.

72. Eck, *Ains Judenbüchlins Verlegung*, sig. T²–V³ᵛ.

because of this. I saw the child with my own eyes, about four weeks after the murder; and with my fingers I held and touched the prick wounds. I also saw the execution of the father in Buchen; he died confessing that the Jews had stabbed his child to death. . . .

Moreover, I saw the Christian, who took the blood from the Jews in Waldkirch and carried it to Alsace, and who was sentenced to death by the noble and honorable city council of Freiburg im Breisgau and later executed. He carried the blood of the child from Buchen to the Jews of Alsace. Many hundreds of people heard this confession.[73]

Like the two headless corpses in Endingen, like little Michael Pisenharter in Sappenfeld, this dead boy in Freiburg was also put on display, both as a sign of the murderous magic of the Jews and as an object of Christian devotion. For Eck and his contemporaries, the boys proved that miracles still happened; they were living relics, embodiments of a salvific source that dispensed grace to their beholders.[74] Beholding and touching represented the most powerful ways of feeling and expressing piety; the sacred was made flesh, and it was through the human body that the promise of salvation became materially real.

The very sensuality of Eck's description of the corpse belies the inaccuracy of his memory; he remembered the year wrong. But the important thing was the intense feeling this memory conjured in him thirty-six years later. The little corpse, completely bled white, symbolized the very image of death and redemption; the boy, like the crucified Christ, was a sacrificial victim of the Jews. In the cathedral of Colmar, across the Rhine from Freiburg, hangs Matthias Grünewald's powerful painting of the crucifixion. It is a human Christ, bled completely white,

73. "Ich will hernach völligklich thun [give a full account of the history of ritual murder]: vnd jetz allain ain vorlass geben: Nit von hören sagen/sondern das ich mit mein augen gesehen: als man zalt 1503. jar/vnd ich von Cöln auff das studium zu Freiburg jetz zogen war: ward ain kind verlorn under lang Dentzlingen auf ainem hof: das ain nachbaur durch brellen der ochsen gefunden im holtz. Vnlang darnach kam des kinds vatter ein zu Buchen/vmb verdacht ains diebstals: vnnd do ehr seins Kinds halb bespracht ward/wollt er nichts darumb wissen: Als bald aber das kind im fürtragen: hat ehr angefangen zu schwaissen: hat der vatter/on alle peinliche frag bekent/wie er sein kind vieriärig zwaien juden von Waltkirch umb v gulden verkaufft hab: wiewol sie im zugesagt/das kind wurd nit sterben/allain wolten sie von jm das blut fahen: das laider anders geraten/vnnd das kind daran gestorben: das kindle hab ich gesehen mit mein augen/die stich des kinds/etwa vier wochen nach dem mordt/mit meinen fingern griffen vnd angerüert: Hab auch den vatter gesehen zu Buch richtenn: der darauff bestendiglich gestorben ist/die judenn haben sein kind zu tod gestupft. . . . Ferner hab ich gesehen/den Christen der das blut von juden genommen zu Waltkirch hat/vnnd den juden bracht im Elsass/das er durch vrtayldes Edlen vnd Erberen raths zu Freiburg im Brissgei/ist gericht worden: vnnd darauff gestorben/Er hab des Kindlins vonn Buche blut den Juden ihns Elsas tragen: sollich bekantnus haben vil hundert menschenn gehört" (Eck, *Ains Judenbüchlins Verlegung*, sig. B[3v]–B[4v]).

74. Mayer, "Die heilbringende Schau."

all bloody and full of pain; the immense suffering of a man is vividly expressed in the grim contortions of the body. Grünewald's crucifixion reflected a trend in this genre that transformed the heavily allegorical crucifixion scenes of the Middle Ages into realistic, gruesome, and human depictions of torture and death.

In Eck's memory of Freiburg, in the salvific display at Sappenfeld, the images of Christ, the dead boy, and the Eucharist all blended into a single symbol of Christian sacrifice. All three were tortured by the Jews; all bled. When the corpse of the Sappenfeld boy bled after five weeks on display, it was no different from the bleeding Eucharist tortured by the Jews. Human flesh, tortured, became divine and created an immediate salvific presence "showing God's mercy" to the beholders. This process meant nothing less than a eucharistic sacrifice, a ritualistic variation of the Crucifixion, and a social mass, enacted in a drama and discourse, with a language drawn partly from the liturgy of the ecclesiastical hierarchy and partly from the vocabulary of popular magical beliefs. The set of interlocutors in this social-divine drama encompassed the Christian community, its victims and saviors, and the demonic "other," the Jews, and resulted in the reaffirmation of a secure salvific boundary for the collectivity of faith and emotional reassurance for the individual beholder.

The centrality of Eck's personal experience in Freiburg was also manifest in a sermon he wrote for Good Friday. Christ's blood cries out for vengeance against the Jews, Eck preached, just as the blood of Abel cried out against Cain. As a result of these blood feuds, God dispersed the Jews and made them suffer great terror and contempt. Citing Saint Augustine, Eck reminded his flock that the blood curse caused Jewish men to suffer menstruation and that to cure it they had to seek Christian blood by murdering children.[75] As notorious examples of ritual murder, he singled out Trent and Freiburg.

To Eck, Christian persecutions of Jews became actions of legitimate self-defense; the 1298 Rindfleisch pogroms in Franconia, the massacres in the wake of the Black Death, and the expulsions of Jews from France and Spain all resulted from Jewish evil.[76] Just as insidious, in Eck's view, was

---

75. Johannes Eck, *Christliche Auslegung der Evangelien von der Zeit/durch das gantz Jar/nach gemeynem verstand der Kirchen und heiligen väter von der selbigen angenommen . . . Der erste Teyl vom Advent biss Ostern . . . Der andern Teyl vom Ostern biss auff den Advent* (Tübingen, 1531), folio 158c: "Wann das heilig blut IHESU Christi schreyt rach über sie wie das blut Abel über seinen bruder/Sie empfinden des fluchs wol/das sie also flüchtig unnd schwaiffent durch die gantzen welt zerstrewt sindt/ unnd allenthalb in grosser forcht und verachtung. Es sagt Augustinus das die juden von dem fluch (auch die man) leiden die kranckheit der frawen (patiuntur menstrua) und haben kein ertzney denn Christen blut wie man sagt. Da her kombt es das sie die unschuldigen Christenkind als offt getödt haben."

76. Eck, *Ains Judenbüchlins Verlegung*, sig. O⁴⁻⁴ᵛ.

Osiander's denial of ritual murder, for it undermined the entire theological, or one may say magical, foundations upon which salvific sacrifice and Christian redemption were based. Eck slanders the composer of the antiritual murder tract as "the father of Jews (*Judenvater*)," who has taken bribes from them.[77] He also attacks Luther's doctrine of *sola fides*[78] and accuses Lutherans of stirring up the peasant revolts of 1525[79] and for insisting that the study of Hebrew is essential for recovering the true Christian faith.[80] From Eck's perspective, Lutherans and Jews were allies in the war against the true church: the Lutheran "desecration" of the sacrament of Eucharist was similar to Jewish Host desecrations;[81] lately, the iconoclasts of the Reformation have learned from the Jews.[82] How dare the Judenvater doubt the veracity of ritual murders: does he want to slander Christianity by accusing Christians of murdering innocent Jews? In essence, Eck charges, Osiander is accusing Christians of murder, magic, and lies by defending Jews against the blood libel.[83]

MARTIN LUTHER: THE REFORMER AS EXORCIST

Magic and countermagic, false and true faith, superstition and religion: these were some of the central themes of theological discourse in the generations preceding and following the Reformation. Whereas for Johann Eck, Protestant heresy and Jewish magic went hand in hand, for Luther, Catholic superstition and Jewish magic equally represented the old, false religion that was to be overcome by the new, true evangelical faith.

No one embodied the ambivalence toward magic more vividly than the Wittenberg professor himself: Luther both believed in magic and condemned it. From his off-the-cuff table talks, scribbled down by his many students at meals, there emerges a picture of the reformer that rounds out the image of the passionate theologian and writer of vehement anti-Jewish treatises.[84] Especially in his later years, Luther was

77. Eck, *Ains Judenbüchlins Verlegung*, sig. R²ᵛ.
78. Eck, *Ains Judenbüchlins Verlegung*, sig. G².
79. Eck, *Ains Judenbüchlins Verlegung*, sig. N⁴.
80. Eck, *Ains Judenbüchlins Verlegung*, sig. P⁴ᵛ–Q²ᵛ.
81. Eck, *Ains Judenbüchlins Verlegung*, sig. V⁴.
82. Eck, *Ains Judenbüchlins Verlegung*, sig. T¹ᵛ.
83. Eck, *Ains Judenbüchlins Verlegung*, sig. Z⁴⁻⁴ᵛ.
84. For the most important publications on Luther and the Jews, see Reinhold Lewin, *Luthers Stellung zu den Juden* (Berlin, 1911; reprint, 1933); C. Bernd Sucher, *Luthers Stellung zu den Juden: Eine Interpretation aus germanischen Sicht* (Nieukoop, 1977); Walther Bienert, ed., *Martin Luther und die Juden: Ein Quellenbuch mit zeitgenössischen Illustrationen, mit Einführungen und Erläuterungen* (Frankfurt, 1982); and Mark U. Edwards, *Luther's Last Battles: Politics and Polemics, 1531–46* (Ithaca, 1983).

preoccupied with the malevolent forces of magic, particularly Jewish magic. In *On the Ineffable Name, Vom Schem Hamphoras* (1543), a work that attacks the Kabbalah as mere superstition and word magic, Luther exclaims that "a Jew fabricates as much idolatry and magic as the hair on nine cows, that is, countless and infinite."[85] He had believed for some time that Jews were poisoners, influenced no doubt by legends of well poisonings by Jews before the Black Death.[86] Moreover, to Luther, the Jews seemed to have singled him out as their enemy. In a letter to his wife, Katherina, Luther described a journey through Eisleben in 1543:

> I became ill on my way just before reaching Eisleben. It was really my own fault. But if you were there, you would have said that it must have been the fault of the Jews or their God. We had to pass through a village before reaching Eisleben which was inhabited by many Jews. Perhaps they were blowing hard at me [*hart anblasen*] . . . and it was done. When I passed through the village, a cold draft came into the wagon and almost froze my head, I swear.[87]

Needless to add, Luther came down with a severe cold that put him in bed for several days after reaching Eisleben.

For the sixteenth century, piety and health, religion and medicine, were of course related. If Jews used black magic to harm Christians, they also practiced medicine in order to kill Christians, Luther cautions.[88] But it was really the Jews' superstitions (*Aberglaube*) which put them alongside the "papists." For Luther, the "Jewish danger" was the product of a mind which placed true, evangelical faith (*Glaube*) on one side, and all opponents of the reform, real or imaginary, on the other. Thus, in *On the Jews and Their Lies* (1543), Luther attacks Jews, papists, and Turks in one breath:

> And if I had not had experience with my papists,
> it would have been impossible for me to believe,
> that such evil people could exist on earth, who
> knowingly oppose the open, known truth, that
> is, to oppose God himself in his face. I should have
> seen such hardened feelings not in the heart of
> men, but only in the heart of the Devil. But now,
> I do not wonder, neither about the Turks nor the
> Jews, about their blindness, hardness, wickedness,
> because I see them in the most holy fathers of
> the church, in the popes, cardinals, and bishops.[89]

85. *WA* 53, p. 602.
86. *WA Br* 3, p. 821.
87. *WA Br* 11, no. 4195.
88. *WA Tr* 4, no. 4485.
89. *WA* 53, p. 449.

In short, Jews, Catholics, and Turks were all idolaters, blind believers in the false religion of the flesh; their beliefs killed the living spirit of the evangelical faith.

But Jews killed more than the spirit, exclaimed Luther; they actually kidnapped and murdered Christian children. Luther raises the charge of ritual murder many times in *On the Ineffable Name* and *On the Jews and Their Lies*. He repeats over and over again that he has learned from history that Jews had often been burnt for poisoning wells and murdering Christian children for their blood; they had done it at Trent and Weissensee and are still doing it in his day.[90] They are the Devil's children, Luther writes:

> I have read and heard many stories [*Historien*] about
> the Jews. . . . Namely, how they poisoned wells, murdered
> in secret, stole children. . . . For example, how a Jew sent
> another Jew over field a jar of blood, and also by a
> Christian. . . . And for stealing children they have often
> been burnt and chased out, as I have said earlier.
> I know well that they deny all of this. But all of this
> agrees with the judgment of Christ, that they are
> poisonous, bitter, vengeful, deceitful snakes, assassins,
> and the Devil's children, who stab and do harm secretly,
> because they dare not do it in the open.[91]

When Luther wrote this passage in *On the Jews and Their Lies*, he had already worked himself up to a frenzy, being convinced (and trying to convince his reader) that Jews would never convert; but if we take a closer look at his first mention of ritual murder in the text, we see a revealing tension in Luther's language. After attacking the Jews for rejecting Christ as the Messiah and putting all their stock on blood and circumcision, Luther writes: "That is why one often accuses them in the histories that they had poisoned wells, stolen children and killed them with pins. . . . They deny this. That may or may not be [*Es sey oder nicht*], but I know well, that they do not lack the full, whole, and ready will, wherever they could come to do it, in secret or openly."[92]

The ambivalence of this passage may seem insignificant in comparison with the full blast of his vehemence, but it is enough of a reminder that there was still something of the younger Luther left, a Luther who wrote a compassionate pamphlet in 1523 with the title *That Jesus Christ Was a Born Jew*.[93] Hoping for a rapid spread of the evangelical message among Jews, Luther excoriated past Christian persecutions

90. See *WA* 53, pp. 482, 520, 522, 538.
91. *WA* 53, p. 530.
92. *WA* 52, p. 482.
93. *WA* 2, "Dass Jesus Christus ein geborner Jude sei."

born of ignorance and superstitions and even exclaimed that if he were a
Jew he would never have converted. Nothing on ritual murder or blood
magic but plenty on "papist" superstitions can be found in the 1523
work. In his later anti-Jewish writings of 1543, Luther emphasizes the
murderous intent and not the acts of which he had read in histories; if
Jews had murdered Christians, it was out of hatred and revenge, not for
the purpose of magic. When Luther mentions blood superstitions, it is in
the context of Jewish dietary laws, nothing similar to Eck's litany of
beliefs associating ritual murder with circumcision, menstruation, childbirth, and all sorts of magical purposes. In other words, Luther's discourse against Jews does not really speak the language of sympathetic
magic, which expressed itself unconsciously in Eck's treatise on ritual
murder; Luther's theological grammar is quite different. The 1543 anti-
Jewish polemics constituted an antimagical discourse, directed not only
at the Jews but also against Catholic magic and superstitions; while the
vocabulary may in part be magical, the language is that of disenchantment.

To free Christianity from magic and superstitions, both Jews and
Catholics had to be combated. For Luther, the task of the Reformation
was particularly onerous because there was much in medieval Christianity that the Jews considered magical and superstitious. On one hand
Luther was outraged that the Jews would call Jesus a magician;[94] on the
other, he had to defend Christianity against Jewish charges of word
magic: "They [the Jews] may say this: but you Christians do this too,
utter words over water, and it is baptism, which wash away all sins and
render people newborn. Also, with words you turn bread and wine into
body and blood. Also, you put your hands on the head of a sinner and
with words free him from sins."[95] What better defense than a preemptive
strike? After denying that true evangelical Christianity is a religion of
empty, meaningless letters (Buchstaben), Luther goes on to attack Catholic word magic. Whereas the evangelicals understand rites as suffused
by the Holy Spirit, "the pope and his whole church has filled the entire
world with swindle, magic, idolatry, for he has his special Schem Hamphoras [the ineffable name of God] . . . enchants [bezaubert] water with
wanton, mere meaningless letters, says it is holy water which washes
away sins, chases away the devil, and has many virtues." "He also
enchants cowls and tonsures and the whole world with mere words or
letters," Luther continues, "so that they become monks, nuns, and
priests, who say and sell mass, invoke and celebrate saints, peddle
indulgences, worship dead bones, serve the devil, and through their

94. WA 53, p. 513.
95. WA 53, p. 592.

own work deserve heaven, namely the heaven where the devil abbot and pope are in."[96]

For Luther, the essence of magic is in words: witches, Turks, Catholics, and Jews all practice it, "and thus the devil fills the whole world with magic, idolatry, and swindle." The Hebrew Kabbalah becomes the sign of a demonic language of enchantment. When Jews practice magic, it is "to make angels and gods out of letters" and thus to impress foolish Christians with their power.[97]

Jewish folk medicine actually used many Hebrew incantations: benedictions were used to keep away illnesses; Hebrew words written down on scraps of paper or inscribed on objects and blessed by rabbis were worn to ward away misfortune and evil. The making and use of talismans was a central fact of Jewish life and religion; their adoption by Christians represented an act of cultural influence that Luther wanted to stamp out.[98] Hebrew incantatory formulas, often debased in a completely nonsensical form, constituted part of the language of the magical handbooks of the sixteenth century; the works of Cornelius Agrippa von Nettersheim, the best known Christian magus of the Renaissance, are full of them.[99] Agrippa's writings and other magical handbooks circulated widely among princes, magistrates, townsfolk, and clerics. Even Protestant pastors were implicated in this penchant for the occult. Some twenty years after the promulgation of an evangelical church ordinance for Ernestine Saxony, the home province of the Reformation was still permeated with Jewish magic. In 1543 Luther recalled with anger the 1527/28 Visitation of the Saxon Church, which turned up many magical books in the possession of village pastors and churchwardens; these forbidden prints contained the tetragrammaton—the Hebrew word for the ineffable name of God—names of angels and demons, and many prayers and incantations in Hebrew.[100]

The specter of Jewish magic haunted Luther in his new evangelical order and not only in the Catholic church. If the Devil had enchanted the world with his magical language and his magical people, then the mission of true Christianity must be disenchantment. If the essence of Jewish magic, or of magic in general, was in words, then the weapons of true religion must be the unmasking and destruction of this magical language. For the Protestant Reformation it was no longer blood that held the power of magic but the language of the Jews.

96. WA 53, p. 593–94.
97. WA 53, p. 602.
98. On talismans, see Schrire, *Hebrew Amulets*, and Josephy, *Magic and Superstition*.
99. See chap. 1, note 25.
100. WA 53, p. 614.

CHAPTER SEVEN

Christianity Disenchanted

N HIS ANTI-JUDAIC WRITINGS, LUTHER IDENTIFIED THE essence of Jewish magic as the use of the Hebrew language as a system of magical signs. The belief in the power of blood, so crucial in ritual murder and Host desecration discourses, was undermined by the theological revolution of the Reformation. When miracles, pilgrimages, Marian devotion, and the veneration of saints became points of ridicule, manifestations of old superstitions, and fabrications of an unscrupulous Roman clergy, as the Protestants charged; when the eucharistic doctrine of transubstantiation was challenged by the symbolic interpretations of the sacrament, as Karlstadt, Zwingli, Müntzer, and others reasoned; when salvation depended on God's grace rather than on human sacrifice, as Luther himself taught; when all forms of magic were attacked, by Protestants as well as by Catholics, the psychological and intellectual foundations of ritual murder discourse also began to disintegrate among the clerical and magisterial elites, although the *popular* discourse on ritual murder was to persist well into the Enlightenment.

ANDREAS OSIANDER: DECONSTRUCTING RITUAL MURDER

The first attempt by a Christian to systematically refute the veracity of ritual murder discourse also brought on a vehement defense by Johann Eck, as we have seen. The anonymously published booklet against which Eck poured out his outraged rhetoric came from the pen of Andreas Osiander, the most prominent evangelical reformer in Nuremberg.[1] Os-

---

1. The anonymously published treatise, *Ob es war vnd glaublich sey/dass die Juden der Christen Kinder heymlich erwürgen/vnd jr blut gebrauchen/ein treffenliche Schrifft/auff eines yeden vrteyl gestelt* was republished by Moritz Stern as *Andreas Osianders Schrift über die Blutbeschuldigung* (Kiel, 1893, reprint, Berlin, 1903). See also chap. 6. For a recent discussion of Osiander's theology and attitude toward Jews, see Gerhard Philipp Wolf, "Osiander und

iander composed his booklet as a response to an inquiry by an unnamed nobleman about the credibility of ritual murder charges, specifically the 1529 Poesing ritual murder trial in Hungary. Osiander's long letter to the nobleman remained at first only in manuscript. In 1540, in the village of Sappenfeld, not far from Weissenburg, a ritual murder trial resulted in the arrests and executions of Jews in the diocese of Eichstätt by its bishop, Moritz von Hutten. A supporting argument against the Jews cited the 1529 Poesing trial, in which the Jews allegedly used the blood of a Christian child to anoint their "priest"; thirty Hungarian Jews were burnt.[2] To exorcize the ghost of Poesing, two Jews from Sulzbach published Osiander's manuscript in defense of their accused brethren in the 1540 Sappenfeld case.[3]

Divided into three parts, Osiander's treatise first refutes general arguments supporting the blood libel; it then examines the particulars of the Poesing trial and ends by suggesting alternative explanations for cases of missing and dead children. In his opening statements, Osiander justifies his booklet with an appeal to conscience: ritual murder trials are about justice and violence, and all Christians must examine their conscience as to whether they are doing Jews an injustice through their uncritical credulity. One stands before a choice of right or wrong, as Osiander cautions: "Either the Jews are slaughtering Christian children most cruelly, or the Christians are slaughtering innocent Jews most shamefully, which a Christian not only should not do, but if he sees others doing it, he must not keep silent or agree to it."[4] No baptized Jew has ever brought forth ritual murder charges against his former coreligionists. And for himself, Osiander explains:

> I have not been able to find, to think of, or to hear of anything which could have moved me to believe such suspicion and accusation. Rather, I have found, on the contrary, so many circumstances and reasons which I hold to be completely true and certain (but without injury to anyone) that injustice has been done to the Jews in this matter. However, I would excuse the authorities because it is possible that they were misled into believing nothing else but that the Jews were guilty when such suspicions befell the Jews and they confessed to them due to their faintheartedness and heavy torture.[5]

---

die Juden im Kontext seiner Theologie," *Zeitschrift für bayerische Kirchengeschichte* 53 (1984), pp. 49–77; for a short summary of the anti-ritual murder treatise, see pp. 59–64.

    2. Count Wolf von Poesing, who owed the Jew Esslein Ausch a large sum of money, apparently instigated a ritual murder charge against the Jews of Poesing, a town near Pressburg. Later, the allegedly murdered boy was found in Venice. See Stern, *Josel of Rosheim*, pp. 80–81.

    3. Stern, *Josel of Rosheim*, pp. 180–82.

    4. Osiander, pp. 5–6. The paginations refer to the edition by Moritz Stern.

    5. Osiander, pp. 6–7.

To prove that such "voluntary" confessions have nothing to do with the truth, Osiander lists twenty reasons demonstrating that ritual murder discourse is based not on reality but on fabrication:[6]

1. Mosaic Law—that is, divine commandment—forbids the shedding of innocent blood; the injunction against the spilling of innocent blood is repeated over and over in the Old Testament.

2. The dietary laws of the Jews, which they observe even to this day, forbid the drinking of blood and the eating of unclean flesh.

3. Not only do the laws of the Jews forbide the spilling of blood, "it is also implanted in the hearts of all people, due to the nature of man, that the spilling of blood is unjust."[7]

4. Even animals spare the lives of innocent children, as the wolves nurtured Romulus and Remus instead of devouring them. In war, women and children are spared. How can anyone suspect the Jews of such unnatural and cruel crimes when one does not even hear of them committing murders?

5. The Jews believe in eternal life and would certainly shy away from infanticide in order to gain salvation.

6. There is no reason to believe that Jews bear hatred against Gentiles without cause. Even during their exile in Egypt and Babylon, Moses and Daniel urged the people to obey the authorities, so there is much more reason to believe that Jews are friendly to Christians in this "milder exile."

7. No people on earth are more meek and frightened than the Jews. How can anyone believe that the Jews, who feel uncertain about their own lives from hour to hour, would murder children?

8. Some say that Jews are driven to murder because they need the blood of children. Thus, during the Poesing trial, the Jews were accused of using the blood of a Christian child to annoint their priests. This is patently a lie. Since the destruction of Jerusalem and their diaspora, the Jews have only rabbis, who are teachers and judges, and no longer anoint priests. Others claim that Jews need Christian blood to stop their own hemorrhaging; this is also a lie. How can the Jews hide their bleeding, especially when some of them have been imprisoned for years? Still others suggest that Jews need Christian blood to heal diseases inflicted upon them by God. "But I say this is in many ways contrary to God's Word, against nature and human reason because if God were to punish them with

6. Osiander, pp. 7–31.

7. "Zum dritten/so ist das gepot nicht allein den Juden in schrifften geben/sonder es ist auch von natur allen menschen in das hertz eingepflanzet/das blut vergiessen vnrecht vnd verpoten ist" (Osiander, pp. 9–10).

a special disease, no human could heal it." If some people think that a child's blood is so salutary, why doesn't one hear of Turkish children being murdered by Jews?

9. Even if the blood of children were salutary, the Jews could very well have obtained it without murder. Whoever is ready to believe such devilish fantasy (*teuffelisch gespenst*) is also against God's Word, Nature, and Reason.

10. There are many Jews in lands without Christians. How then do they remain healthy? How then do they practice their religion without Christian blood?

11. It is equally unreasonable to believe that Jews know their own religion to be wicked and seek Christian blood merely to prove the evil of their faith and the goodness of Christianity. It makes no sense that they should murder only in order to discover Christian truth and then convert.

12. Baptized Jews and Jews shunned by their brethren do not report ritual murders even though they have every reason to hate their fellow Jews. Pfefferkorn and the friars in Cologne would have raised this charge of ritual murder if it had any grounding in reality. Doctor Paul Ricius, who has converted from Judaism to evangelical Christianity, denies that Jews have ever practiced ritual murders.

13. The accusation of ritual murder first appeared two or three hundred years ago, "when monks and priests instituted all sorts of roguery and deceit, with pilgrimages and other false miracles, when they openly fooled and deceived Christians." Precisely because the Jews knew the Scriptures better than they did, the monks and priests singled them out as objects of hatred and persecution. But God would not allow the Jews to be exterminated "for the good of Christianity," and through the Hebrew language Christians have once again come to a correct understanding of their faith. These "Jewhaters" are equally capable of inventing lies against Christians, whom they call Lutherans.

14. In the early history of the church, pagans accused Christians of child murders.

15. The confessions of the Jews are often contradictory and have nothing to do with the truth because they have always been obtained under heavy torture. "I have often asked the Jews why they are so desperate and confess to something which threaten their lives and bring their people into such dangerous suspicions. They answered me thus: when a Jew is being tortured, it doesn't matter whether he speaks the truth or not because his tormentors would not stop until they have heard what they want to hear. It is enough for us [Jews] that God will punish our tormentors and that every reasonable man may judge for himself whether such confessions are

lies or truths. . . . Many years ago [1476], the Jews of Regensburg were tortured into confessing to a ritual murder, however, the Emperor intervened to save them. But now, the Jews of Poesing are executed for similar lies. How can we find it mysterious that the Jews confess, when they are put under torture? But nowadays, many pious Christian princes and authorities do not have credence in such lies . . . especially the authorities of Nuremberg, so I hear, who, for a long time and still today, do not build a case out of nothing unless they have proof."

16. Some say this whole thing is the result of God's anger with the Jews. But why would God punish the Jews in such a way as to drive them further away from him and commit more murders?

17. Some say this is God's scourge for us Christians, that he sends the Jews to take away what is most precious to us on earth—namely, our children, especially our boys. "But I ask you, if one believes in a merciful and righteous father in heaven, how can one think that God has singled out his own people, us Christians, for such cruel punishments?"

18. As Saint Paul in his Roman Epistles (chapters 9–11) reminds us, Christians and Jews are brothers, and one day Jews will be joined to us in one flock under the true shepherd.

19. It should suffice for every Christian that none other than a pope and an emperor have condemned the blood libel and the persecution of Jews.[8]

20. In the Talmud, money is often referred to as blood, both being essential to life. Perhaps some semilearned man, either Jew or Christian, overheard the rabbis referring to this word and misunderstood it to mean that Jews need blood. Somehow, perhaps, the rumor was started and it spread until some evil men used it for their own wicked ends.

In the next section of his treatise, Osiander sets out to discredit the accusation against the Poesing Jews by examining the circumstances of the alleged ritual murder. Osiander's most devastating charge is that the instigator of the prosecution, the count of Poesing, was a tyrant: he had unjustly imprisoned a merchant and took the poor man's wife as his mistress; it is also well known that he owed the Jews an enormous sum of money. Osiander refrains from accusing the count of staging a show trial, but he concludes with the perhaps more damaging observation that "what we want to see and desire, we also believe willingly."[9]

8. Here, Osiander publishes the full text of Emperor Friedrich III's condemnation of Margrave Karl of Baden for his part in the 1470 Endingen ritual murder trial.
9. Osiander, p. 32.

The judicial procedures, Osiander goes on to charge, appeared highly irregular. On the same day the Jews were arrested, the count went searching for witnesses and confiscated the possessions of the Jews. Put under torture, the Jews steadfastly maintained their innocence. Moreover, the corpus delicti never turned up, the testimonies of witnesses were unreliable, and the manner in which the eight-year-old boy was allegedly murdered made no medical sense. The author of these fabrications was really the Devil, "the Father of lies," as Osiander calls him. The interrogations, confessions, and convictions all took place within eight short days; the indiscriminate executions of Jews immediately followed the hasty trial: altogether, twelve Jews were arrested, six confessed, but thirty died at the stake, including women and children. These cruel burnings, Osiander exclaims, were "contrary to Divine, Natural, and Imperial Law";[10] such injustice brings great shame to Christianity among Turks and unbelievers.[11]

In the final section, Osiander addressed himself to the logical question. If he does not believe in the guilt of the Jews, who then is responsible? He writes:

> On account of my simplicity and ignorance, I cannot really suspect anyone, but would rather excuse everyone, particularly the authorities [die Obrigkeit]. For I am of the opinion that they cannot be held accountable in this matter, except for believing too lightly the enemies of the Jews and for putting too much trust in false counsel, which of course they themselves did not know as such. I will, nonetheless, offer some indications by which one can find the suspects.[12]

Osiander then lists seven indications to discover the truth behind these allegations of ritual murder:[13]

1. One should pay close attention to whether the lord is "a miserable, ambitious tyrant" who is addicted to drinking, gambling, and whoring or whether he is an inopportune warrior.

2. If the lord happens to be a pious and God-fearing man, one should see whether his councillors, officials, courtiers, judges, and bailiffs are wicked.

3. One must question "whether priests or monks do not long to whip up great miracles and institute new pilgrimages in order to gain the appearance of greater sanctity, or whether they are wont to exterminate the Jews."

10. Osiander, p. 39.
11. Osiander, pp. 40–41.
12. Osiander, pp. 41–42.
13. Osiander, pp. 42–44.

4. One should find out whether the subjects are heavily indebted to the Jews and would thus save their household and honor if the Jews are ruined.

5. One must investigate whether magicians, soothsayers, conjurers of demons, treasure hunters, or other sorts of indecent people who commerce with evil spirits are not in the same place, who may hope to murder children for their magic and have the Jews take the blame for it.

6. Perhaps some children are killed in accidents: for example, they could have been run over by a wagon, and the driver, afraid to report the death, disguised it as a ritual murder.

7. Perhaps some negligent parents are responsible: the children could have fallen on knives or were drowned, and in fear of possible punishment and shame, the parents blame it on the Jews.

In closing, Osiander adds that the wealth of Jews further make them a tempting target, citing a Jewish proverb, "A rich Jew and a poor nobleman are not good together," to prove his point. If the cause of death cannot be found among the seven reasons listed above, Osiander concedes he would perhaps have reason to believe in the guilt of the Jews, which until now he firmly denies.

Written with passion and wit and flawlessly argued, Osiander's treatise is a brilliant tour de force. The truth behind ritual murder accusations, according to him, was revealed by human reason, endowed by Nature with an innate sense of justice. This "Natural Reason" was further aided by the knowledge of God, made accessible to the pious through his Word, the Scriptures, and by adherence to human, positive laws.[14] Thus, nowhere in the Old or New Testaments, or in canon and roman law, can one find reason to suspect Jews of ritual murders. On the contrary, both imperial and papal decrees (here, Osiander was referring to the condemnations of ritual murder trials by Emperors Friedrich II and Friedrich III and by Pope Innocent IV) explicitly forbade ritual murder trials. To accuse, imprison, torture, and execute Jews on unproven crimes, on charges that stood against "God's Word, Nature, and Human Reason," was to do the work of the Devil, "the Father of Lies." The true

14. On the history of Natural Law, see Otto Gierke, *Natural Law and the Theory of Society, 1500 to 1800*, trans. Ernest Baker, 2 vols. (Cambridge, 1934). This translation is based on parts of Gierke's multivolume work, *Das Deutsche Genossenschaftsrecht* (1868–). Gierke's analysis focuses heavily on constitutional theories; for an essay arguing from the perspective of theology, see Brian Tierney, *Religion, Law, and the Growth of Constitutional Thought, 1150–1650* (Cambridge, 1982). For a brief description of the Greek and Roman roots of the idea of Natural Law, see Helmut Coing, "Naturrecht als wissenschaftliches Problem," in his *Gesammelte Aufsätze zu Rechtsgeschichte, Rechtsphilosophie und Zivilrecht, 1947–1975*, vol. 2 (Frankfurt, 1982), pp. 23–49; here, pp. 23–26.

culprit, Osiander pointed out, was the fabrication of evil men, which found credence with the superstitious masses and the vainglorious and greedy Roman clergy.

Turning the ritual murder discourse inside out, Osiander instead condemned Christians of murder and magic, a charge that infuriated Johann Eck. Other reformers, notably Wolfgang Capito of Strasbourg,[15] shared Osiander's sympathy for the Jews, but philo-Semitism was by no means a general phenomenon among German Protestants.[16] Quite the opposite. Martin Bucer, colleague of Capito, reformer, and superintendent of the Protestant church in Strasbourg, clamored in his letter to Philip of Hesse for the expulsion of Jews from evangelical Christian communities.[17] Nevertheless, the theological thinking implicit in Osiander's defense of the Jews fundamentally undermined the structure of ritual murder discourse. The faith in a "true religion" and the exposition of "the magic and superstitions" of the Roman church were intellectual commonplaces of all reformers—including the implacable foes of Jews, who would continue to raise accusations of usury, blasphemy, and greed against Jews—but the charges of magic and murder would gradually fade into a faint echo.

THE DISENCHANTMENT OF MAGIC

In this "rite" of disenchantment, by which the reformers exorcised the magical and superstitious demons of the Roman church from the reconstituted Body Religious of evangelical Christians, the spell of ritual murder was also broken. Three components were essential to this historical ritual of purification:[18] the exposition of popular magic, the demystification of Hebrew and Jewish rituals, and a new concern with the family in Protestant theology.

15. For Capito's Hebraic studies, see James M. Kittelson, *Wolfgang Capito: From Humanist to Reformer* (Leiden, 1975), pp. 21–22. See also Capito's letter to Luther on behalf of Josel of Rosheim, *WA* 8, no. 3152.

16. See Klaus Deppermann, "Judenhass und Judenfreundschaft im frühen Protestantismus," in Bernd Martin and Ernst Schulin, eds., *Die Juden als Minderheit in der Geschichte* (Munich, 1981), pp. 110–30.

17. Martin Bucer, *Von den Juden ob/vnd wie die vnder den Christen zu halten sind/ein Rathschlag/durch die Gelerten am Ende dis Büchlins verzeichnet/zugericht. Item Ein weitere Erklerung vnd Beschirmung des selbigen Rahtschlags* [Strasbourg, 1539]. A 1539 Erfurt edition appeared under the title: *Ratschlag ob Christlicher Obrigkeit gebüren müge/das sie die Juden/unter den Christen zu wonen gedulen/welcher gestalt und mass.* Bucer's advice was rejected by Philip of Hesse.

18. For a persuasive argument that supporters of the Reformation saw their attack of the Catholic church as rites of purification, see Robert W. Scribner, "Reformation and Ritual," in Hsia, ed., *The German People and the Reformation*.

Among the "true grounds" behind ritual murder trials, Osiander lists two having to do with magic: the greed of the Roman clergy to invent miracles, and the practice of black magic by sorcerers, witches, diviners, and other "indecent people." What he condemned was that vast gray area between the official rituals and doctrines of the Catholic church and the ways in which these were understood, appropriated, and creatively adopted in popular religion.[19] In spite of repeated denunciations by the reformers and by the vigorous catechismic efforts of the Lutheran clergy, popular religion, with its magical and material views of the cosmos, persisted well past the Reformation century.[20]

In the second half of the sixteenth century, the physician Johann Weyer (1515–88), famous for his criticism of witchhunts, compiled a vast catalog of popular beliefs in demons, devils, and witches and of practices in the magical arts.[21] His purpose in collecting these anecdotes and episodes of popular magic was not to formulate a theory of witchcraft but rather to expose these practices and beliefs for what they really were— namely, the "superstitions" and delusions of the common people. There were no real witches, only deluded, melancholic women, Weyer writes:

> And on these other points [of witchcraft], which will be refuted later, I will, for now, hold my peace, but it is a coarse and shameless lie, sheer devilish insinuation, and a roguish superstition, [to believe] that young children are sometimes killed in ceremonies. Also, [to believe] that they [the witches] secretly dig [the children] out of their graves is nothing but the false delusion of the Devil, which has its source in the imagination, which in [these women] has gone wild or has sunken into a deep sleep.[22]

This passage referred to the belief that witches murdered small children or stole their corpses in order to use their bodies and bones as ingredients for magical potions. Substitute "Jews" for "witches," exchange "blood" for "bodies and bones," and one has, in essence, the notions underlying beliefs in ritual murders.

19. See Robert W. Scribner, "Ritual and Popular Religion in Catholic Germany at the Time of the Reformation," *Journal of Ecclesiastical History* 35 (1984), pp. 47–77.

20. On the persistence of magic in the villages of Protestant Germany, see Gerald Strauss, *Luther's House of Learning: Indoctrination of the Young in the German Reformation* (Baltimore, 1978), pp. 303–5; see also his "The Reformation and Its Public in an Age of Orthodoxy," in Hsia, ed., *The German People and the Reformation*.

21. See Johann Weyer, *De praestigiis daemonum. Von Teuffelsgespenst, Zauberern und Gifftbereytern, Schwarzkünstlern, Hexen und Unholden, darzu ihrer Straff, auch von den Bezauberten vnnd wie ihnen zu helfen sey* (Frankfurt: Nicolaus Basseum, 1586). Two other works, *De Lamiis. Von Teuffelsgespenst, Zaubern und Gifftbereytern . . .* and *Theatrum de Veneficis. Von Teuffelsgespenst, Zauberen, Gifftbereyten und Unholden Schwarzkünstlern . . .* , were also published in 1586 in Frankfurt.

There existed, in fact, numerous popular beliefs about the salutary powers of blood. Weyer cites the following examples: to stop bleeding, add three drops of blood to a cup of cold water, recite "Our Father" and "Hail Mary" between each dropping, and when asking the patient who the helper is, the patient is to answer, "the Virgin Mary"; use human blood to write the words "consummatum est" on the forehead of the bleeding patient to stop the blood flow; or recite the following incantation:

> Blood, stay in yourself, just as Christ in himself.
> Blood, stay in your veins, just as Christ in his pain.
> Blood, stay fixed, just as Christ was to his crucifix.[23]

In addition to the salutary power of human blood, whose efficacy ultimately reflected the forces of a sympathetic substance—the higher potency of the blood of Christ—the Eucharist, Christ's body, was also applied as a magical medicament in popular religion. A particularly rigorous medical regimen specified that, to cure a sickness, the patient should swallow three consecrated Hosts. On the first one, the following words were to be written: "As the Father is, so is life"; on the second, "As the Son is, so is the Sacred"; and on the third, "As the Holy Ghost is, so is medicine." The three Hosts were to be given to the sick on three consecutive evenings; the patients meanwhile prepared themselves by fasting and prayers—fifteen "Our Fathers" and fifteen "Hail Marys" every evening.[24]

Weyer cited these examples as evidence of the "scandalous abuses of holy Scripture and of the precious Name of God for magical cures of the sick." They belonged to the widespread practice of folk medicine and popular magic in the Rhineland, which proved highly resilient to suppression by ecclesiastical authorities.[25] Besides the Eucharist, many other consecrated ecclesiastical objects doubled as devices in magical operations, items such as holy salt and water, candles, cassocks, and so on.[26] In addition, blood magic enjoyed a long history in folk medicine, and this particular technique was applied with numerous incantation formulas to heal diseases.[27] Used for prophylactic and medical purposes, the magical

22. Weyer, De praestigiis daemonum, bk. 3, chap. 4, p. 152.

23. Weyer, De praestigiis daemonum, bk. 5, chap. 4, pp. 311f. The Latin incantation reads: Sanguis mane in te, sicut fecit Christus in se.

Sanguis mane in tua vena, sicut Christus in sua poena.

Sanguis mane fixus, sicut Christus quando fuit crucifixus.

24. Weyer, De praestigiis daemonum, bk. 3, chap. 4, pp. 311f.

25. See Rudolf van Nahl, Zauberglaube und Hexenwahn im Gebiet von Rhein und Maas: Spätmittelalterlicher Volksglaube im Werk Johann Weyers (1515–1588) (Bonn, 1983).

26. Nahl, Zauberglaube, p. 127.

27. On blood magic and the use of magical incantations to stop bleeding in Germanic

application of blood in folk medicine was in itself something purely instrumental; it represented a technique, differing in category but not in function from the many para-ecclesiastical rituals that grew around the sacraments of the medieval church. While these beliefs and practices in folk medicine formed the soil on which luxuriant magical notions were projected onto Jews and their rituals, it was a neutral environment— receptive of diverse cultures, including elements from Jewish folk medi- cine, such as the use of talismans—and did not, by itself, sustain accusa- tions of ritual murders and Host desecrations. External agents were needed to nurture the growth in blood libel.

Until the 1530s and 1540s, both the theological discourse on Jews and Judaism and the legal system helped to create an intellectual and political climate that encouraged the discourse on ritual murder. But the changes in midcentury, to be discussed later in this chapter, were crucial in dismantling the practice and discourse of ritual murder accusations. Before moving on, one last observation about Weyer is in order: in his catalog of popular magic and in his exposition of fraud and superstitions, nowhere did he mention Jews; not one word about ritual murders or Jewish Host desecrations appears in his writings. This silence points to the great changes in learned discourse of the two generations before the publication of De praestigiis daemonum: women in particular, not Jews, were now identified as potential witches, demon conjurers, and mur- derers, accused of kidnapping and murdering children in rituals of witchcraft, denounced as consorts of the Devil and practitioners of blood magic. It was in defense of these poor women that Weyer took up the pen, arguing against the vast array of legal and theological authorities who demanded "justice" and suppression.[28]

In this Protestant campaign of "true religion" against "magic and superstition," the sacraments of the Catholic church were primary tar- gets. The second generation of reformers began to collect stories of late medieval legends in order to hold Catholic sacraments and rituals up for ridicule; one of the best known collections, One Hundred Selected Papist Lies (Hundert auserwählte papistische Lügen), was compiled by Hieronymus

folklore, see Nahl, Zauberglaube, pp. 134f., 138. For examples of such incantations, see Irmgard Hampp, Beschwörung-Segen-Gebet: Untersuchungen zum Zauberspruch aus dem Bereich der Volksheilkunde (Stuttgart, 1961), pp. 31ff., 40–47, and Arthur F. Hälsig, Der Zauberspruch bei den Germanen bis um die Mitte des XVI. Jahrhunderts (Leipzig, 1910), pp. 39–40.

28. Cf. H.-C. Erik Midelfort, Witchhunting in Southwestern Germany, 1562–1684: The Social and Intellectual Foundations (Stanford, 1972), pp. 25–26. This analysis is taken up in fuller detail in Midelfort's "Johann Weyer and the Transformation of the Insanity Defense," in Hsia, ed., The German People and the Reformation. The debate over whether the witchhunts were directed specifically against women cannot be answered here. It is sufficient to note that the majority of victims were women.

Rauscher (1515–64/65).[29] A native of Nuremberg, Rauscher studied at the University of Wittenberg from 1534 to 1539 before returning to his native city to serve as deacon under Andreas Osiander. In 1552 he became preacher in Neumark; in 1554 Count Wolfgang von Zweibrücken appointed him court preacher in Amberg, a post he held until his death. *The Hundred Selected Papist Lies*, first printed in 1562, offered Protestant readers, as its title indicated, one hundred Catholic legends as examples of the superstitions of the Roman church. Central to this "unmasking" was the ridicule of Catholic legends about the power of the Mass and the Eucharist. Miraculous legends testifying to the power of the Eucharist were transformed, in Rauscher's confessional polemic, into superstitious tales of "papist" magic: thus, stories about the transformation of the Eucharist into the Child Jesus, the consecrated Host that bleeds, and the apparitions of Christ were but "papist lies." The practitioners of these deceptions were none other than the Roman clergy, as one might expect from the pen of a Lutheran pastor, and the credulous, superstitious folk who appeared frequently in these selected legends were often women and Jews. Rauscher recounted many tales: a priest placed a boy on the *corporale* and he turned into bread; a monk felt that he was eating the Child Jesus when taking communion; the Child Jesus refused to be eaten by a sinful priest; a Jew in Cologne stole the Eucharist but was caught by virtue of Christ's apparition; some witches stole the Eucharist but it became a living child. Or take the story of the woman of Prussia: skeptical of the doctrine of real presence, she stole the Eucharist to feed her swines, but instead of chewing the Host the animals bent their knees in worship; when she then roasted the Host over a fire, it began to bleed; finally she buried it underground, but the blood streamed through the earth like a well, thus moving her to confess her sins.[30]

Rauscher's compilation enjoyed enormous success. After the publication of the original work in 1562, another four editions of further "hundred papist lies" were compiled and printed.[31] Although two generations of Protestant confessional polemics against the Catholic church could not eradicate the long tradition of Christian anti-Judaism—indeed, stories of Jewish magic persisted in Protestant Germany, as I will show in the last two chapters—the Lutheran Reformation succeeded in altering the terms of the anti-Judaic and anti-Semitic discourse. By undermining the sacramental and magical foundations of late medieval Christianity on which ritual murder trials were based, the Lutheran pastors concentrated their attack instead on Jewish injury to the Christian moral economy. The

29. See Schenda, "Hieronymus Rauscher," pp. 179–259.
30. Schenda, "Hieronymus Rauscher," pp. 230–34.
31. For a listing of the different editions, see Schenda, "Hieronymous Rauscher."

image of the Jewish moneylender eventually replaced that of the Jewish magician.

FROM MAGICAL SIGNS TO SACRED LANGUAGE

Without a system of signs, magic cannot function, and a magical language, in Marcel Mauss's analysis, consists of signs understood by only a small circle of practitioners. Once a magical language is dissected and studied, it loses its force of enchantment.[32] The study of Hebrew by Protestants in the sixteenth century represented precisely such a process of disenchantment. What began as an attempt to recover the heritage of the Old Testament for Christianity resulted in a new Christian knowledge of Jewish rites and writings; no longer feared as a system of mysterious, magical signs, as it was sometimes crudely applied in popular magic, Hebrew came to be treasured as a divine language in the service of the Reformation. In the "disenchantment" of Hebrew and Jewish rites, converts to Christianity in the early sixteenth century played an important role in introducing to Christians, albeit in a polemical and biased manner, the basic tenets of Judaism and knowledge of its rites.

Perhaps the most influential introduction of Judaism to the early Lutheran church was the book *The Entire Jewish Faith*, written by the convert Anthonius Margaritha.[33] Son of Rabbi Jacob Margolis of Regensburg, whom Johann Reuchlin consulted concerning the Kabbalah,[34] Margaritha grew up in the Jewish quarter of Regensburg, a community not only threatened by the unrelenting hostility of the magistrates and Christian citizens after the unsuccessful ritual murder trial of 1476–80 but also torn apart by internal strife as different Jewish families jostled for positions of power and leadership. Margaritha himself was to recall with particular poignancy an acrimonious conflict between the newcomer Mosse and the established leading families of the community.[35] In 1521 Margaritha converted in Wasserburg; he made his living among Chris-

---

32. On the theoretical formulation of the properties of magical languages, see Mauss, *Magic*, pp. 57–58, 60–62, 86–87.

33. The first edition was printed in 1530 in Augsburg; the copy I used is a 1531 Augsburg edition, *Der Gantz Judisch Glaub mit sampt eyner grundtlichtenn und warhasstigen anzeygunge, aller satzungen, Ceremonien, gebetten, heymliche und offentliche gebreuch, deren sich die Juden halten, durch das gantz Jar, mit schonen unnd gegrundten Argumenten wider iren glauben, durch Anthonium Margaritham/Hebreyschen Leser/der löblichen Vniversitet und fürstlichen Stat Leyptzigk/beschryben und an tag gegeben* [Augsburg: Heinrich Steiner?], 1531. For an evaluation of this work and a biography of Margaritha, see Josef Mieses, *Die älteste gedruckte deutsche Übersetzung des jüdischen Gebetbuchs aus dem Jahre 1530 und ihr Autor Antonius Margaritha* (Vienna, 1916).

34. Straus, *Regensburg and Augsburg*, pp. 68–69.

35. See Margaritha, *Der Gantz Judisch Glaub*, L³ᵛ⁻⁴ᵛ. Margaritha was a boy of 13 then.

tians by teaching Hebrew, first in Augsburg, and later in Leipzig and Vienna.[36]

The intention of composing *The Entire Jewish Faith*, as Margaritha informed his readers, was to depict the ceremonies, prayers, and customs of the Jews based on their own books; he wanted to "expose" the "false beliefs" of the Jews and to show how they curse the Holy Roman Empire and Christians in their liturgy. Margaritha's ultimate goal was the conversion of his fellow brethren to the new faith, which he himself had accepted.[37] The main body of the book consists of a German translation of the liturgy and prayers used by the Jewish communities in the Holy Roman Empire, spiced with extensive commentaries on the history and meanings of Jewish feasts, ceremonies, and customs, lengthy diatribes against usury and rabbinic authority, and a cornucopia of anecdotes and descriptions of contemporary Jewish communal life. For the first time, Christians could read in German the liturgy and prayers of Jews; find out in detail the observance of the Sabbath, the Passover, Yom Kippur, the performance of circumcision, Jewish dietary laws, the social structure of Jewish communities, Jewish folk medicine, and the essence of the Kabbalah and the Talmud (from Margaritha's perspective, naturally); and learn how Jews behaved toward one another, what they thought of Christians, what they ate, how they dressed, bathed, and cured themselves, and how they prepared for death.

The book represented, to Germans of the early sixteenth century, a sort of encyclopedia of Judaism. Although it has been observed that Margaritha's translation is not without grammatical errors and inaccuracies and that the fervor of the convert is abundantly manifest in his anti-Judaic rhetoric,[38] *The Entire Jewish Faith* had a significance that far surpassed the works of earlier Jewish converts: it is completely silent on the blood libel. Drawing on his own childhood and adolescent experiences, Margaritha ridicules the "superstitions" of the Jews; their folkways, medicine, and beliefs blind them to faith in Christ, which Margaritha has come to endorse. But an obstinate nation does not make a murderous people. To be sure, Margaritha admits that Jews, like all other peoples, have murderers, adulterers, and other common criminals among them, but the greatest crime committed by Jews was the hatred they bore one another and their willingness to betray one another to Christian authorities.[39] The work mentions magic only in reference to the

36. Margaritha, *Der Gantz Judisch Glaub*, Dd⁴ʳ; Stern, *Josel of Rosheim*, p. 103.

37. Margaritha, *Der Gantz Judisch Glaub*, A¹ᵛ⁻²ʳ.

38. On criticisms of Margaritha's translation, see Stern, *Josel of Rosheim*, pp. 97–100. On Margaritha's Christian polemic, see *Der Gantz Judisch Glaub*, esp. Dd³ʳ–Dd⁴ʳ.

39. Margaritha, *Der Gantz Judisch Glaub*, L²ᵛ⁻³ʳ.

Kabbalah; Margaritha dismisses this as the magic of the Jews, a superstition that does them no good, for "there is no people on earth who gets run over, robbed, and killed more often on the open roads than Jews."[40] Not a word on blood magic. Nothing on ritual murders or Host desecrations. This silence, coupled with the seemingly factual descriptions of Jewish rites by an avowed partisan of Christianity who had had personal experiences with Judaism, must have made a deep impression on Christian readers of *The Entire Jewish Faith*: once the magical mysteries surrounding circumcision and the Passover were dispelled, any notion of ritual murder would be difficult to sustain. Many passages in Margaritha's work indicate that he was deeply concerned by the crisis that threatened the Jewish communities of the Holy Roman Empire; his solution sounded similar to Pfefferkorn's before him—namely, social, cultural, and religious assimilation. In Margaritha's heart, a chance to silence forever the chorus of cries of ritual murders and Host desecrations and to listen to the message of hope and redemption in the evangelical movement must have seemed encouragement enough for conversion.

Growing up in the generation before the Reformation, Margaritha, like some Jews and many Christians, must have experienced a profound crisis of faith. In the early years of the evangelical movement, when the reformers were attacking the magic and rituals of the Roman church, condemning the persecutions of Jews, and advocating the study of Hebrew and the Old Testament, many Jews interpreted the schism in Christianity as the sign of their own imminent messianic deliverance.[41] Luther's *Table Talks* tells the story of a visit by three rabbis in 1540; they wanted to understand why Protestants were studying Hebrew. Rabbi Samaria told Luther that the Jews rejoiced that Christians were studying their language and reading their books. But his hope that Christians would convert to Judaism met with an angry retort by Luther.[42] In any event, there was a profound sense that pogroms against Jews, based on accusations of Jewish magic, had been swept away by the reformers' attack of medieval Christian magic.

As expected, Margaritha's book caused a great stir in the Jewish communities. By asserting that his erstwhile brethren were praying for the destruction of the Holy Roman Empire, Margaritha lent support to men like Konrad Peutinger, the Augsburg patrician who accused Jews of

40. Margaritha, *Der Gantz Judisch Glaub*, Y⁴ᵛ.
41. Stern, *Josel of Rosheim*, p. 96; for a discussion of the interpretation of the Reformation in Jewish historiography, see Mordechai Breuer, "Modernism and Traditionalism in Sixteenth-Century Jewish Historiography: A Study of David Gans' Tzemah David," in *Jewish Thought in the Sixteenth Century*, ed. Bernard Cooperman (Cambridge, Mass., 1983), pp. 49–88; here, pp. 72–76.
42. *WA Tr*, no. 5026.

treasonous communication with the Ottomans, who were then driving the imperial forces back on the Hungarian Plain.[43] After the publication of *The Entire Jewish Faith*, many rabbis gathered under the leadership of Chief Rabbi Samuel of Worms to plan strategies for countering Margaritha's arguments.[44] In Augsburg, where the Imperial Diet convened in 1530, Josel of Rosheim successfully defended Jews against Margaritha before Charles V.[45] After his expulsion from the imperial city, Margaritha went to Leipzig, where he taught Hebrew and met Luther.

The Entire Jewish Faith exerted a profound influence on the evaluation of Jews by the new Lutheran church: Luther read it, praised it, recommended it, and was confirmed in his belief that both Jews and Catholics were superstitious and relied foolishly on good works for their salvation.[46] After the first Augsburg edition of 1530, Margaritha's book went through at least five more printings: 1531 in Augsburg, a 1544 Frankfurt edition in quarto, a 1561 Frankfurt edition in octavo, a 1689 Frankfurt edition in octavo, and a 1713 reprint in Leipzig.[47] The significance of Margaritha's book (and of the changes in the Reformation) was not in winning toleration for Judaism—that was never the author's intention—but in shifting the focus of Protestant anti-Judaism away from the late medieval obsession with Jewish magic and sacrifice to new forms of intolerance, which, however repressive, did not match the full fury of the ritual murder discourse they replaced.

DISCOURSES ON CHILD MURDERS

Roughly contemporaneous with the first criticism of ritual murder discourse, stories of real child murders began to appear in print. These chapbooks depicting gruesome murders for popular entertainment may have pointed to a new sensitivity toward child abuse, as exemplified by a new concern for family harmony so prominent in the writings of Luther,

43. See Stern, *Josel of Rosheim*, p. 92; for perceptions of the Turkish threat in 16th-century Germany, see Wilfried Schulze, *Reich und Türkengefahr im späten 16. Jahrhundert* (Munich, 1978).

44. Margaritha, *Der Gantz Judisch Glaub*, Dd³ᵛ.

45. Stern, *Josel of Rosheim*, pp. 101–2; Josel of Rosheim, "Journal," no. 15, p. 98.

46. *WA Tr* 5, 5504.

47. The 1531 edition is apparently identical to the 1530 editio princeps, although I have been unable to locate a copy of the first edition. The 1544 and 1561 Frankfurt editions are identical in content, except that the original woodcuts (which were lifted from Pfefferkorn's *Eyn buchlijn der iudenbeicht* [Cologne: Johann van Landen, 1508]) were left out in the 1561 edition. The 1713 reprint, published by Friedrich Lanckischen's heirs, has a forward by a Magister Christian Reineccius, bachelor of theology, who testified to the important influence the treatise had on Luther and on successive generations of Lutheran theologians and pastors.

Osiander, and other reformers.[48] This is not to say that before the Reformation parents abused children more or loved them less, but one can discern a clear line of development from the humanists to the reformers, who seemed to have expressed a greater concern for the proper upbringing of children in their writings. Coupled with the multiple prescriptions and instructions on bringing up children to be disciplined, obedient, loving, hardworking, God-fearing, well-mannered, and decorous was also a greater sensitivity toward child abuse; bourgeois parents of sixteenth-century Germany knew the distinction between spanking and maltreating children.[49] Examples of deep parental grief at the loss of a child abound in family chronicles, private letters, and autobiographies.[50]

But what implication does this have for changes in ritual murder discourse? The blood libel was, after all, a way of representing child murders: by the 1480s, the discourse had standardized to the point where the victims were all depicted as boys around the age of seven. In defending Jews against the blood libel, Osiander did not deny that children were killed but stated that they either died from natural or accidental causes or fell victim to negligent parents and vicious sorcerers. In other words, the blood libel was *one* of the ways in which a society understood violence against children, in which the discourse on ritual murder functioned both to conceal other causes of child murders and to satisfy a reflexive demand for "justice" by providing a Jewish scapegoat for the collective catharsis of vengeance on the part of a Christian community.

The enhanced sensitivity toward child abuse manifest in the writings of the humanists and reformers suggests a shift in the understanding and representation of violence toward children. It is instructive in this regard to examine the prosecution of infanticide in Reformation Germany.[51]

48. For humanist and Protestant attitudes toward child rearing and education, see Steven E. Ozment, *When Fathers Ruled: Family Life in Reformation Europe* (Cambridge, Mass., 1983), pp. 148–50.

49. "Direct evidence of widespread brutality or even harsh treatment of children by sixteenth-century Protestants has yet to be presented" (Ozment, *When Fathers Ruled*, p. 150). On the 'bourgeois" aspirations behind humanist concerns for good manners, see Norbert Elias's discussion of Erasmus in *The Civilizing Process*, vol. 1 (New York, 1978).

50. Ozment, *When Fathers Ruled*, pp. 167–69; see also his *Magdalena and Balthasar: An Intimate Portrait of Life in Sixteenth-Century Europe Revealed in the Letters of a Nuremberg Husband and Wife* (New York, 1986), pp. 96–101.

51. There is, as yet, no definitive study on the history of infanticide in late medieval and early modern Germany. For two valuable local studies, see H. Bode, "Die Kindestötung und ihre Strafe im Nürnberg des Mittelalters," in *Archiv für Strafrecht und Strafprozess* 61 (1914), pp. 430–81, which covers the period from the 14th to the late 18th centuries; and Alfons Felber, *Unzucht und Kindsmord in der Rechtsprechung der freien Reichsstadt Nördlingen vom 15. bis 19. Jahrhundert* (Bonn, 1961). For a historiographical introduction to the research on infanticide, see William L. Langer, "Infanticide: A Historical Survey," *History of Childhood Quarterly* 1:3 (1974), pp. 353–65, and Langer, "Further Notes on the History of Infanticide," *History of Childhood Quarterly* 2:1 (1974), pp. 129–34.

TABLE 2. Executions for Infanticide in Nuremberg, 1500–1700

Years	N	Years	N
1500–1510	0	1601–1610	4
1511–1520	1	1611–1620	5
1521–1530	2	1621–1630	4
1531–1540	1	1631–1640	1
1541–1550	0	1641–1650	7
1551–1560	5	1651–1660	4
1561–1570	1	1661–1670	5
1571–1580	8	1671–1680	1
1581–1590	5	1681–1690	5
1591–1600	1	1691–1700	3

Source: Adapted from Bode, "Kindestötung," pp. 431–32.

Based on the extensive surviving judicial records of the imperial cities of Nuremberg and Nördlingen, two scholars have analyzed the prosecution of infanticide between the fourteenth and nineteenth centuries. Two major conclusions can be drawn from these studies: first, the public prosecution of abortions and infanticide was practically unknown before 1500, whereas the number of trials rose steadily throughout the sixteenth century and remained constant into the late eighteenth century; second, the punishments meted out to offenders also became more severe during the course of the sixteenth century until capital punishment was established as the norm in sentencing. In Nördlingen, infanticide as a punishable crime was unknown before 1400; for the entire fifteenth century, one case was prosecuted; for the sixteenth century, four women were condemned for the crime; by the seventeenth and eighteenth centuries the record of convictions had risen four times.[52] For Nuremberg, punishments for infanticide were relatively mild until the 1510s: the women were either banished for a number of years or for life, and in one case the offender was actually pardoned.[53] The first execution for infanticide took place in 1510, and the dramatic jump occurred between the first half and the second half of the century (table 2).

Different explanations have been advanced to explain the criminalization of infanticide. Child abandonment, especially the exposure of in-

52. Felber, Unzucht und Kindsmord, pp. 95–96. Felber argues that his statistics are accurate because documentation from the 15th century onward is almost fully extant; moreover, in a city of several thousand inhabitants, infanticide was a crime that could hardly be concealed.
53. Bode, "Kindestötung," p. 463.

fant girls, was a common practice in pre-Christian Germanic society.[54] After the adoption of Christianity, canon law prohibited infanticide—in the Decretum of Gratian (1140) and the Decretals of Pope Gregory IX (1234)—but the church was powerless to prevent widespread infanticide in the rural areas.[55] In the late Middle Ages, with the increasing extension of civic secular jurisdiction into moral and family matters previously under the competence of the ecclesiastical courts, and with the replacement of the accusatory system of justice (when the injured party initiated the lawsuit) by an inquisitorial one (when the magistrates initiated the prosecution in defense of public peace and morality), the prosecution of sexual misdemeanors, including the related crimes of infanticide and child murders, also became more rigorous.[56]

While infanticides involved the killing of newborn infants or children slightly older, usually by mothers who could not and did not want to raise their illegitimate children,[57] purposeful neglect or even intentional abandonment or the killing of older children could occur within the structure of a family, most often in rural areas, commonly in response to food crises or to conflicts generated by remarriages.[58] Child abandonment is a central motif in German folktales: the archetypal "cruel father," "mean stepmother," and "unkind mother-in-law" are familiar types in the folktales collected by the brothers Grimm in the nineteenth century; the tales also tell of children being sold to the Devil or abandoned to wild animals and the elements.[59]

54. Ingeborg Weber-Kellermann, Die deutsche Familie: Versuch einer Sozialgeschichte (Frankfurt, 1974), pp. 27–28; HWDA 4, c. 1388.

55. The best evidence of rural infanticide comes from 15th-century southeast England; see R. H. Helmholz, "Infanticide in the Province of Canterbury during the Fifteenth Century," History of Childhood Quarterly 2:3 (1975), pp. 379–90.

56. Felber, Unzucht und Kindsmord, pp. 32ff.

57. For a detailed examination of the motivations and circumstances leading up to infanticide, the social dynamic of denunciation, and the state apparatus of repression, there is an excellent study of infanticide in the Bavarian countryside between 1878 and 1910. See Regina Schulte, "Kindsmörderinnen auf dem Lande," in Emotionen und materielle Interessen, ed. Hans Medick and David W. Sabean (Göttingen, 1984), pp. 113–42.

58. Child abandonment and infanticide as methods of birth control and as responses to economic and subsistence crises have been demonstrated for quattrocento Florence; see Richard C. Trexler, "Infanticide in Florence: New Sources and First Results," History of Childhood Quarterly 1:1 (1973), pp. 98–116; Trexler, "The Foundlings of Florence, 1395–1455," History of Childhood Quarterly 1:2 (1973), pp. 259–84.

59. Weber-Kellermann, Die deutsche Familie, p. 37; Stith Thompson, The Folktale (1946; reprint, Berkeley, 1977), "Motif-Index of Folk Literature" (pp. 488–500), under (S. Unnatural Cruelty), motifs S. 11, S. 31, S. 51, S. 211, S. 301; Margarethe W. Sparing, The Perception of Reality in the Volksmärchen of Schleswig-Holstein (Lanham, 1984), pp. 51–56, 66, 69–73, 138. Sparing analyzes with great care the motifs of child abuse in these folktales and concludes that they reflect the power structure in the patriarchal family of rural North Germany.

Seen in this context, the new sensitivity toward children and family harmony in the writings of the humanists and reformers assumes a new social significance. These were treatises written, published, disseminated, and read in cities; the intended audience consisted of the solid burgher families whom Luther admonished to live a companionable, Christian marriage and rear children with a firm but loving hand; the enforcers of this new ideal of the family were the godly magistrates whom Luther exhorted to found schools and root out immorality. Surrounding this solid core of civic morality were the forces of moral and social disruption: servant girls, chambermaids, city women of loose morals, apprentices, journeymen, young village males, rough landless laborers, and marginal squatters, who enjoyed little stability of family and property, unlike the solid peasant farmer and burgher, and who represented potential killers of infants and children born out of respectable wedlock.

Concomitant with the decline of ritual murder trials after 1540, cases of child murders began to be publicized in Germany. In 1556, in the small town of Obernehen (Obernai), three miles from Strasbourg, a vintner, Adam Stegman, flew into a mad rage and stabbed his seven-year-old daughter, his four-year-old boy, and a baby boy just under two to death. Before Easter, the man had borrowed money from his landlord for work in the vineyard but had gambled most of it away. He had also hurt his leg earlier and was unable to work. For the murders, he was branded and then broken on the wheel.[60] Yet another murder was described in lurid detail in a chapbook published in Frankfurt. In 1570 a young man asked the pastor of the village of Sprendenlingen for lodging, claiming that he was a student. When the pastor went out of his house, the young man brutally murdered his daughter and young son; he was later apprehended and executed in Frankfurt.[61]

What significance did these stories have? Would a sixteenth-century reader draw moral lessons besides perhaps being entertained by the gruesome details of murderous furies? Three observations can be made. First, the urban/rural contrast is important. In the case of Obernehen, the murder took place in a small wine-growing community just outside the great city of Strasbourg; in Sprendenlingen, the crime again took place in

60. See *Drey grausamer erschröcklicher mordt, der sich in der Stat Obernehen im Elsass, drey meyl von Strassburg gelegen, zugetragen hat, von einem Vater, der seiner eigener Kinder drey jemmerlich hat ermordt und umbracht, am 10. tag Aprilis, Anno 1556. Auch was er für eine Straffe darob empfangen hat, geschehen den 24. Aprilis, 1556 jar.* 1556.
61. See Johann Schwanfelder, *Warhafftiger Bericht von dem jämmerlichen und erbärmlichen Mordt, so zu Sprendenlingen in der Dreyeych an zweyen kindern im Pfarhof am 26. tag dess Jenners in diesem jetzlauffenden 1570. jar begangen, und wie nachmals der Thäter allhie zu Franckfurt am Meyn, den 24. Hornungs ist gericht worden* (Frankfurt, 1570).

a village on the outskirts of a big city. The common theme seems to be that brutality and violence were the staple of country life, which, in these two cases, because of their proximity, proved particularly threatening to the peace and security of urban society. Second, to invoke the model of a ritual murder discourse developed in chapter 2, many elements in these murders could have served to trigger an accusation against Jews in a different historical context, had the real culprits and the circumstances of the murders not been identified immediately. The third and final observation points to the opposition between the themes of familial harmony and unnatural violence that underlie the tales. In Obernehen, the father was the murderer; his addiction to gambling epitomized the defect in his moral character. Having failed to live up to his moral duty as *Hausvater*, the head and provider for his family, the father succumbed to rage and despair and committed the unnatural crime of killing his own children. In Sprendenlingen, the father was now the victim as a pious Christian family in a small village fell prey to a brutal vagabond; this story reminded its readers of the forces of violence that threatened the stability and sanctity of family life, forces embodied by vagabonds, gypsies, marauding soldiers, and all sorts of wandering folks.

Irrespective of confessional differences, governments also began to exercise greater caution in investigating ritual murder charges. Two official inquests, one in Catholic Austrian Alsace, the other in Protestant Brunswick, indicated both the tighter control of local magistrates by central government officials and the intrusion of the state into the conflicts of rural society.

In 1537 two Jews in an Alsatian village near Ensisheim were accused of stabbing a Christian boy and drawing blood from him; the grandmother of the boy and the two Jews had previously argued over the repayment of a loan. The bailiff (*Schultheiss*) at Ensisheim arrested the suspects and interrogated them but also questioned many villagers; unable to adjudicate the case, he sent the documents to the archducal government in Innsbruck for further instructions. On 19 May the Innsbruck chancery wrote back to the bailiff in Ensisheim, expressing doubts concerning the charge.[62] To continue the investigation, the bailiff was to take the boy away from his parents for a day or two and then question him closely whether anyone had put him up to the accusation; the bailiff was also to show the Jews various instruments of torture, "but on no account were they to be strung up"; if they were proven innocent, he must release them.[63] Meanwhile, the Alsatian Jewish communities

62. HStA Stuttgart, B17, 2 (1537), folios 73^{r-v}.
63. Letter of Hapsburg chancery, Innsbruck, to Ensisheim, 19 May 1537: "[Folio 73^r] Wir haben Euer schreiben, den xi tag dits monats Maij ausganngen die zween Juden

rallied to the defense of the two; the bailiff had put the suspects under a strict regime of bread and water because they refused to eat nonkosher meat in prison. On 26 May, on receiving a petition from the *Gemein Judischait* of upper Alsace, Charles V instructed the bailiff to free the two after carrying out the instructions for questioning mentioned in the letter of 19 May. The emperor also rebuked the bailiff for starving the Jews, "for if one wants to tolerate Jews amongst Christians, one should not force them to disobey their laws."[64]

Six years later, in Protestant Brunswick, magistrates were equally skeptical about another purported ritual murder; their investigation uncovered a twisted tale of village conflict. In 1544 a peasant by the name of Weimar Weimar who lived in the village of Volkerode, near Göttingen, declared a feud against all Jews in Brunswick. Torching the houses of Jews and ambushing them on open roads, this highwayman became a threat to public peace in the borderlands between Brunswick and Hesse.[65] His menace prompted Duchess Elisabeth of Brunswick to seek aid from Philip of Hesse in a joint manhunt.[66]

Weimar swore vengeance because a shepherd had accused the Jews of putting him up to the murder of Weimar's son. Back in 1543, two women found the five-year-old boy in a field outside Volkerode, a rope of green cloth wrapped tightly around his neck. The bailiff summoned all

betreffennt, *so auf ain Red und Verdacht* [italics mine] das Sy ain Cristen kneblin in lr der Juden behausung gestochen, und das plutt von ime genomen haben sollen fennigklichen angenomen werden sein mit sambt des beschehen Inquisition und erkundigung von etlichen personen nach der lenng vernomen. Vnd wiewol wir nun soll erfarung vnd kundtschafften etwas weittleuffig, auch vngleich befinden, also das nit wol darauf zufuessen ist auch vnder anderm darinn angezogen wirdet, das des kinds gross muetter auch der Juden aine entlonung vnains vnd neydig ainander geweest seyen, so ist doch auf soll Euer [73ᵛ] schreiben und begeren, zu noch merer vnd grundtlicher erfarung, damit nyemand unrecht beschehe, unnser gutbedunckhen, das ir yemands den is achten taugenlich zu sein bevollen, das gemelt kynnd so also gestochen worden sein soll etwan vnwissender ding seiner Vatter vnd Muetter an ain annder ort zu bringen, vnd ain tag oder zwen haimlichen zuenthalten, vnd das kynnd mit guete zufragen, wer es angelernet, vnd ob auch was man ime verhaissen, oder geschenncket, das es gesagt hab, die Juden haben es gestochen, aus welhem man gewar wirdet, ob es auf den Reden, wie die Kuntschafften zum tail lautten beleiben, oder die Enndern vnd anderst sagen wurdt. Zum andern, so mögt lr die gemelten zwen Juden solhes verdachts halben ernnstlich besprechen, auch auf die Tortur vnd warsagerin [a torture instrument] troen [?] vnd zaigen, aber noch zu malen nit aufziehen ob sy heraus liessen, das sy dermassen mit dem kynnd gehanndelt und gestochen hetten. Vnd so lr sy aber in solhen ernnstlicher besprechung unschuldig fynnden würden, als dann mögen lr sy gegen gebürlicher vrfehd wider ledig lassen" (HStA Stuttgart, B17, 2 [1537]).

64. Letter of Charles V to Ensisheim, HStA Stuttgart, B17, 2, folio 74ʳ.

65. Letter of petition of *Gemeine Judenschaft* to Elisabeth, duchess of Brunswick, 3 Dec. 1544, StA Mb, PA 1638, folio 2ʳ-3ᵛ.

66. Six letters between Elisabeth and Philip and his chancellor, 2 Dec. 1544–15 Jan. 1545, StA Mb, PA 1638, folios 1ʳ-ᵛ, 4ʳ-5ᵛ, 6ʳ-ᵛ, 9ʳ-15ᵛ.

men and women over ten years of age from the village to the scene of the crime. Upon examining the corpse, he found that the foreskin of the penis had been cut off and saw prick marks on both arms. Returning to the village the next morning for further questioning, the bailiff saw a shepherd running away into the woods. With the help of four hundred villagers, he caught the fugitive, Heinrich the shepherd, who immediately blamed Jacob the Jew of putting him up to the murder. While being conducted back to Münden Castle, the shepherd claimed that Klingen's daughter was also involved and that he would recognize Jacob on sight. Wisely, the bailiff presented Heinrich with the gatekeeper of the castle, whom the suspect mistook as Jacob. The shepherd also confessed that he had hidden a jar of blood, but the officials could not find it at the indicated spot. After a few days in the dungeon, Heinrich withdrew his accusations of Jacob and Klingen's daughter. He had hated her for a long time because his dog had bitten her swine, and he had been forced to pay half a mark in damages. The one who had informed on Heinrich was Andreas Bethen, who naturally reaped the shepherd's enmity; Heinrich plotted to kill Bethen's son but lacked the opportunity for action. Thus, he turned to Weimar's son, who was the nephew of Bethen's wife, and choked him to death in the woods. After the murder, Heinrich returned to the corpse, cut off the boy's foreskin and drew some blood from the corpse. He was planning to sell the blood to the Jews and to frame them for murder. Sentenced to death, Heinrich publicly confessed to the innocence of the Jews before his execution, but apparently Weimar was still bent on revenge.[67]

The two murder cases revealed the raw material of ritual murder discourse in rural society: petty quarrels in villages—communities riddled by personal hatred and conflicts over money—frequently gave rise to violence. In the struggles between factions, families, and individuals, the weakest were the first victims; the boys in these child murders, like the old, single women in witchhunts, had few means to defend themselves against the violence of unscrupulous men. The discourse of ritual murder provided the perfect scenario for a cover-up, and criminals could count on village gossip to spread false suspicions of Jews. More interesting, however, was the attitude of the officials. Skeptical, cautious, and judicious, they demonstrated an awareness of the gap between the discourse and reality of ritual murder. The sixteenth century saw the beginning of a long process of political centralization whereby the authority of the state would gradually impose itself on the rural communities of early modern Germany. The extension of state authority into the villages of the

67. Reports of the case by Johann Koch of Homberg and Heinrich Hoystede, Amtmann and Schultheiss in Münden, StA Mb, PA 1638, folios 15ʳ–17ʳ.

Holy Roman Empire ensured the institutional hegemony of elite ideas in the campaign to control popular culture. The suppression of ritual murder trials in Reformation Germany would depend in large measure on the success of this cultural institutionalization.[68]

Beginning with the early sixteenth century, then, humanists and reformers showed an increasing concern for pedagogy, child rearing, and family harmony. At the same time, with the greater concentration of jurisdiction in the hands of the civic magistrates—a trend that culminated in the Reformation—and with the call for social and moral reform, a greater number of sexual and familial matters came under the purview of the secular courts. As a result, the criminalization of infanticide expressed itself both in the growing number of convictions and in the increasing severity of punishments. These developments concentrated in the cities and widened the distance between urban and rural views of justice and criminality. The chapbooks that described child murders narrated these acts of violence not as magical and ritualistic representations but in ways closer to our readings of similar events. Toward the end of the sixteenth century, however, the criminalization of infanticide also took on a theological character in Protestant cities. In a legal brief written in 1600 by the jurors of Nuremberg (who were trained in roman law) for the city council regarding the case of an Anna Kiessingin, accused of infanticide, Jean Bodin's *De la daemonomanie* was cited to counter the defender's claim that her child was stillborn.[69] In many cases of infanticide trials, the legal defense of the accused was to plead *insania* or delusion by the Devil.[70] In sum, the rise of a new discourse on the family and the consolidation of the discourse on infanticide and witchcraft appropriated crucial elements that had formerly constituted the ritual murder discourse. Violence against children was not a preserve of the Jews; evil lurked in the hearts of all. Nor could one think of Jews as the chief servants of Satan when numerous examples of Christian men and women who abandoned or killed children could now be counted among the nefarious undertakings of the Devil. While the blood libel persisted in spite of these changes, especially in the countryside, the judicial mechanism by which rumors of a ritual murder discourse could be transformed into a trial was being dismantled.

68. Two works are particularly helpful in the analysis of state control and popular culture in rural society: Sabean, *Power in the Blood*, provides illuminating examples of patterns of resistance to and collaboration with state power in early modern Württemberg; the successful integration of peasant households into the feudal regime of Hapsburg Lower Austria is described in Hermann Rebel, *Peasant Classes: The Bureaucratization of Property and Family Relations under Early Habsburg Absolutism, 1511–1626* (Princeton, 1983).

69. This document is transcribed in Bode, "Kindestötung," pp. 439–40.

70. Bode, "Kindestötung," pp. 444*ff.*

THE EMPEROR AND THE JEWS

The increase in anti-Semitism in the decades before the Reformation met with a greater effort on the part of the Jewish communities in the empire to defend themselves. Their efforts to counter the charges of ritual murder and Host desecration coincided with the reassertion of imperial authority under Maximilian I and Charles V and took the form of appeals to the emerging imperial institutions of law, primarily the Imperial Chamber Court (Reichskammergericht), which functioned under the authority of the Imperial Estates, and, later, the Imperial Aulic Court (Reichshofrat), directly under the Austrian Hapsburgs.

Within the empire, Jewish communities developed an informal corporate institution to represent their common interest. In 1521 Charles V appointed Rabbi Samuel of Worms to be *Reichsrabbiner*,[71] but the real spokesman for the Jewish communities was Josel of Rosheim, whose great-uncles were victims of the 1470 Endingen ritual murder trial.[72] Having successfully lobbied for the interest of Alsatian Jews for many years, Josel was elected "commander" in 1529 to plead on behalf of all Jewish communities when the Poesing ritual murder trial in Hungary brought home to the German Jews the common danger they faced.[73] When the Imperial Estates met in Augsburg in 1530 to discuss grievances of usury and monopolies and the question of religious reform, Josel summoned delegates from Jewish communities throughout the empire to a parallel meeting to draw up guidelines for regulating moneylending in order to blunt potential charges against Jews.[74] The confirmation of privileges for Jews by Charles V at the 1530 Augsburg Imperial Diet represented an initial success for the Jewish lobby, but the turning point in the campaign against ritual murder trials came a decade later, in Frankfurt and Speyer.

In 1539 many leading Protestant princes and church leaders gathered at Frankfurt to discuss the confessional situation in the empire. Among the participants were Martin Bucer, Philip Melanchthon, Landgrave Philip of Hesse, and two electors, Johann Friedrich of Saxony and Joachim II of Brandenburg. It was in Frankfurt that Josel met and convinced Melanchthon, who then presented reliable evidence to the other participants that the thirty-eight Brandenburg Jews executed for Host desecration in 1510 were innocent. Just before his execution, the Christian suspect who had made the accusation against the Jews told his confessor of the falsity of the charges. Driven by his conscience, the priest

71. Stern, *Josel of Rosheim*, p. 65.
72. See chap. 2.
73. Stern, *Josel of Rosheim*, pp. 81–83.
74. Stern, *Josel of Rosheim*, pp. 116–19.

reported this confession to Bishop Jerome of Brandenburg, but the bishop ordered him to keep silent. The former priest had become a Protestant and was living in Württemberg when he unburdened himself of this secret from the past. As a result of this shattering revelation, Josel secured permission from Joachim II to allow Jews to settle in Brandenburg.[75]

The test case came four years later. In 1543 a Jewish man, three women, and a young girl of sixteen were arrested by the bishop of Würzburg on a charge of ritual murder voiced by a man who had tried in vain to seduce the girl.[76] Josel first interceded with the bishop but failed to gain their release. When the Imperial Estates met in Speyer the following year, Josel petitioned Emperor Charles V to intervene. On 3 March, Charles sent a letter asking the bishop to be merciful toward the imprisoned Jews since "more than enough violence has been done to them by the common, ignorant men (*gemeinen unverstendigen man*)." It was brought to his attention, the emperor continued in his letter, that among the arrested were several women and a young girl of sixteen; not only had they been held for a long time and were being fed on nothing but bread and water, but when relatives tried to bring food and clothes to the prisoners they were turned away. In view of their long imprisonment and the peril to their health, and given the fact that the Jews were being held against their freedom and in violation of imperial law, the emperor asked the bishop to free them.[77]

Toward the conclusion of the Imperial Diet, Charles V issued a mandate, dated 3 April 1544, in which he reaffirmed all previous imperial and papal privileges bestowed on the Jews of the Holy Roman Empire and explicitly placed all Jews in the empire under his personal protection.[78] Specifically, Charles V granted Jews safe-conduct to travel anywhere within the empire; forbade the closing of synagogues and the expulsion of Jews; stipulated that no Jew should be forced to wear Jewish badges outside of their places of residence (lest they should stand out as marked prey on the open roads); allowed Jews to charge higher interests on loans since they also had to pay higher taxes to the emperor; and strongly condemned violence against Jews and spoliation of their prop-

75. Stern, *Josel of Rosheim*, pp. 171–72.

76. Stern, *Josel of Rosheim*, pp. 200–201, which is based on Josel's memoirs. I have been unable to find records of this case in Staatsarchiv Würzburg; the only other document related to the Würzburg ritual murder trial I have located is in HHHStA Vienna, RHR Antiqua 1159, no. 6. It is the draft (almost illegible) of an imperial letter to the bishop of Würzburg, 3 Mar. 1544.

77. HHHStA Vienna, RHR Antiqua 1159, no. 6.

78. A copy of the imperial mandate is in StdA Worms 2030, folios 214–36 (foliation added by archivist).

erty. On the matter of the blood libel, Charles prohibited future trials of Jews on pretexts of alleged child kidnappings and murders.[79] Citing the condemnation of ritual murder trials and blood superstition by Pope Innocent IV and Emperor Friedrich III's decree that all trials of "ritual murders" must be referred to imperial authority, Charles decreed to the Imperial Estates and to his subjects that in the future no Jew should be charged with ritual murder or interrogated without the consent of the emperor. A heavy fine of fifty mark *löttig* gold (five hundred grams) was imposed for any unauthorized imprisonment and trial of Jews on account of ritual murder; the fine was to be doubled if the Jews were found innocent.[80]

Speyer signaled a decisive turn in the fortunes of German Jews. Based on mutual interests, the emperor and the Jewish communities forged a new alliance: Charles needed all the money he could get to finance the dynastic ambitions of the Hapsburgs, an enterprise which his bankers, the Fuggers, could no longer single-handedly underwrite, and the Jews turned to the emperor for protection against political trials staged by princes, bishops, and magistrates, often at the instigation of "the common men." In 1545 the Jews of the empire contributed three thousand guldens to help finance Charles's campaign against France, but the first fruit of this community of interest was only manifest in the Schmalkaldic War (1547–48), in which Charles defeated the league of Protestant princes and cities. During the war, the Jews prayed for imperial victory, offered money to pay the Charles's Spanish *tercios*, and in return were spared the ravages of the soldiers and even benefited from the war economy.[81]

If the Protestants thought they were disenchanting Christianity of "papist" and Jewish magic, the Jews realized their protection lay in imperial law, a system of justice that separated religion from jurisprudence. But what changes in judicial institutions and in legal thought discredited ritual murder trials? And how did the reassertion of imperial authority lead to the suppression of anti-Jewish persecutions? With these questions in mind, we will turn our attention to the second half of the sixteenth century and trace the further fortunes of the blood libel.

79. StdA Worms, 2030, folios 223–24.
80. StdA Worms, 2030, folios 228–30, 235.
81. Stern, *Josel of Rosheim*, pp. 206–7, 210–16.

CHAPTER EIGHT **Worms**

HE JEWISH COMMUNITY IN WORMS HAD A LONG, CONTIN-
uous, and venerable history, dating back to the elev-
enth century, and despite many persecutions the community survived and flourished in the early modern
period.[1] The Jewish cemetery, a monument to this long
tradition, still exists today, across town from the former ghetto, which now constitutes a clearly recogniz-
able neighborhood in postwar, industrial Worms.[2] After the expulsion of
Jews from Regensburg in 1519, few imperial cities tolerated Jews; among
these, Worms and Frankfurt protected the largest urban concentrations
of Jews during the sixteenth and seventeenth centuries.

In 1563 a ritual murder trial divided burghers and Jews.[3] It arose in
the middle of a conflict between the city and the bishop of Worms over
the right to tax Jews and heightened tensions in the civic community,
which was petitioning Emperor Ferdinand I for permission to rescind
protection and residence permits from the Jewish community.[4] Unlike

1. For a recent survey of the history of the Worms Jewish community, see the
volume by the city archivist Fritz Reuter, *Warmasia: 1000 Jahre Juden in Worms* (Worms,
1984).

2. For a plan of the ghetto from 1500, see Reuter, *Warmasia*, p. 92.

3. There is a brief notice of this trial in Paul Wigand, *Wetzlar'sche Beiträge für
Geschichte und Rechtsalterthümer*, vol. 3 (Giessen, 1850), pp. 260–62.

4. The plan to expel Jews from Worms was hatched in the city council by 1558 at the
latest, apparently under pressure from the guildsmen, who were complaining of economic
competition. On 17 Dec. 1558, the city obtained permission from Emperor Ferdinand I to
expel the Jewish community, a right contested by the bishop of Worms, who claimed
violation of his own rights over the Wormser Jews. Different imperial commissions were
boycotted by the city and the bishop in turn, and the dispute dragged on unresolved until
1570. The Jews were not expelled. This episode is noted in passing by Reuter, *Warmasia*,
pp. 75–76; it is discussed in more detail by Sabine Frey, *Rechtsschutz der Juden gegen
Ausweisungen im 16. Jahrhundert* (Frankfurt, 1983), pp. 108–14. Besides relevant documents
in Worms, materials are also to be found in HHHStA Vienna, RHR Antiqua 1143.

the earlier ritual murder trials we have examined, some of which were little more than hasty judicial murders, the magistrates in Worms apparently took their duties most diligently in investigating this case; the copious records they left behind enable us to probe deeper into the structure of a ritual murder trial, to see how judicial institutions and thinking worked behind the investigation, and to descend into the inner recesses of the men and women swept up by this episode, to share their anxieties, fears, and pain. The subsequent appeal of the case at the Imperial Chamber Court in Speyer further illuminates the clash between imperial and civic authorities, the two systems of jurisdiction, and the two types of legal discourse.[5]

THE ACCUSATION

On 18 March 1563, a Thursday, a twenty-year-old saddler journeyman named Hans Vlean reported "a crime" he had witnessed to the magistrates: he claimed to have seen the Jew Abraham zum Bock purchase a boy from a woman, a camp follower (*Kriegsfrau*), hide the boy under his overcoat, and take him into the ghetto. The magistrates immediately arrested Abraham and also detained Hans for further questioning.[6] The next day, Friday, 19 March, the magistrates put Hans under close examination in the city hall. The clerk noted that the young man showed himself in "an unfrightened, knowing, and steady mood (*Hierauff er gantz unerschrocken, kenklich und standhafftiges gemüts angezaigt*)" before the magistrates and gave them the following sworn testimony:

> [On Thursday] in the early morning, he was sitting in a room in the house of Michael Schnitzler the saddler, his master, and was waiting for work to begin. And in the morning light he saw a Jew and a woman coming down the Kämmergasse, in the vicinity of the Judengasse and St. Martin's Gate. [See fig. 10.] The Jew was carrying a young child under his overcoat; and the child had on a white bonnet or a little cap, like the French (*Welschen*) are wont to wear around the head. Then the Jew began to talk to the woman—Hans could not hear the words, he could only see that they were talking to one another; the Jew looked at the child and again covered it with his overcoat, which was gray and had a yellow circle [the Jewish badge] on it [see fig. 11]. He then went with the child into the ghetto, the woman followed them, and was constantly wiping her eyes with a piece of cloth as if to stop crying. Also, before the Jew went into the ghetto, he looked all around him, but perhaps he did not see the saddler journeyman [Hans] or anyone else because almost

5. The documents generated by this trial are deposited in StdA Worms 1 V (Judenschaft), 2030. The ca. 350 folios of letters, interrogation records, legal briefs, summons, and petitions are numbered consecutively.

6. StdA Worms, 2030, folio 4.

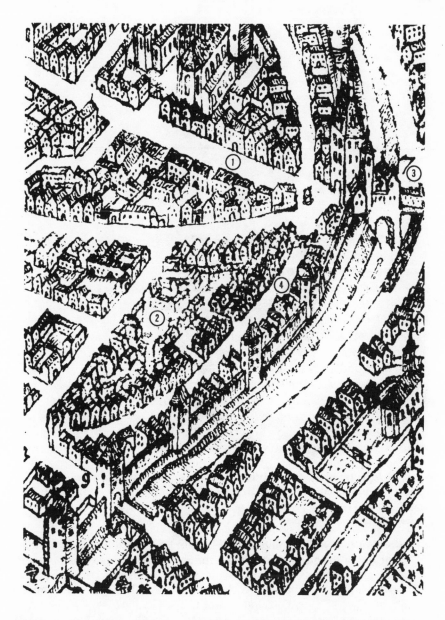

Figure 10. The Ghetto at Worms, 1630. Noted on the woodcut are: (1) Kammergasse; (2) the Ghetto; (3) Saint Martin's Gate; and (4) Judengasse. Excerpted from the city plan by Peter Hamman. Reproduced courtesy of Stadtarchiv Worms.

Figure 11. Male Jewish costume, sixteenth-century Worms. The money bag and garlic represent Jewish moneylending and dietary habits. Note the yellow ring: "the Jewish badge." From "Thesaurus picturarum" of Mark zum Lamm (1544–1606). Reproduced courtesy of Stadtarchiv Worms.

everyone was still sleeping. About an hour later, the Jew and the woman came out of the ghetto but without the child. The woman was tumbling along as if she were half full of wine; she also looked terrible, sad, and inconsolable; and when she reached the house of the Sackmaker, she fell down. Then she went on alone toward "The Golden Swan" [apparently an inn]. But he [Hans] does not know whither she went. He wanted to show his master the woman but could not find him in the house, so afterwards he told his master what he saw. His master warned him right away, and said one must not lie about things like this. But Hans stuck to his story.[7]

7. StdA Worms, 2030, folios 4–5.

After his testimony, Hans was led out of the chamber. The magistrates then had Abraham brought in for questioning.

They first asked Abraham how early the gate to the ghetto was opened, to which he answered at about five in the morning. Asked when he left the ghetto, Abraham said he went out of the ghetto for the first time that Thursday between seven and eight in the morning. He told the magistrates he first sold some corn to the baker, after which he walked to the *Obermarkt* to buy wood.[8] Pressing on with the questioning, the magistrates asked Abraham: Whom did he meet outside of the ghetto? Abraham answered, "Nobody." Did he meet a woman with a child? "He said, unfrightened, no (*Sagt unverschrockenn Nein*)." Was he wearing different clothes from what he has on now? Abraham replied he did not have another overcoat. Getting nowhere with these preliminary probes, the magistrates repeatedly questioned Abraham about the child and threatened him with judicial torture if he did not tell the truth. But Abraham did not admit to anything, even when the magistrates told him that someone had seen him with a child.[9] The clerk recorded verbatim Abraham's answer to this last question:

> He answered: here are his life and goods, and one can do with him whatever one wants, but one would be doing him an injustice. He knows nothing about this matter, which he has heard often enough before, on which he is supposed to have done something with our children. And people have tried to pin the same thing on them [the Jews] but have never proved it to be true. Moreover, imperial and royal privileges have supported them against these accusations; and nothing can be found in their own writings which shows that they need and share Christian blood.[10]

These courageous words failed to convince the magistrates. Admonished once more to speak the truth or face the pain of torture, Abraham steadfastly maintained his innocence.[11]

His accuser, Hans Vlean, was then brought into the chamber, and upon first seeing Abraham, the clerk recorded, "he said right away, without any fear or fright, I think this is the Jew." The journeyman then approached Abraham, looked him in the eye and said,

> You are the right Jew [*du bist der recht Jud*] and this is the cloak that I saw you wearing, and you wrapped a child in your arm. [The clerk adds here: "he means the left arm of the Jew."] There was also a French

8. StdA Worms, 2030, folio 17.
9. StdA Worms, 2030, folio 18.
10. StdA Worms, 2030, folio 18.
11. StdA Worms, 2030, folio 19.

[*Welsche*] woman with you. . . . you went into the ghetto with the child
and later the woman came out looking very sad.[12]

Having heard this, Abraham replied in a hardened tone (*gantz verstockens
gemüts*): "May God send his power into this room and be a witness to you
and to me and show that you are lying!" Turning to the magistrates,
Hans swore an oath that he was telling the truth. According to law,
Abraham pointed out, his accusor should be questioned under torture; it
would turn out, he predicted to the magistrates, that Hans gave false
testimony. Although the journeyman wanted to retort, he was escorted
out of the chamber. The judges were ready to apply torture.[13]

In vain, Abraham pled with the magistrates to be of good will and
inquire into the matter before proceeding with the interrogation. His
hands and feet tied in the manner of the strappada, Abraham was
hoisted up twice but refused to confess. Instead, he said that "they [the
magistrates] were doing him an injustice, just like the Jews in Engenn."[14]
Pausing a moment to take counsel, the judges decided to place three
stones in front of Abraham while he was being suspended in midair with
bound limbs and to act as if they were going to add the extra weight to his
feet. At first, Abraham did not confess. Eventually, when fear and pain
overcame him, he said that there was a Jew in Worms recently who
looked like him; this man had a sick child and perhaps had carried it into
the ghetto with him on his arm.[15] At this point, the judges ended the
investigation for the day.

The next day, Saturday, 20 March, the judges again summoned
Hans Vlean to be questioned; he had been locked up in the tower for the
night to reflect on his testimony. The magistrates informed Hans that
they had questioned Abraham with and without torture (*gutlich und
peinlich gefragt*) but that the Jew maintained his innocence. He was then
asked as to whether he had denounced the Jew "on someone's instruc-
tion," "out of envy," and whether his master owed money to Abraham
or to other Jews. The young journeyman replied that no Jew had ever
done him an injury, nobody gave him instructions, and his master had
not borrowed money from the Jews. He then repeated his previous
statement.[16]

A few details emerged from Hans's second testimony: after he had

12. StdA Worms, 2030, folio 19.
13. StdA Worms, 2030, folio 20.
14. StdA Worms, 2030, folio 21. This refers to the 1495 ritual murder charge in Engen,
a small town near Constance; see *HWDA* 7, "Ritualmord," c. 730.
15. StdA Worms, 2030, folio 21.
16. StdA Worms, 2030, folios 6–7.

allegedly witnessed the incident, he told it to his master's wife. She went
out to tell her brother, the shoemaker, whose house was nearby. The two
then came back and questioned Hans, who stuck to his story. Convinced
that the youth was telling the truth, the shoemaker and Hans's master,
who had by then arrived on the scene, advised him to report the incident
to the authorities in order to save the poor child's life. But the supposed
eyewitness now wavered on one point: he was uncertain about Abraham's cloak, which just yesterday he had readily identified.[17] Somewhat
shaken by this, the magistrates asked Hans to take time to think about his
testimony; if he should have done Abraham an injustice, there would be
grave consequences for the Jew as well as for his own soul. At this, Hans
answered firmly that he had actually seen the Jew with a child in his arm
and affirmed his previous statement. When asked whether he recognized Abraham, Hans replied that when several Jews came out of the
ghetto later that day, he spotted Abraham in their company; he then
described the clothes Abraham was wearing.[18]

The child transaction supposedly took place on Thursday; by Friday,
rumors filled the city. Two female camp followers (*Kriegerin, Kriegsweiber*)
traveling through Worms claimed they knew the woman who had allegedly sold the child to Abraham. After the Saturday morning session
with Hans Vlean, the judges decided to summon other witnesses to
ascertain these rumors. Three citizens were called in: Hans Mosnler, the
butcher, Leonhard Maier, the innkeeper of Zum Weissen Rösslein, and
Maier's wife, Magdelene.

On Friday night, at two in the morning, Mosnler and a friend, Hans
Mertz, the innkeeper of Zum Weissen Löwen, went drinking from tavern
to tavern, until they came to Zum Weissen Rösslein. He saw the two
women camp followers with a child. The guests in the inn were talking
excitedly about the case, and Mosnler overheard the two women calling
the alleged child seller "a saucy bitch (*ein verweg breckin*)." They knew her
well, so the two claimed, and she had committed many misdeeds for
which she was punished. After her return to army camp, someone asked
her whether she had sold the child to the Jews, to which she said yes.
From their intonation, Mosnler surmised the two women were Nether-
landers; one wore a black cloak, the other a green coat. They left Worms
with two servants early Saturday for Oppenheim.[19]

Next Leonhard Maier and his wife, Magdelene, testified before the

17. StdA Worms, 2030, folios 8–9.
18. StdA Worms, 2030, folio 10; see folios 12–16 for another copy of this second
examination.
19. StdA Worms, 2030, folios 111–12.

magistrates. Last night, the innkeeper was sitting among his guests when the two women came in with a child. They chatted a lot with some women in the tavern. One of the two told the others she knew the "tramp" who sold the boy to the Jew: she came from Thuringia or Oberland and had two other children at home; this "tramp" had tried to sell a child for a long time and once refused an offer of ten kronen by a nobleman; she also said she would rather sell her child to a Christian than a Jew. At this point, the woman who was telling this story to the other tavern guests began to cry.[20]

Magdelene had a different story to tell. When she was working in the inn on Friday, a camp follower in a black coat carrying a baby girl came begging for food at the inn. Magdelene asked the beggar whether she was going to sell the baby to the Jews. The other woman answered that she would never sell her own flesh and blood; and even if she were to do it she would not deal with Jews, a nobleman would buy it for nine kronen. When Magdelene told the beggar that another child had been sold, the woman said she knew this child seller well, that she was from Oberland and had a boy and a girl at home, and that she and her boy had once stayed with her for two nights. Out of sympathy for the child's fate, the beggar woman began to weep in front of Magdelene.[21]

Faced with these conflicting and confusing stories, the magistrates decided to bring in more witnesses. On Sunday, 21 March, they summoned nine people, in addition to recalling Mosnler and Maier. Altogether nine men and two women gave sworn statements on that day (see fig. 12). Called into a room in the *Rathaus* one by one, the witnesses were enjoined by the magistrates to tell the truth, and the citizens, the nine men, were further reminded of their burgher oath to aid the city council in the execution of its official duties.[22]

The first to testify was Jost Glashewr, a barber-surgeon by trade. Asked under oath whether he had bandaged a child this past Thursday morning in his house, Glashewr replied that he had often healed bleeding children who were brought to him, but he could not recall attending anyone on Thursday, nor did his apprentice bind any wounds on that day.[23]

Michael Schnitzler the saddler was the second to testify that day. As the master of the only eyewitness of the purported crime, Hans Vlean, his testimony was crucial. The saddler repeated what his journeyman

20. StdA Worms, 2030, folios 112–13.
21. StdA Worms, 2030, folios 113–14.
22. For the original transcript of the questioning, see StdA Worms, 2030, folios 94–101. For a clean copy of the proceedings (which omitted Jost Glashewr's testimony), see folios 104–9.
23. StdA Worms, 2030, folio 94.

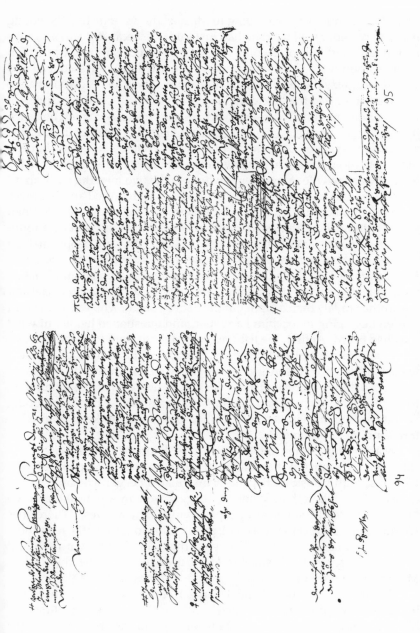

Figure 12. Transcript of witnesses' testimonies, Worms, 1563. Reproduced courtesy of Stadtarchiv Worms.

told him on Thursday. According to Michael, he admonished the young man "to consider well what he had just said . . . because it was a serious matter, and nothing good would follow, if it should come to the attention of the authorities." The youth, however, insisted he witnessed it all and would recognize the Jew if he saw him again. It was on his own initiative that Hans reported the "incident" to the city council. On the business of the two women camp followers, Michael had this to say: when he heard the rumor about them, he and his neighbor [his brother-in-law, the shoemaker, Wendel Gerlach] went to Zum Weissen Rösslein, but the innkeeper did not want to say anything and instead directed them to his wife. It was the wife, Magdelene, who told the two men the story about the two women and their claim. Finally, Michael reported another piece of hearsay that originated from a fisherwoman. On Friday, some women were chatting about the "sold child" while doing their wash by a fountain, and a young Jewish girl supposedly said, "Why are people making such a fuss about this child? It's still alive! (*Was man viel wesens von diesem kindt dörfft mach, es lebe doch noch*)." An older Jewish woman immediately scolded her for saying stupid things and told her to shut up. Michael and his brother-in-law then sought out the fisherwoman, who was living on a garden belonging to Joachim Landauer, and questioned her about what they had heard. At first, the fisherwoman did not want to speak to them; eventually, she confirmed the story, but added that "the young Jewess was a foolish, poor person and was not quite right in the head (*aber es were die junge Judin ein töricht arm menschen und nit wol bei samen*)." Other than this, the fisherwoman had nothing more to say. After questioning Schnitzler, the magistrates admonished the saddler to keep silence before sending him home.[24]

Martin Pfungsräter, the third witness, happened to be a city councillor. He remembered that one time, when he was standing in front of his house with Hans Buschel and Hans Hilat, a beggar woman went up to his wife to talk to her. When the beggar woman was walking down "the Speyer Road," she heard people saying to themselves, "There goes another camp follower with a child; she is going to sell it to the Jews too!" She shouted back, "May God prevent this! This is my own flesh and blood; how could I sell something so dear to me?" She then asked Martin's wife why people would say such things to her.[25]

The next witness was Wendel Gerlach, shoemaker and neighbor and brother-in-law of Michael Schnitzler. When the journeyman first told him the story, he thought the youth was lying and warned him that if this

24. StdA Worms, 2030, folios 94–95a.
25. StdA Worms, 2030, folio 95.

should come before the authorities it would have grave consequences. Other than this, his testimony simply corroborated Michael's sworn statement.[26]

Next came the cooper, Erhard Reyher. He lacked firsthand knowledge of the incident, knowing only that after he had opened shop on Thursday, Hans Vlean came and told him the story of the Jew and the woman, "at which he warned him [Hans] several times with all seriousness, and asked him to take cognizance of what he was saying, and if it was really so, it would have to be reported to the authorities." Upon Hans's insistence, Erhard went to the market but did not see the Jew. He had also heard rumors about the stories told by the two women tavern guests and by the fisherwoman.[27]

Wendel Fertgin, a fishmonger, also heard the story secondhand from Michael Schnitzler and Wendel Gerlach. He knew the young Jewish girl, too; she was supposed to be "somewhat foolish."[28]

When Hans Mosnler the butcher was recalled to testify, he repeated his statement from Saturday, as did Leonhard Maier, the innkeeper at Zum Weissen Rösslein.[29]

The two women were the last to appear before the magistrates. The Jewish girl who had been mentioned by several witnesses was called in first. Her name was Ruffgen (Ruthy). Nervous and frightened, Ruffgen denied saying anything at the fountain about a child; she had been working in the ghetto and could not remember what she was doing. But when the magistrates questioned her sternly, she confessed to saying what was reported by the other witnesses and for which she was punished by the older Jewish woman (see fig. 13). Earlier, she had heard people in the ghetto say that "he is going to live" but had no idea of whom or what they were talking about. Otherwise, she knew nothing.[30]

The last witness, Sara, a servant girl from Strasbourg, was working in the house of a vintner in the parish of Saint Andrea, when she heard the following story from a schoolboy, Endres Krug, whose father was living in Mainz. A woman came to the house of Krug's schoolmaster and said that a Jew and a woman were seen at Saint Martin's Gate standing and talking for almost an hour. But whenever anyone approached, they stopped talking. Finally, the Jew gave her ten guldens and the boy an apple, placed the boy under his overcoat, and went inside the ghetto.

26. StdA Worms, 2030, folio 96.
27. StdA Worms, 2030, folio 97.
28. StdA Worms, 2030, folio 99.
29. StdA Worms, 2030, folios 98–100.
30. StdA Worms, 2030, folio 100.

Figure 13. Female Jewish costume, sixteenth-century Worms. From "Thesaurus picturarum" of Mark zum Lamm (1544–1606). Reproduced courtesy of Stadtarchiv Worms.

The woman went away by herself.[31] After Sara's testimony, the judges adjourned.

Where did the case stand after the hearings on Sunday? What legal grounds did the magistrates have for continuing the investigation? What crime had been committed? The entire case was initiated by the denunciation of a single eyewitness, the journeyman Hans Vlean, but what did he see? Even if he was telling the truth, he witnessed nothing more than an alleged transaction, in the course of which apparently Abraham gave

31. StdA Worms, 2030, folio 101.

money to the woman for the child. Nonetheless, he, his master, other artisans, and the judges assumed immediately that the alleged episode was the prelude to a ritual murder, although the judicial documents never explicitly stated this. The magistrates' only evidence was simply the sworn testimony of a youth of twenty who was not even a burgher of Worms; the testimonies of all the other witnesses, including Sara, amounted to nothing but hearsay. Even when the rumors seemed to suggest that a child had been sold, they pointed to the shadowy existence of a woman; nothing implicated Abraham himself. Moreover, the circumstances reported in the hearsay were inevitably full of contradictions: Hans swore that a Jew and a woman were alone on the street; Sara reported the story of a Jew and a woman seen by several people who interrupted their conversation; at least two beggar women appeared in the testimonies as potential child sellers; differing reports of what the two camp followers said in the tavern Zum Weissen Rösslein gave an inconsistent picture; and Magdelene Maier's statement contradicted that of her husband's on several points.

What about the judicial conduct of the magistrates? Was it proper? According to the roman-canon law of proof, as reflected in the 1532 *Carolina*, specific guidelines were set for the investigation of cases where blood sanctions (capital punishments or maimings) might be involved. To condemn a suspect, full proof was required—that is, either the sworn testimonies of two credible witnesses or a voluntary and full confession of the suspect.[32] If only one eyewitness stepped forward, the judges needed to have reasonable doubt, based on circumstances (*indicia*) of the crime, before subjecting the suspect to judicial torture in order to extract a confession. The *Carolina* contains detailed guidelines regarding the conditions under which judicial torture could be applied; the method, degree, and suitability of judicial torture also belonged to the realm of learned jurisprudence.[33] Torture was not meant to be arbitrary, at least in juristic theory. Seen against this background, the judges acted at best in an ambiguous manner: they had one eyewitness whose testimony they trusted; no corpus delicti, however, was found, nor did it seem that the magistrates tried to find it, which means that no suspected murder was linked to this alleged child buying; the testimonies of all the nine men and women added up to nothing but hearsay and could certainly not be construed as circumstantial evidence. On two points of procedure, the judges acted inappropriately: judicial torture was applied without in-

32. John H. Langbein, *Prosecuting Crime in the Renaissance: England, Germany, France* (Cambridge, Mass., 1974), pp. 181–82; Appendix B is a partial translation of the *Carolina*, see pp. 259–308.

33. Langbein, *Prosecuting Crime*, pp. 183–86.

dicia, contrary to roman-canon jurisprudence, and without further investigation into the matter, as Abraham himself requested; the examination
of the suspect was improper when the magistrates repeatedly interrogated Abraham about buying the child, suggesting clearly the confession
they wanted to hear.

The eagerness of the magistrates to proceed with the trial reflected
the power of the ritual murder discourse: Hans Vlean's sworn testimony
activated the emotions and anxieties embedded in the community's belief in the reality of ritual murder; most people assumed the alleged sale
of the child would lead to its eventual death. And once the journeyman
began his discourse (the people who first heard this tale from him
warned him of the gravity of his *"Rede"*), the entire community became
the teller of tales. Rumors spread like wildfire: Hans's story triggered
memories and personal experiences, which in turn helped to produce
new stories and variants on the theme of selling children; tales, hearsay,
and words taken out of context were adapted by different "storytellers"
to embellish the discourse on ritual murder. Even the Jews themselves
were not immune. Thus the dull-witted Jewish girl Ruffgen picked up
something she had heard (namely, that someone was sick or dying, but
was still living) and repeated it in a completely different context, which
was misunderstood by the listeners as referring to the imaginary child.
Likewise, the two women camp followers traveling through Worms
claimed they knew a woman who would have sold her child to the Jews
because the story they heard in Worms triggered off this association of
themes and personalities. The association of personalities by the two
women, touched off by hearing the story, completely unsubstantiated
and quite out of context, in turn provided new episodes and supporting
themes for this collective telling of the ritual murder tale.

From the way in which these rumors began and spread, we can
define the central feature of this particular ritual murder discourse as
follows: it was an act of narration, initiated by a member of a community,
which was then taken up by other members of the community, who
added on fresh material based on personal remembrance and experience;
storytelling thus represented simultaneously a social act of both con-
sumption and creation that depended on the cohesiveness of the community for its perpetuation. In this particular case, a division of labor
between the sexes can be observed. Both the originator of the tale and
those who first lent it credence were men: although Michael Schnitzler,
Wendel Gerlach, and Erhard Reyher at first doubted Hans Vlean, (and
Gerlach actually accused the journeyman of lying), they were finally
convinced; by virtue of their status as artisans, married men, and citizens, their belief in fact validated the story of a younger man, who was
not a native of the city and did not enjoy an independent economic and

social status of his own. If the men had been skeptical, Hans would not have felt encouraged and emboldened to go before the magistrates. Women, however, played a much more important function in the telling and further embellishment of the story once it had been created: the Jewish girl Ruthy, the fisherwoman, Magdelene Maier, Sara, the two camp followers, the women washing their clothes by the fountain— these women represented the collective tellers of the story. In the case of Ruffgen, the fisherwoman, and Sara, they merely repeated what they had heard; but Magdelene and the campfollowers played a creative role in adding new details and twists to the original story of ritual murder.

An analysis of the spatial themes mentioned in the various testimonies suggests that the act of ritual murder discourse was a social, hence, public activity, and that it functioned to define more sharply that sense of social and geographical space. Hans Vlean told the initial tale in his master's house, but storytelling spilled out into the streets right away when Michael Schnitzler's wife went to her neighbor, shoemaker Wendel Gerlach. Likewise, Hans himself went to Erhard Reyher's shop to tell his story. Thus, one way of transmission was from house to house, as when a woman went to tell her story to the master of the schoolboy Endres Krug and the boy, in turn, repeated the tale to Sara the servant girl. The more important arena of discourse was in public: at the fountain, where the women exchanged gossip over their wash, at the tavern, where the two alien women told the Wormsers their tale, and finally, of course, in the city council chamber, where the discourse was set down in writing. For the burghers of Worms, danger lurked in unfamiliar, marginal space: at Saint Martin's Gate, where the alleged transaction took place, in the open roads, where beggar women came wandering with their children, and in the ghetto, with its gate, a dangerous zone for small Christian children.

Clearly then, the judges' attitudes were colored by the social discourse of ritual murder surrounding them; as magistrates and as members of the same civic community, they shared to some degree the ideas of their fellow citizens. Crucial to the case was their trust in Hans Vlean: the scrivener who recorded the examinations in the interrogation chamber described the journeyman as "unafraid," "without fear," speaking "without hesitation" and "calmly." Magisterial confidence in the eyewitness rested on Hans's oath; he was putting eternal salvation on the line. The magistrates, however, were in a quandary: on one hand, they were inclined to believe Hans; on the other, the testimony of one eyewitness amounted to only half proof; not only did they find no circumstantial evidence, but Abraham had refused to confess under judicial torture. Without full proof, there could be no conviction. And, by the terms of the *Carolina*, a suspect who maintained his innocence under torture must be released.[34] One obvious solution would be to torture Abraham into confessing, as the Regensburg and Freiburg magistrates had done in similar cases in 1476 and 1504, but that would be a flagrant violation of the principles of jurisprudence. Another option would be to search the ghetto for the corpus delicti, but to do so would exceed the reasonable actions mandated by the case because there was no plaintiff and no murder. Moreover, the city had been embroiled for five years with the bishop in a lawsuit at the Imperial Aulic Court over the proposed expulsion of the Jews; any action directed against anyone other than the accused would put the city council in a bad light. Above all, the magistrates wanted to avoid the appearance of using this as an excuse to persecute and expel the Jewish community. Since minutes of the council meetings no longer exist, we can only speculate as to what the magistrates might have entertained in the secrecy of the council chamber deliberations. But it is not unreasonable to assume that for some, the case represented a tempting opportunity to expel the Jews, while others would have urged caution and extreme discretion for fear of incurring the charge of injustice, and perhaps still others might have argued for the release of Abraham.[35]

THE APPEAL

In any event, for the city fathers of Worms, matters soon got out of hand. A letter to the city council, delivered on 26 March, struck the magistrates like a bolt of lightning. It was delivered by a messenger of the Imperial Chamber Court in Speyer, half a day's journey south of Worms, and was, in fact, a summons citing the Stettmeister, the Bürgermeister, and the city council of Worms as *defendants* in a lawsuit filed at the Imperial Chamber Court.[36] The plaintiff was one Moses von Orb, brother-in-law of Abraham zum Bock, and the charge was the miscarriage of justice. Doctor David Capito, procurator at the Imperial Chamber Court, had been retained by Moses to represent the imprisoned Abraham. On 19 April, Capito drew up a complaint with twenty-nine points of grievances against the defendant, the city of Worms, and presented it at the Chamber Court.[37]

The main charge was the arbitrary violence done to Abraham contrary to the ordinances of the Holy Roman Empire. Doctor Capito pre-

---

34. Langbein, *Torture*, p. 16.
35. The 1563 ritual murder trial was mentioned briefly by Reuter, who suggests that the magistrates were going to free Abraham anyway. This argument is improbable in light of the council's subsequent actions. See Reuter, *Warmasia*, p. 76.
36. StdA Worms, 2030, folio 32.
37. StdA Worms, 2030, folios 38–48, "Libellus Nullitatis Articulatis."

sented the following points in his legal brief to the Chamber Court: On 18 March, the day of Abraham's arrest, Moses appeared before the city council protesting his brother-in-law's innocence, but the magistrates ignored him; Moses further charged that the magistrates tortured Abraham on 19 March not once but three times, "until [he] almost died from torture";[38] the investigation occurred because of a longstanding embitterment (*Erbitterung*) and was not founded on any reasonable suspicion or evidential proof; the judges had no other reason to torture Abraham other than the fabricated testimony of a scoundrel saddler journeyman; there was no report of a missing child; the judges should have inquired as to whether a child was missing before undertaking an inquisition; the Christian neighbors of the Jews were also questioned but nobody had knowledge of this matter; the street on which the journeyman allegedly saw the clandestine transaction was a main thoroughfare where many come and go; the arrest of Abraham was based on one false testimony without any sufficient reason or circumstance for suspicion (*ohne Mutmassung und Inditien*); without a shred of material evidence, Abraham was tortured three times and almost to death, yet he maintained his innocence; in other cases where Jews had also been arrested after similar malicious accusations, they had been released without fines; the judicial torture of Abraham was "against all Natural Rights and Equity (*wider alle Naturliche Recht und Billihait*)";[39] the late emperor (Charles V) had condemned the false belief that Jews need Christian blood and had forbidden the arrest and judicial torture of any Jew for ritual murder without imperial permission on penalty of fifty mark gold; and, finally, not only had the city council of Worms behaved contrary to imperial mandate but it still held Abraham in prison. In conclusion, Capito summarized the grievances in two major points: judicial torture was applied without the warranty of circumstantial evidence (*Indicien*) contrary to all natural rights, and the trial itself was held against explicit imperial interdict. To seek justice (*Richtigkeit*), the plaintiff now turned to the Imperial Chamber Court, the highest court of appeals in "all matters pertaining to blood sanctions," to ask for the righting of wrongs and the imposition of a fine of three thousand dalers on the city council.[40]

Back in Worms, the magistrates tried to build a stronger case by seeking other witnesses. The key figure, it seemed to them, was the woman who had allegedly sold the child to Abraham, but she was nowhere to be found. There were also, however, the two women in the tavern Friday night who claimed to know the whole thing. The city

38. Art. 2, StdA Worms, 2030, folio 40, "fast bis uf dem todt gemarterdt."
39. Art. 18, StdA Worms, 2030, folio 43.
40. StdA Worms, 2030, folios 46–48.

council sent word to neighboring authorities of the case, and a report came back that two women camp followers had been detained in Friedberg, an imperial city northeast of Frankfurt. The Worms magistrates requested information on the two women from their Friedberg colleagues. In their letter to Friedberg, dated 3 April (Saturday Judica) 1563, the Worms city fathers explained why they placed such a significance on the two women: the suspect Abraham refused to confess; but his accusor, Hans, was sticking to his story and did not show any fear even though the magistrates were still holding him and had threatened him with corporal punishment. It was Hans whom they believed, the Wormsers continued, and they hoped that the testimonies of the two women held in Friedberg would corroborate the journeyman's sworn statement. That would clinch the case. A copy of Hans's testimony was sent along, with the request that the Friedbergers check the women's clothing against the description in the transcript. Furthermore, the magistrates of Worms reminded their colleagues in Friedberg of their right as *Obrigkeit* to use torture to seek the truth—it being the only way—and they should have no qualms about its application. They also entreated the Friedbergers to proceed with all earnesty in their investigation "for truth," for "Holy Christendom," and on account of "innocent Christian blood."[41]

The Friedbergers, in turn, replied on 27 April asking the Wormsers to send someone to Friedberg to hear their findings and to discuss matters of mutual concern.[42] On 3 May the city council of Worms sent the city clerk (*Stadtschreiber*) to Friedberg.[43] Setting out on 3 May and passing through Oppenheim, the clerk arrived in Frankfurt the next day; after an overnight stay, he resumed his trip to the north. Arriving in Friedberg, the clerk entered the imposing *Reichsburg*, which overlooks the city. He first met with the *Burggraf*, the castellan who coadministered justice with the Friedberg magistrates, and tried to persuade him of the importance of the two women as potential witnesses against the Jew Abraham. The Wormser's position hinged on the argument that there were sufficient circumstances to warrant the judicial torture of the two women; he, as city clerk representing Worms, and an official of the castellan, would take part in the examination. The Burggraf objected to the clerk's presence during the interrogation but promised to tell him the results of the questioning.[44]

When the clerk returned to his lodging to write out his report, he

41. StdA Worms, 2030, folios 116–23.

42. Letter of Bürgermeister and City Council of Friedberg to Bürgermeister and City Council of Worms, 27 Apr. 1563, StdA Worms, 2030, folio 125.

43. The report (*relatio*) of the negotiations with the Friedberg city council, 8 May 1563, was written in the first person; see StdA Worms, 2030, folios 132–52.

44. StdA Worms, 2030, folios 132–37.

saw the Friedberg magistrates emerging from the Ratshaus and caught a glimpse of the two women, who did not seem to match the descriptions in the trial transcripts from Worms. A committee had been appointed to question the two women, who, incidentally, were not incarcerated but were staying in an inn at the city's expense.[45] The next day, after lunch, the clerk was summoned to the Ratshaus. The Friedberg magistrates had interrogated the women but had not put them under judicial torture. Questioned about the child, the women insisted they knew nothing about the incident in Worms. The clerk complained that he did not have a copy of the questions (*Fragstück*); the Friedbergers then agreed to provide a copy of the interrogation record for their visitor.

As it turned out, the two women, Thrina von Berbera and Greta of Aÿnpeck, were soldiers' wives. Thrina, who had a child with her, was married to a Hans Haberbuch of Hildesheim; Greta, the driver of the wagon on which they were traveling, had a husband called Claus of Reckenhausen. They had traveled widely and were recently in Livonia but had not been in Worms.[46] They claimed it was a case of mistaken identity.

Without any grounds to hold them, the Friedbergers wanted to free them on a sworn oath, but the Wormser objected, insisting that if they should be freed "the matter [meaning the ritual murder trial] cannot otherwise be resolved soon." He urged repeatedly that the women be subjected to judicial torture.[47]

Apparently the clerk's interference had worn thin the Friedbergers' collegiality. When he was summoned back to the Ratshaus the next morning, the two women had already signed an oath of truce (*Urfehde*), promising not to discuss the case for a year, after which they were freed.[48] The Wormser's request for a copy of the city council's deliberations on the case was flatly denied.[49] What started as a promising lead for the magistrates of Worms turned out to be a dead end.

Meanwhile, before the city clerk's return to Worms on 8 May, the magistrates got themselves another potential witness. A *Landsknecht* by the name of Wilhelm Schryer, a Wormser by birth but who grew up in Mainz, was traveling from Frankfurt to Worms. He was heard in public

45. An undated note was sent by an innkeeper who complained that he could no longer keep the two women at his own cost; on the back of the note was the permission of the city council (of Friedberg?) to send him 20 guldens (StdA Worms, 2030, folio 126).
46. StdA Worms, 2030, folios 144, 152.
47. StdA Worms, 2030, folios 144–46.
48. An Urfehde was commonly required of those acquitted of charges who would swear that they would not undertake to seek redress against the magistrates for false arrest. For the women's Urfehde, see StdA Worms, 2030, folio 150.
49. StdA Worms, 2030, folio 151.

many times to have said that he had knowledge of this matter of the sold child and boasted that he knew the woman, the child seller, too.[50] The magistrates arrested him on the pretext that he was a vagabond.[51]

After Moses had filed a lawsuit against them, the city fathers retained Doctor Conrad Offenbach to represent them in Speyer. On 6 May, when Wilhelm Schryer turned out to be a potential witness, the Wormsers immediately informed their attorney of the new development.[52] In his reply, Offenbach advised the magistrates to interrogate Schryer once more to ascertain the veracity of his accusations against the woman, the mysterious Kriegsfrau we have heard so much about. More importantly, they should concentrate their efforts in finding her and, if she could be located, serve her a summons; only if she refused to cooperate should she be imprisoned. Moreover, she and the soldier should be questioned separately, with particular attention to checking her clothing. Concerning another question raised by the city councillors, the learned lawyer advised against putting Schryer under judicial torture, after having consulted with his colleagues at the Imperial Chamber Court. A confession extracted under torture in Worms and forwarded to Speyer would cast a shadow of suspicion on the city council, Offenbach warned; instead, a notary from the court should be sent to Worms to preside over future interrogations of the soldier.[53] Offenbach further suggested that he should compose a petition to the Chamber Court on the basis of Schryer's testimony, in order to win permission for continuing the trial in Worms. On the question of Hans Vlean, Offenbach regretted that the journeyman's testimony would be inadmissible for the hearing at the Chamber Court. The magistrates should also hold Hans in custody until after examining Wilhelm because freeing the journeyman on bail would again cause suspicion and bad talk. At the end of his letter, Offenbach inquired about the latest development in Friedberg.[54]

In their reply to Offenbach, the magistrates expressed their frustration with the whole Friedberg affair: the city clerk had a very difficult time negotiating with the Friedbergers, and a great deal of effort had been

50. The details about Wilhelm Schnyr are mentioned in a petition of 19 May 1563 (draft), composed by Dr. Conrad Offenbach, who was representing Worms at the Imperial Chamber Court (StdA Worms, 2030, folio 55): When Schnyr was in Worms, "zum mehren malen offentlich hören lassen, das er solicher des verstricken Judens mishandlung von wegen des erkauften Kindes guete wissenschaft hette. Auch dafür des weib, so dz kindt dem Juden verkauft wol bekenth [this last sentence was crossed out in the draft].

51. This was the justification given by Offenbach's petition of 19 May to the Imperial Chamber Court; see StdA Worms, 2030, folios 55–57.

52. This communication was sent by a messenger from Worms to Speyer; see the letter from Offenbach to the city council of Worms, 7 May 1563, StdA Worms, 2030, folio 70.

53. StdA Worms, 2030, folio 72.

54. StdA Worms, 2030, folios 73–74.

wasted on a wild goose's chase, since the two women did not match the
descriptions. They thanked Offenbach for his legal advice and agreed to
his suggestions; particularly gratifying for the city fathers was Offenbach's plan to draw up a petition to the Chamber Court.[55]

On 19 May the magistrates once more questioned Wilhelm the soldier and Hans the journeyman.[56] A list of questions concerning the
details of the alleged event of 18 March was prepared, apparently for
crossexamining Hans; Wilhelm's testimony, on the other hand, focused
on the mysterious woman. He had an even more curious tale to tell: the
Kriegsfrau was not the real mother of the child; the boy's parents were a
French soldier and his wife. Some years ago, the poor mother drowned in
a waterfall; the bereft father, not knowing what to do with his child, gave
his boy to the Kriegsfrau. This woman took the child with her on her
many wanderings in France and in Germany. Often she complained of
her misfortunes and wondered what she should do with the child. When
she left camp to go to Worms, she had this child with her. Upon her return
to camp, Wilhelm reproached her for leaving the child in Worms. She
began to weep bitterly, told him that she had sold the child for six dalers to
a Jew, and, although it was not her own flesh and blood, she felt great
sorrow. At this Wilhelm flew into a rage, grabbed his sword, and was
about to run her through with it, but the woman slipped away. These
articles, Wilhelm "confessed openly to the city council of Worms."[57] A
copy of this confession was made and sent to Offenbach, who then filed a
petition with the Imperial Chamber Court on 19 May on the ground that
the new testimony of Schryer justified allowing the magistrates to proceed with their trial in Worms.[58]

The trial had ground to a halt in Worms while the magistrates and
Abraham's relatives awaited the slow judicial procedure at the Imperial
Chamber Court to move forward. On 26 June the syndic of the city
council, Dr. Johann Deschler, drew up a long and detailed defense of the
city's position and submitted it to the judges at the court.[59] Apparently,
on 6 June, Worms had submitted a petition in Speyer against the lawsuit
filed by Moses, but the latter would not withdraw his complaint. The
syndic accuses Moses von Orb of "shamelessly fabricating lies" against

55. See letter of city council of Worms to Offenbach, 8 May 1563, StdA Worms, 2030,
folios 76–79.
56. See the Articuli Probatorii (the questions put to Wilhelm Schnyr) and his testimony, StdA Worms, 2030, folios 58–64.
57. StdA Worms, 2030, folios 61–63.
58. See letter of Offenbach to city council requesting copies of the testimonies of Hans
Vlean and Wilhelm Schnyr, 15 May 1563, StdA Worms, 2030, folios 51–53, and draft of his
petition on behalf of Worms, 19 May 1563, StdA Worms, folios 54–57.
59. StdA Worms, 2030, folios 161–83.

the city of Worms and obstructing the laws of the empire. It was not true that Abraham was arrested without probable cause, the letter continued; there was, in fact, a great outcry against this crime in Worms and in neighboring places. A saddler journeyman who had nothing to do with the Jew first denounced him. Thereafter, the city council interrogated many witnesses and had ascertained that the said woman actually came to Worms to sell the child, a point confirmed by the testimony of the Landsknecht. The said woman was supposed to have sold other children in Worms in the past.[60] Moreover, the magistrates had questioned Hans Vlean twice and warned him of the consequences of false testimony; the third time, he was made to confront the Jew. Every time, the youth appeared to be "unfrightened and constant" and said that his conscience was clear, that he would rather sacrifice his own life in the attempt to discover the truth. When the magistrates questioned Hans for the fourth time and threatened him with torture, the unflinching journeyman stood by his testimony; when a pastor was sent to remind him of his salvation, the young man exclaimed that he wanted to bring this matter before the Supreme Judge, God Himself, and that he would willingly suffer all tortures and even undergo death.[61] Thus, the syndic wrote: "On account of all this, the Honorable City Council, as the properly constituted Authority, did not want the suspicion of negligence to be imputed to it, as if it were to turn a blind eye to truth; rather, it desired that the truth should come to light and such an evil deed, wherever it may be found, must not remain unpunished."[62] Regarding the charge of heavy torture, the syndic explained, it was applied judiciously and lightly. The assertion that Abraham almost died under torture was false, and if he were to swear to a notary on his Jewish faith, the syndic claimed, he would have to confess to this truth. The magistrates gave the Jew every opportunity to prove his innocence, but thus far no contrary evidence has come up to support his claim of innocence. It fell within the authority of the city council to hold Abraham in custody while searching further evidence. And although enough circumstantial evidence existed to interrogate the suspect again under torture, the magistrates have refrained from this action. The appeal filed by Moses on behalf of Abraham was "whimsical (*mutwillig*)" and based on "fabrication (*Erdictung*)."[63]

60. StdA Worms, 2030, folios 163–65.
61. StdA Worms, 2030, folios 165–67. The transcript of Hans's interrogation mentions neither the threat of judicial torture nor the presence of a pastor.
62. "Durch welches alles Einer Ersamen Räth als die ordentliche Obrigkaith damit deroselben ainiger Vermiss und böhser Argwen, als wolte man durch die finger sehenn, nit beygelegt würde, sonder viel mehr die warhait an Tagk kheme, und eine solche grosse Ubelthat, wo sich die also befunndenn wurde, nit ungestraft pleibe" (StdA Worms, 2030, folio 167).
63. StdA Worms, 2030, folios 166–67.

According to the petition, the magistrates only carried out due judicial process "according to natural reason and law"; the trial should not be obstructed by Moses's lawsuit. Moreover, the city council has always been impartial in judgment, to Jews as well as Christians, a reputation well known among the Jewish community in Worms. Acting within its properly constituted authority, the magistrates were following the guidelines of the *Carolina* in this criminal case; they have done nothing wrong and were willing to wait for the Imperial Chamber Court to hand down its decision.[64] The syndic then asked the court to "remit" the case back to Worms, since the magistrates have not disobeyed His Majesty, nor have they broken the laws of the empire, but the Jews were behaving as if they enjoyed a privilege that exempted them from the due process of law. This privilege (meaning Charles V's condemnation of ritual murder trials) was unknown to the city council, the petition claimed; the magistrates have no intention of quibbling over its terms but asked only that it must yield to "the common written laws and the criminal code [that is, the *Carolina*] of the Holy Roman Empire."[65] It was certainly not the wish of the emperor that by granting a privilege to the Jews, it should cancel out the legal authority of the Imperial Estates and declare the Jews unpunishable to the detriment of Christians. The common laws of Worms further prohibited the mingling of Christians and Jews for fear that Christians, especially young children, might be led astray by Jewish idolatry.[66] An imperial privilege must not undermine the laws of the empire.

After justifying the actions of the city council in uncompromising legal language, the letter changed its tone to put the magistrates' treatment of Abraham in a better light: his prison cell was well lit and ventilated; Abraham had every provision he might need; he was fed from his own kitchen "as if he were at home"; he could move about freely and was not chained in irons; it was untrue that Abraham was rotting and dying in jail. However, regarding the request that Abraham should be freed on bail, the syndic replied that criminals were simply not released like that; moreover, the Jew would then have all sorts of opportunities to invent false testimonies and plant evidence. Hardening his tone once more, Deschler declared: not release on bond but further punishment was warranted for his "whimsical, frivolous complaint" to obstruct justice. The syndic concluded his long petition by asking the Imperial Chamber Court to deny Abraham's request for bail, to refuse a hearing, and to turn the case back to Worms.[67]

On 13 July, Moses again appealed to have Speyer hear the case. On

64. StdA Worms, 2030, folios 170–73.
65. StdA Worms, 2030, folios 173–74.
66. StdA Worms, 2030, folio 175.
67. StdA Worms, 2030, folios 177–81.

19 July, the Imperial Chamber Court decided to reject the city's request to dismiss the case; in view of the new testimony of Wilhelm Schryer, the judges at Speyer wanted to examine the soldier themselves and issued a summons to have Schryer appear at the Imperial Chamber Court for the morning court session of 24 July.[68]

By midsummer Abraham and Hans had been languishing in jail for over four months. The magistrates in Worms were extremely annoyed with the appeal at Speyer and equally frustrated that they could not proceed with the trial. Abraham's family and the entire Jewish community were understandably apprehensive of the outcome. The lawyers, notaries, and scriveners in Speyer were the only ones who clearly benefited from the drawn-out lawsuit. On the city's side, besides retaining Offenbach, money had to be paid out for copying and certifying documents, petitions, and letters.[69] On the other side, in addition to Capito's fees, Moses was stuck with even higher stationary bills: he hired the notary Christian Dreer to copy and notarize the imperial mandate of Charles V (3 April 1544) and its confirmation by his brother, Ferdinand (19 January 1562), which forbade ritual murder trials. The notary's large and beautiful handwriting stretched the relatively short texts of the imperial mandates to fill out twenty-nine folio sheets (scriveners were paid by the folio for their work).[70]

In this war of words in Speyer, waged with paper, ink, and legal wit, Moses was gaining the upper hand. On 20 August, his attorney, Dr. David Capito, submitted a legal brief in which he refuted the arguments of Dr. Johann Deschler, the syndic of Worms, for dismissal of the case.[71] Capito discredited the chief witness, Hans Vlean, as a young man of lowly status and "bad reputation" and as "a deadly enemy of Abraham." On his unreliable testimony alone, and without any material evidence for suspicion, the magistrates tortured Abraham three times. It made no sense for the city council to search for witnesses in Worms and in neighboring places because nobody had any knowledge of this supposed crime. To build a case, the judges should have several credible witnesses; but not only was Hans Vlean untrustworthy, the woman who supposedly sold the child was nowhere to be found, and the two women

68. See summons prepared by Dr. Bartholomys Egem, notary at the Imperial Chamber Court, served to the Bürgermeister and Council of Worms, 19 July 1563, StdA Worms, 2030, folio 207.
69. See the correspondence on money matters between Dr. Johann Deschler, syndic of Worms, Dr. Conrad Offenbach, and Lic. Martin Veyhardt, who worked as a scrivener and notary for Worms at the Imperial Chamber Court, 20, 24 July 1563, StdA Worms, 2030, folios 208–11.
70. StdA Worms, 2030, folios 213–42.
71. StdA Worms, 2030, folios 251–64.

detained in Friedberg in conjunction with the case had been questioned and freed. Turning to the journeyman's testimony, Capito argued that it was inconceivable that nobody else saw Abraham and the woman on such a busy street; moreover, people simply did not carry children under their cloak. Also, the magistrates did not treat Abraham and Hans even-handedly: the saddler journeyman was provided with food in jail, he could freely receive visitors, and merely on his bravado that he would willingly sacrifice his life in seeking the truth, he was not subjected to judicial torture. When only one witness testified, Capito invoked the *Carolina*, it was the responsibility of the magistrates first to examine the credibility of the witness and to investigate the background, rather than torture the suspect and then investigate, as they had done. The Worm-sers were trying to play down their use of torture; in truth, Abraham was badly tortured three times, and many had heard his screams of pain. He was never given a chance to defend himself against Hans Vlean's charges and was tortured right away; even so, he maintained his innocence. Only after repeated petitions from the Jewish community did the city council allow a physician to visit Abraham in prison: the poor man was found in chains and in poor health, and only on the advice of the physician was Abraham removed to another cell and unfettered. It was a far cry from being "almost at home." The entire Jewish community in Worms, the attorney went on to say, had pledged their lives and properties as bond for Abraham. These were the reasons why Moses and Abraham ap-pealed to the Imperial Chamber Court for a fair trial. The Wormsers, however, had repeatedly asked for a postponement because they still wanted to proceed with their trial. Capito ended his petition with a plea for a hearing in Speyer in the near future.

In Worms, after recovering from the initial shock, the Jewish com-munity had rallied to Abraham's defense. On 20 July the community leaders wrote to the city council, disclaiming responsibility and fore-knowledge of the lawsuit at the Imperial Chamber Court. They be-seeched the magistrates not to vent their anger at the community and pledged their properties and lives to vouchsafe Abraham's innocence; in addition, they offered to raise money for his bail, should the magistrates agree to set one. The magistrates, however, believed in the complicity of the Jewish elders.[72] No bond was set, and Abraham continued to lan-guish in prison.

By September, the city council still did not want to give up. A list of

72. Letter of the *Judenschaft* of Worms to the city council, 20 July 1563, StdA Worms, 2030, folios 246–48. On the back of the letter was a note by the city secretary: "Man lässt es bey der angefangen handlung pleiben und kann ein E. Rath nit gedencken, dz es [i.e., the appeal to Speyer] one der Supplicanten wissen oder willen bescheen."

questions was sent to Speyer for Offenbach's legal advice.[73] The magistrates wanted to know whether, on the basis of the saddler's and the soldier's testimonies, they could have a free hand (*uff freiem fuess gesetzt*) to resume judicial torture. The Wormsers were especially concerned that they would be penalized for violation of the imperial mandate, especially since the council was well aware of the privileges for Jews. On the issue of releasing Abraham, the letter asked Offenbach the following questions: Should the council accept bail from the Jewish community? Was it possible that the Imperial Chamber Court would order the city to pay damages to Abraham? How could Hans Vlean be released if he could not raise bail money? Should the journeyman be freed after swearing an oath of loyalty to the city? Should Abraham's prior consent be sought? If the Jews in Worms could not come up with the requisite sum, should Frankfurt Jews be accepted as bondsmen? The magistrates were now quite worried about the financial consequences for their city; the resolve to press on with the trial seemed weak. While the city fathers worried about fines and costs, others were afflicted with a deeper anguish.

No one shared Abraham's sufferings more than his wife, Trine. After waiting patiently for half a year for the release of her husband, Trine turned her grief into action. On 10 September she submitted a petition to the magistrates, blaming Hans Vlean for denouncing her husband "out of envy and whim."[74] Abraham's imprisonment caused her and her relatives great suffering on account of his innocence. Moreover, she was anxious about his health:

> Since Abraham my husband . . . has been in strict confinement for a long time, which brings him great pain, and it is not to be doubted (regardless of his innocence) that he would rather wish for a timely death than to lie in prison any longer; and now the wintry airs are getting stronger by the day, which would bring even greater suffering, pain, and anguish to the poor man who has been imprisoned for so long, I am thus petitioning on behalf of my poor children.[75]

Trine further explained that she and her relatives knew nothing of the lawsuit at Speyer. Moses von Orb had filed the complaint entirely on his own accord without anyone's knowledge or consent. She asked that the magistrates not be angry with her and her family. Toward the end of her petition, Trine pointed out the many Jewish leaders who were willing to pledge their lives and properties as bond for Abraham's release.[76] On the

73. "Frag Puntel an dem Hern D. Offenbach," 1 Sept. 1563, StdA Worms, 2030, folios 284–87.

74. StdA Worms, 2030, folios 276–79.

75. StdA Worms, 2030, folio 277.

76. The city council (the Inner Council of Thirteen) was prepared to come to some sort

same day when she wrote the petition to the magistrates, Trine also appealed in person to the rabbis and leaders of the Jewish community to enlist their help in freeing her husband.[77]

Moved by her tears and convinced of Abraham's innocence, the Jewish leaders wrote to the city council on 15 September.[78] They were willing to pledge their eternal salvation and their possessions to vouch for Abraham's innocence: "And when this most secure bail we offer is accepted, may it come to pass that the aforementioned Abraham might be mercifully released from prison, [in time] for the New Year Festival, which in accordance with our customs, will be celebrated this coming Saturday; may he be allowed to enjoy himself and refresh his spirits after such a lengthy imprisonment with the merciful restoration of a new beginning."[79] Signed by Rabbi Jacob, Rabbi Haym, and Rabbi Lew, together with twelve men, this eloquent plea expressed the collective solidarity of the Jewish community at Worms.[80]

Abraham spent Rosh Hashanah in prison. The pride of the magistrates prevented a quick pardon. In fact, Abraham had to wait out the entire winter in his cell. Finally, on 26 January 1564, the magistrates accepted the offer of bail from the Jewish community.[81] On 10 March twenty-three Jewish leaders appeared in the synagogue to pledge themselves as bondsmen for Abraham with a promise to raise twenty thousand guldens.[82] Dr. Johann Capito from Speyer was given power of

---

of settlement after consultation with the Common Council. On the back of Trine's letter, the city secretary noted: "Entschlossen diese sach zum besten, auch mit andern rath, nachzu wie man in alle d. sach möchte abkommen, und solichs mit alt und neuen Räth zu verrichten" (StdA Worms, 2030, folio 279).

77. StdA Worms, 2030, folio 280.

78. StdA Worms, 2030, folios 280–83.

79. StdA Worms, 2030, folio 282.

80. The other 12 were: Samson zum Bern, Jacob zum Affen, Abraham zur Gron, David zur Rosen, Leser zum Wolff, Johel zum Gulden Schwan, Leb zur Flesch, Judman zum halben Mon, Leser (Mayer's grandson), David zum Han, Salmon zum Eichel, and Nathan zum Ring.

81. See the *Burgschaft* for Abraham by the *Judenschaft* of Worms (copy), 26 Jan. 1564, StdA Worms, 2030, folios 324–27; another copy, with the date 6 Feb. 1564, was sent to David Capito in Speyer (StdA Worms, 2030, folios 328–21).

82. See the notarized sworn statement, written down by Philip Kühler of Kaiserslautern, notary of the bishopric of Worms, 20 Mar. 1564, StdA Worms, 2030, folios 332–42. The 23 were: Jacob, chief rabbi, Jacob zum Affen (the Jewish "bishop," a position created by the city council), David zur Rosen, Leser zum Wolff, Pelt zum Gulden Schwan, Leb zur Fleschen, Moses zur Eicheln, Nathan zum Prag, Leb zum Giessen, Kieffe zum Pffauen, Isaac zum Pflug, Leb zur Gens, Mose zum Korb, Palm zum Eicheln, David zum Eicheln, Secklin zum Stern, Anselm zum Weissen Ross, Abraham zum Kanten, Simon zum Höchst, Leser (Mayer's grandson), Isaac zur Waagen, Samson zum Bären, and Judman zum Halben Mon.

attorney to arrange for Abraham's bail and release; Anton Barth, procurator of the Imperial Chamber Court, Mathias Gedeleus, notary in Worms, and Philip Kühler of Kaiserslautern, notary of the bishopric of Worms, served as witnesses. On 25 April, more than thirteen months after his arrest, Abraham was freed on a bail of twenty thousand guldens. Hans Vlean was likewise released: as an alien journeyman, he could not raise enough bail money, nor was his master willing to act as guarantor, given the strict conditions of the bond; he was freed only after swearing a solemn oath that he would not leave Worms before the final verdict of the Imperial Chamber Court and that if imprisonment was ordered, he would comply with the command; Abraham also agreed to the terms of the journeyman's bail.[83] Although the documents end here, the verdict of the Imperial Chamber Court was not in doubt; Abraham's long ordeal was over.

THE NEW LEGAL DISCOURSE

Created in 1495 as part of Maximilian I's plan to reform the constitution of the Holy Roman Empire, the Imperial Chamber Court was to stand as the highest appellate bench to render judgments "in accordance with the common laws of the Empire."[84] These imperial written laws, the *ius commune*, which incorporated much of roman law, served as the legal corpus by which the judges and assessors of the Imperial Chamber Court, all doctors of civil law, relied on to pronounce verdicts. The most distinctive feature of the court was its thoroughly professional staffing: aside from the judges and assessors who rendered judgments, some thirty procurators (attorneys) and advocates (legal councillors) represented the litigants in and out of court, and a host of protonotaries, notaries, scriveners, and messengers, in addition to the fiscal and chancery officials in the service of the court, completed the large judicial apparatus.[85]

Much has been made of the so-called reception of roman law in the Holy Roman Empire around the turn of the sixteenth century.[86] It has been argued that the recourse to the corpus of roman law and the application of medieval Italian jurisprudence in Germany contributed to the

83. StdA Worms, 2030, folios 346–49.
84. Cf. Strauss, *Law, Resistance, and the State*, p. 65. For the creation, constitution, and early history of the Imperial Chamber Court, see Rudolf Smend, *Das Reichskammergericht, I. Teil: Geschichte und Verfassung* (Weimar, 1911), pp. 23ff.
85. For the structure of the Chamber Court and the function of its different personnel, see Smend, *Das Reichskammergericht*, p. 243ff.
86. For a historiographical survey, see Strauss, *Law, Resistance, and the State*, pp. 56–58.

better recognition of the equal legal status of Jews in the empire.[87] Could a case be made that the ritual murder trial in Worms and the Imperial Chamber Court's intervention represented indeed the triumph of roman-civil law over the customs of a local city court? To answer this, we need to analyze the legal language of the case more closely.

Both parties in the litigation, Capito representing Moses and Abraham and Offenbach representing Worms at the Chamber Court, spoke a similar language: they invoked the 1532 *Carolina*, argued fine points of the law of evidence (*Indizienlehre*), discussed the propriety of the use of judicial torture, and referred to "natural law." And in spite of the accusation that the magistrates were too ready to believe in Hans Vlean and to resort to torture—a charge that contained a core of truth—the magistrates were not acting in an arbitrary manner. In other words, there is no evidence to imply that the Wormsers were deliberately engaged in a political trial without regard to any principle of jurisprudence. But what system of law were the judges following? The legal code in use at Worms in 1563 dated from 1498, when the city instituted a legal reform, the so-called *Wormser Reformation*.[88] The last of the six books of the *Wormser Reformation* deals with the procedures of criminal law and stipulates:

> (1) An introductory statement of Inquisitionsprozess. Because it happens that crimes are committed whose authorship is not clear, save that "general repute or strong suspicion or credible indication" may suggest the guilt of someone, the Bürgermeister and Council are directed to investigate diligently and to take report from witnesses or those with knowledge or understanding of the matter. They may jail a suspect and question him. Should he fail to confess, there shall be inquiry of the accusors looking to whether there is sufficient indication to justify questioning the accused by torture.
> (2) Upon what grounds there may be examination under torture. Before there may be examination under torture, there needs be sufficient indication. Now this determination defies precise formulation. There can be "no certainty or rule established, rather it depends upon the judgment of each judge."[89]

Other subsections give guidelines on the proper conduct of judicial torture, on when witnesses, as opposed to suspects, may be examined under torture, and on other circumstances limiting and defining the use of torture.

The notion that the reception of roman law introduced into Germany

---

87. Wilhelm Güde, *Die rechtliche Stellung der Juden in den Schriften deutscher Juristen des 16. und 17. Jahrhunderts* (Sigmaringen, 1981).

88. Langbein, *Prosecuting Crime*, pp. 159–62.

89. *Wormser Reformation 1498*, bk. 6, pt. 2, cited by Langbein, *Prosecuting Crime*, p. 160.

the widespread sanction of judicial torture has long been discarded.[90] Torture was applied indiscriminately in the wake of the Black Death to extort confessions from Jews that they had poisoned wells, and by the fifteenth century, magistrates used torture to elicit confessions for a wide variety of crimes. The promulgation of the *Carolina* in 1532, itself based essentially on the 1507 Bamberg Criminal Code, was meant to create a standard set of guidelines in order to limit the use of judicial torture and to curb its excesses. Described as a law primer by one legal historian, the *Carolina* expresses a distrust of the competence of lay judges;[91] many articles recommend the reliance on expert witnesses, such as midwives and physicians in cases of suspected infanticides (Articles 35, 36). For almost two centuries before the promulgation of the *Carolina*, the discretionary use of judicial torture by judges was widespread in local courts in the empire. This inquisitorial process of criminal law, by which representatives of public authority, in lieu of private injured parties, initiated the investigation, gathered evidence, and prosecuted the offender, was crucial in sanctioning the use of judicial torture in extracting confessions for sentencing. It also made possible the criminalization of behavior that the magistrates deemed threatening to the social order, including, as we have seen, the purported magical murders of the Jews, one of the many various crimes against Christianity. An example of this magisterial initiative in prosecuting crimes against society was the judicial institution in Freiburg. Before the adoption of the new legal code in 1520 (in which Zasius played a prominent role), the Freiburg city council appointed a commission of "secret councillors" (*heimliche Räte*) to denounce criminals, and judicial torture was an integral part of the criminal legal system.[92]

Compared to the behavior of the Freiburg magistrates in 1504 (on which admittedly documentation was not as abundant), the judges in Worms were far more circumspect. Yet, the transcript of the 1563 investigation indicated they were not proceeding "by the book." The reason is simple. The magistrates, including the judicial commissioners, were all laymen and not professional jurists; it was not until the seventeenth century when jurists routinely sat on city councils.[93] As citizens elected to serve without pay, the juristic learning of the magistrates was limited

90. See Eberhard Schmidt, *Inquisitionsprozess und Rezeption* (Leipzig, 1940); Langbein, *Prosecuting Crime*, pp. 141–55.

91. Langbein, *Prosecuting Crime*, pp. 167–202.

92. See Joseph Willmann, "Die Strafgerichtsverfassung und die Hauptbeweismittel im Strafverfahren der Stadt Freiburg i. Br. bis zur Einführung des neuen Stadtrechts (1520)," ZGF 33 (1917), pp. 1–106.

93. Strauss, *Law, Resistance, and the State*, pp. 183–89; R. Po-chia Hsia, *Society and Religion in Münster, 1535–1618* (New Haven and London, 1984), pp. 111–24.

compared to professional judges; moreover, their sense of justice inevitably reflected in part the emotions of the body politic in which they were both heads and members. Hence, despite the elaborate guidelines on the application of torture and on the gathering of evidence in the *Wormser Reformation*, it was too easy for the magistrates to be swayed by "public outcry" and to lose sight of their magisterial discretion in investigating the blood libel against Abraham.

What distinguished the proceedings in Speyer from those in Worms was the strict adherence to legal procedure at the Imperial Chamber Court, a judicial body staffed by a professional judicial corps who did things by the book, as opposed to the laymen in Worms, whose judicial conduct and judgments were compromised by the prejudices in the community. If we turn from Offenbach's arguments to those of his clients, the city council of Worms, an important difference is immediately apparent. While the learned doctor spoke the language of the Chamber Court in defense of his clients, a language based on the Justinian Code, on the *Carolina*, and on medieval Italian glosses, the magistrates in Worms still thought in medieval legal terms.

Under roman law, Jews were recognized as *cives romani* (C.1.9.8.) who enjoyed the same rights as the other citizens of the empire;[94] central to roman law was the power of the emperor and the equality of all Roman citizens under the law. The concept of legal equality was expressed by the term *aequalitas* (equity), or *Billigkeit*, as it was translated into German.[95] It was a term Capito invoked on behalf of Abraham, in that the Wormsers acted against the principle of equity. If a continuous development can be discerned in the history of judicial torture and the evolving inquisitorial process between late medieval German jurisprudence and the reception of roman law in the early sixteenth century, then the idea of equity—namely, the recognition of equal legal status for Jews in court—indeed appeared as a revolutionary break. It ran contrary to the essence of late medieval German jurisprudence, as manifest in the two thirteenth-century codes, the *Sachsenspiegel* (composed between 1221 and 1224) and the *Swabenspiegel* (1274–75), in which different legal status was ascribed to different social groups; and in the case of the Jews, it implied a legal handicap, since they were effectively discriminated against in courts on account of their faith. Thus Christian and Jewish oaths were accorded different values, especially humiliating forms of executions were re-

94. In Germany, Reuchlin was the first to stress the legal status of Jews as "Roman citizens" in the Holy Roman Empire; he made this point in defending Jews against Pfefferkorn. See Reuchlin, *Augenspiegel*, cited in Güde, *Die rechtliche Stellung der Juden*, p. 61, n. 71.

95. Güde, *Die rechtliche Stellung der Juden*, pp. 54–55.

served for Jewish criminals, and some courts even forbade Jews from testifying at all.[96] Legal discrimination, grounded in religious difference, was fundamentally still at work in sixteenth-century Worms. To return to the transcript of the investigation once more, it was Hans Vlean's sworn oath "as a Christian" and his firmness when reminded of the perils to his soul by a pastor that finally convinced the magistrates of his reliability as a witness; conversely, the power of the blood libel discredited Abraham's sworn testimony from the beginning even though he maintained his innocence under torture. The language of the city council's correspondence with their colleagues in Friedberg and with the Chamber Court judges in Speyer revealed as much: it spoke of the need to render justice to "Christian blood" and of the danger of contacts between Jews and Christians, particularly for Christian children.

This 1563 case of appeal did indeed represent the conflict between two systems of justice, but it was less the tension between roman law and the customary laws of Worms than it was a contest between a professional judicial corps of a high court of appeals, guided by roman and imperial law, and the magistrates of a civic community, in which religious and juristic assumptions together constituted a sense of "justice." With few exceptions, notably in the case of Ulrich Zasius, academic jurists of roman law in the empire acknowledged legal equality for Jews,[97] and the change in legal thought clearly influenced the workings of the Chamber Court and other high courts staffed by professional jurists. In addition to this 1563 case, the Chamber Court showed impartiality in handling other cases where Jews were involved. In a decision publicized by Joachim Mynsinger's selection of case studies from the Imperial Chamber Court, a compilation published in 1576, the judges adjudicated a case in favor of "the Jews [who were] Roman citizens according to the customs of Germany and the jurisdiction of the Chamber Court."[98]

96. On statutes related to Jews in the *Sachsenspiegel* and in the *Swabenspiegel*, and for a history of the legal status of Jews in late medieval Germany, see Guido Kisch, *The Jews in Medieval Germany: A Study of Their Legal and Social Status* (Chicago, 1949), pp. 34–41; see also his *Jewry Law in Medieval Germany: Laws and Court Decisions concerning Jews* (New York, 1949); for forms of executions for Jews, see Güde, *Die rechtliche Stellung der Juden*, pp. 58–60.

97. The violent anti-Semitism of Zasius puts him in an extreme position among the spectrum of learned juristic discourse on Jews in 16th- and 17th-century Germany; see Güde, *Die rechtliche Stellung der Juden*, esp. pp. 33–34. Kisch's statement that roman law was misinterpreted and abused by jurists to serve anti-Semitic politics is based on his intensive study of Zasius; it needs to be modified in light of Güde's research. See Kisch, *Jews in Medieval Germany*, p. 360.

98. "Verum in Camera Imperiali contra supra dictum ius commune est iudicatum in causa Hansi Weinschenck contra Berlin Juden: et allegata fuit in hoc consuetudo Germaniae stylusque Camerae, cum Iudaei habeantur pro civibus Romanis" (*Ioachimi Mynsingeri a Frundeck Singularium Observationum Iudicij Imp. Camerae Centuriae V. Observatio VI*, p. 421, cited in Güde, *Die rechtliche Stellung der Juden*, p. 65, n. 95).

In treating the Jews in an even-handed manner, the Chamber Court became one of the main instruments by which the imperial condemnation of ritual murder trials could be enforced.[99] The second half of the sixteenth century has been described as a high point in the influence of the Chamber Court.[100] Unlike in the Imperial Aulic Court, the Chamber Court judges, who were roughly divided between Catholics and Protestants, tried to maintain confessional impartiality in pronouncing judgments in the difficult decades between 1555 and 1618.[101] The court's prestige was associated with the assertion of constitutional law in the empire. Its efforts at upholding imperial authority, however, met with resistance from many estates in the empire. The chagrin of the Wormser magistrates at being cited before the Chamber Court was shared by many other princes, counts, and city councillors who tried to forbid their subjects from appealing to Speyer. The territorial rulers sometimes exerted political pressure and inflicted illegal punishments in order to hinder appellations to the Chamber Court.[102] In the sixteenth century, many imperial cities tried to prevent their citizens from appealing to the Chamber Court, among them Aachen, Bremen, Dortmund, Hamburg, and Rottweil.[103] The fears of retribution on the part of the Jewish community in Worms were not unfounded.

One last observation about the 1563 case in Worms is in order. Curiously, the language of blood magic is conspicuously absent. Blood was mentioned once, in fact by the accused, Abraham zum Bock, when he defended his people against the legend of ritual murder; otherwise, the documents are silent on this point. Why? Was it because everyone already assumed that Jews needed blood for their rituals?

By 1563 Worms was a thoroughly Lutheran city; its citizens had eagerly supported the evangelical movement in the 1520s. The silence of blood magic in the Lutheran community reflected the transformation of the ritual murder discourse at a deeper level. Although the magical assumptions that gave rise to the blood libel in the Middle Ages were attacked by the reformers as superstitions of the Roman church, popular belief in ritual murder in Protestant areas persisted. But, like the new Christianity, which had been disenchanted of Roman magic, ritual murder discourse in this Lutheran community also underwent a "rite of disenchantment." The real meaning of this purported crime was no longer a disguised eucharistic sacrifice or an imitation of the Crucifixion;

99. On the evenhanded treatment of Jews at the Chamber Court related to all sorts of litigation, see Güde, *Die rechtliche Stellung der Juden*, p. 50.

100. Smend, *Das Reichskammergericht*, pp. 181ff.

101. Smend, *Das Reichskammergericht*, pp. 181, 188–90, 197.

102. See Jürgen Weitzel, *Der Kampf um die Appellation aus Reichskammergericht: Zur politischen Geschichte der Rechtsmittel in Deutschland* (Cologne, 1976), pp. 329ff.

103. Weitzel, *Der Kampf um die Appellation aus Reichskammergericht*, pp. 213–31.

magic had been displaced by the more prosaic fear of child kidnappings and murders. Less spectacular perhaps than the representations of ritual murders before the Reformation, the emotions conjured by a community's fear for its children proved no less powerful. The image of the Jew as evil magician would receive a second life as bogeyman in the folklore of Protestant Germany. The suppression of ritual murder trials in courts would not banish the specter of the Jewish child murderer.

CHAPTER NINE **The Stuff of Legends**

OSES VON ORB WAS NOT THE ONLY JEW TO APPEAL ON behalf of his relative at the Imperial Chamber Court. In the second half of the sixteenth century, other Jews implicated in ritual murder trials voiced petitions all the way up to the emperors. The explicit condemnation of ritual murder trials by Charles V in 1544, renewed by Ferdinand I in 1562, Maximilian II in 1566, and Rudolf II in 1577, provided the legal bulwark in the Jews' defense against the blood libel.[1] The imperial courts—the Chamber Court in Speyer and the Aulic Court (Reichshofrat) in Prague (later Vienna)—represented the institutional channels for legal appeals.[2] Vigorous imperial intervention represented the attempt to reclaim regalian rights lost to the estates during the fourteenth and fifteenth centuries, one of which was the regalia over the Jews. The Hapsburg plan to strengthen imperial authority, however, ran into stiff opposition from the princes of the empire, who wanted to restrict the constitutional rights of the emperor while extending their own sovereignty. The decades leading up to the Thirty Years' War saw an intense effort of state building in the German territories, with both Catholic and Protestant rulers bent on extending their authority over all their subjects, Christians and Jews alike. As a result, the fortunes of the Jews were inseparable from the conflict between the emperor and the territorial princes, and the campaign to suppress the blood libel was long and arduous. Just how tenacious the

1. Ferdinand I's confirmation of Charles V's mandate condemning ritual murder trials was dated 19 Jan. 1562; for a copy, see StdA Worms, 2030, folios 213–41. Maximilian II renewed it on 8 Mar. 1566, and Rudolf II confirmed all provisions in this imperial mandate for the Jews of the empire on 15 June 1577. For a printed copy of Rudolf's mandate, see StdA Ff Ugb E46y.
2. On the Imperial Aulic Court and other institutions in the Holy Roman Empire, see Hanns Gross, "The Holy Roman Empire in Modern Times: Constitutional Reality and Legal Theory," in Vann and Rowan, eds., *The Old Reich*.

blood libel was can be seen in the investigations and trials that persisted in the second half of the sixteenth century. In spite of imperial condemnation, not all ritual murder trials could be suppressed, due to the political fragmentation of the empire, and in the face of popular beliefs in Jewish child murders, Hapsburg authority had a clear limit. Nevertheless, the second half of the sixteenth century represented a turning point in the history of German Jewry.

LAW VERSUS RELIGION

When Moses von Orb appealed on behalf of Abraham zum Bock before the Imperial Chamber Court, the judges in Speyer were already well acquainted with ritual murder trials in the territorial courts. Just a year before, in 1562, two cases of appeal regarding ritual murder trials came before the imperial high court of appeals.[3]

In the part of the Neckar valley that belonged to the Teutonic Knights, a criminal accused Aaron of Gysheim of murdering a child. Wolfgang Schutzlar, master of the Teutonic Knights at Neckersulm, arrested Aaron and put him under judicial torture. Shortly before the man who had denounced Aaron was sentenced, he retracted his accusation when a pastor reminded him to heed his salvation and die with a clear conscience.[4] Meanwhile, Aaron's relative, a Joseph of Gundelsheim, had filed a lawsuit at the Chamber Court against Wolfgang Schutzlar. The summons from Speyer, dated 20 February 1562, invoked an imperial mandate of Ferdinand I that placed all Jews under the emperor's protection; moreover, the interdiction of ritual murder trials by any imperial estate was once again reiterated. For violating the terms of the imperial *Judenprivilegien*, Wolfgang was summoned to appear in Speyer to answer charges.[5] The master of the Teutonic Knights retained Licentiate Pantheleon Klein at the Chamber Court to argue his case. On 6 March his attorney asked for the repeal of the summons on three grounds: first, Joseph gave false testimony and misleading information about the case; second, both imperial and canon law prohibited contacts between Christians and Jews; third, Wolfgang was simply carrying out his duty as a magistrate.[6] Further details of the case are unknown, but Wolfgang

3. There are brief summaries of these two trials in Wigand, *Wetzlar'sche Beiträge*, pp. 253–60.
4. The outline of this case is summarized in the summons issued to Wolfgang Schutzlar by the Chamber Court, 20 Feb. 1562; see StA Lu B342 U229 (a sealed Urkunde), the first half of which is a verbatim copy of the original Chamber Court citation.
5. StA Lu B342 U229.
6. StA Lu B342 U229.

retained a Doctor Capito to represent him at the Chamber Court.[7] On 8 June, on Capito's petition, the court dismissed Joseph's appeal and absolved Wolfgang from the citation to answer charges in Speyer.[8] There is no information on Aaron's fate. Presumably he was released without compensation.

At almost the same time, another appeal was filed by Josel of Berlichingen on behalf of his father, Moses, against the brothers the noblemen Ludwig Kasimir and Eberhard, count von Hohenlohe and Langenberg.[9] Moses' ordeal began when a subject of Count Eberhard, the laborer Leonhard Wümpffhaymer of Sulm, accused Moses and another Jew "from Löwenstein" of buying a four-year-old boy from him and then murdering the child. The scenario is familiar enough from the history of ritual murder trials: most probably, Wümpffhaymer was either covering up a crime he himself had committed by accusing the Jews or had actually tried to sell a boy to Moses and Löwenstein. In fact, the accusor was first arrested because he struck his mother and was suspected of several murders. In any event, the count's officials arrested the two Jews and tortured them into confessing their "guilt."

According to a report forwarded to the Chamber Court by the Hohenlohe chancery, Moses of Berlichingen confessed to six articles of crime on 12 February: (1) that he had betrayed Löwenstein as an accomplice, that the two had given Wümpffhaymer twenty guldens to lie in order to get themselves off the hook, that they had urged a pastor to persuade the imprisoned Leonhard not to do them an injustice, and that the two had sent presents to Wümpffhaymer's wife; (2) that Wümpffhaymer sold him and Löwenstein a four-year-old boy whose veins were cut open by the Jews at Sulm, and that the blood was then sent to the rabbis of Frankfurt; (3) that four years back, the soldier Hans of Worms sold a child to the Jews of Bingen for twenty guldens; (4) that he himself paid five guldens for a child to Wendel Höringer, a farm worker and that Würzburg Jews were present during the ritual killing; (5) that three years earlier, he paid five guldens for a four-year-old child of Wilhelm Durberger of Berlichingen and that he killed the child in his own room and buried the body in his garden; and 6) that the reason why Jews need Christian blood is this: just as the angels slew all the firstborn of the Egyptians and spared only those households painted with the lamb's

7. It would be interesting to ascertain whether this Dr. Capito was in fact David Capito, who represented Moses and Abraham against the city of Worms the next year. Perhaps the irony was not lost on contemporaries that lawyers were equally skilled in arguing both sides of the fence.

8. StA Lu B342 U230.

9. HStA St C3 J1277.

blood, so the Jews also want to paint their dead with Christian blood in order that God would be more merciful to them at the Last Judgment.[10]

This confession, like all ritual murder confessions, reflected a remarkable mixture of fact and fantasy. Moses probably tried to buy off Wümpffhaymer with presents, but it was an act of a frightened and foolish man rather than that of a master criminal. According to Josel's version of the story, Wümpffhaymer actually retracted his accusations before receiving communion from a pastor but was tortured again by the officials into sticking to his original testimony.[11] The other "murders" confessed to by Moses not only implicated the Jews of Bingen, Frankfurt, and Würzburg but also provided solutions to earlier unsolved child murders in the region, a perfect resolution, as far as the magistrates were concerned. The alleged motive of ritual murder represented nothing less than an inversion of the Christian-Jewish themes of sacrifice and triumph, with the Jews depicted as wanting to sacrifice Christian martyrs in order to gain resurrection and salvation by power of their blood. The Hohenlohe trial of 1562 reminds us how deeply entrenched ritual murder discourse was and the extent to which religious and magical ideas may still underpin the judicial process at the local courts. Perhaps a hidden political agenda was also at work, the ritual murder trial being the pretext and prelude to an expulsion of Jews, but this cannot be documented from the sources available.

In any event, Moses' son, Josel, tried to save his father by filing a lawsuit in Speyer on 23 February. A summons ordering the cessation of the trial was served, and Dr. Jacob Bobhart (alias Schütz), Count Eberhard's chancellor, got into trouble with the Chamber Court for his contemptuous behavior toward the messenger who delivered the summons and for threatening to torture Moses again the next day, openly flaunting the court's authority. For this, Bobhart had to write an abject letter of apology to the judges of the Chamber Court in which he excused the episode by claiming that the messenger had not understood his "joking talk."[12]

Both Count Ludwig Kasimir and Count Eberhard appointed attorneys to plead their cases in Speyer: Ludwig retained Dr. Matthias Ramninger, advocate at the Chamber Court, and Eberhard appointed his

10. See copy of Moses' confession forwarded to the Chamber Court by the Hohenlohe chancery; the confession, dated 12 February was sent on 8 Apr. 1562 (HStA St C3 J1277).

11. Josel of Berlichingen's appeal is no longer extant, but the main points can be deduced by the rebuttal composed by the lawyer representing Count Eberhard; see his "Protestation to the Chamber Court," dated 8 Apr. 1562, HStA St C3 J1277.

12. See letter of Dr. Jacob Bobhart, Hohenlohe chancellor, to the judge and assessors of the Imperial Chamber Court, 2 Apr. 1562, HStA St C3 J1277.

chancellor, Jacob Bobhart, as legal representative.[13] On 8 April Bobhart composed a long letter to the Chamber Court, protesting the judicial interdiction placed on the case and asking for a dismissal of Josel's appeal.[14] Josel's major argument was that the arrest and torture of his father proceeded without any circumstantial evidence (*inditia*) and "contrary to all natural laws and all equity." Bobhart protested the acceptance of the case by the Chamber Court, accused Josel of obstructing justice, and excused the count by arguing that his master was simply acting out of magisterial duty and as a member of the empire in dealing with a "notorious crime." If a Jew could run to the Chamber Court at any time and file an appeal, Bobhart continued, then all authorities in the Holy Roman Empire must fear an "inhibition" of justice, injury to the regalian rights of the Imperial Estates, and violation of the traditions of the German nation. Moreover, Bobhart claimed, his lord was merely acting in accordance with the *Carolina*. The plaintiff, Josel of Berlichingen, told lies to support his case, "which is in the nature of the Jews," as Bobhart now turned to vituperation, and magisterial rights have been violated in a case where the accused had already confessed. Referring to the copy of Moses' confession attached to his letter, Bobhart announced that the guilt of the two Jews was "clearer than the midday sun." He maintained that the whole case was handled *"ex officio"* and *"de iure magistratu"* and that torture was applied in accordance with the *Carolina*, supported by legitimate proofs and in conformity with godly command. Furthermore, Count Eberhard enjoyed the counsel of many jurists (Bobhart was no doubt referring to himself in the first place), who were learned in the *Carolina* and in the "common written laws of the Empire"; it could not be insinuated that he was acting contrary to jurisprudence. In conclusion, Bobhart asked the Chamber Court again to dismiss the appeal and allow justice to run its course in Hohenlohe. Unfortunately, the decision of the Chamber Court in this case is not known.

Whatever the outcome at Speyer, the remarkable thing was that the Chamber Court would routinely hear appeals to halt ritual murder trials conducted by local city and territorial courts. The judicial language of the two 1562 cases is similar to the legal discourse of "Moses von Orb versus the City of Worms." For the Jews, the imperial mandates prohibiting ritual murder trials formed the bulwark of their constitutional rights and legal defense; their attorneys spoke the language of roman law, invoking concepts of "natural laws" and "equity" on behalf of their clients. For the

13. For letters of appointment, see HStA St C3 J1277.
14. The letter was unsigned, but the writer identified himself as Count Eberhard's attorney; see HStA St C3 J1277.

defendants—the city magistrates, the counts, and the territorial lords—the crux was the propriety of their own judicial conduct and their juris-dictional autonomy; the arguments of their lawyers stressed that the magistrates were strictly following the *Carolina* and the common laws of the empire; their magisterial duty allowed them no recourse. In these instances of judicial disputes, which indicated the development of the blood libel in the second half of the sixteenth century, ritual murder had been condensed into a conflict of legal discourse. When the voice of blood magic and Judaic/satanic sacrifice was heard, as in the confession of Moses of Berlichingen, it emitted a faint sound amid the chorus of legal rhetoric. Unlike the blood libel trials of earlier generations, the con-fessions of the Jews no longer formed the "canon" of the ritual murder discourse; these central "texts" of the Christian-Jewish sacrificial dialectic had been displaced by the much more voluminous legal documents contesting the very legality of the trials.

One of the most poignant examples of this conflict between law and religion in the handling of ritual murder cases was the 1569/70 trial in the bishopric of Würzburg.[15] In 1569 the body of a twelve-year-old boy was discovered near the road between the villages of Hollenbach and Al-ringen, in the territory of the prince-bishop of Würzburg. According to the bailiff who examined the corpse, needle marks were visible on one side of the neck and the veins had been cut open, but little blood could be found near the body. Inhabitants of the two communities were sum-moned by the officials to a meeting, and everyone in turn was told to touch the body of the boy. Finally, it came to Gumprecht and Moses, Jews of Dertzbach, and when they touched the body, according to the episcopal letter to the emperor, the body began "anew to sweat and bleed *(von frischen zu schweissen und pluten),*" a divine sign demonstrating the Jews' guilt, as everyone present assumed.[16]

The authorities arrested Moses and Gumprecht and put them under judicial torture, but in the meantime, another suspect turned up. A potter of Rinderfelt, Ulrich Seidenschwartz (alias Steurieth), was arrested in Röttingen on suspicion of murdering the boy. Seidenschwartz, how-ever, maintained his innocence, and the testimonies of other witnesses seemed to corroborate his statement. After several days in jail, Bishop Friedrich of Würzburg ordered his release without requiring bail. At the same time, in order that "their [the Jews'] Satan leader and relatives" may not complain of injustice, in Bishop Friedrich's own words, he

15. For documents related to this case, see HHHStA Vienna, RHR Antiqua 1157/4.

16. Details reported in a letter by Friedrich, bishop of Würzburg, to Emperor Max-imilian II, defending his interrogation of the two Jews, 14 Oct. 1570, HHHStA Vienna, RHR Antiqua 1157/4.

agreed to set a bail of four hundred dalers for Moses and Gumprecht. Due to difficulties and differences in arranging for bondsmen and bail, the two were still in prison when the Jews filed a petition at the Imperial Aulic Court against the bishop.

Three imperial letters were sent to Bishop Friedrich (on 13 June, 5 August, and 26 September 1570) outlining the charges against him—of false imprisonment and torture without probable cause—and ordering the release of the two Jews. In his reply, dated 14 October, Bishop Friedrich defended himself by pointing out that the Jews had already been released on bail and that they had been tortured only once, in accordance with proper judicial procedure. He defended his actions by stating he was simply doing his duty and his conscience was clear before God. The complaint againt the bishop was eventually dismissed by the Aulic Court on 3 November 1570.[17] The Würzburg ritual murder trial took place amid an anti-Jewish policy adopted by the prince-bishops Friedrich and his successor, Julius Echter von Mespelbrunn, who expelled Jews from the bishopric and tried to prevent their resettlement on adjacent noble estates. Unlike the master of the Teutonic Knights and the count of Hohenlohe, who bowed to the authority of the Imperial Chamber Court, the bishops were powerful princes who could afford to ignore imperial wishes.[18]

THE DECLINE OF RITUAL MURDER TRIALS

While vigorous imperial intervention in the later sixteenth century contributed to the suppression of ritual murder trials in the central lands of the Holy Roman Empire—a process accompanied by the gradual disintegration of the ritual murder discourse as articulated in the two generations before the Reformation—the blood libel began to plague the Jewish communities in the eastern periphery of the empire during the last quarter of the sixteenth century, from whence the charge of blood magic would spread eastward into the Slavic lands. In 1574 two women were charged with stealing a seven-year-old girl in the Bohemian town of Litomischel (Litoměricě).[19] Under judicial torture, they claimed that two

17. On the back of Bishop Friedrich's letter is notated: "Die Juden simpliciter abzuweisen, 3 Nov, 1570" (HHHStA Vienna, RHR Antiqua 1157/4).
18. Frey, Rechtsschutz der Juden, pp. 115–18.
19. See the broadsheet with woodcut, Warhafftiger bericht von zweyen Juden die zwey Weiber bestelt haben/das sie inen ein Christen Kind solten bringen/vnd wie die sach offenbar ist worden/und die Weiber sampt den Juden sind gericht worden/in der Stat Litomischel/in der Kron Behem gelegen/den dreyzehenden Januarii 1574. The woodcut, which depicts the executions of the two Jews, was by Michael Peterle of Prague. The broadsheet is reproduced in Walter L. Strauss, The German Single-Leaf Woodcut, 1550–1600, 3 vols. (New York, 1975), vol. 2, p. 831.

Jews had commissioned the kidnapping in order to supply a victim for ritual killing during Passover. For their crime, the two women were buried alive, and the two Jews, forced to confess after suffering horrendous torture, were also executed. Their forced confession implicated the Jews of Cracow and Breslau. But, more interestingly, the notion of blood magic, already on the wane in ritual murder discourses of the central German lands, emerged as a central motif in this Bohemian trial.

Within the central lands of the empire, a significant development is discernible in investigations of ritual murder charges. Compared to the period of consolidation at the end of the fifteenth century, when the ritual murder discourse took on definite motifs—the identification of the victims as prepubescent boys, the conflation of images of ritual murders and eucharistic sacrifices, and the salvific power of Christian blood—the representations of blood libel cases in the late sixteenth century became more diffuse in their discursive structures. Children of all ages, not only prepubescent boys, once again became identified as potential victims of ritual murders, the miraculous identification of the sacrificial children and the Eucharist was completely absent in all accounts of ritual murder after 1540, and the magical potency of Christian blood disappeared as a prominent motif in the trials. One could describe this process as the disintegration of the tripartite structure of ritual murder discourse: magical notions about Jews did not necessarily lead to accusations and interrogations, and the trials themselves were suppressed by imperial mandate. In other words, the ritual murder discourse was beginning to lose its former coherence, its narrative structure, and its power of persuasion. During this last phase, dissonant motifs appeared as fragments that did not quite add up to a coherent whole: the dead child, the blood collected in jars, and the ritual of death dangle like individual symbols in the documentary accounts; they appear as signs isolated from a larger field of meaning, vestiges of a discourse that had lost a part of its social audience. Under pressure from the elites, the popular discourse of ritual murder began to lose its former coherence, a process similar to the gradual dissolution of the agrarian cult of the *benandanti* in Friuli as a result of suppression by the Counter-Reformation clergy.[20] To analyze this phase of disintegration during the last decades of the sixteenth century, let us now examine three cases of blood libel between 1584 and 1593.

In the sixteenth century, many Jews found protection under noblemen, who valued the wealth and business acumen of this religious minority. In exchange for an annual "protection money," these *Schutz-*

20. See Carlo Ginzburg, *The Night Battles: Witchcraft and Agrarian Cults in the Sixteenth and Seventeenth Centuries* (Baltimore, 1983).

juden enjoyed the right of residence and legal protection under their noble lords. A rich Jew and a poor nobleman, however, were a poor mix, as a contemporary proverb says, and for some impoverished lords, the temptation to confiscate the wealth of their Jews to meet debt payments proved too great. In 1585 Schmul of Grumbach addressed a petition to the emperor accusing his former lord of unjust imprisonment.[21] For a number of years, Schmul and his family had been the Schutzjuden of the nobleman Conrad von Grumbach in Franconia, who received forty guldens a year in protection money. But in 1584, under the pretext that Schmul had murdered a Christian child and had minted false coins, Grumbach and his men forced their way into Schmul's house, took all his possessions, threw Schmul into jail, and tried to torture him into confessing to the charge. This desperate measure to improve his finances helped only in the short run. By 1598 Conrad von Grumbach could not pay his debtors. His assets were seized and inventoried by officials of the bishop of Würzburg, showing outstanding debts of 208,197 guldens, including money he still owed Schmul.[22]

While the imprisonment of Schmul was a flagrant act of injustice, with scant effort to represent it as a ritual murder case, a magisterial investigation in the same year (1584) in Worms showed greater judicial caution. The details of the case are worth examining, for they reveal the connections between suspicions of ritual murder and infanticide.

In the morning of 24 June 1584, Kunnigund, Eckhart Keullen's wife, took her small son, Peter, out to her garden. The Keullens lived right next to the Jewish cemetery, just outside the city wall, within clear sight of the spires of the magnificent Romanesque Cathedral of Worms. From a distance, she saw two broken bricks at the foot of the city wall. When she approached the spot, she discovered a half-buried infant and fainted from fright. When she came to, she ran to her neighbors and told them the horrible discovery.[23] The magistrates, after hearing Kunnigund's testimony, also questioned her neighbors: Anna, Jacob Scheckler's wife, Catharina, Hans Kampen's wife, and Anna, Hans Branntmayer's wife.[24] The three women told the city fathers they had looked at the body: it was a baby girl of about age six weeks, some blood drops could still be detected on the forehead and head of the corpse, and they were of the opinion that the baby did not die a natural death. A physician summoned

21. StA Wü, Hochstift Würzburg, Adel 1369, folios 9ʳ–14ᵛ.
22. StA Wü, Hochstift Würzburg, Adel 1369, folios 63ʳ–70ʳ.
23. Testimony of Kunnigundt Keullen in the city council, 24 June 1584, StdA Worms, 2031/1, folios 2–3.
24. Witnesses 3–5, StdA Worms, 2031/1, folio 3.

by the magistrates, Dr. Theodorus, had also examined the baby. He discovered seventeen prick marks on the knees and feet and concurred with the women that the infant had not died a natural death.

Four other witnesses testified. Eckhart Keullen had nothing to add to his wife's testimony.[25] Georg Gauch, a citizen, claimed he saw a Jew passing by his door the day before who looked as if he was carrying something under his cloak. When Gauch asked the Jew what he was carrying, the man simply ignored him and walked on. Gauch also said he had no animosity against the Jews and could not remember what the man looked like.[26] Next, two young men testified. Hans Neirbeyer from Bern was an apprentice with the blacksmith, Hans Selden, under whom he had been working for five weeks. He told the magistrates this story: yesterday, 23 June, his master's servant rushed up to him at seven in the morning and pointed out to him that a Jew was burying something between two bricks at the foot of the city wall. Earlier in the day, Hans had seen a Jew digging a hole in the very same spot. He could not, however, give an accurate description of the Jew, except that he was a tall man with a long beard and a long coat. The miller's servant also witnessed the whole thing. At the end, Hans swore to the magistrates that he was telling the truth.[27] Hans's companion, Deobalt Kefler, the blacksmith's servant, confirmed the apprentice's statement in each detail.[28]

Next to testify were two leaders from the Jewish community, Isaac zur Samen and Lewr zur Genuss.[29] On 14 June, Nathan's wife had given birth to twins in the hospital of the ghetto. Barbara Adloff was the midwife. One of the baby girls died and was buried yesterday by the *Spitalmeister* Abraham. Isaac and Lewr asked the magistrates for permission to rebury the child.

After a short deliberation, the Bürgermeister sent for Barbara the midwife and Nathan, the father of the baby girl. The midwife confirmed that she did indeed deliver the twins; one girl was born very weak but got stronger. Questioned about the cuts on the infant, she suggested that the couple must have known about this. Barbara also mentioned in passing the marital quarrels between husband and wife, suggesting to the magistrates, perhaps, a motive for child abuse and accidental infanticide.[30] Nathan recognized the dead infant as his and told the magistrates that it had died on June 22; he then asked Abraham to bury the child in a corner of the Jewish cemetery, according to their customs. Nathan claimed to

25. StdA Worms, 2031/1, folio 4.
26. StdA Worms, 2031/1, folios 2, 5.
27. StdA Worms, 2031/1, folios 3–4.
28. StdA Worms, 2031/1, folios 4–5.
29. StdA Worms, 2031/1, folios 5–6.
30. StdA Worms, 2031/1, folios 5–6.

know nothing about the cuts and said he would ask his wife about them. But the magistrates held him in custody.[31]

The next day, 25 June, the magistrates resumed their investigation. Abraham the Spitalmeister was cleared of all charges.[32] The next step was to question Nathan's wife, the mother of the dead child. Master Steffan Frantzen, barber surgeon, accompanied the magistrates into the ghetto as expert witness. Mergen, the mother, was bedridden after childbirth and could hardly eat or drink for three weeks. The magistrates showed her the dead baby girl and put the twins side by side on a table. Mergen identified the dead infant as her daughter. When asked about the cut marks, she said there were none on the baby when it was carried away to be buried. Still suspicious, the magistrates lay the dead child beside her on the bed. Mergen put her hand on its chest but no blood could be seen, "hence one could recognize that she was guilty for its death," concludes the official inquiry.[33] Once again, Mergen protested her ignorance of the cut marks and suggested that perhaps the body had been bruised by bricks when it was buried. The record of the inquest ends with a magisterial order to rebury the infant.[34] Nothing more is known about the fate of Nathan and Mergen.

How did the infant girl get those cuts? Was she abused by her parents? Was her body bruised during burial? Or did someone dig up the baby, inflict prick wounds, and try to frame the Jews? Did Hans Neirbeyer and Deobalt Kefler secretly dig up the child and plant false evidence of "ritual murder" during the night of 24 June before the body was discovered in the morning? Or were they simply telling the truth, since they did not make any specific accusations against the Jews? Tantalizing as these questions may be, one can only speculate about possible answers, given the lack of documentation. But one point can be reasonably surmised from the records: the judicial thinking of the magistrates is revealed by the turn in the investigation; what began as an inquiry into a possible ritual murder ended up as a suspected case of infanticide. The cut marks, a buried child in the Jewish cemetery, and a mysterious Jewish gravedigger—these were the motifs that sustained the initial suspicion of ritual murder. But when the dead infant turned out to be Jewish, and when the parents readily identified the child as theirs, the magistrates transformed the ritual murder investigation into an infanticide case. Instead of seeing other possible explanations for the cut marks on the body of the infant girl, the city fathers were convinced of its violent

31. StdA Worms, 2031/1, folio 7.
32. StdA Worms, 2031/2, folios 1–2.
33. StdA Worms, 2031/2, folios 3–5.
34. StdA Worms, 2031/2, folio 5.

death. The strength of the initial ritual murder suspicion carried the investigation into the realm of infanticide, an act that became criminalized during the course of the sixteenth century.

The third case took place in 1593. In that year, Abraham of Lublin came to Frankfurt from Poland and asked for charity from the most prosperous and numerous Jewish community in the Holy Roman Empire. Having received the token sum of one and a half dalers and being openly scorned by the Frankfurt Jews for his foreign appearance, Abraham plotted vengeance to make the Frankfurt Jews pay for their snobbery. He bought oxen blood from a butcher, hid the bottle of blood in the synagogue, and tipped off the authorities. The truth came out during the official inquest; imprisoned for a time by the magistrates, Abraham was eventually released.[35]

These three cases reflected the spent fury of ritual murder *trials* in the last decades of the sixteenth century. Too many false accusations and mistrials in the past had undermined the credibility of further prosecutions. But while the decline of the magical discourse of blood libel and its replacement by a legal discourse dissolved the foundations of court convictions, the popular belief that Jews had actually murdered Christian children in the past persisted in collective memory. This process of remembering, this cultural preservation, was achieved by the creation of a historicity, a history of ritual murders, or, more accurately speaking, of a myth of Jewish child murders. Thus, ritual murder passed from the realm of the functional—where beliefs and actual accusations could lead to inquests, trials, sentencing, or dismissal—into that nebulous region of myth—where fragments of past events and contemporary imagination flowed in and out of a unifying structure of cohesive signs and meanings—thus creating a knowledge to be transmitted under the guise of history. In this process of cultural preservation and transmission, both Lutheran and Catholic Germany were involved, and the commemoration of past Jewish "crimes" against Christianity worked in different ways to strengthen a sense of confessional identity. In Lutheran Germany, this process took the form of the study of Judaism and manifested itself most strongly in a confessional historical consciousness in which Protestant Christianity identified itself as the New Israel; in Counter-Reformation Germany, beginning with a popular religious revival in the seventeenth century, past Jewish "crimes" served to fuel new devotional practices and to establish a bond between baroque and medieval Catholicism. Transcending the confessional divide, ballads, tales, and paintings

35. StdA Ff Ugb E47p.

helped to preserve memories of Host desecration and child murders in collective folk memory.

Jews as magicians, as child murderers, became an archetype and a derogative ethnic slur. Even when ritual murder trials went out of fashion, the discourse of Jewish magic lingered on in print here and there. In 1573, when the Brandenburg elector Johann Georg sentenced the Jew Leopold to be broken on the wheel and quartered, on charges of poisoning the old elector Joachim II and minting false coins, a litany of "crimes" was attributed to him in a pamphlet: described as a "conjuror of the Devil," a fornicator who slept with Christian women, a murderer, thief, traitor, and magician, Leopold was the very embodiment of Evil.[36] In fact, Leopold of Prague was the mint master and tax collector of the recently deceased Joachim II, and his judicial murder resulted from popular hatred against his fiscal measures. Politics, not magic, was the cause of Leopold's downfall.[37]

Other examples abound. In 1591 Johann Georg Gödelmann, a doctor of canon and civil law, accused Jews of being a blasphemous and magical people in his learned Latin treatise on how to recognize and punish magicians and witches.[38] In 1595 the printer Arnd Westhoff of Dortmund published an anti-Jewish booklet that was in essence a compilation and condensation of Luther's major writings against the Jews.[39] Among the accusations against the Jews, the blood libel was mentioned. The publication of this booklet served as a prelude to the expulsion of the small Jewish community from the Lutheran imperial city of Dortmund in Westphalia. On strong protest from the Frankfurt Jews, particularly in regard to the charge of ritual murder, Emperor Rudolf II ordered the confiscation and ban of the booklet and the arrest of the printer, apparently to no avail.[40]

36. See L.T.Z.T. [pseud.], *Warhaftige Geschicht vnd Execution Leupoldt Judens/welche an ihme seiner wolverdienten grausamen und unmenschlichen thaten halben (so er an dem unschuldigen Christlichen Blut begangen) den 28. Jenners/1573 zu Berlyn/nach innhalt Götliches und Keyserliches Rechten vollnzogen worden ist* (1573), sig. A².

37. For the pro-Jewish elector Joachim II, see chap. 7. After the execution of Leopold, his widow appealed to the Imperial Aulic Court to no avail. See Frey, *Rechtsschutz der Juden,* pp. 107–8.

38. *De magis veneficis et lamiis recte cognoscendis et puniendis libri tres* (Frankfurt: Nicolaus Bassaeus, 1591), quoted in Lynn Thorndike, *A History of Magic and Experimental Magic,* vol. 6 (New York, 1941), pp. 535–37.

39. *Christlicher Unterricht D. Mart. Lutheri/von den Jüden Lügen wider die Person unsers Herren Jesu Christi/seiner Lieben Murter Maria/und aller Christen/hochnötig zu lesen. Dar aus ein jeder Christ liechtlich schliessen kan/ob man die Jüden billich bey sich leiden solle oder nicht* (Dortmund: Arnd Westhoff, s.d.). A copy of this booklet in octavo is bound with other folios in StdA Ff Ugb E46 ad J1, folios 13–54.

40. The ban, however, had limited success. For a discussion of this censorship case, see R. Po-chia Hsia, "Printing, Censorship, and Anti-Semitism in Reformation Germany,"

THE LEGACY

Censorship could control only expressions, not thoughts. Forced out of the law courts by imperial mandate, the ritual murder discourse lodged itself in the historical consciousness of Lutheran and Catholic Germany. If the 1470 Endingen trial records provided historical "proof" of the magical crimes of the Jews, when the confessions were copied verbatim in the *Kopialbuch* of the city council of Freiburg, serving eventually as a historical reference for the 1504 Freiburg trial, a very different approach to ritual murders as "history" can be discerned in the early seventeenth century, when the Catholic officials of an ecclesiastical state sought cooperation from the Lutheran magistrates of an imperial city.

On 9 September 1611, the officials of the Cologne archiepiscopal government in Arnsberg wrote to the city council of Frankfurt to ask for cooperation in a crime investigation.[41] In their letter, the Cologne officials reported on the arrest of several Jews accused of torturing and murdering a child in the Westphalian town of Brilon. Further charges that Frankfurt Jews had committed similar crimes were brought to their attention. The imprisoned Jews, however, maintained their innocence and begged the officials of the archbishop to write to Frankfurt, so that the city fathers "might open up their old and new protocol and find out for themselves whether such stories had ever been recorded."[42] After spending more than a month examining the records of the city council for the last hundred and fifty years, the Frankfurters wrote back on 7 October.[43] On thorough research in their own archive, the city fathers found only two cases in the past: in 1504 the shoemaker Bryhenn killed his stepson and falsely accused Gumprecht;[44] and in 1593 the Polish Jew Abraham of Lublin planted false evidence to cast suspicion on the Frankfurt Jews.[45] Other than these two incidents in a period of 150 years, the Frankfurters reported, they could find nothing else on ritual murders in the city records. Regarding the painting under the arch of the Brückenturm Gate (which depicted the alleged 1474 ritual murder in Trent), the magistrates had this to say: the picture did not refer to a real event in Frankfurt but to a murder in foreign Trent, committed many years ago.[46] At the further

---

in *The Process of Change in Early Modern Europe: Essays in Honor of Miriam Usher Chrisman*, ed. Sherrin Marshall and Philip N. Bebb (Athens, Ohio, 1988).

41. This letter, together with the reply of the Frankfurt magistrates, is deposited in StdA Ff Ugb E47p.

42. "Sie wolten Ihre alte unndt neuwe Prothocolla aufschlagen unndt sich darauss erkundigen lassen, ob solch geschicht sich daselbst jemahls zugetragen" StdA Ff Ugb E47p.

43. Letter of City Council to the Cologne officials at Arnsberg, 7 Oct. 1611, StdA Ff Ugb E47p.

44. See chap. 5.

45. See n. 35.

46. See fig. 13.

request of the Frankfurt Jewish community, the magistrates enclosed with their reply a copy of the 1577 imperial mandate of Rudolf II, wherein all privileges of Jews in the Holy Roman Empire were confirmed and all ritual murder trials by territorial authorities outlawed.[47]

In their reply, the Frankfurt magistrates clearly denied a Frankfurt connection to the alleged Brilon child murder; in fact, the tone of their letter tended to discredit ritual murder trials in general. But these were the same men who had rejected a 1609 petition by the Jewish community to remove the painting of Simon of Trent's "martyrdom" at the entrance of the Brückenturm Gate.[48] To the city fathers, perhaps, the ritual murder at Trent was a historical event just as real and as irrefutable as the innocence of the Frankfurt Jews; both "facts" were attested to by written discourse—in one case by chronicles, histories, pamphlets, and by the very painting on their own city gate, in the other by the carefully kept records of the city council. Ritual murder was a part of history.

For the Frankfurt Jews, however, the painting did not represent a historical event and harmless myth. To them it meant literally a matter of life and death. In their 1609 petition, the Committee of Ten of the Jewish Community (Zehender der Judischeit) described the effect of the painting on Christian treatment of Jews:

> And since the painting had been standing under the Brückenturm (with a naked child tortured to death with awls by Jews), we poor folks have to suffer all sorts of injuries and curses, from someone here and another there in passing, and have been condemned to numerous tortures and pains that one can always invent; and afflicted with such fear and fright, we know not how we should behave in such great anxiety. The common rabble can assume from such a daring painting that we Jews need to have Christian blood at all times, and that our ceremonies and faith are such, that we have to purchase or kidnap Christian children and murder them slowly. And since this is such a cruel and repulsive vengeance, it would be unchristian and unfair, that a single Jew should be left alive; rather, one should attack them, torture and kill them like inhumans [unmenschen] and slaughter them with less mercy than one would slaughter dogs.[49]

The Jewish leaders then reminded the magistrates that during past church councils, scholars had examined their books and found nothing therein to lend credence to the blood libel. The emperors, too, had condemned ritual murder beliefs.

The common people, however, were the deadly enemies of the

47. Another copy of Rudolf II's mandate can be found in StdA Ff Ugb E46y.

48. See letter of petition by the *Judischeit* (the organization of the Jewish community) to the city council of Frankfurt, 21 Nov. 1609 (StdA Ff Ugb E46y).

49. Letter of the Baumeister and Zehender of the Judischeit to the city council of Frankfurt, 21 Nov. 1609 (StdA Ff Ugb E46y).

Jews, and the painting must be removed, as the petition went on to say: "Not least because the unreasoning common crowd [der Gemein unverstendige Hauff] are wrapped up in misunderstanding, and hold this painting in such power, as if the authorities themselves had rendered judgement, that everyone is allowed to pursue revenge with the sword."[50] The petition reminded the magistrates how easy it would be for blood to be spilled, if the city fathers had not always acted firmly against the common people. The Jewish leaders "still remember with horror" the events of 1607, when an imperial commission was investigating the so-called Frankfurt Rabbinic Conspiracy,[51] and the mob used the pretext of a fire to try to plunder the ghetto.

If the magistrates would remove the inflammatory painting, the "fury of the mob" would be contained, peace would be preserved, and the Jews would continue to enjoy the patronage and protection of the city council, "and could live securely without fear of bodily danger to themselves." Moreover, since "the depiction of this inhuman event does not refer to an event in this city, and it is uncertain whether it took place in Vienna or Weissenburg," the petitioners continued, it would be best to remove the picture and not to further agitate "the common mob" with such dangerous material. If any Jew were actually guilty of such a heinous crime, the Jewish leaders would gladly assist the magistrates in finding the culprit. But in the meantime, the Jews begged the authorities to believe in their innocence and to protect them against "attacks, revolts, and seditions."[52]

This passionate and urgent appeal from the ghetto fell on deaf ears in the Ratshaus on the Römer. Two years later, Moses zum Schwan and Hirsch zum grünem Schild again appealed to the city council. In their letter, dated 30 April 1612, they asked the Bürgermeister and magistrates to remove the painting, or at least cover it, on account of the forthcoming gathering of the electors, "since different nations and foreign peoples would come here, and we [the Jews] might find ourselves in great danger

50. StdA Ff Ugb E46y.

51. The so-called Frankfurter Rabinerverschwörung of 1603 was instigated by Archbishop Ferdinand of Cologne. In that year, the Frankfurt rabbis invited other Jewish communities to send delegates to a meeting in Frankfurt in order to deliberate on establishing an organization to represent the interests of all the Jews in the Holy Roman Empire. Archbishop Ferdinand accused the Jews of planning an illicit political organization; an imperial commission was preoccupied with the investigation for the next few years. For a thorough discussion of the incident, see Volker Press, "Kaiser Rudolph II und der Zusammenschluss der deutschen Judenheit: Die sogenannte Frankfurter Rabinerverschwörung von 1603 und ihre Folgen," in Zur Geschichte der Juden im Deutschland des späten Mittelalters und der frühen Neuzeit, ed. Alfred Haverkamp (Stuttgart, 1981), pp. 243–93.

52. StdA Ff Ugb E46y.

on account of the said painting."[53] On this occasion, the city fathers favored the petition and ordered the painting to be covered over the Election.[54]

The reprieve was temporary. Not only did the painting continue to stand in plain view of anyone passing through the Brückenturm Gate, but it was renovated in 1678, the occasion of which gave rise to the printing of a scurillous and disgusting broadsheet, with picture and verse commemorating the renovation (fig. 14). The top portion of the illustration reproduces the gruesome wall painting that depicts the boy Simon lying on a board, bloody with wounds pierced by awls. The bottom two-thirds presents a scene with the Brückenturm in the background. A man dressed as a rabbi gazes at the wall painting on the arch under the tower and mutters gibberish that is obviously supposed to be Hebrew. Occupying the central foreground are two rabbis. One is sitting on a sow (the accompanying text calls him Rabbi Schilo) and flipping its tail, while the other eats its feces. A child is sucking from the breasts of the sow. To the left, the rabbi's wife rides on a goat, which bears a clear resemblance to the Devil, who smiles and watches the scene. The scatological verses describe how Jews derive their nourishment from the excrement and milk of the sow and how the woman can ride on the two-horned scapegoat and fly through the air. The rabbi calls forth all Jews to return to the Holy Land,[55] for the "Goyim" are making an end of them on account of Trent. The Jews deserve the gallows and the wheel because they have no remorse and are damned.

Demonization is the central theme. As one of the animals symbolizing the Devil, the *Judensau* became one of the most repellent creations of anti-Semitism.[56] The goat, again a demonic animal, symbolizes lust and featured prominently in representations of witchcraft. Suckling the milk of the Judensau, Jewish children thus learn the demonic ways of their fathers; the eating of feces reflects the popular belief that devils fed on feces, a motif that appears frequently in Luther's writings.[57] The ico-

53. Letter of Mosche zum Schwan und Hirtz (Hirsch), Baumeister of the Jewish community to the Bürgermeister and city council, 30 Apr. 1612, StdA Ff Ugb E46y.

54. On the back of the petition is notated: "Lect. 30. Aprilis, Ao 1612. Relect. 7. Maij Ao 1612 und beschlossen, solcher Gemälte den Wahltag über zuzuhalten." See also StdA Ff Bgmb 1612 30 April and 7 May, and Kracauer, *Geschichte der Juden in Frankfurt*, vol. 1, p. 369.

55. A satirical reference, no doubt, to the messianic movement among the European Jewry generated by the self-proclaimed Messiah Sabbetai Zevi (1626–76).

56. See Isaiah Shachar, *The Judensau: A Medieval Anti-Jewish Motif and Its History* (London, 1974).

57. The identification of feces with demonic pollution is well known in Luther's writings. The reformer's scatology, in fact, reflects the popular cultural and symbolic structures of the age. In the much read chapbook of the adventures of Til Ulenspiegel, there is an episode where the peasant rogue tricked some Frankfurt Jews into buying his feces as

nography is crude and direct: to the authors of the broadsheet the Jews embodied a demonic species; they were enemies of Christians and children of the Antichrist.[58] It took almost another century after 1678 before the authorities would obliterate this painting of Simon of Trent.

Until the nineteenth century, when Berlin grew to be the leading center of German Jewry after the emancipation of Jews, Frankfurt remained the most populous, the wealthiest, and the most powerful Jewish community in the Holy Roman Empire. In the seventeenth century, this Lutheran city on the Main became the leading center of Jewish publishing in the empire; the vibrancy of its Jewish community also nourished an incipient academic interest on Jews and Judaism by German scholars.

One of the best known German students of Judaism in the seventeenth century was Johann Jacob Schudt (1664–1722).[59] Born in Frankfurt to a Lutheran pastor, Schudt studied at the *Gymnasium* in his home town before enrolling at the University of Wittenberg. He returned to teach at his alma mater in Frankfurt, eventually becoming its rector in 1717. We owe much of our knowledge of contemporary Jewish life to his many observances and anecdotes, compiled and published in a massive four-part work, *Jewish Curiosities* (1714–17).[60] He remarked that in his own day, Christians still suspected Jews of kidnapping and murdering children; thus, when a child ran away or was lost, its parents would be most anxious, lest it would enter the ghetto and fall prey to the Jews.[61] Schudt himself, however, in spite of his general hostility toward Jews, emphatically denied that Jews had killed Christians for blood.[62]

This scholarly skepticism of the reality of ritual murders was shared by another Lutheran professor. Christof Wagenseil (1633–1705) was born in Nuremberg to a prominent merchant family. After studies at Altdorf and Orléans, he served for some years as tutor to various Austrian noblemen before returning as professor of Oriental languages to Alt-

---

rare medicament (thirty-fifth story). During the early evangelical movement, Luther's Franciscan foe, Thomas Murner, lampooned the reformer with literary and pictorial feces in a polemical tract, *Von dem Grossen Lutherischen Narren;* see *Thomas Murners Deutsche Schriften,* ed. Paul Merker, vol. 9 (Strasbourg, 1918), p. 267.

58. Trachtenberg, *The Devil and the Jews.*

59. *ADB,* vol. 32, pp. 652–63.

60. *Jüdische Merckwürdigkeiten,* 4 parts (Frankfurt and Leipzig, 1714–17; reprint, Berlin, 1922), with continuous pagination.

61. "Und weil dann diese Beschuldigung wider die Juden noch heut zu Tage währet/dahero auch/wann sich in dieser Stadt ein kind verläufft oder verliehrt/ist der Eltern grösste Sorge/es möge in die Judengasse gekommen/und von Juden umgebracht worden seyn" (Schudt, *Jüdische Merckwürdigkeiten,* p. 1335).

62. Schudt, *Jüdische Merckwürdigkeiten,* pt. 2, bk. 36, sect. 4 (p. 1355), and pt. 4, bk. 36, sect. 4 (p. 2587).

Figure 14. The Brückenturm in Frankfurt. From a 1678 broadsheet commemorating the renovation of the Brückenturm. The scurrilous verses mimick "Jewish curses" of Christians. To the left, the rabbis and their family are depicted as the Devil's servants; to the right, standing under the Brückenturm passage, a rabbi looks at the painting of Simon of Trent, which is reproduced in detail at the top of the broadsheet. Reproduced courtesy of the Historisches Museum Frankfurt. Photograph kindly supplied by Frau Ursula Seitz-Gray.

dorf.[63] In his many writings on Judaism, Wagenseil tried to educate at least the learned reader of the falsity of ritual murder charges, although his books are otherwise filled with criticisms of the economic practices, religion, and character of German Jewry.[64] Wagenseil singled out for praise Count Palatine Christian August of Sulzbach (1622–1708) for his justice: twice in his land, in 1682 and 1692, charges of Jewish child murders were raised, and, after thorough investigations proved the falsity of the accusations, Christian ordered corporal punishment for anyone bringing false accusations against Jews.[65]

In the same decades that Schudt and Wagenseil were cautiously offering Protestant Germany a relatively more accurate picture of Jewish life and history, another Protestant *érudit*, Johann Andreas Eisenmenger (1654–1704), professor of Oriental languages at Heidelberg, was much more ambivalent in his attitude toward the blood libel. In his massive and pretentious tome, *Judaism Discovered* (1700), Eisenmenger affirmed the historical veracity of the blood libel: he recounted the history of ritual murders from the fifth century onward, mentioning Trent (1475), Regensburg (1486 [sic]), Pösing (1509 [sic]), and Sappenfeld (1540), among others.[66] In addition to the many history books and theological treatises, Eisenmenger cited as authority the Brückenturm painting depicting the death of Simon of Trent. After giving contemporary examples of alleged ritual murders in Poland, Eisenmenger conceded:

> One does not hear nowadays any more of these gruesome acts in Germany, except that, if I remember correctly, I had read in the newspaper

63. *ADB*, vol. 40, pp. 481–83.

64. In his *Benachrichtigungen wegen einiger die Judenschafft angehenden wichtigen Sachen*, pt. 1 (Frankfurt, 1705), p. 126*ff.*, Wagenseil discredits the blood libel: "Der Denen Juden fälschlich beymessene Gebrauch der Christen-Bluts. Das ist Unwidersprechliche Widerlegung der entsetzlichen Unwarheit, dass die Juden zu ihrer Bedurfnis Christen-Blut haben müssen, welche so viel tausend dieser unschuldigen Leute um Haab, Leib und Leben gebracht."

65. Wagenseil, *Hofnung der Erlösung Israelis, oder Klarer Beweiss der annoch bevorstehenden . . . grossen Jüden-Bekehrung*, 2d ed. (Nuremberg and Altdorf, 1706), pp. 28*f*. The count Palatine was also the patron of the leading Christian Hebraist of the age, Christian Knorr von Rosenroth (1636–89), author and compiler of the 1,400 folio thick *Kabbala denudata*. Christian August later converted from Lutheranism to Catholicism. See Manfred Finke, "Toleranz und 'Discrete' Frömmigkeit nach 1650: Pfalzgraf Christian August von Sulzbach und Ernst von Hessen-Rheinfels," in *Frömmigkeit in der frühen Neuzeit: Studien zur religiösen Literatur des 17. Jahrhunderts in Deutschland*, ed. Dieter Breuer (Amsterdam, 1984), pp. 193–212.

66. *Entdecktes Judenthum: oder Gründlicher und Wahrhaffter Bericht, welchergestalt die verstockte Juden die Hochheilige Dreyeinigkeit . . . erschrecklicher Weise lästern und verunehren, die Heil. Mutter Christi verschmähen . . . Dabey noch viele andere, bishero unter den Christen entweder gar nicht, oder nur zum Theil bekantgewesene Dinge und Grosse Irrthüme der Jüdischen Religion und Theologie, wie auch viel lächerliche und kurtzweilige Fabeln und andere ungereimte Sachen an den Tag kommen: Alles aus ihren eigenen . . . Büchern* (Frankfurt, 1700), pp. 220–24.

some years ago that in Franconia a murdered child was found and therefore the Jews were held on suspicion. But since one has in the past dealt most stringently with the Jews wherever such things were committed, it is thus beyond doubt that they refrain from such bloodshed out of fear of punishment, although their hatred of Christians is just as great now as it might have been at any time in the past.[67]

Eisenmenger repeated the catalog of magical beliefs surrounding blood; he speculated that perhaps rabbis used Christian blood in writing spells on amulets.[68] At the end of his discussion, Eisenmenger grudingly admitted that perhaps in the past some instances of injustice were involved in the handling of ritual murder accusations, but he himself was inclined to believe in a core element of truth in these charges because so many authorities had written about them and so many examples had been cited. He concluded "that Jews committed child murders mostly during Easter . . . because our Savior Christ was crucified at Easter, and they did this to scorn him."[69]

From the perspective of Protestant Germany in the late seventeenth century, it seemed that Christians were finally disenchanted from Jewish magic. Deprived of their murderous power, exposed as superstitious, Jews remained nonetheless an alien and potentially dangerous element due to their wealth. The academic study of Judaism and Jewish life in Protestant Germany served only in passing to dispel popular legends; for many, its chief function was to document and ridicule Jewish superstitions and to celebrate the triumph of evangelical Christianity over medieval magic, a victory achieved by the heroic struggles of the Reformation at the cost of a divided Christendom.

If books and theology kept alive the myth of Jewish magic in Protestant Germany, the ritual murder discourse was rejuvenated by the popular Catholic revival beginning in the mid-seventeenth century.[70] One

---

67. "Mann höret aber jetziger Zeit nichts mehr von solchen grausamen thaten in Teutschland/ausser dem das ich/wann ich mich recht erinnere/vor etlichen jahren in der zeitung gelesen hab/dass in Franckenland ein ermordtetes kind seye gefunden worden/ und habe man die Juden desswegen im verdacht gehabt: dann weil mann vor diesem mit den Juden sehr scharff verfahren ist/allwo solche dinge seind begangen worden/so ist nicht zu zweiffelen/sie auss furcht vor der straff/sich nun solches blutvergiessens enthalten/ wiewohl ihr hass gegen die Christen eben so gross ist/als er jemahls vor diesem gewesen sein mag" (Eisenmenger, *Entdecktes Judenthum*, pp. 224–25).

68. Eisenmenger, *Entdecktes Judenthum*, p. 225.

69. Eisenmenger, *Entdecktes Judenthum*, p. 227.

70. The scholarship on the Counter-Reformation has focused so far on the institutions of the Tridentine church and on the major ecclesiastical leaders. A popular Catholic revival, especially in Bavaria and Austria, began relatively late, but a revival of pilgrimages and devotional practices after the Thirty Years' War made popular Catholicism of the 17th and 18th centuries a topic highly deserving of study.

way of combating the Protestant Reformation, in the eyes of the Catholic church, was to reclaim the heritage of the late medieval church; the Roman church could offer what the Lutherans and Calvinists could not, namely, miracles, new saints, and sacred legends.

Sanctity and patriotism were united in the work of Matthaeus Rader (1561–1634), the Tyrolean Jesuit who helped to give Bavarian self-image its distinctive blend of international baroque Catholicism and provincial Bavarian patriotism. Born in Innichen, Tirol, Rader studied at the Jesuit college in Munich before joining the Society of Jesus at the age of twenty. As one of the most prominent clerics in the Bavarian Counter-Reformation, Rader counted among his friends the leading Catholic intellectuals, among them the great scholar Justus Lipsius, the Jesuit Martin Delrio, and the Capuchin Francesco Valerian de Magni, court preacher in Vienna.[71]

Rader's fame was secured by his publication of *Bavaria Sancta*, a four-volume compilation of hagiographies and biographies of saints, monks, bishops, holy women, martyred children, and pious Bavarian dukes and duchesses from the time of the conversions of the Germanic peoples to his own day.[72] Dedicated to Duke Maximilian I, whom Rader compared to Constantine the Great, the book equates Bavarian history with the history of Christianization, a process begun under Charlemagne in Germany and brought to perfect fruition at last under the Wittelsbach dukes, with the selfless dedication of the Jesuits. Saints and martyrs peopled this heroic missionary saga: a place of honor was created for the alleged victims of ritual murder in Rader's story of Christian testimony and Catholic vitality. Local heroes mentioned in this tale of Holy-Bavarian-Land include a boy of Munich, martyred in 1285, the boy Heinrich of Munich, also an alleged victim of ritual murder, the six boys of Regensburg, martyred in 1486 (here, Rader got his dates of the Regensburg trial mixed up), and Michael of Sappenfeld, killed in 1540.[73] Engravings depict these little boy martyrs: the corporal sensuality of pious suffering brings to mind Rubenesque cherubs, redemptive flesh in the sensuous iconography of baroque Catholicism (see figs. 15, 16, and 17).

Not only were old legends recorded in seventeenth-century Catholic Germany, new ones were also being made. The most successful example of this was the creation of the Judenstein legend.[74] According to oral

71. *ADB*, vol. 27, p. 118.

72. *Bavaria Sancta*, 3 parts (Munich, 1615). German translations were published in Augsburg (1714), Straubing (1840), and Munich (1861–62) under the title of *Heiliges Bayer-Land*.

73. *Bavaria Sancta*, book 2, pp. 315–16, 331–33; book 3, pp. 172–75, 176–80.

74. See Strack, *The Jew and Human Sacrifice*, p. 91f., and Nadine Hauer, *Judenstein:*

Figure 15. The killing of Michael of Sappenfeld. From Matthaeus Rader, *Bavaria Sancta*. Reproduced by permission of the Houghton Library, Harvard University.

tradition, on 12 July 1462, the three-year-old boy Andreas Oxner, son of Simon and Maria, who lived in Rinn, a village near Innsbruck, was sold by his godfather to some traveling merchants and was then cruelly murdered by them in the nearby forest. After the Trent ritual murder trial of 1475, the tale took on new details: the traveling merchants became

Legende ohne Ende? (Vienna, 1985). In 1984 and 1985 Hauer investigated the suppression of the cult of Judenstein by the bishop of Innsbruck; her report includes journalistic interviews, historical background, and bibliographical references. I wish to thank Professor Ruth Angress of Princeton University for sending me a copy of this report.

Submiffa eft mihi forma & magnitudo corporis S. hujus
pueri Eyftadio per Nob. & Excell. D. Doct. Thomam Thiermair
Medicum, quam placuit hic ad nonam proportionem propter

MICHAEL PVER. M. 1540

Fórma et modus corpufculi S. Pueri et M. Michaëlis trimuli
et femestris in Hietingensi pago ab Iudæis crudelifsimè
excarnificati et interfecti ex nona proportione iurtæ staturæ.

magnitudinem imaginis redactam, repræfentare. Interim in 3.
Vol. Bau. S. p. 176. v. vlt. pro Titingensi, l. Hietingensi. Et p. 179.
v. 5. eand. vocem eod. modo corrige, Martyriü ipsü habes p. 173.

Figure 16. Michael of Sappenfeld as corpse and relic. This portrait was purportedly
based on a medical description of the prick marks and wounds. From Matthaeus
Rader, *Bavaria Sancta*. Reproduced by permission of the Houghton Library, Harvard
University.

Jews, the murder turned into a ritual sacrifice, and the village adopted
the toponymic name of Judenstein, after the stone on which Andreas was
allegedly murdered. The bones of the boy were reburied in the parish
church as relics for a local cult, and an inscription commemorated him as
a victim of ritual murder.

But the tradition was not committed to writing until the seventeenth
century. Dr. Hippolytus Guarinoni (1571–1654), physician of a cloister in

DE PVERIS RATISPONENS.   173

SEX PVERI RATISPONÆ AB IVDÆIS INTERFECTI.

En iterum nostras perfundit sanguine cunas
Vespus et exhaustâ turget hirudo cute.
Quis tandem vobis tam diri criminis auctor?
Sanguinis aut nostri tam grauis vnde sitis?

Primâns primævi soboles infanda parentis
Tam sævum docuit cæde patrare nefas?
An qui Bethlemios rex est grassatus in agnos?
Non poterant atauos hi docuisse suos?

Figure 17. The six children of Regensburg. The alleged victims of ritual murder, found in Rabbi Jossel's basement in Regensburg. From Matthaeus Rader, *Bavaria Sancta*. Reproduced by permission of the Houghton Library, Harvard University.

Hall, Tirol, took a deep interest in the legend of Andreas. He inquired about the legend from the local clergy, collected oral stories from the older people of Rinn, and discovered the 1475 inscription recording the event. By writing down his personal antiquarian quest, Guarinoni endowed this local cult with universal salvific meaning and elevated an oral folk tradition to a festival worthy of wider Catholic recognition. In 1670 a pilgrimage church was built to honor this little martyr boy; Adrian Kember, the abbot of Wilton, the Premonstratensian monastery that had jurisdiction over Judenstein, compiled the "Acta pro veritate martyrii corporis et cultus publici B. Andreae Rinnensis pueruli . . . ";[75] in 1753 Pope Benedict XIV sanctioned the use of a particular breviary and mass liturgy in honor of the blessed martyr; and in 1754 plenary indulgence was granted to those visiting the church at Rinn on 12 July, Andreas's feast day. Andreas of Rinn and Simon of Trent became the only two purported victims of ritual murder to be officially recognized by the papacy.[76]

Likewise, the revival of pilgrimages in the diocese of Passau, which grew in the seventeenth century and reached its zenith in the eighteenth, also drew strength from the 1477 legend of Host desecration.[77] The "crime" and the eucharistic triumph were celebrated in two as yet unidentified paintings of the seventeenth century: one depicts the Jews stabbing the Host; the other shows four Jews trying to burn the stolen Host in the synagogue, while angels and doves fly out of the oven.[78] The purported instrument of torture, a long curved dagger, was placed in a reliquary for display in Saint Salvator (formerly the synagogue),[79] and in 1800, the 1477 broadsheet commemorating Passau, with woodcuts and verses describing the Host desecration and sold to pilgrims of earlier generations, was reprinted for pilgrims of a later age.[80] A song commemorating 1477, composed by a local cleric, was immortalized in the romantic movement. The poet Clemens Brentano (1778–1842), like others of his generation who drew creative fantasy from medieval Catholicism, se-

75. Cf. Hayn, *Übersicht*, no. 62.

76. See the report by Cardinal Lorenzo Ganganelli (later Pope Clement XIV) on ritual murder (1759), in Cecil Roth, ed., *The Ritual Murder Libel and the Jew: The Report by Cardinal Lorenzo Ganganelli (Pope Clement XIV)* (London, 1934), original Italian text with English translation, pp. 53–55. For a German translation of Ganganelli's report (published with the Italian original), see Moritz Stern, ed., *Die päpstlichen Bullen gegen die Blutbeschuldigung* (Berlin, 1893). The cult persisted until 1985, with the sanction of the ecclesiastical hierarchy. Under the National Socialists, the legend of Judenstein was used for racial anti-Semitic propaganda. In 1984, Reinhold, bishop of Innsbruck, ordered the suppression of the cult. This led to confrontations between the clergy and the parishioners, who rallied to a defense of their "Anderl of Rinn." See Joachim Riedl, "Das Anderl vom Judenstein," in *Die Zeit* 38 (13 Sept. 1985), p. 74.

77. See Franz Mader, *Wallfahrten im Bistum Passau* (Munich, 1984); *Wallfahrten im Bistum Passau: Ausstellung im grossen Hofsaal der Neuen Residenz in Passau. 3. Mai bis 25. Oktober 1986* (Passau, 1986); and Walter Hartinger, *Mariahilf ob Passau: Volkskundliche Untersuchung der Passauer Wallfahrt und der Mariahilf-Verehrung im deutschsprachigen Raum* (Passau, 1985).

78. The paintings are in the Museum Veste Oberhaus, Passau; they are identified as museum inventory numbers 1750 and 1750a.

79. A photograph of the reliquary is reproduced in Mader, *Wallfahrten*, p. 31.

80. A copy is on display in the Museum Veste Oberhaus, inventory no. 822a.

lected it for his collection of German folk songs, *Des Knaben Wunderhorn*.[81] Not surprisingly, the revival of Catholicism in Bavaria sustained a climate of ritual murder suspicion. As late as 1732, five Jews were arrested on the accusation of a Kilian Bentgraf, who had murdered an eleven-year-old boy near Ried. Although the accused Jews had ironclad alibis, the jurists at the University of Ingolstadt, to whom the officials turned for legal advice, still claimed that "it was still a general opinion of this time that the Jews need Christian blood."[82]

For many Lutherans and Catholics of the eighteenth century, ritual murder was a historical reality: documented in old chronicles, judicial records, and past writings, it lived on as the stuff of legends. For the Jews, too, the blood libel provided a powerful motif in storytelling; they would create a myth of magical tales. In the first half of the eighteenth century, Jewish communities in Poland were threatened by a wave of blood accusations.[83] For the Eastern European Jewry, it was also a time of growing fascination with mysticism and the occult.[84] Many supernatural tales that extolled the power of cabalistic magic centered on a historical figure, the Great Rabbi Loew of Prague.

According to a family chronicle compiled by his descendants in 1727, the Great Rabbi Loew was born in 1512 in Worms. After serving Jewish communities in Moravia and Posen, he moved to Prague, where his profound cabalistic learning won him numerous students and great fame.[85]

In 1592, Emperor Rudolf II, who was more interested in the occult arts than in administration, summoned Rabbi Loew for an audience; this brief interview was to give rise to many fantastic legends of the rabbi's influence at court.[86] The first supernatural story about Rabbi Loew ap-

81. Compiled by Clemens Brentano and Ludwig Achim von Arnim and originally published between 1808 and 1854 in Heidelberg. The song, "Die Juden in Passau," consists of 21 strophes of four verses each and narrates the theft of the Host by Christoph Eisenhammer, its torture by the Jews, and their execution. I used the 1891 Halle reprint of the Heidelberg edition, pp. 59–61.

82. Güde, *Die rechtliche Stellung der Juden*, pp. 13f.

83. Roth, *Ritual Murder Libel*, pp. 24–26. The report by Cardinal Ganganelli, which condemned the Polish ritual murder trials, was occasioned by a petition to the Vatican from the Jewish communities in Poland.

84. Scholem, *Mysticism*, pp. 321ff.

85. Frederic Thieberger, *The Great Rabbi Loew of Prague* (London, 1955), pp. 8–9, 20–22.

86. Thieberger, *Rabbi Loew*, pp. 38–40. For a valiant effort in reconstructing the intellectual climate at the court of Rudolf II, see Robert J. W. Evans, *Rudolf II and His World: A Study in Intellectual History, 1576–1612* (Oxford, 1973).

peared in 1709, and between 1710 and 1730, the Great Rabbi became more and more a central figure of cabalistic legends.[87]

The most fascinating figure in these Rabbi Loew legends was the Golem, an artificial man created by cabalistic magic, using hidden formulas and secret knowledge of the ineffable name of God—the Schem, or tetragrammaton.[88] Jewish word magic, as it was applied throughout the Middle Ages, centered on the use of magical formulas in the making of talismans and amulets as charms against evil demons and illness.[89] In the fantasy world of these cabalistic legends, the prophylactic function of the sacred word was extended to protect the Jews against the blood libel. In the Jewish discourse on ritual murder, word magic was used to ward off blood magic.

Already the birth of the Great Rabbi portended luck and charm for his people, according to the first of these thirty-three legends about the great scholar: the occasion of his difficult birth foils an attempt to smuggle a dead child into the ghetto of Worms.[90] When he became chief rabbi in Prague, Loew was disturbed by the many ritual murder accusations against his people. A divine message was given to Rabbi Loew in a dream, and, using the ineffable name of God, he created the Golem out of a lump of earth, just as God had created Adam in the beginning. Disguised as one of his many household servants, the Golem, often made invisible by amulets prepared by the rabbi, would wander in the streets of the Prague ghetto at night to catch Jew-haters, who tried to implant false evidence of ritual murders.[91] All the expected motifs are present in these tales: the Jewish renegade who wants to ingratiate

87. Thieberger, *Rabbi Loew*, p. 79. These legends were first collected and published by Jüdel Rosenberg in 1909 under the title *Niphloath ha-Maharal* with a German translation by Chaim Bloch.

88. See Jean Marquès-Rivière, *Amulettes, talismans et pantacles dan les traditions orientales et occidentales* (Paris, 1972), p. 54: "La création artificielle d'un être vivant, d'un *Golem*, était une chose possible, pour la tradition kabbalistique, tant était puisante, pour elle, l'action du "mot" convenablement utilisé. On trouve l'histoire d'un Golem dans toutes les communautés juives médiévales." The 13th-century German *Hasidim* were especially intrigued by the problem of generating a human being; from them comes the use of the word *golem* to designate a homunculus created by the magical invocation of names; see Trachtenberg, *Jewish Magic*, pp. 84–86. For the role of the golem in Jewish mystical thought, see Scholem, *Mysticism*, pp. 98–99.

89. Amulets are essentially talismans with inscriptions. For definitions of the two, see Marquès-Rivière, *Amulettes*, p. 8. For an introduction to medieval Jewish amulets and magical practices, see Josephy, *Magic*, passim (unpaginated). This volume is the catalog of an exhibition of Jewish magic and superstition at the Spertus Museum of Judaica and contains many illustrations of amulets.

90. Chayim Bloch, *The Golem: Legends of the Ghetto of Prague*, trans. Harry Schneiderman (Vienna, 1925), story 4.

91. Bloch, *The Golem*, story 8.

himself with his new patrons; the fanatical monk Thaddeus who stoops to framing the Jews; the resentful journeymen who envy the wealth of their employer; the just Emperor and conscientious magistrates; and, of course, the Great Rabbi Loew, pious, wise, and skillful, and his mute assistant, the Golem with superhuman strength. When the "last" ritual murder case was exposed in 1589, the Great Rabbi turns the Golem back into a lump of clay.[92]

In these legends about the life of Loew of Prague, the storm of persecutions is dispersed by piety and learning; rays of divine light break through the dark clouds of bigotry to illuminate the hope for the future. For the Jews of Eastern Europe, who had to endure the reality of anti-Jewish violence, these imaginary tales of a heroic age in a civilized Holy Roman Empire gave strength to the powerless and hope to the fearful.

92. Bloch, *The Golem*, story 23.

Conclusion

In the two generations before the Reformation, ritual murder and Host desecration trials reached a climax in the Holy Roman Empire. For princes and magistrates, one trial fed into another and past convictions justified new suspicions, until the blood libel took on an overwhelming momentum of its own. The individual trials represented much more than instances of crime and punishment. As symbols of the murderous magic of Jews, the trials furnished the historical "reality" for the articulation and consolidation of a discourse of ritual murder, which in turn sustained new accusations, inquests, and convictions.

During this phase, there was a broad consensus in Christian society on the magical nature of Jews. A wide spectrum of opinion, ranging from learned theological and legal discourse in the universities, through a vernacular culture of books, sermons, and prints in the towns, reached down to the lowest sectors of rural society, where the belief of ritual murder motivated criminals to murder children and initiate blood transactions with Jews. The essential mentality underlying ritual murder discourse was the Christian belief in sacrifice, the dominant form of its representation being the story of Christ's Passion. In accusing Jews of child murders, and in extracting confessions from the suspects, the magistrates and the people thus created repetitions and variations on the theme of Christian sacrifice. The tortured Christian children, the bleeding little martyrs, and the abused Eucharist became symbols by which a society created its own moments and loci of sanctity. In acting out this sacred drama of human redemption, everyone was assured a role: the innocent Christian martyrs, the murderous Jews, the conscientious magistrates, the treacherous Christians who kidnapped and murdered children for money, and the entire Christian community, which participated both in witnessing the execution of the Jews and in receiving the fruits of divine redemption. The murdered children, like Christ, became sacrificial gifts. The offering of their blood through the double sacrifice of Jewish murder and Christian vengeance was meant to create a bond of exchange between heaven and earth for assuring the incessant flow of divine grace. When the new sites of Christian martyrdom drew pilgrims, when miracles attracted visitors, when sacrifice earned renown and wealth, the bond between piety and material well-being was firmly established. This theme of sacrifice, vengeance, and divine benefaction repeated itself in a multitude of cultural artifacts: carnival farces, passion plays, ballads, popular tales, woodcuts, chronicles, and sermons told and retold this story of salvation.

The coherence of this narrative of ritual murder, however, depended on the collective solidarity of Christian society. In the suppression of ritual murder trials, the Reformation proved to be a turning point, undermining the foundations of late medieval piety. During the two decades before the Reformation, the effort to suppress ritual murder trials was limited to the political sphere. Protecting the rights of Jews became a contestation of political will as Emperor Friedrich III asserted the regalian rights over Jews in the empire against princes and the magistrates of imperial cities. In this conflict between the power of the emperor and of the Imperial Estates, the outcome was equivocal: in 1470 Friedrich acted too late to save the Endingen Jews; in 1476 a determined effort to suppress ritual murder trials rescued the Jews of Regensburg. The enforcement of an imperial policy of Judenschutz was more effective in lands directly ruled by the Hapsburgs; thus, in spite of the virulent anti-Semitism in the Austrian lands of the Upper Rhine, no Jew was executed for ritual murder or Host desecration after 1470.

Before the appearance of the obscure Saxon monk Martin Luther, the "Jewish question" had already occupied a central place in the debates over religion and polity in the Holy Roman Empire. Luther's criticism of the doctrines and practices of the late medieval church reflected a strong current of discontent before the Reformation, a force most noticeable among the ranks of the clerical professionals and the humanists. The reformers concentrated their attack on the "human fabrications" of Roman doctrines and rituals; they professed "true faith" over "human superstitions" and "religion" over "magic." To strip Christianity of its Roman encrustations, the reformers called for the return to its origins. In attacking late medieval magic and in advocating the study of Hebrew, the Reformation provided another force to undermine ritual murder discourse.

In the middle decades of the sixteenth century, the conjunction of new discourses in theology and law challenged the ideological foundations of ritual murder discourse. In the same period, German Jews intensified their collective efforts at self-defense: their spokesmen appealed directly to the emperors, communities armed themselves with imperial privileges and legal writs, and relatives of the accused filed lawsuits at the Imperial Chamber Court or petitioned the Imperial Aulic Court. Gradually but unmistakably, ritual murder discourse lost its credibility among the elites: for civil lawyers, imperial and roman laws clearly recognized the constitutional rights of Jews and prohibited ritual murder trials; for some princes and magistrates, they exercised greater caution in investigating the charges of child murders; for some Protestant reformers, ritual murder discourse was but a product of "papist lies" and "popular superstitions."

Elite and popular discourses of ritual murder began to part ways. The official inquests into ritual murder accusations during these decades emphasized jurisprudence and practicality, in stark contrast to the strongly religious coloring of pre-Reformation trials. Investigations into ritual murder accusations began to merge into prosecutions for child murders: the religious, magical, and sacrificial motifs became less prominent, whereas the attention to child murders in general grew stronger. Like many aspects of social life after the Reformation, child murders also became secularized. The examination of the attitude of magistrates in the prosecution of crimes during the sixteenth century reveals a clear chronological pattern of declining ritual murder trials and rising rates of infanticide convictions. One of the manifestations of this transformation was the greater emphasis of ritual child murders in witchcraft discourses of the late sixteenth century, as witches seemed to have replaced Jews as the most dangerous enemies within Christian society.

This transformation in learned ritual murder discourse had a limited impact on popular perceptions of Jews. The magical reputation of Jews did not seem to have diminished much among the rural folk, to whom the Jews represented not only a disliked alien element but also part of a world in which everything was perceived as either harmful or beneficial. The villagers of early modern Germany continued to traffic with Jews: horses, oxen, meat, leather, clothes, jewelry, coins, loans, talismans, and amulets were the main commodities; but, from time to time, blood and children appeared as products for sale.

Even though ritual murder trials were by and large successfully suppressed by the turn of the seventeenth century, the discourse of ritual murder retained much of its cohesion and force of persuasion. In popular culture, the lore of child murders passed on in ballads and legends. Village gossip, street talk, chapbooks, broadsheets, and woodcuts were some of the most important media of cultural transmission. Long after the suppression of ritual murder trials, the telling of tales of Jewish magic served an important function: the continued discourse of ritual murder justified past persecutions of Jews and obstructed critical self-examination; it also validated an anti-Semitism based on economic competition and political resentment. After the mid-sixteenth century, the revolutions of the common man had failed to transform the social and political structures of the empire; the territorial states, the princes, and magistrates had emerged victorious. In the realignment of social forces, the Jews threw in their lot with the authorities and invoked the forces of law and order against the prejudices of peasants and artisans. During the carnage of the Thirty Years' War, from which few Germans escaped unscathed, the Jews actually profited from the war economy and enjoyed special protection under different armies of occupation.[1] For precisely this reason, certain forms of anti-Semitism took on the mantle of popular culture and politics in early modern Germany, the 1614 Fettmilch Uprising in Frankfurt being the most notable example, with popular resentment of Jews continuing after the rise of the figure of the "court Jew" in the service of the Old Regime.[2]

In Lutheran Germany, ritual murder discourse survived primarily as a historical discourse to strengthen confessional identity. On one hand, medieval persecutions of Jews were blamed on the superstitions and greed of the Roman clergy, who whipped up charges of Jewish magic to disguise their own "papist" magic. On the other, Lutheran Germany remained deeply ambiguous about Jews, in spite of an undercurrent of philo-Semitism. The skepticism of ritual murder discourse expressed in the writings of Lutheran scholars like Schudt and Wagenseil did not remove the basis of anti-Semitism; for the Lutheran church, Jews still believed in a false religion, and the Jew as moneylender was perhaps just as hateful as the Jew as magician.

For Catholic Germany, ritual murder and Host desecration discourses mirrored an age when miracles and sainthood seemed more abundant than the difficult times of confessional strife. In Judenstein and Passau, these discourses stimulated the revival of pilgrimages during the seventeenth and eighteenth centuries; they provided counterpoints of specific folk piety in a baroque Catholicism whose worldview came to reflect that of the social elites and whose ecclesiastical leadership became increasingly aristocratic.

For the Jews of the Holy Roman Empire, the suppression of ritual murder trials signaled the dawn of an age of relative security and prosperity. Although still occasionally haunted by the specter of blood libel charges, not one Jew within the German-speaking lands of the empire was executed for ritual murder after the sixteenth century. In the next

---

1. See Jonathan Israel, "Central European Jewry during the Thirty Years' War," *Central European History* 16 (1983), pp. 3–30; the same point is reiterated in his *European Jewry in the Age of Mercantilism, 1550–1750* (Oxford, 1985), pp. 87–122.

2. See Christopher R. Friedrichs, "Politics or Pogrom? The Fettmilch Uprising in German and Jewish History," *Central European History* 19 (1986), pp. 186–28.

two hundred years, German Jews enjoyed uncontestable constitutional rights even when they had to face discrimination in daily life. Their numbers increased, as did their wealth. And their presence was firmly established as a part of the bedazzling patchwork of polities and social groups in the world of the Old Reich.

Sources

Manuscripts

Frankfurt, Stadtarchiv
Ugb: E44t, E46 adJ1, E46y, E47p
Freiburg, Stadtarchiv
A1 (Urkunden) XIIc nos. 25–31
B5 (P) XIIIa no. 9, Ratsprotokolle 1504
C (Akten) 1, Judensachen
Ludwigsburg, Staatsarchiv
B342 (Deutschorden Neckeroberamt): U229, U230
Marburg, Hessisches Staatsarchiv
Politisches Archiv des Landgrafen Philipp: 1638
Nürnberg, Staatsarchiv
Reichsstadt Nürnberg: Repertorium 2b, Urkunden 3414, 3415, 3419, 3460
Stuttgart, Württembergisches Hauptstaatsarchiv
B17 (Vorderösterreichische Regierung): Bd. 2
C3 (Reichskammergericht): J1277
Vienna Österreichisches Haus-, Hof-, und Hauptstaatsarchiv
Reichshofrat Antiqua 1143, 1157/4, 1159/6
Worms, Stadtarchiv
1, V (Judenschaft): 2030, 2031/1–2
Würzburg, Staatsarchiv
Hochstift Würzburg Adel 1369

Printed Sources

Amira, Karl von, ed. *Das Endinger Judenspiel.* Halle, 1883.
Benz, Richard, ed. *Historia von D. Johann Fausten dem Weitbeschreyten Zauberer und Schwarzkünstler.* Stuttgart, 1977.
Brentano, Clemens, and Ludwig Achim von Arnim, comps. *Des Knaben Wunderhorn.* Heidelberg, 1808–54.
Bucer, Martin. *Von den Juden ob/vnd wie die vnder den Christen zu halten sind/ein Rathschlag/durch die Gelerten am Ende dis Büchlins verzeichnet/zugericht. Item Ein weitere Erklerung vnd Beschirmung des selbigen Rathschlags.* [Strasbourg, 1539.]

Chmel, Joseph, ed. *Actenstücke und Briefe zur Geschichte des Hauses Habsburg im Zeitalter Maximilian's I*. Vol. 3. Vienna, 1858.

————. *Sammlung von Actenstücken und Briefen zur Geschichte des Hauses Habsburg in dem Zeitraum von 1473 bis 1576. 1. Abteilung: Das Zeitalter Maximilian's I*. Vol. 2. Vienna, 1855.

Christlicher Unterricht D. Mart. Lutheri/von den Juden Lügen wider die Person unsers Herren Jesu Christi/seiner Lieben Murter Maria/und aller Christen/hochnötig zu lesen. Dar aus ein jeder Christ liechtlich schliessen kan/ob man die Jüden billich bey sich leiden solle oder nicht. Dortmund: Arnd Westhoff [1591?].

Die Chroniken der westfälischen und niederrheinischen Städte. Bd. I: *Dortmund, Neuss* = [*Die Chroniken der deutschen Städte vom 14. bis ins 16. Jahrhundert* Bd. 20.] Ed. Historische Kommission bei der Bayerischen Königlichen Akademie der Wissenschaften. Leipzig, 1887.

Crämer, Ulrich, ed. "Eine Reise durch Schwaben, Tirol und die Rheinlande im Jahre 1503." *Alemannisches Jahrbuch* (1956), pp. 371–403.

Drey grausamer erschröcklicher mordt, der sich in der Stat Obernehen im Elsass drey meyl von Strassburg gelegen, zugetragen hat, von einem Vater, der siner eigener Kinder drey jemmerlich hat ermordt und umbracht am 10. tag Aprilis, Anno 1556. Auch was er für eine Straffe darob empfangen hat. geschehen den 24. Aprilis, 1556 jar.

Eck, Johannes. *Ains Judenbüchlins Verlegung: darin ain Christ/gantzer Christenhait zu schmach/will es geschehe den Juden unrecht in bezichtigung der Christen kinder mordt*. Ingolstadt: Alexander Weissenhorn, 1541.

————. *Christliche Auslegung der Evangelien von der Zeit/durch das gantz Jar/nach gemeynem verstand der Kirchen und heiligen väter von der selbigen angenommen . . . Der erste Teyl vom Advent biss Ostern . . . Der andern Teyl vom Ostern biss auff den Advent*. Tübingen, 1531.

————. *Schutz Red Kindtlicher Unschuld wider den Catechisten Andre Hosander/unnd sein schmach buchlin. . . . 1540*.

Ein grausame Geschicht von einem verrucktem Christen man. der sein natürliches kind den seellosen Juden verkauft hat. 1504.

Ein hübsch new lied von Zweyen Juden/vnd einem Kind/zu Sappenfelt newlich geschehen. [s.l., 1540?]

Ein wunderbarlich geschichte. Wye die Merckischen Juden das hochwirdig Sacrament gekaufft vnd zu martern sich vnderstanden. Anno domini 1510. Nuremberg: Hieronymus Höltzel.

Einblattdrucke des XV. Jahrhunderts. Ein bibliographisches Verzeichnis. Ed. Kommission für den Gesamtkatalog der Wiegendrucke. Halle, 1914.

Eisenmenger, Johann Andreas. *Entdecktes Judenthum: oder Gründlicher und Wahrhaffter Bericht, welchergestalt die verstockte Juden die Hochheilige Dreyeinigkeit . . . erschrecklicher Weise lästern und verunehren, die Heil. Mutter Christi verschmähen . . . Dabey noch viele andere bishero unter den Christen entweder gar nicht, oder nur zum Theil bekantgewesene Dinge und Grosse Irrthüme der Jüdischen Religion und Theologie, wie auch viel lächerliche und kurtzweilige Fabeln und andere ungereimte Sachen an den Tag kommen: Alles aus ihren eigenen . . . Büchern*. Frankfurt, 1700.

Fischer, Hanns, ed. *Hans Folz: Die Reimpaarsprüche*. Munich, 1961.

Gemeiner, Carl Theodor. *Der Regensburgischen Chronik*. Vol. 3. Regensburg, 1821.

Hoffmann, Conrad, ed. *Quellen zur Geschichte Friedrichs des Siegreichen.* Vol. 1. Munich, 1862.

Keller, A. von, ed. *Fastnachtspiele aus dem fünfzehnten Jahrhundert.* 3 vols. [Bibliothek des litterarischen Vereins in Stuttgart, vols. 28–30.] Stuttgart, 1853.

Kohler, Josef, and Willy Scheel, eds. *Die peinliche Gerichtsordnung Kaiser Karls V. Constitutio Criminalis Carolina [Die Carolina und ihre Vorgängerinnen: Text, Erläuterung, Geschichte I.]* Halle, 1900; reprint, 1968.

Kracauer, Isidor. "L'affaire des juifs d'Endingen de 1470: Prétendu meurte de chrétiens par des juifs." *Revue des études juifs* 17 (1888), pp. 236–45.

―――. "Rabbi Joselmann de Rosheim" (The memoirs of Josel of Rosheim). *Revue des études Juifs* 17 (1888): pp. 84–105.

L. T. Z. T. [pseud.]. *Warhaftige Geschicht vnd Execution Leupoldt Judens/welche an ihme seiner wolverdienten grausamen und unmenschlichen thaten halben (so er an dem unschuldigen Christlichen Blut begangen) den 28. Jenners/1573 zu Berlyn/nach innhalt Götliches und Keyserliches Rechten vollnzogen worden ist.* s.l., 1573.

Liliencron, Rocus von, ed. *Die historischen Volkslieder der Deutschen vom 13. bis 16. Jahrhundert.* 5 vols. in 4. Leipzig, 1867.

Luther, Martin. *D. Martin Luthers Werke. Kritische Gesamtausgabe.* Weimar, 1883–.

Margaritha, Anton, *Der Gantz Judisch Glaub mit sampt eyner grundtlichenn und warhasstigen anzeygunge, aller satzungen. Ceremonien, gebetten, heymliche und offentliche gebreuch, deren sich die Juden halten, durch das gantz Jar, mit schonen unnd gegrundten Argumenten wider iren glauben, durch Anthonium Margaritham/Hebreyschen Leser/der löblichen Vniversitet und fürstlichen Stat Leyptzigk/beschryben und an tag gegeben.* [Augsburg: Heinrich Steiner?], 1531.

Martin, Ernst, ed. *Freiburger Passionsspiele des XVI. Jahrhunderts.* Freiburg, 1872.

Maurer, Heinrich, ed. "Urkunden zur Geschichte der Herrschaft Üsenberg," *Zeitschrift der Gesellschaft für Beförderung der Geschichts-, Altertums- und Volkskunde von Freiburg* 5 (1879–82), pp. 193–326.

Mayer, August L., ed. *Die Meisterlieder des Hans Folz.* Berlin, 1908.

Merker, Payl, ed. *Thomas Murners Deutsche Schriften.* Vol. 9. Strasbourg, 1918.

[Osiander, Andreas]. *Ob es war vnd glaublich sey/dass die juden der Christen Kinder heymlich erwürgen/vnd ir blut gebrauchen/ein treffenliche schrifft/auff eines yeden vrteyl gestellt.* Republished by Moritz Stern as *Andreas Osianders Schrift über die Blutbeschuldigung.* Kiel, 1893.

Osiander, Andreas. *Verantwortung des Nürnbergischen Catechismi, wider Johannes Eck.* Nuremberg: L. Milchtaler, 1539.

Pfaff, Fridrich, ed. "Die Kindermorde zu Benzhausen und Waldkirch im Breisgau. Ein Gedicht aus dem Anfang des 16. Jahrhunderts." *Alemannia* 27 (1899), pp. 247–92.

Pfefferkorn, Johannes. *Brantspiegell. Abzotraibenn und auszuleschen eines ungegrunten laster buechleyn mit namen Augenspiegell.* Cologne: Hermann Gutschaiff, 1512.

―――. *Handt Spiegel wider und gegen die Jüden.* [Mainz: J. Schoeffer, 1511.]

―――. *Eyn buchlijn der iudenbeicht.* Cologne: Johann van Landen, 1508.

―――. *Speculum adhortationis iudaice ad Christum.* [Speyer: C. Hist, 1507.]

―――. *Zu lob und Ere des aller durchleichtigsten und grossmechtigsten Fursten und herren, Herr Maximilian . . . Römischen Kaiser. . . .* Augsburg: Erhard Oglein, 1510.

Phareta catholice fidei: siue ydonea disputatio inter Christianos et Judeos. Ulm, 1495; Cologne: Heinrich Quentell, 1495; Landshut: Johann Weissenburg, 1518.

Rader, Matthaeus, S. J. *Bavaria Sancta.* 3 parts. Munich, 1615.

Reuchlin, Johannes. *Augenspiegel. Warhafftige Entschuldigung gegen und wider ains getaufften iuden genant Pfefferkorn vormals getruckt ussgangen unwarhaftigs Schmachbüchlin.* [Tübingen: Thomas Anselm, 1511.]

———. *Tütsch Missive. Warumb die Juden so lang im ellend sind.* [Pforzheim: Thomas Anselm, 1505.]

Roth, Cecil, ed. *The Ritual Murder Libel and the Jew: The Report by Cardinal Lorenzo Ganganelli (Pope Clement XIV).* London, 1934.

Rowan, Steven, ed. "Die Jahresrechnungen eines Freiburger Kaufmanns 1487/88." In *Stadt und Umland,* ed. Erich Maschke and Jürgen Sydow, pp. 227–77, Stuttgart, 1974.

Schedel, Hartmann. *Liber Chronicarum cum figuris et imaginibus ab initio mundi.* Nuremberg: Anton Koberger, 1493.

Schreiber, Heinrich, ed. *Urkundenbuch der Stadt Freiburg im Breisgau.* 2 vols. Freiburg, 1829.

Schudt, Johann Jacob. *Jüdische Merckwürdigkeiten.* 4 parts. Frankfurt and Leipzig, 1714–17; reprint, Berlin, 1922.

Schwanfelder, Johann. *Warhafftiger Bericht von dem jämmerlichen und erbärmlichen Mordt, so zu Sprendenlingen in der Dreyeych an zweyen kindern im Pfarhof am 26. tag dess Jenners in diesem jetzlauffenden 1570. jar begangen. und wie nachmals der Thäter allhie zu Franckfurt am Meyn den 24. Hornungs ist gericht worden.* Frankfurt, 1570.

Schwarz [Nigrius], Peter, O. P. *Der Stern des Meschiah.* Esslingen: Conrad Fyner, 1477.

———. *Tractatus contra perfidos Judaeos de conditionibus veri Messie.* Esslingen: Conrad Fyner, 1475.

Simon ain kind bin ich genant/zu triendt wol in dem wälschen lant. [Ulm: Johann Zainer, 1498?]

Stern, Moritz, ed. *Die päpstlichen Bullen gegen die Blutbeschuldigung.* Berlin, 1893.

———. *Urkundliche Beiträge über die Stellung der Päpste zu den Juden.* Kiel, 1893.

Straus, Raphael, ed. *Urkunden und Aktenstücke zur Geschichte der Juden in Regensburg, 1453–1738.* Munich, 1960.

Strauss, Walter L. *The German Single-Leaf Woodcut, 1550–1600.* 3 vols. New York, 1975.

Von Tegkendorff das geschicht wie die Iuden das hailig sacrament haben zugericht. [Augsburg: S. Otmar, 1520.]

Wagenseil, Christof. *Benachrichtigungen wegen einiger die Judenschafft angehenden wichtigen Sachen.* Part 1. Frankfurt, 1705.

———. *Hofnung der Erlösung Israelis, oder Klarer Beweiss der annoch bevorstehenden . . . grossen Jüden-Bekehrung.* 2d ed. Nuremberg and Altdorf, 1706.

Weyer, Johann. *De Lamiis, Von Teuffelsgespenst, Zaubern und Gifftbereytern. . . .* Frankfurt: Nicolaus Basseum, 1586.

———. *De praestigiis daemonum. Vom Teuffelsgespenst, Zauberern und Gifftbereytern,*

Schwarzkünstlern, Hexen und Unholden, darzu ihrer Straff, auch von den Bezauberten vnnd wie ihnen zu helfen sey. Frankfurt: Nicolaus Basseum, 1586.

———. *Theatrum de Veneficis. Von Teuffelsgespenst, Zaubern, Gifftbereyten und Unholden, Schwarzkünstlern. . . .* Frankfurt: Nicolaus Basseum, 1586.

Wolfram, Georg, "Prozessakten eines angeblich durch Juden verübten Christenmords zu Endingen." *ZGO* N.F. 2 [41] (1887), pp. 313–21.

Wuttke, Dieter, ed. *Fastnachtspiele des 15. und 16. Jahrhunderts.* Stuttgart, 1973.

Zasius, Ulrich. *Opera Omnia V.* Lyon: Sebastian Gryphius, 1550; reprint, 1966.

———. *Nüwe Stattrechten und Statuten der loblichen Statt Fryburg im Bryszgow gelegen.* [*Zasius Opera Omnia Supplementum.*] Freiburg, 1520.

Zoepfl, Heinrich, ed. *Die Peinliche Gerichtsordnung Kaiser Karls V. nebst der Bamberger und der Brandenburger Halsgerichtsordnung . . . mit den Projecten der peinlichen Gerichtsordnung Kaiser Karls V. von den Jahren 1521 und 1529.* Heidelberg, 1842.

Secondary Works

Ackermann, A. *Geschichte der Juden in Brandenburg.* Berlin, 1906.

Amman, Hektor. "Freiburg und der Breisgau in der mittelalterlichen Wirtschaft." *Oberrheinische Heimat* 28 (1941), pp. 248–59.

Andreas, Willy. *Deutschland vor der Reformation.* Stuttgart, 1959.

Bauer, Clemens. "Wirtschaftsgeschichte der Stadt Freiburg im Mittelalter," In *Freiburg im Mittelalter,* ed. Wolfgang Müller, pp. 50–76. Bühl, 1970.

Beemelmans, Wilhelm. "Die Organisation der vorderösterreichischen Behörden in Ensisheim im 16. Jahrhundert," *ZGO* N.F. 22 [61] (1907), pp. 52–92, 627–56; ibid., N.F. 23 [62] (1908), pp. 195–220.

Bienert, Walther, ed. *Martin Luther und die Juden: Ein Quellenbuch mit zeitgenössischen Illustrationen, mit Einführungen und Erläuterungen.* Frankfurt, 1982.

Blickle, Peter. *Gemeindereformation: Die Menschen des 16. Jahrhunderts auf dem Weg zum Heil.* Munich, 1985.

Bloch, Chayim. *The Golem: Legends of the Ghetto of Prague.* Trans. Harry Schneiderman. Vienna, 1925.

Bode, H. "Die Kindestötung und ihre Strafe im Nürnberg des Mittelalters." *Archiv für Strafrecht und Strafprozess* 61 (1914), pp. 430–81.

Bossy, John H. *Christianity in the West, 1400–1700.* Oxford, 1985.

Brady, Thomas A. *Turning Swiss: Cities and Empire, 1450–1550.* Cambridge, 1985.

Brednich, Rolf W. "The Song as a Commodity." In *German Volkskunde: A Decade of Theoretical Confrontation, Debate, and Reorientation (1967–1977),* ed. James R. Dow and Hannjost Lixfeld, pp. 203–11. Bloomington, 1986.

Breuer, Mordechai. "Modernism and Traditionalism in Sixteenth-Century Jewish Historiography: A Study of David Gans' Tzemah David." In *Jewish Thought in the Sixteenth Century,* ed. Bernard Cooperman, pp. 49–88. Cambridge, Mass., 1983.

Brod, Max. *Johannes Reuchlin und sein Kampf.* Stuttgart, 1965.

Browe, Peter. "Die Eucharistie als Zaubermittel im Mittelalter." *Archiv für Kulturgeschichte* 20 (1930), pp. 134–54.

————. *Die Eucharistischen Wunder des Mittelalters.* Breslau, 1938.

————. "Die Hostienschändungen der Juden im Mittelalter." *Römische Quartalschrift für christliche Altertumskunde und Kirchengeschichte* 34 (1926), pp. 167–97.

————. *Die Judenmission im Mittelalter und die Päpste.* Rome, 1942.

————. *Die Verehrung der Eucharistie im Mittelalter.* Munich, 1933; reprint, Rome, 1967.

Brückner, Wolfgang, ed. *Volkserzählung und Reformation: Ein Handbuch zur Tradierung und Funktion von Erzählstoffen und Erzählliteratur im Protestantismus.* Berlin, 1974.

————. "Historien und Historie: Erzählliteratur des 16. und 17. Jahrhunderts als Forschungsaufgabe." In *Volkserzählung und Reformation,* ed. Wolfgang Brückner, pp. 13–123. Berlin, 1974.

Bücking, Jürgen. "Das Geschlecht Stürtzel von Buchheim (1491–1790): Ein Versuch zur Sozial- und Wirtschaftsgeschichte des Breisgauer Adels in der frühen Neuzeit." *ZGO* 18 (1970), pp. 239–78.

Chwolson, Daniel. *Die Blutanklage und sonstige mittelalterliche Beschuldigungen der Juden: Eine historische Untersuchung nach den Quellen.* Frankfurt, 1901.

Cohen, Jeremy. *The Friars and the Jews: The Evolution of Medieval Anti-Judaism.* Ithaca, 1982.

Coing, Helmut. *Gesammelte Aufsätze zu Rechtsgeschichte, Rechtsphilosophie und Zivilrecht, 1947–1975.* Vol. 2. Frankfurt, 1982.

Dammann, Günther. *Die Juden in der Zauberkunst.* 2d ed. Berlin, 1933.

Dégh, Linda. *Folktales and Society: Story-Telling in a Hungarian Peasant Community.* Trans. Emily M. Schossberger. Bloomington, 1969.

Deppermann, Klaus. "Judenhass und Judenfreundschaft im frühen Protestantismus." In *Die Juden als Minderheit in der Geschichte.,* ed. Bernd Martin and Ernst Schulin, pp. 110–30. Munich, 1981.

Dow, James R., and Hannjost Lixfeld, eds. and trans. *German Volkskunde: A Decade of Theoretical Confrontation, Debate, and Reorientation (1967–1977).* Bloomington, 1986.

Dülmen, Richard van. *Theater des Schreckens: Gerichtspraxis und Strafrituale in der frühen Neuzeit.* Munich, 1985.

Edwards, Mark U. *Luther's Last Battles: Politics and Polemics, 1531–46.* Ithaca, 1983.

Eisenstein, Elizabeth N. *The Printing Press as an Agent of Change: Communications and Cultural Transformations in Early Modern Europe.* 2 vols. Cambridge, 1979.

Evans, Robert J. W. *The Making of the Habsburg Monarchy, 1550–1700.* Oxford, 1979.

————. *Rudolf II and His World: A Study in Intellectual History, 1576–1612.* Oxford, 1973.

Felber, Alfons, *Unzucht und Kindsmord in der Rechtsprechung der freien Reichsstadt Nördlingen vom 15. bis 19. Jahrhundert.* Bonn, 1961.

Finke, Manfred. "Toleranz und 'Discrete' Frömmigkeit nach 1650: Pfalzgraf Christian August von Sulzbach und Ernst von Hessen-Rheinfels." In *Frömmigkeit in der frühen Neuzeit. Studien zur religiösen Literatur des 17. Jahrhunderts in Deutschland,* ed. Dieter Breuer, pp. 193–212. Amsterdam, 1984.

Fox, Nikolaus. *Saarländische Volkskunde.* Bonn, 1927.

Franz, Adolph. *Die kirchlichen Benediktionen im Mittelalter.* 2 vols. Freiburg, 1909.
———. *Die Messe im deutschen Mittelalter: Beiträge zur Geschichte der Liturgie und des religiösen Volkslebens.* Freiburg, 1902.
Freimann, Aron. "Aus der Geschichte der Juden in Regensburg von der Mitte des 15. Jahrhunderts bis zur Vertreibung im Jahre 1519." In *Beiträge zur Geschichte der deutschen Juden: Festschrift zum 70. Geburtstage Martin Philippsons,* pp. 79–95. Leipzig, 1916.
———, ed. *Stadtbibliothek Frankfurt a. M. Katalog der Judaica und Hebraica.* Vol. 1. Frankfurt, 1932.
Frey, Sabine. *Rechtsschutz der Juden gegen Ausweisungen im 16. Jahrhundert.* Frankfurt, 1983.
Friedman, Jerome. *The Most Ancient Testimony: Sixteenth Century Christian Hebraica in the Age of Renaissance Nostalgia.* Athens, Ohio, 1983.
Friedrichs, Christopher R. "Politics or Pogrom? The Fettmilch Uprising in German and Jewish History." *Central European History* 19 (1986), pp. 186–228.
Gager, John. *The Origins of Anti-Semitism.* New York, 1983.
Geiger, Ludwig. *Johann Reuchlin, sein Leben und seine Werke.* Leipzig, 1871.
Gierke, Otto. *Natural Law and the Theory of Society, 1500–1800.* 2 vols. Trans. Ernest Barker. Cambridge, 1934.
Ginzburg, Carlo. *The Night Battles: Witchcraft and Agrarian Cults in the Sixteenth and Seventeenth Centuries.* Trans. John and Anne Tedeschi. Baltimore, 1983.
Graetz, Heinrich. *Geschichte der Juden von den ältesten Zeiten bis auf die Gegenwart.* Vol. 9. Leipzig, 1891.
Gross, Hanns. "The Holy Roman Empire in Modern Times: Constitutional Reality and Legal Theory." In *The Old Reich: Essays on German Political Institutions, 1495–1806,* ed. James A. Vann and Steven W. Rowan, pp. 1–29. Brussels, 1974.
Güde, Wilhelm. *Die rechtliche Stellung der Juden in den Schriften deutscher Juristen des 16. und 17. Jahrhunderts.* Sigmaringen, 1981.
Gugitz, Gustav. *Österreichs Gnadenstätten in Kult und Brauch,* Vol. 3: *Tirol und Vorarlberg.* Vienna, 1956.
Hälsig, Arthur F. *Der Zauberspruch bei den Germanen bis um die Mitte des XVI. Jahrhunderts.* Leipzig, 1910.
Hampp, Irmgard. *Beschwörung-Segen-Gebet: Untersuchungen zum Zauberspruch aus dem Bereich der Volksheilkunde.* Stuttgart, 1961.
Hartinger, Walter. *Mariahilf ob Passau: Volkskundliche Untersuchung der Passauer Wallfahrt und der Mariahilf-Verehrung im deutschsprachigen Raum.* Passau, 1985.
Hauer, Nadine. *Judenstein: Legende ohne Ende?* Vienna, 1985.
Haverkamp, Alfred, ed. *Zur Geschichte der Juden im Deutschland des späten Mittelalters und der frühen Neuzeit.* Stuttgart, 1981.
———. "Die Judenverfolgungen zur Zeit des Schwarzen Todes im Gesellschaftsgefüge deutscher Städte." In *Zur Geschichte der Juden im Deutschland des späten Mittelalters und der frühen Neuzeit,* ed. Alfred Haverkamp, pp. 27–93. Stuttgart, 1981.
Hayn, Hugo, ed. *Übersicht der (meist in Deutschland erschienenen) Literatur über die angeblich von Juden verübten Ritualmorde und Hostienfrevel.* Jena, 1906.
Hefele, Friedrich. "Freiburg als vorderösterreichische Stadt." In *Vorderösterreich: Eine geschichtliche Landeskunde,* vol. 2, pp. 326–47. Freiburg, 1959.

Helmholz, R. H. "Infanticide in the Province of Canterbury during the Fifteenth Century." *History of Childhood Quarterly* 2:3 (1975), pp. 379–90.

Hsia, R. Po-chia. "Die Juden im Alten Reich: Einige Bemerkungen zu einer Forschungsaufgabe." In Georg Schmidt, ed., *Stände und Gesellschaft im Alten Reich*. Wiesbaden, forthcoming.

———. "Printing, Censorship and Antisemitism in Reformation Germany." In *The Process of Change in Early Modern Europe: Essays in Honor of Miriam Usher Chrisman*, Ed. Sherrin Marshall and Philip N. Bebb, Athens, Ohio, 1988.

———. *Society and Religion in Münster, 1535–1618*. New Haven and London, 1984.

———, ed. *The German People and the Reformation*. Ithaca, 1988.

Israel, Jonathan. "Central European Jewry during the Thirty Years' War." *Central European History* 16 (1983), pp. 3–30.

———. *European Jewry in the Age of Mercantilism, 1550–1750*. Oxford, 1985.

Janda, Elsbeth, and Fritz Nötzoldt. *Die Moritat vom Bänkelsang, oder das Lied der Strasse*. Munich, 1959.

Josephy, Marcia Reines. *Magic and Superstition in the Jewish Tradition*. Chicago, 1975.

Kellenbenz, Hermann. *The Rise of the European Economy: An Economic History of Continental Europe from the Fifteenth to the Eighteenth Century*. London, 1976.

Keyser, Erich, ed. *Badisches Städtebuch*. [*Deutsches Städtebuch: Handbuch städtischer Geschichte*, Bd. IV:2:1.] Stuttgart, 1959.

Kisch, Guido. *Jewry Law in Medieval Germany: Laws and Court Decisions concerning Jews*. New York, 1949.

———. *The Jews in Medieval Germany: A Study of Their Legal and Social Status*. Chicago, 1949.

———. *Zasius und Reuchlin: Eine rechtsgeschichtlich-vergleichende Studie zum Toleranzproblem im 16. Jahrhundert*. Stuttgart, 1961.

Kittelson, James M. *Wolfgang Capito: From Humanist to Reformer*. Leiden, 1975.

Kracauer, Isidor. *Geschichte der Juden in Frankfurt a. M. (1150–1824)*. 2 vols. Frankfurt, 1925–27.

Langbein, John H. *Prosecuting Crime in the Renaissance: England, Germany, and France*. Cambridge, Mass., 1974.

———. *Torture and the Law of Proof: Europe and England in the Ancien Régime*. Chicago, 1976.

Langer, William L. "Further Notes on the History of Infanticide." *History of Childhood Quarterly* 2:1 (1974), pp. 129–34.

———. "Infanticide: A Historical Survey." *History of Childhood Quarterly* 1:3 (1974), pp. 353–65.

Lea, Henry C. *Superstition and Force: Essays on the Wager of Law—the Wager of Battle—the Ordeal—Torture*. Philadelphia, 1866.

Lewin, Adolf. *Die Juden in Freiburg i. Breisgau*. Trier, 1890.

Lewin, Reinhold. *Luthers Stellung zu den Juden*. Berlin, 1911; reprint, 1933.

Lowry, Martin. *The World of Aldus Manutius*. Ithaca, 1979.

Mader, Franz. *Wallfahrten im Bistum Passau*. Munich, 1984.

Marquès-Rivière, Jean. *Amulettes, talismans et pantacles dan les traditions orientales et occidentales*. Paris, 1972.

Martin, Bernd, and Ernst Schulin, eds. *Die Juden als Minderheit in der Geschichte.* Munich, 1981.

Mauss, Marcel. *A General Theory of Magic.* Trans. Robert Brain. London, 1972.

Mayer, Anton L. "Die heilbringende Schau in Sitte und Kult." In *Heilige Überlieferung: Festschrift für Ildefons Herwegen,* pp. 234–62. Münster, 1938.

———. "Die Gründung von St. Salvator in Passau—Geschichte und Legende." *Zeitschrift für bayerische Landesgeschichte* 18 (1955), pp. 256–78.

Mayer, Hermann. "Zur Geschichte der Freiburger Fronleichnamsprozession." *Freiburger Diözesan-Archiv* N.F. 12 (1911), pp. 338–61.

Midelfort, H.-C. Erik. "Johann Weyer and the Transformation of the Insantiy Defense." In *The German People and the Reformation,* ed. R. Po-chia Hsia. Ithaca, 1988.

———. *Witchhunting in Southwestern Germany, 1562–1684: The Social and Intellectual Foundations.* Stanford, 1972.

Mieses, Josef. *Die älteste gedruckte deutsche Übersetzung des jüdischen Gebetbuchs aus dem Jahre 1530 und ihr Autor Antonius Margaritha.* Vienna, 1916.

Mone, L. J. "Zur Geschichte der Viehzucht vom 14. bis 16. Jahrhundert in Baden, Wirtenberg, Elsass, Baiern." *ZGO* 3 (1852), pp. 398–414.

———. "Zur Geschichte des Weinbaues vom 14. bis 16. Jahrhundert in der Schweiz, Wirtenberg, Baden, Hessen und Rheinpreussen," *ZGO* 3 (1852), pp. 257–99.

Moser-Rath, Elfriede. "Some Thoughts on Historical Narrative Research." *German Volkskunde: A Decade of Theoretical Confrontation, Debate, and Reorientation (1967–1977),* Ed. and trans. James R. Dow and Hannjost Lixfeld, pp. 212–28. Bloomington, 1986.

Müller, Arnd. *Die Geschichte der Juden in Nürnberg, 1146–1945.* Nuremberg, 1968.

Nahl, Rudolf van. *Zauberglaube und Hexenwahn im Gebiet von Rhein und Maas: Spätmittelalterlicher Volksglaube im Werk Johann Weyers (1515–1588).* Bonn, 1983.

Nauck, Ernst T. *Zur Geschichte des medizinischen Lehrplans und Unterrichts der Universität Freiburg i. Br.* Freiburg, 1952.

Nauert, Charles. *Agrippa and the Crisis of Renaissance Thought.* Urbana, 1965.

Oberman, Heiko A. *Wurzeln des Antisemitismus: Christenangst und Judenplage im Zeitalter von Humanismus und Reformation.* Berlin, 1981.

———. "Zwischen Agitation und Reformation: Die Flugschriften als 'Judenspiegel.'" In *Flugschriften als Massenmedium der Reformationszeit,* ed. Hans-Joachim Köhler, pp. 269–88. Stuttgart, 1981.

Overdick, Renate. *Die rechtliche und wirtschaftliche Stellung der Juden in Südwestdeutschland im 15. und 16. Jahrhundert dargestellt an den Reichsstädten Konstanz und Esslingen und an der Markgraftschaft Baden.* Konstanz, 1965.

Overfeld, James H. *Humanism and Scholasticism in Late Medieval Germany.* Princeton, 1984.

Ozment, Steven E. *Magdalena and Balthasar: An Intimate Portrait of Life in Sixteenth-Century Europe Revealed in the Letters of a Nuremberg Husband and Wife.* New York, 1986.

———. *When Fathers Ruled: Family Life in Reformation Europe.* Cambridge, Mass., 1983.

Peters, Edward. *The Magician, the Witch and the Law.* Philadelphia, 1978.

————. *Torture*. New York, 1985.

Peuckert, Will-Erich. *Die grosse Wende: Das apokalyptische Saeculum und Luther.* Hamburg, 1948.

Press, Volker. "Kaiser Rudolph II und der Zusammenschluss der deutschen Judenheit: Die sogenannte Frankfurter Rabinerverschwörung von 1603 und ihre Folgen." In *Zur Geschichte der Juden in Deutschland des späten Mittelalters und der frühen Neuzeit*, ed. Alfred Haverkamp, pp. 243–93. Stuttgart, 1981.

Pressel, Friedrich. *Geschichte der Juden in Ulm.* Ulm, 1873.

Rebel, Hermann. *Peasant Classes: The Bureaucratization of Property and Family Relations under Early Habsburg Absolutism, 1511–1626.* Princeton, 1983.

Reuter, Fritz. *Warmasia: 1000 Jahre Juden in Worms.* Worms, 1984.

Rickert, Leo A. *Freiburg: Aus der Geschichte einer Stadt.* Karlsruhe, 1964.

Roth, Cecil. *The Jews in the Renaissance.* Philadelphia, 1977.

Rowan, Steven W. "A Reichstag in the Reform Era: Freiburg im Breisgau, 1497–98." in *The Old Reich: Essays on German Political Institutions, 1495–1806*, ed. James A. Vann and Steven W. Rowan, pp. 31–57. Brussels, 1974.

————. "The Guilds of Freiburg im Breisgau as Social and Political Entities." Ph.D. diss., Harvard University, 1970.

————. "Ulrich Zasius and the Baptism of Jewish Children." *SCJ* 6 (1975), pp. 3–25.

Sabean, David W. *Power in the Blood: Popular Culture and Village Discourse in Early Modern Germany.* Cambridge, 1985.

Schenda, Rudolf. "Hieronymus Rauscher und die Protestantisch-Katholische Legendenpolemik." In *Volkserzählung und Reformation*, ed. Wolfgang Brückner, pp. 179–259. Berlin, 1974.

Schmid, W. M. "Zur Geschichte der Juden in Passau." *Zeitschrift für die Geschichte der Juden in Deutschland* 1:2 (1929), pp. 119–35.

Schmidt, Eberhard. *Inquisitionsprozess und Rezeption.* Leipzig, 1940.

Schmidt, Heinrich. *Die Deutschen Städtechroniken als Spiegel der bürgerlichen Selbstverständnisses im Spätmittelalter.* Göttingen, 1958.

Schmidt, Leopold. *Volksgesang und Volkslied: Proben und Probleme.* Berlin, 1970.

Scholem, Gershom. *Major Trends in Jewish Mysticism.* New York, 1974.

————. *On the Kabbalah and Its Symbolism.* New York, 1965.

————, ed. *Zohar: The Book of Splendor.* New York, 1949.

Schrire, T. *Hebrew Amulets: Their Decipherment and Interpretation.* London, 1966.

Schulte, Regina. "Kindsmörderinnen auf dem Lande." In *Emotionen und materielle Interessen*, ed. Hans Medick and David Sabean, pp. 113–42. Göttingen, 1984.

Schulze, Wilfried. *Reich und Türkengefahr im späten 16. Jahrhundert.* Munich, 1978.

Scribner, Robert W. *For the Sake of Simple Folk: Popular Propaganda for the German Reformation.* Cambridge, 1981.

————. "Incombustible Luther: The Image of the Reformer in Early Modern Germany." *Past and Present* 110 (1986), pp. 38–68.

————. "Reformation and Ritual." In *The German People and the Reformation*, ed. R. Po-chia Hsia. Ithaca, 1988.

————. "Ritual and Popular Religion in Catholic Germany at the Time of the Reformation." *Journal of Ecclesiastical History* 35:1 (1984), pp. 47–77.

Schacher, Isaiah. *The Judensau: A Medieval Anti-Jewish Motif and Its History.* London, 1974.

Smend, Rudolf. *Das Reichskammergericht, I. Teil: Geschichte und Verfassung.* Weimar, 1911.

Sparing, Margarethe W. *The Perception of Reality in the Volksmärchen of Schleswig-Holstein.* Lanham, 1984.

Stern, Selma. *Josel of Rosheim: Commander of Jewry in the Holy Roman Empire of the German Nation.* Trans. Gertrude Hirschler. Philadelphia, 1965.

Stintzing, Heinrich. *Ulrich Zasius: Ein Beitrag zur Geschichte der Rechtswissenschaft im Zeitalter der Reformation.* Basel, 1857.

Straus, Raphael. *Die Judengemeinde Regensburg im ausgehenden Mittelalter.* Heidelberg, 1932.

———. *Regensburg and Augsburg.* Trans. Felix N. Gerson (Jewish Communities Series). Philadelphia, 1939.

Strauss, Gerald. *Law, Resistance, and the State: The Opposition to Roman Law in Reformation Germany.* Princeton, 1986.

———. *Luther's House of Learning: Indoctrination of the Young in the German Reformation.* Baltimore, 1978.

———. *Nuremberg in the Sixteenth Century.* Bloomington, 1976.

———. "The Reformation and Its Public in an Age of Orthodoxy." In *The German People and the Reformation,* ed. R. Po-chia Hsia. Ithaca, 1988.

Sucher, C. Bernd. *Luthers Stellung zu den Juden: Eine Interpretation aus germanischer Sicht.* Nieuwkoop, 1977.

Thieberger, Frederic. *The Great Rabbi Leow of Prague.* London, 1955.

Thiele, Folkmar. *Die Freiburger Stadtschreiber im Mittelalter.* Freiburg, 1973.

Thieme, Hans. "Zasius und Freiburg." In *Aus der Geschichte der Rechts- und Staatswissenschaften zu Freiburg i. Br.,* ed. Hans J. Wolff, pp. 9–22. Freiburg, 1957.

Thomas, Keith V. *Religion and the Decline of Magic.* New York, 1971.

Thompson, Stith, *The Folktale.* Bloomington, 1946; reprint, Berkeley, 1977.

Thorndike, Lynn. *A History of Magic and Experimental Magic.* Vol. 6. New York, 1941.

Tierney, Brian. *Religion, Law, and the Growth of Constitutional Thought, 1150–1650.* Cambridge, 1982.

Trachtenberg, Joshua. *The Devil and the Jews.* New Haven, 1943.

———. *Jewish Magic and Superstition: A Study in Folk Religion.* Philadelphia, 1939.

Trexler, Richard C. "The Foundlings of Florence, 1395–1455." *History of Childhood Quarterly* 1:2 (1973), pp. 259–84.

———. "Infanticide in Florence: New Sources and First Results." *History of Childhood Quarterly* 1:1 (1973), pp. 98–116.

Vann, James A., and Steven W. Rowan, eds. *The Old Reich: Essays on German Political Institutions, 1495–1806.* Brussels, 1974.

Von den Brincken, Anna-Dorothee. "Die Juden in der Kölnischen Chronistik des 15. Jahrhunderts." In *Köln und das rheinische Judentum: Festschrift Germania Judaica, 1959–1984.* Ed. Jutta Bohnke-Kollwitz et al., pp. 63–74. Cologne, 1984.

Wallfahrten im Bistum Passau: Ausstellung im grossen Hofsaal der Neuen Residenz in Passau, 3. Mai bis 25. Oktober 1986. Passau, 1986.

Weber-Kellermann, Ingeborg. *Die deutsche Familie: Versuch einer Sozialgeschichte.* Frankfurt, 1974.

Weitzel, Jürgen. *Der Kampf um die Appellation aus Reichskammergericht: Zur politischen Geschichte der Rechtsmittel in Deutschland.* Cologne, 1976.

Wenninger, Markus J. *Man bedarf keiner Juden mehr: Ursachen und Hintergründe ihrer Vertreibung aus der deutschen Reichsstädten im 15. Jahrhundert.* Cologne, 1981.

Wigand, Paul. *Wetzlar'sche Beiträge für Geschichte und Rechtsalterthümer.* Vol. 3. Giessen, 1850.

Willmann, Joseph. "Die Strafgerichtsverfassung und die Hauptbeweismittel im Strafverfahren der Stadt Freiburg i. Br. bis zur Einführung des neuen Stadtrechts (1520)." *ZGF* 33 (1917), pp. 1–106.

Wilson, Adrian, and Joyce Lancaster. *The Making of the Nuremberg Chronicle.* Amsterdam, 1976.

Wolf, Gerhard Philipp. "Osiander und die Juden im Kontext seiner Theologie." *Zeitschrift für bayerische Kirchengeschichte* 53 (1984), pp. 49–77.

Yates, Frances A. *Giordano Bruno and the Hermetic Tradition.* Chicago, 1964.

———. *The Occult Philosophy in the Elizabethan Age.* London, 1979.

Zahn, Peter. *Neue Funde zur Entstehung der Schedelschen Weltchronik.* Nuremberg, 1974.

Zehnter, J. A. "Zur Geschichte der Juden in der Markgrafschaft Baden-Baden." *ZGO* N.F. 11 [50] (1896), pp. 337–441.

Zimmels, H. J. *Magicians, Theologians, and Doctors: Studies in Folk-medicine and Folklore as Reflected in the Rabbinical Responsa (Twelfth-Nineteenth Centuries).* London, 1952.

Index

Aachen, 195
Aaron of Gysheim, 198–99
Abraham of Endingen, 35, 38
Abraham of Kitzing, 73n, 74–75
Abraham of Lublin, 208, 210
Abraham of Worms, 206, 207
Abraham zum Bock of Worms, 164, 167–69, 175–80, 183–91, 193, 195, 198
Agrippa, Cornelius, 8, 135
Albrecht, duke of Bavaria, 123, 128
Alringen, 202
Alt, Georg, 47
Altdorf, 214–15
Amberg, 147
Amerbach, Boniface, 118
Amulets, 6–8, 135, 217, 224, 228
Anne, Saint, 11
Antichrist, 63–64, 214
Aquinas, Thomas, 114
Arnsberg, 210
Aron, rabbi of Regensburg, 68
Augsburg, 44, 48, 51, 67, 149–51, 160
Augustine, Saint, 118, 130

Baden, 8, 17, 79
Bader, Philip, 90–91, 93–95, 101, 104, 110
Bamberg, 24, 67, 70
Bamberg Criminal Code (1507), 23–24, 192
Baptism, 21, 51, 112–17, 134. See also Conversions
Basel, 14, 39, 88, 99, 109
Benzhausen, 90, 96, 108
Berlin, 214
Bern, 70
Berthold of Regensburg, 10
Black Death, 3, 15, 47, 88, 130, 132, 192
Blood, 6, 19, 20, 35, 48, 94, 111, 134, 138; folklore of, 8–9, 94, 145; uses of, 9–10, 20–22, 29–30, 75, 127–28, 217; Christian, 38, 44, 75, 88, 92, 108, 116, 121, 127–28, 138–39, 180, 194, 199–200, 204, 223

Bobhart, Dr. Jacob, 200–201
Bodin, Jean, 159
Boldwiler, 93, 95, 97, 99
Bones, human, 17, 21, 33, 38, 76, 79, 103, 134, 144, 220
Brandenburg, 56, 70, 128
Breisach, 88, 99–100
Breisgau, 14–16, 34, 85–86, 88, 90, 97, 102, 107
Bremen, 195
Brentano, Clemens, 222–23
Breslau, 204
Brilon, 210–11
Bryhenn of Frankfurt, 94, 210
Bucer, Martin, 143, 160
Buchheim, 90, 92–93
Budapest, 48
Byman, rabbi of Regensburg, 68

Canon law, 113–14, 117, 142, 154, 175–76, 198
Capistrano, St. John, 66
Capito, Dr. David, 178–79, 186–87, 189, 191, 193, 199
Capito, Wolfgang, 143
Carben, Victor von, 123
Carnival, 64. See also Plays, carnival
Carolina (1532), 23, 24, 175, 177, 185, 187, 191–93, 201–2
Charles V, Emperor, 22, 41, 157, 160–62, 179, 185, 186, 197
Children: abuse of, 151–52, 159; as relic, 36, 56, 126, 129, 204; Jewish, 112, 114–18; martyrs, 12, 43, 48, 54, 56, 116, 222, 226; murder of, 2–4, 13, 18–21, 28–29, 55, 91, 96, 98, 116, 125–26, 144, 152, 155, 157–58, 199, 202; rhymes, 1; selling of, 35, 56, 75, 84, 96, 98, 167–72, 183, 199; stories, 2. See also Infanticide
Christian August, Count Palatine of Sulzbach, 216
Christoph, bishop of Trent, 126

243